PCTIPS 3000

I0473954

Microsoft Windows 7

A Complete How-To Guide

Vivek Nayyar

http://www.pctips3000.com

Microsoft Windows 7 - A Complete How-To Guide by Vivek Nayyar

This book is dedicated to my loving dad **Mr. V. K. Nayyar**

whose abilities have always inspired me to do something different

and in the loving memory of my mom **Late Mrs. Indu Nayyar**

who always wanted me to rise and shine.

- Vivek Nayyar

Acknowledgements

I am thankful to all those who devoted their time and shared their experiences during the creation of this book. Entire credit for the success of this book goes to them only.

Avijit Palival
Network Engineer

Chirag Nangia
Nestle India

Csaba Kissi
PCTIPS3000
Site Owner

Irshad Alam
Team Lead, Ship Corp.
Kolkata

Kunwer Shoeb Rana
T.G.T.
Natural Science

Lou Cordova
Medical Administrator
Toronto, Ontario

Navneet Mehta
State Head
R.G. Global

Preeti Rai
Govt. of India
Lucknow

Rakesh Tiwari
Dealing Assistant
ESIC, Govt. of India

Riza Rosal
Supervisor
Kuwait City

Swagata Bharali
Network Support Engg. Microsoft

Tarun Kandpal
Systems Engineer
ICA

About the Author

Vivek Nayyar

Vivek Nayyar has 8− years' experience in academic and corporate IT training and systems administration on Microsoft and Virtualization platforms.Today he works as Senior Windows Administrator and Chief Editor at PCTIPS3000. He also works as LAN Consultant and provides remote support to various IT oriented organizations around the globe. He has written several IT related blogs and articles on Microsoft and VMware and has been working on Windows since 2001.

Contents at a Glance

Table of Contents

Introduction

Microsoft Windows 7 - A Complete How-To Guide is to help both home users, who want to get familiar with Windows 7, and systems administrators who want to deploy Windows 7 as client operating system in a production network setup.

The guide is in very simple and easy-to-understand language and is deliberately written in this way to let everyone get the most out of it.

This guide covers almost every aspect of Microsoft Windows 7 which will help readers customize the operating system exactly according to their personal, professional and organizational requirements.

After going through this How-To guide readers will learn how to:

1. Install Microsoft Windows 7 operating system.
2. Optimize and personalize Microsoft Windows 7 for home and production environments.
3. Secure Microsoft Winodws 7.
4. Configure Micrcsoft Winodws 7 for Remote Desktops and file sharing.
5. Customize and use Windows Media Center and Windows Media Player in Microsoft Windows 7.
6. Backup and Restore Microsoft Windows 7.
7. Monitor, maintain and troubleshoot Microsoft Windows 7.

As a reader your feedback will help a great deal in improving future books by the author. As per the feedback future improvements may include:

- More simplified language for non-technical home users and corporate employees.
- Technically rich contents for IT professionals.
- More Real World Scenario Tips with more complex and practical examples.
- More screen shots for better understanding.

Readers can send their feedbacks to: **vivek.nayyar1107@gmail.com**

CHAPTER 1

INSTALLING AND PREPARING MICROSOFT WINDOWS 7

How to Install Microsoft Windows 7

Introduction to Microsoft Windows 7

Microsoft Windows 7 as yet another operating system released by Microsoft and is successor of Microsoft Windows Vista. The operating system is based on Windows Vista architecture and inherits almost every feature from its preceding version.

Along with the features that it has inherited from Microsoft Windows Vista, Microsoft Windows 7 has some very advanced features that were not available with any of the previous versions of operating systems released by Microsoft. Some of the advanced features that Microsoft Windows 7 include are creating and attaching VHD files without using any external application such as Virtual PC, installing Microsoft Windows 7 on the attached VHD file and then configuring the VHD file to boot the physical computer with the Windows 7 OS that has been installed on the VHD file, etc.

The best thing that makes Microsoft Windows 7 better than Microsoft Windows Vista is that it is far less resource intensive operating system. Microsoft Windows Vista used to consume decent amount of memory and resources of a computer whereas Microsoft Windows 7 is just the reverse and works quite well even on the computers with low configuration.

Minimum Hardware Requirements for Windows 7

Below is the list of hardware that Windows 7 operating system requires to run successfully on a computer:

- Processor: Pentium III 665 MHz
- RAM: 512 MB
- Graphics: 8 MB
- Hard Disk Drive: 10 GB
- Optical Media Drive: DVD-ROM Drive

The above list contains the bare minimum hardware requirements that must be met in order to get Microsoft Windows 7 installed on a computer and run flawlessly. However the higher the configuration is, the better performance can be expected and experienced from the operating system.

Installing Microsoft Windows 7

Once the minimum hardware requirements of a computer are met below steps must be followed in order to install a fresh copy of Microsoft Windows 7 operating system on a bare metal machine:

1. Power on the computer on which Microsoft Windows 7 has to be installed, make sure that the computer is configured to boot from DVD and insert Windows 7 installation DVD in the DVD drive.

2. On the first screen click **Next.**

3. On the screen that appears next click **Install now** button.

4. On **Select the operating system you want to install** window click to select the appropriate flavor of Windows 7 to install and click **Next.**

5. On **Please read the license terms** window check **I accept the license terms** checkbox and click **Next.**

6. On **Which type of installation do you want** window click **Custom (advanced)** option.

7. On **Where do you want to install Windows** window click to select the hard disk drive on which unallocated disk space is available and click **Next** to dedicate the entire disk space to the Windows 7 system drive (C:). Alternatively, **Drive options (advanced)** option can also be clicked to create multiple volumes on the hard disk drive. If multiple volumes are created, the first volume must be selected before clicking **Next** button to install Windows 7 on the selected partition (volume). (Installation process might require several restarts).

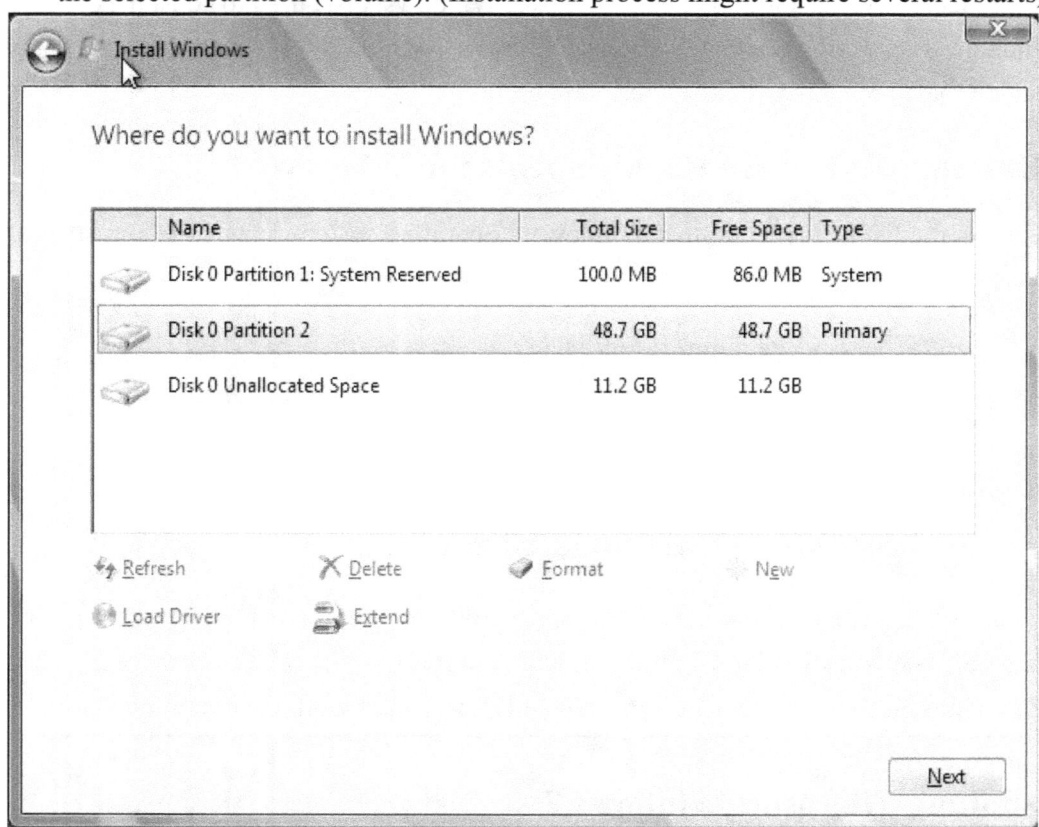

8. After the computer restarts, on the appeared window type a new user name for the computer in **Type a user name (for example, John)** field. User name specified here will have admin rights on the operating system.

9. Operating system automatically specifies a computer name according to the user name specified however administrators can type different name for the computer under **Type a computer name** field.

10. Once both fields are populated with appropriate values click **Next**.

11. On **Set a password for your account** window type and retype the password in respective fields and type password hint in **Type a password hint** field.

12. Click **Next** when done. Alternatively, **Next** button can also be clicked without populating the fields if administrators do not want to specify any password for the user account. This configuration is not at all recommended in production environments.

13. On **Help protect your computer and improve Windows automatically** window click **Use recommended settings** to allow Microsoft Windows 7 automatically receive and install updates from Windows update server. Any of the remaining two options can also be selected as desired.

14. On **Review your time and date settings** window select appropriate time zone from the available drop-down list, adjust system time and click **Next** when done.

15. Wait till the computer restarts again before it becomes available to the users.

PCTIPS 3000

View Product ID

When a Windows 7 operating system is purchased it comes along with its unique product key and a serial number that uniquely identifies that very copy of Windows. These two entities of the operating system allow Microsoft to identify the authenticity of the customer and provide appropriate technical support accordingly. Sometimes users may lose their unique identification information which makes them stand nowhere and the alternative to this might sometimes be that they need to purchase a brand-new copy of Windows if any mishap occurs to their computers. Microsoft understands this problem and to prevent people from investing their money twice for the same product, it allows Windows 7 to view the serial numbers of the OS quite easily. This process does not require any elevated privileges and even standard users can view the serial numbers of Windows 7. As a Windows 7 user if you want to do so you need to follow the steps provided as below:

1. Log on to Windows 7 computer with any account.
2. Click **Start** button and from the menu right click **Computer**.
3. From the available context menu click **Properties**.
4. You can get the serial number of Windows 7 copy under **Windows activation** section and the serial number will be displayed in front of **Product ID**.

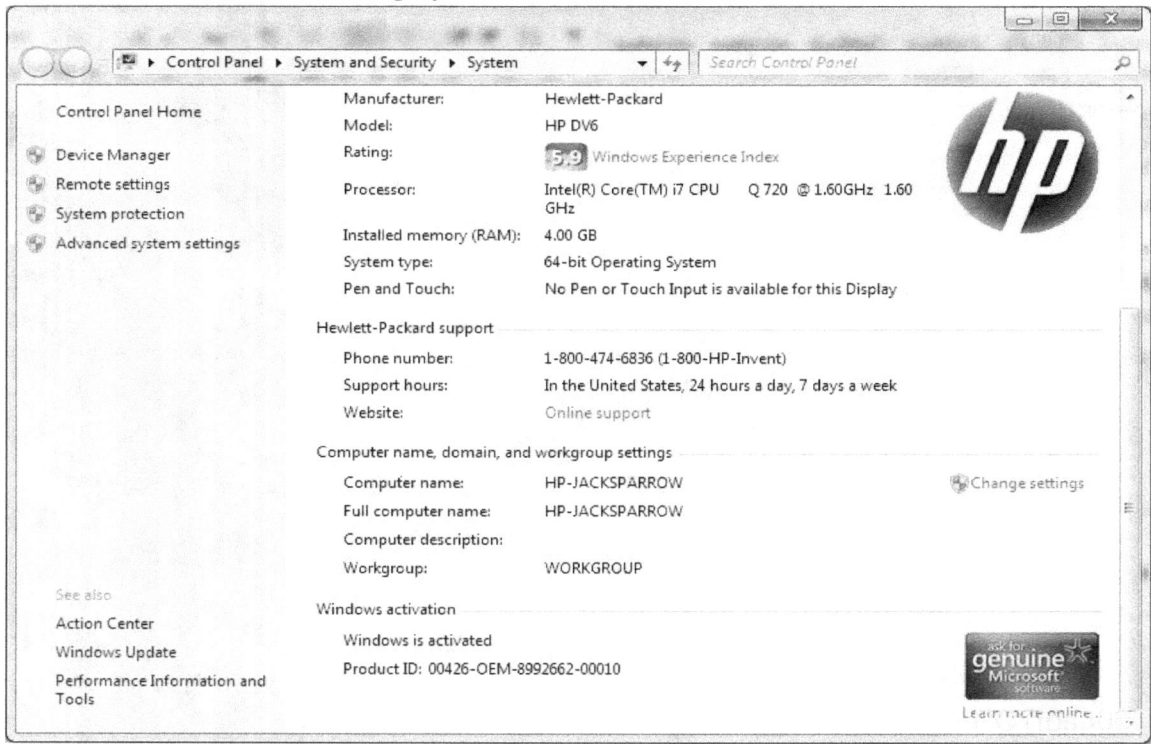

Change Default OEM Logo

When Windows 7 operating system is installed on a computer, the default OEM logo is displayed when you go to system properties. Many users may want to change the default logo for various licensing reasons. Default OEM logo is located at C:\Windows\System32\oobe\info which is a .bmp file of a specific size. In order to modify the OEM logo you need to place another picture of your choice and it should be of the same size. You need to place the picture at the above location and also you need to modify the registry accordingly. You can do so by following the steps given below:

1. Log on to the computer with administrator account and choose the appropriate bitmap image that you want to use as an OEM logo.

2. Place the selected picture at **C:\Windows\System32\oobe\info** location and open **Windows Registry Editor** by typing **REGEDIT** in the search box available at the bottom of start menu.

3. In the registry editor go to

4. **HKEY_LOCAL_MACHINE\SOFTWARE\Microsoft\Windows\CurrentVersion\OEMInformation** and double click **Logo**.

5. In the opened box under **Value data** field leave the entire path intact except replacing the .BMP file name with the new one.

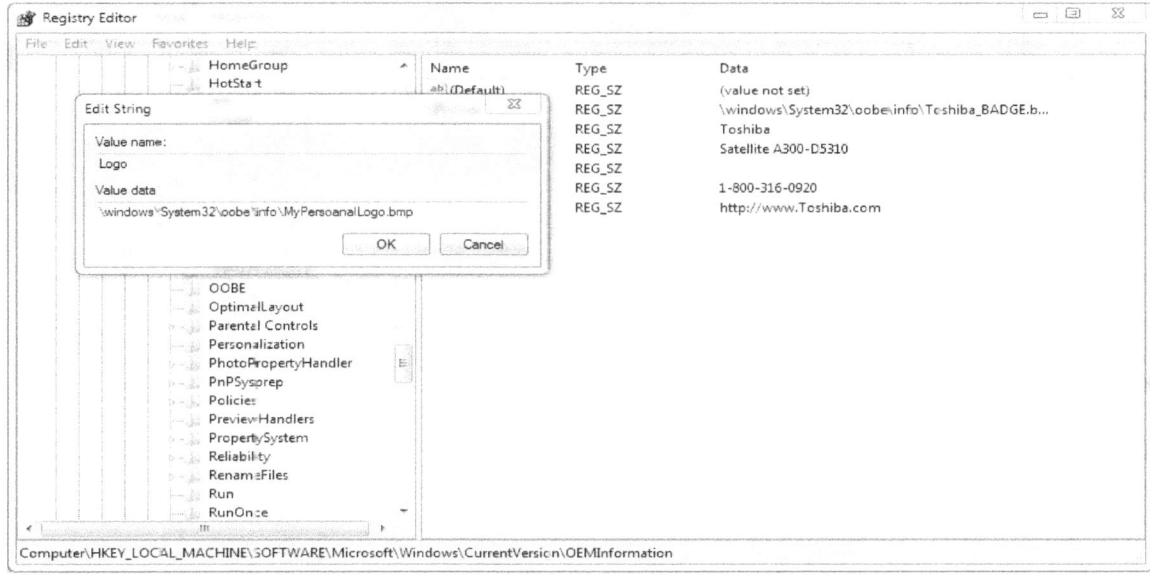

6. Once done, click **Ok** button to accept your changes and close **Windows Registry Editor** window.

7. Restart your computer to allow the changes to take effect.

Customize Logon Sound

Whenever a Windows 7 computer starts it plays a default Windows Logon Sound. This default logon sound can be replaced by any other .wav file which can be any music file of your choice. In order to do so first you need to find a .wav file. If you don't have, you need to convert any audio file to .wav format using any audio converter software application. Once this is done you can follow the steps given below to make your Windows 7 computer to play customized music for you every time it starts:

1. Log on to the computer using administrator account.

2. Click **Start** button.

3. From the start menu click **Control Panel**.

4. From the opened window click **Hardware and Sound** category link.

5. On **Devices and Printers** page click **Sounds** category link.

6. On the opened **Sound** box go to **Sounds** tab to change system default sounds.

7. In the **Program Events** list scroll down and click **Windows Logon** under **Windows** category.

8. Click **Browse** button under **Sounds** section to locate the .wav file and click **Open** button.

9. Back on **Sounds** tab click **Ok** button to confirm your selection. Optionally you can click **Test** button to check if the file is working correctly.

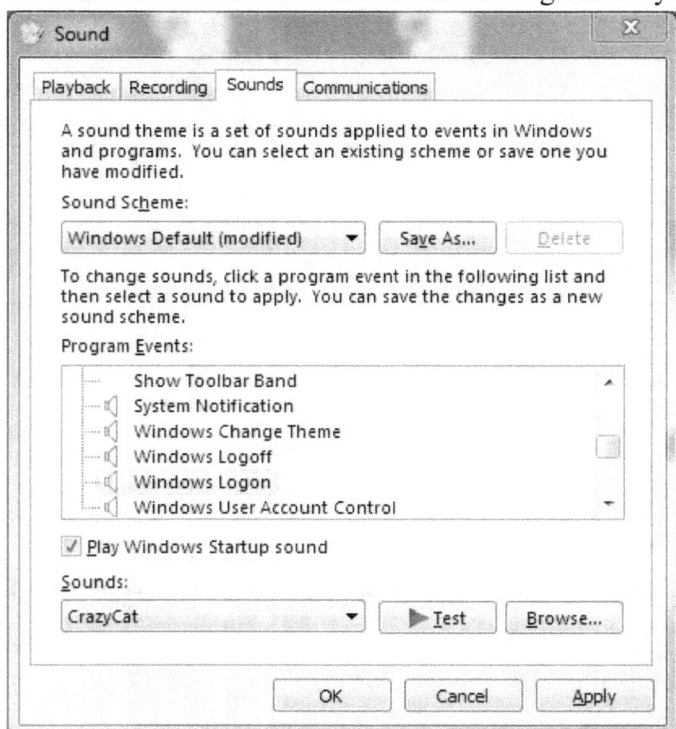

10. Logoff from the computer and re-logon to hear your Windows 7 computer singing a song for you.

Use Special Characters and Symbols

Whenever you use computer, it is expected that you would definitely use it to type any application or a document. Also there might be cases when you would like to type some special characters in your document which are not available on your keyboard. When this is the case, most people rely on Google results and others hire professional computer typists to get the job done. However, many people don't know that they can type special characters in Windows 7 by using Character Map which is a built-in tool that ships along with the operating system. If you want to type some special characters or symbols while working on your documents you can follow the steps given below:

1. Log on to your computer with the account using which you want to type the application or document.

2. Click **Start** button and point to **All Programs**.

3. On the available list click **Accessories** folder and from the expanded list click **System Tools**.

4. From the appeared list click **Character Map** and from the opened box click on the selected symbol that you want to type in the document.

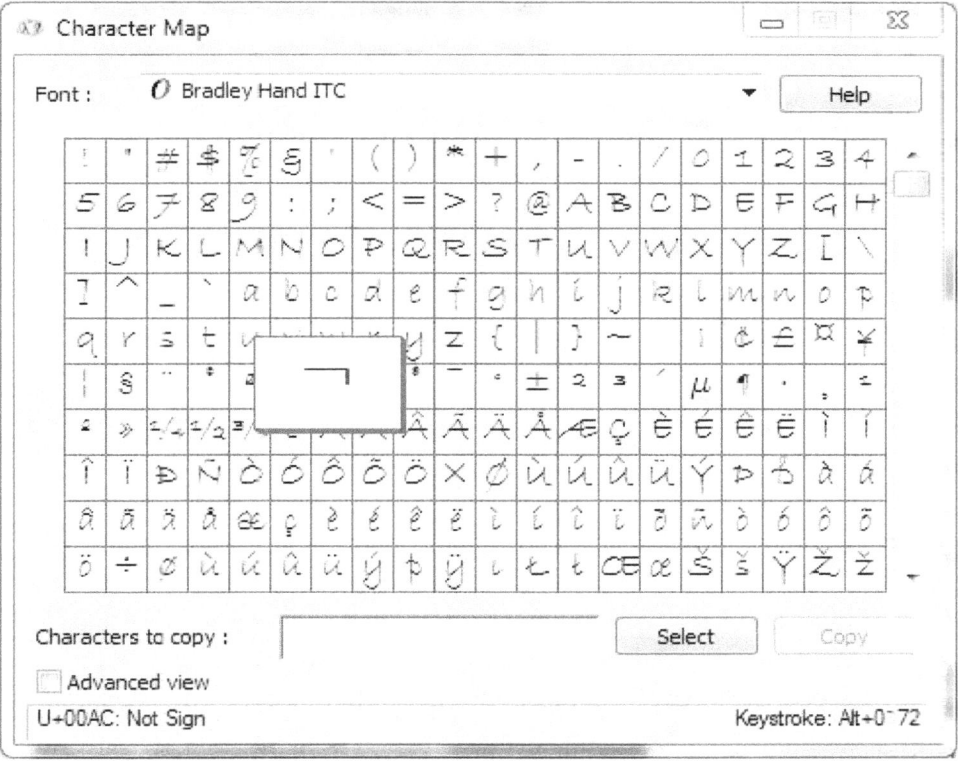

5. Once your selected symbol, you can find its corresponding key combination at the bottom right corner of **Character Map** box. You can use this key combination every time you want to type the selected symbol in your document. (Make sure that you choose the respective font face while typing the key combination for the selected symbol in your document).

Enable Narrator

There are several hidden features Windows 7 operating system which are not yet explored by many users. For example, many users don't know that a Windows 7 computer can speak whatever is displayed on the screen. This built-in feature is known as Narrator and when it is enabled it can be used to make it easier for physically challenged people to work on Windows 7 computer. Users, however, need speakers to use this feature. As a Windows 7 user you can enable narrator by following the steps given below:

1. Log on to the Windows 7 computer with the user account on which you want to turn on the narrator.

2. Right click anywhere on the desktop and from the opened menu point to **Personalize** and click on it.

3. On the opened page at the bottom right corner click **Ease of Access Centre** link.

4. On the next window click **Use the computer without a display** link.

5. On the appeared window under **Hear text read aloud** section check **Turn on Narrator** checkbox.

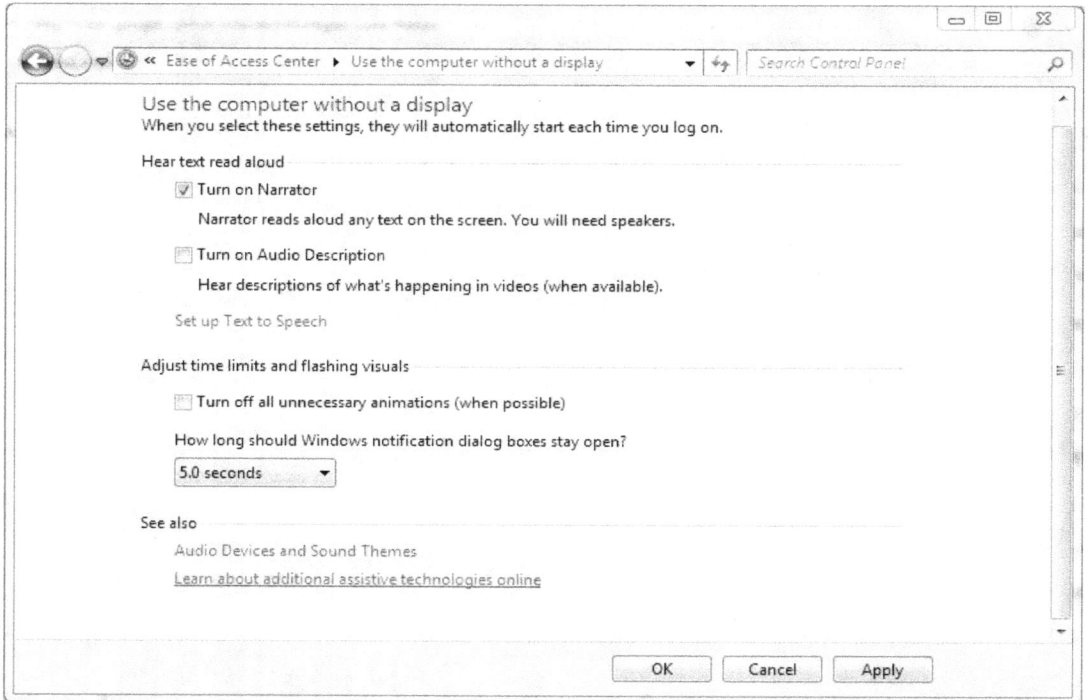

6. Once done, click **Apply** button to test the configuration.

7. When satisfied with the settings, finally click **Ok** button to make the settings persistent.

Create a Customized Power Plan

When Windows 7 is installed By default it is configured to apply Balanced power plan which gives optimum performance as far as the display and power management of the computer is concerned. In some cases, however, users may want to change this default configuration according to their needs and comforts. For example, when Windows 7 is installed on a laptop PC a user may want to modify the display plan when the laptop is running on battery in order to get the optimum brightness of the screen with reduced battery consumption. When this is the case a user can follow the steps given below to create a customized power plan:

1. Log on to the computer and click **Start** button.
2. From the start menu go to **Control Panel** and in the opened window click **Appearance and Personalization** category link.
3. On the next window click **Display** category link and from the opened window in the left bar click **Adjust brightness**.
4. On **Select of power plan** page in the left bar click **Create a power plan** link.
5. On the next page specify a new name for your power plan and click **Next** button.
6. On **Change settings for the plan** page make appropriate changes and click **Create** button.

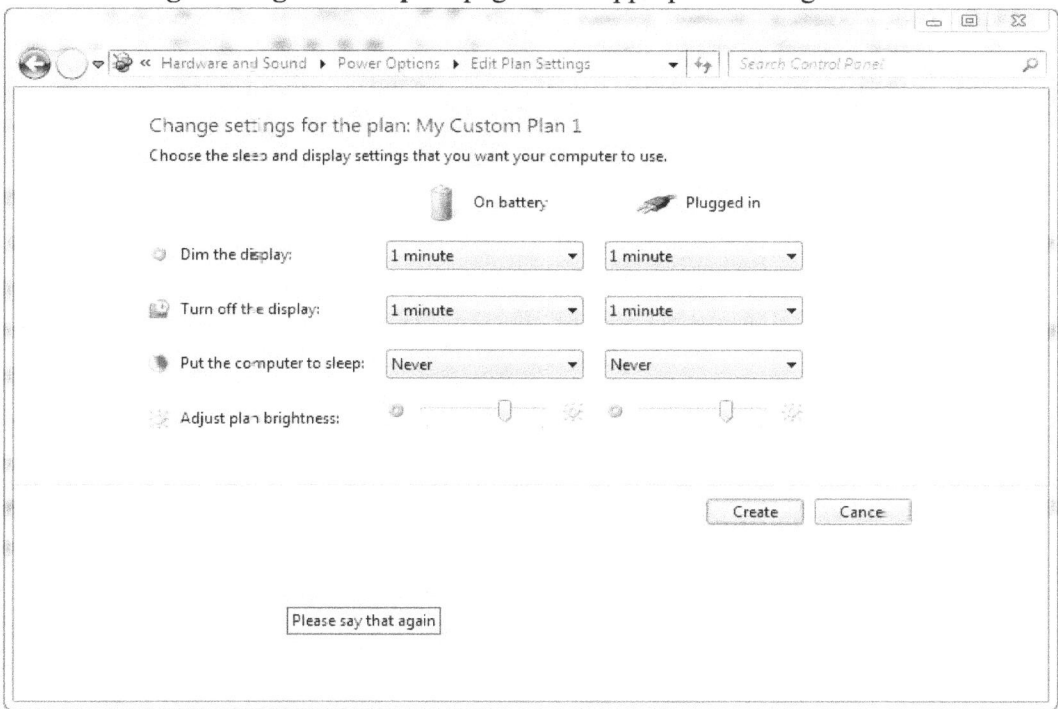

7. Close all the opened Windows.

Customize 'Send to' Menu

When a Windows 7 user right clicks on any object, 'Send to' option is also available in the context menu which allows him to send the copy of that object to the available options in the submenu. The submenu is by default created during the installation of Windows 7 operating system and normally it provides commonly used destinations to send the object. However administrators can customize the options available in the submenu to add or remove destinations as required. As an administrator if you want to do so you need to follow the steps given as below:

1. Log on to Windows 7 computer on which you want to customize **Send To** menu with the account that has administrative privileges.
2. Use **Windows Explorer** to locate
3. **C:\Users\<*Username*>\AppData\Roaming\Microsoft\Windows\SendTo** path.
4. Right click on the destination location object which you want to add to **Send to** menu in another **Windows Explorer** Window and create its shortcut on the desktop.
5. Now copy the shortcut from the desktop and paste it to
6. **C:\Users\<*Username*>\AppData\Roaming\Microsoft\Windows\SendTo location**.

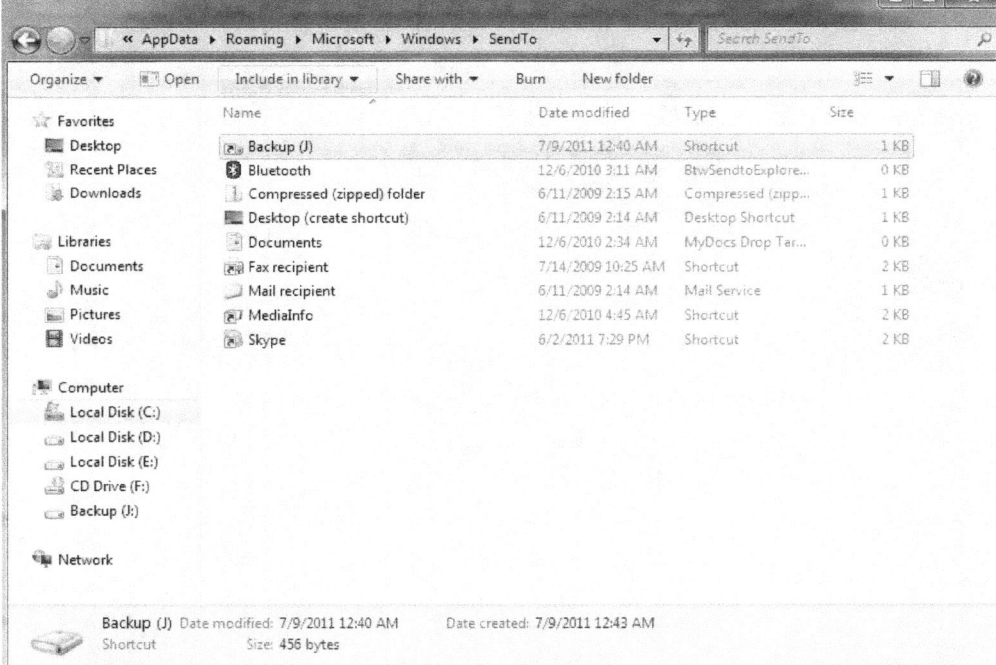

7. In some cases it might be required to restart the computer to allow the changes to take effect.
8. You can test this by right clicking on any object and going to **Sendto** option to find the sub-menu with added entry.

Note: If you want to remove the added destination you just need to delete the shortcut from the above mentioned location.

Display Hidden Locations in 'Send to'

In Windows 7 whenever an object is right clicked and the mouse is pointed to 'Send to' option, the sub-menu which is displayed contains number of locations where the object can be sent as a copy or as a shortcut. This 'Send to' menu can be customized and several other locations can be added to it with the help of few clicks. However the tricky part in Windows 7 is that even if you do not manually customize this option it already contains few other locations but they are normally not visible in the 'Send to' sub-menu. As a Windows 7 user if you want to view other options available in 'Send to' menu you are required to follow the steps given below:

1. Log on to Windows 7 computer with any account.
2. Locate the desired object which you want to send to any specific location.
3. Press **Shift** key and right click on it and from the context menu point the mouse to **Sendto** option.
4. You will be displayed with several other locations and/or location shortcuts to which you can send the desired object.

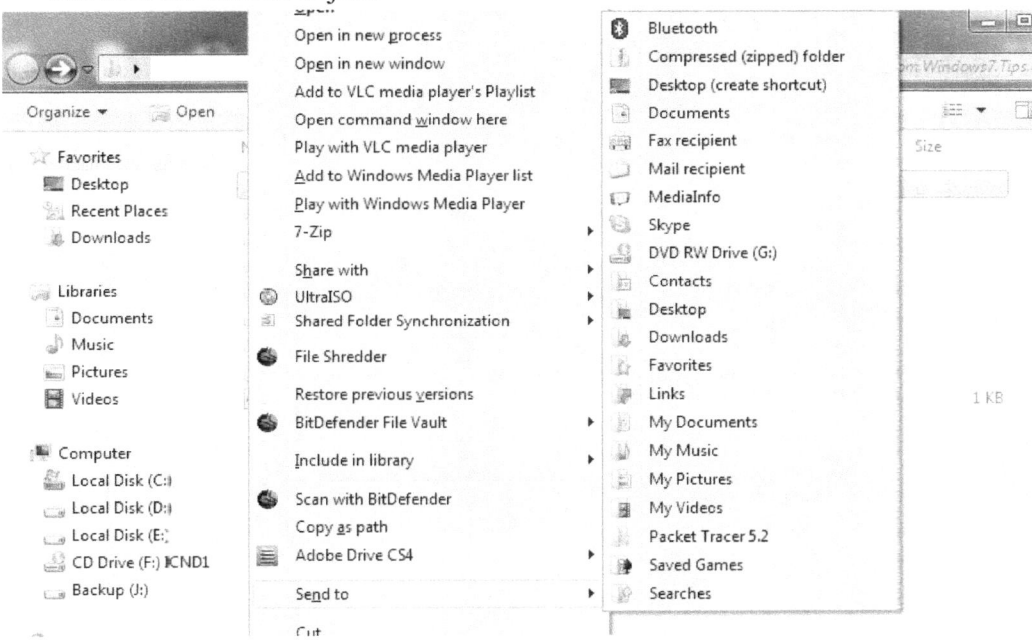

Note: The appeared list of locations is the default list however the menu can still be customized with the help of few tricky clicks.

Enable Run Command Box

With the new interface of Windows 7 many new features are introduced in the operating system. Where some features are added to the OS few of them are eliminated from the interface due to some reasons. Although, these features are not easily seen but are still present and are in active state. Users just need to make them visible before they can use them. Same is the case with Run Command box. Run Command box is by default not present in the Start Menu however it can be enabled by following few simple steps.

In order to make Run Command box visible in Start Menu you need to follow the instructions below:

1. Right click on the taskbar.
2. From the context menu select **Properties**.
3. From the **Taskbar and Start Menu Properties** dialog box go to **Start Menu** tab.
4. On the displayed dialog box click **Customize** button.
5. From the **Customize Start Menu** dialog box search from the list and check **Run Command** checkbox.

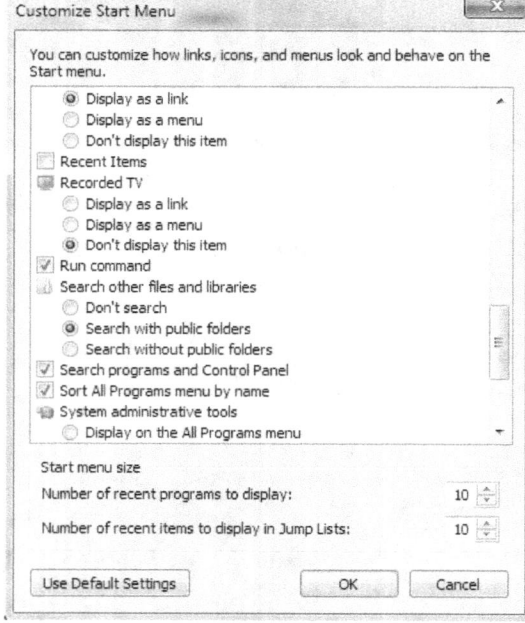

6. Click **Ok** button twice to come back to the desktop.
7. Click **Start** button and you will find **Run** in the list.

Alternatively you can press **Windows Key + R** to pop up **Run Command** box instantaneously.

Although search box is available right at the bottom of start menu which is quite useful as it searches almost everything available in the computer, including files, folders and/orapplications, it does not provide the facility to buffer last used commands. This facility is available only with Run Command box which can be enabled by following the above instructions.

Disable Search Box

Windows 7 ships along with several built in features which were not available in legacy versions of Windows. These features are mostly enabled by default and the ones which are not they can be installed/enabledwith few mouse clicks. One of the main installed features in Windows 7 is Search Box which is available at the bottom of start menu. Search Box works as a real time search program that looks out for the specified file or application in real time. Because Search Box is by default enabled in Windows 7, Microsoft has kept Run command box disabled. If users want they can enable Run command box and they can also disable Search Box so that they can experience the ambience of legacy operating systems. As a Windows 7 user if you want to disable Search Box you are required to follow the steps given as below:

1. Log on to Windows 7 computer with the account that has elevated privileges.
2. Click **Start** button and from the available menu click **Control Panel** option.
3. On the opened window click **Programs** category link.
4. On the next window click **Turn Windows features on or off** link under **Programs and Features** category.
5. On **Windows Features** box uncheck **Windows Search** check box and click **Yes** button on the confirmation box that appears.

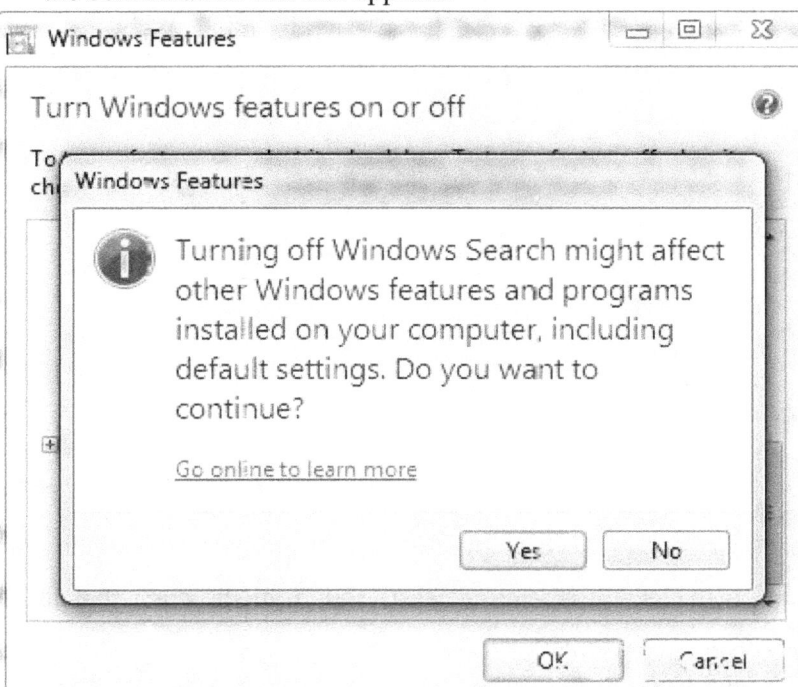

6. Finally click **Ok** button to save the changes you have made.

Pin Run Command Box to Taskbar

Unlike legacy versions of Microsoft operating systems like Windows 2000 and Windows XP, Windows 7 does not have Run command box by default enabled in it. Instead of Run, the operating system contains search box which is available at the bottom of start menu and it is completely indexed and works on real time. This means that as users type the name of an application or command in the search box it keeps on sorting the files according to the typed text and displays the most appropriate object or command available. However search box is still not able to replace Run command box and users still need to enable it in many cases. An added advantage in Windows 7 is that users can pin Run command box to the taskbar so that it can easily be accessed and that too almost instantaneously. As a Windows 7 user if you want to add Run command box to the taskbar you need to follow the steps given as below:

1. Log on to Windows 7 computer with the account on which you want to pin **Run** command box in the taskbar.

2. Right click anywhere on the desktop and from the context menu go to **New**.

3. From the appeared submenu click **Shortcut**.

4. On the opened window type **C:\Windows\explorer.exe shell:::{2559a1f3-21d7-11d4-bdaf-00c04f60b9f0}** in **Type the location of the item** text field and click **Next** button.

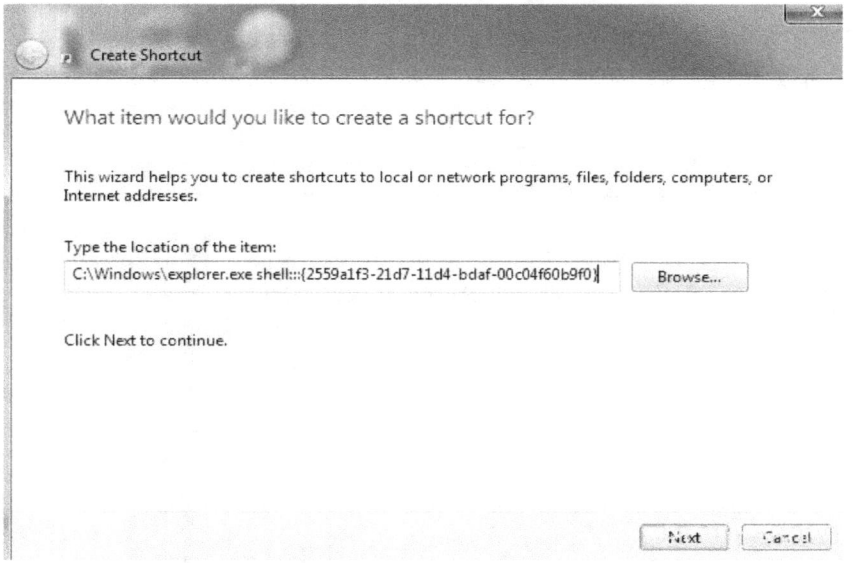

5. On the next page specify the appropriate name for the shortcut and click **Finish** button.

6. Right click on the newly created shortcut and from the context menu click **Properties** option.

7. On the opened box make sure that you are on **Shortcut** tab and from the available drop-down list in front of **Run** section choose **Minimized**.

8. Click **Ok** button when you are done with the configurations mentioned above.

9. Finally drag the shortcut to the taskbar to pin it up there.

Add Sticky Notes Gadget on Desktop

In your busy schedule it is quite normal that you forget your meetings and other important appointments. Many users set reminders in their mobile phones whereas others ask their wives or kids to remind them about their appointments when the time comes. A person using laptop PC or a desktop having Windows 7 installed on it can use the machine as his personal assistant by using Sticky Notes offered by Microsoft. With the help of Sticky Notes users can tag the important tasks on the desktop screens. In a nutshell, Sticky Notes is a tool integrated in Windows 7 on which you can type your To Do list. Since this tool is always placed on the Windows desktop screen it helps users remember their scheduled meetings and appointments. As a busy user you can also prioritize your tasks by placing several Sticky Notes in the order of their precedence. You can start Sticky Notes tool by following the steps given below:

1. Log on to your Windows 7 computer with any user account (this feature does not require any elevated privileges).
2. Click **Start** button and from the start menu point your mouse pointer to **All Programs**.
3. From the appeared list go to **Accessories** and click **Sticky Notes**.
4. Once **Sticky Notes** tool is initiated it will be displayed on your Windows desktop screen and you can start typing your **To Do** list on it.

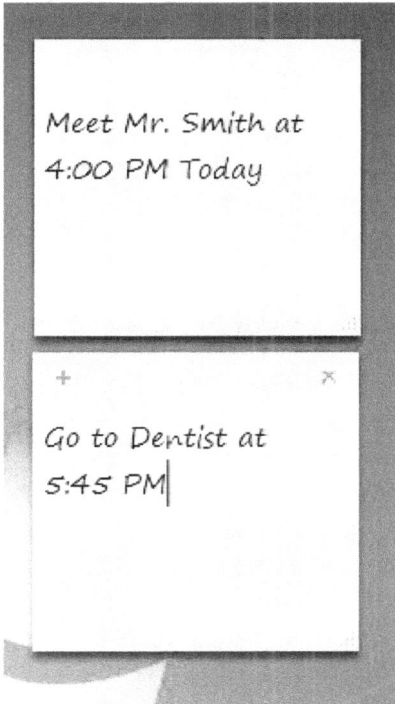

Disabling Gadgets

Windows gadgets are small applications that are developed by Microsoft and are ship and installed along with Microsoft Windows Vista and Windows 7 operating systems. These small applications are capable of connecting automatically to the Internet and gathering information from there. Moreover these applications are lightweight and therefore they require very less processing however they still consume some Internet bandwidth as theycommunicate with web servers to extract and download latest information. In Microsoft Windows Vista entire sidebar was available at the right corner of the desktop which consumed a decent amount of screen space and was considered an unwanted entity. Worst part was that if users wanted to place even single gadget entire sidebar was required to be enabled. In Windows 7 this limitation is removed and individual gadgets can now be placed on the desktop. Also, in Windows 7 users can completely disable gadgets which allow them to save some processing and internet bandwidth. As a Windows 7 user if you want to do so you are required to follow the steps given below:

1. Log on to Windows 7 computer administrator account.

2. Click **Start** button and from the available start menu click **Control Panel**.

3. On the opened window click **Programs** link and on **Adjust your computer's settings** page click **Turn Windows features on or off** link under **Programs and Features** category.

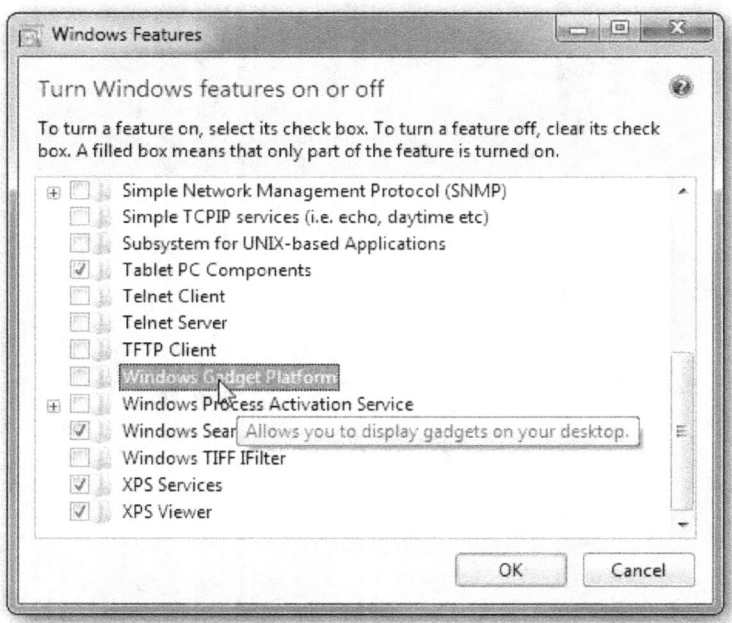

4. On **Windows Features** box uncheck **Windows Gadget Platform** checkbox and click **Ok** button to save the changes.

Customize Manufacturer Info

In Microsoft Windows 7 when properties of Computer are displayed the logo of Original Equipment Manufacturer or OEM is displayed. Default configuration displays the logo of the manufacturer of the machine which helps users identify the vendor to which the machine belongs. In production environments this feature helps administrators a lot as they can easily identify and assess which backup image should be used to restore the operating system on which computer. However in home environments where users normally love to play with operating systems OEM logo can be modified and any other image can be used instead. Modifying OEM logo requires elevated privileges and therefore only users from Administrators group can change the settings. As a Windows 7 administrator in home computers if you want to modify OEM logo in Computer properties box you are required to follow the steps given as below:

1. Log on to Windows 7 computer with any account that has elevated privileges, that is administrator account.

2. From the start menu click on Computer and go to **C:\Windows\System32\OOBE\INFO** folder.

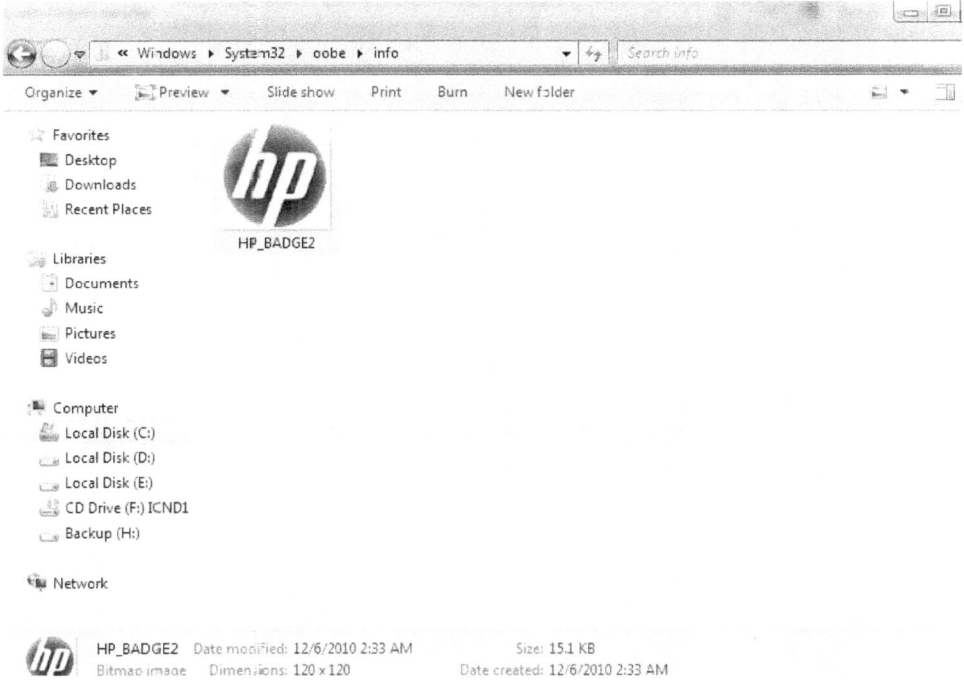

3. Here you are required to modify or replace the file with the new one. In case you are replacing the file make sure that the replaced file is of 120x120 height and width and that you rename it with the name of older file.

4. Once done, restart your computer is required.

Configuring Laptop PC Lid Reaction When Closed

There are times when you need to rush out for some urgent work while you are using your laptop PC. If this is the case the process of shutting down the laptop becomes quite hectic and irritating task to do. If you directly close the lid of your laptop PC, Windows 7 takes it to Sleep Mode which might not be appropriate configuration for everyone. With some added features operating system you can now manage the reaction of your laptop PC when you close its lid. In order to manage the reaction of closing the lid of your laptop you need to follow the steps given below:

1. Log on to the computer using administrator account.
2. Click **Start** button.
3. From the start menu click **Control Panel**.
4. It from the opened window click **Hardware and Sound** category link.
5. On **Devices and Printers** page click **Power Options** category link and **Select a power plan** page in the left bar click **Choose what closing the lid does** link.
6. On **Define power buttons and turn on password protection** page choose appropriate reaction of your laptop PC when you close its lid by selecting best suitable option from the drop-down list in front of **When I close the lid** category.

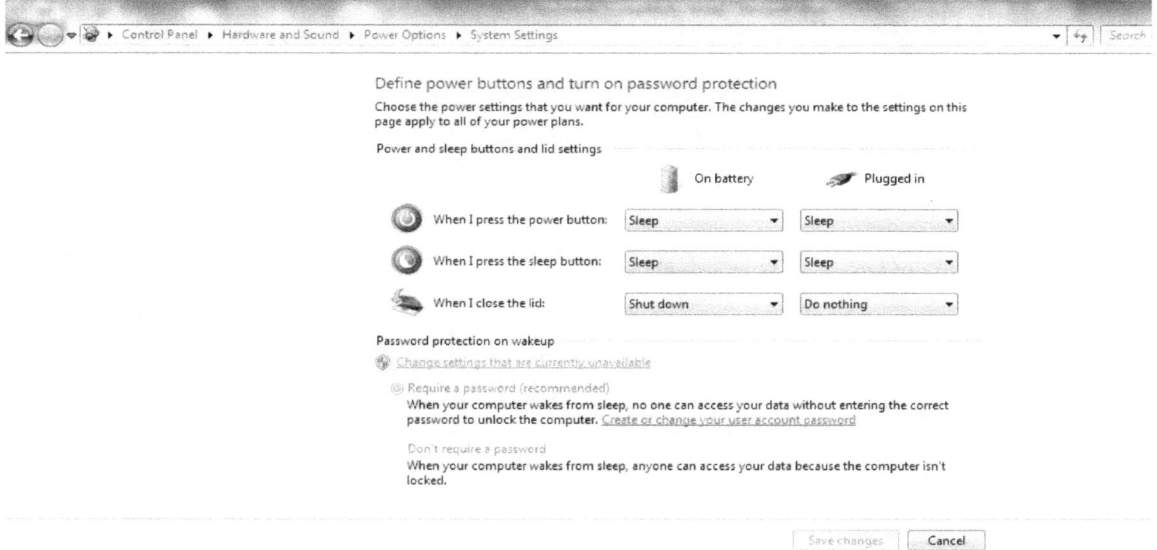

7. Click **Save Changes** button to accept your configuration and close the window.

Add Administrative Tools to Start Menu

Although Windows 7 is developed to be used in both production and home environments, Administrative Tools is the container which is still not available in the start menu as it is in other network operating systems. From Microsoft's point of view Administrative Tools container is not required in any client operating system such as Windows Vista and Windows 7 because it is expected that the operating system will be used by end users who are not technically qualified. Moreover, Administrative Tools provides a one-shop-stop to customize the administrative settings of the computer and if the users are not experienced enough to work with it they may corrupt the entire operating system. In any case if users want to get Administrative Tools in the start menu they can follow the steps given below:

1. Log on to Windows 7 computer with the user account on which you want to add **Administrative Tools** in the start menu.

2. Right click **Taskbar** and from the menu click **Properties**.

3. On **Taskbar and Start Menu Properties** box go to **Start Menu** tab and click **Customize** button.

4. On **Customize Start Menu** box click **Display on All Programs menu and the Start menu** radio button to select it under **System administrative tools** category.

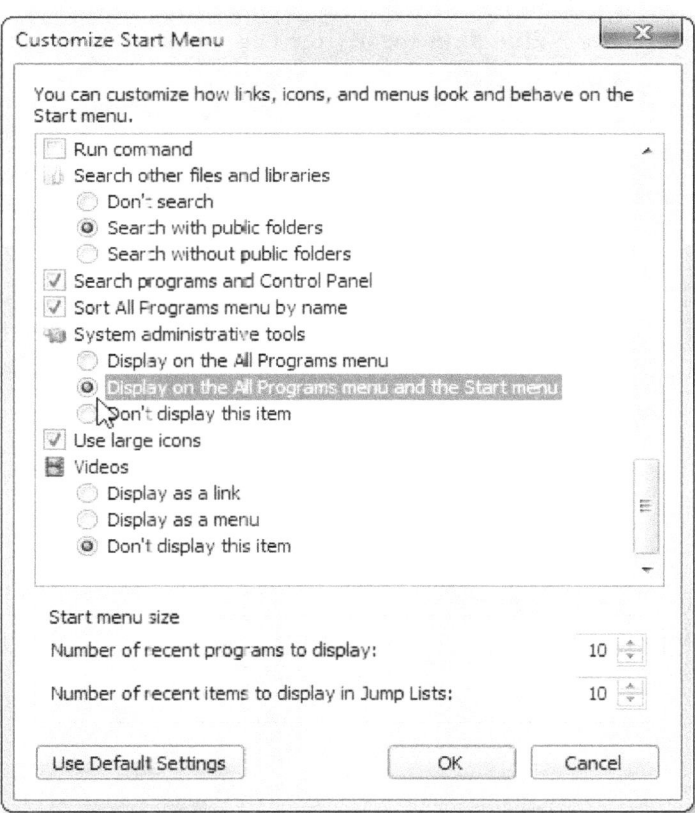

5. Finally click **Ok** button to save the changes you made.

Change Computer Owner Name

In home environments or office network infrastructures many times users or administrators may want to change the names of the owners of computers which are displayed when WINVER command is sent to the Windows 7 computer from either search box or Run Command box. Renaming owner name does not matter much while working on the computer however for the sake of advertisements and individuals' satisfaction sometimes it is necessary to do so. The process requires some modifications in Windows registry and therefore elevated privileges are required in order to perform the task. As an administrator of a Windows 7 computer if you want to change owner name of the computer you need to follow the steps given below:

1. Log on to Windows 7 computer with any account that has administrative privileges.
2. Click **Start** button and in the search box type **REGEDIT** and press enter key.
3. On **User Account Control** confirmation box click **Yes** button to continue.
4. On the opened **Registry Editor** window locate
5. **HKEY_LOCAL_MACHINE\SOFTWARE\Microsoft\Windows   NT\CurrentVersion** from the left pane.
6. On the right pane double-click **RegisteredOwner**.
7. On **Edit String** box under **Value data** specify the new owner's name for the computer and press **Ok** button to save the changes.

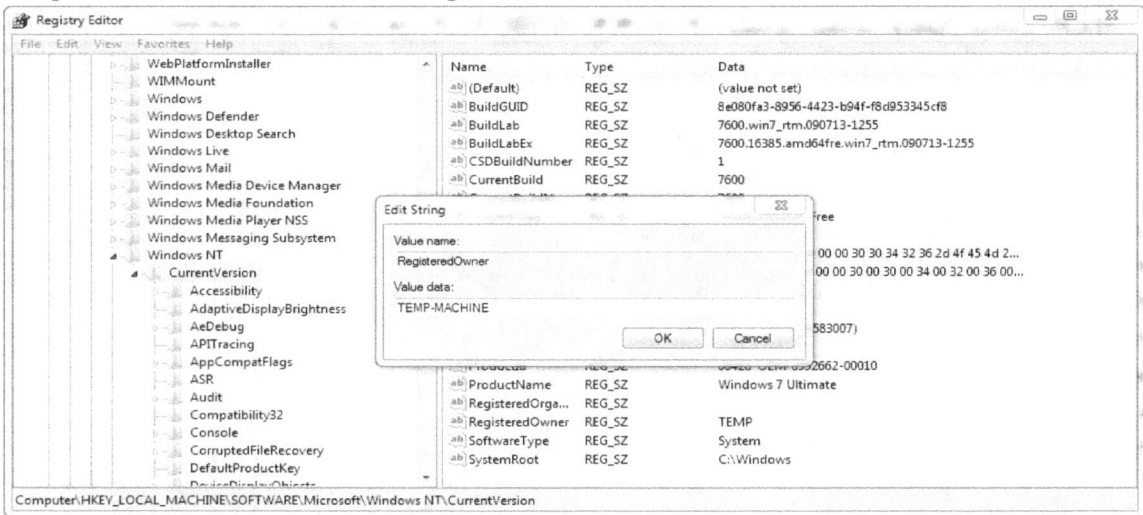

8. Close **Registry Editor** window and type **WINVER** command in search box to see the new name.

Change Registered Organization Name

In almost every production environment there are times when some used machines are purchased so that the organization can save some funds. When such machines are purchased it is likely that the computers will already have operating systems, Windows 7 in this case, installed on them. Also, during the installation the previous owner might have specified his own company name which a person can see by typing WINVER in Run Command box or in search box. This configuration might not be suitable for the new organization and therefore administrators may want to change the organization name of the computer and they would want to do this without reinstalling the operating system. Below are the steps which will tell you (administrator of any organization) how to change the organization name of Windows 7 without doing clean installation:

1. Log on to the Windows 7 computer with the account that has elevated privileges and in the search box of **Start** menu type **REGEDIT** and press enter.

2. Click **Yes** button to confirm UAC prompt.

3. On **Registry Editor** Window go to **HKEY_LOCAL_MACHINE\SOFTWARE\Microsoft\Windows NT\CurrentVersion** location by navigating in the left pane.

4. From the right pane double-click **RegisteredOrganization** key.

5. On **Edit String** box under **Value data** text box type the name of new organization.

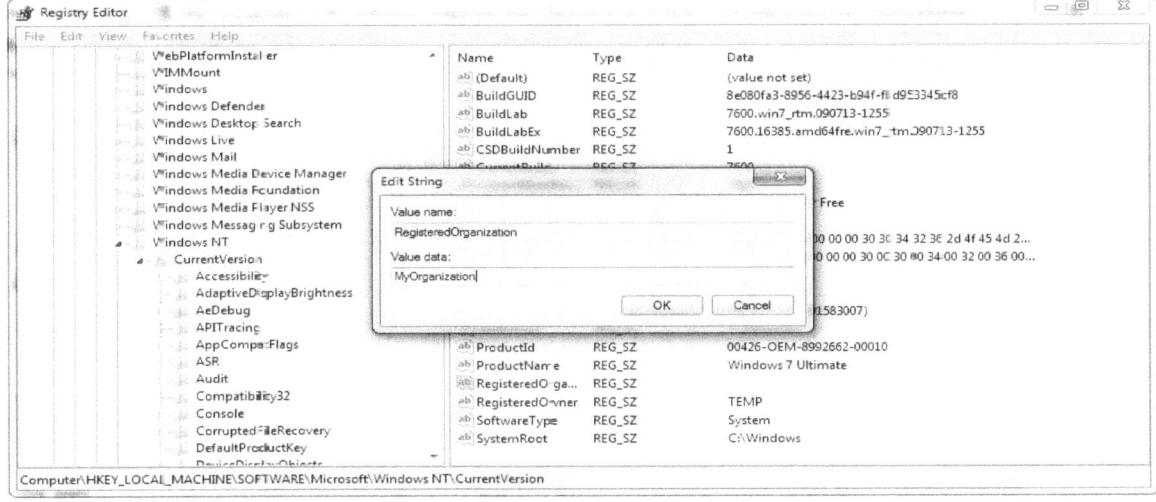

6. Once done, click on button to save the changes and finally close **Registry Editor** Window.

7. You can check new organization name of the computer by typing **WINVER** in the search box.

Keep Num Lock On when Windows 7 Starts

When Windows 7 operating system is installed on any desktop computer, it has default configuration of keeping Num Lock off when the computer boots. This configuration might create a lot of confusion while entering passwords to log on to Windows. The reason behind this is that in most cases users keep complex passwords which contain a combination of special characters, upper and lowercases and numeric digits. If, as default nature of Windows 7, Num Lock is off users may keep on pressing the numbers on the Num Pad not even knowing that numbers are not getting typed. Administrators of these computers can edit the registry and configure Windows 7 machines to have Num Lock on by default when computers start. As an administrator you can do so by following the steps given below:

1. Log on to Windows 7 computer with administrator account.

2. In the search box at the bottom of start menu type **REGEDIT** and press enter key.

3. On **Registry Editor** Window expand **HKEY_USERS > .DEFAULT > KEYBOARD** from the left pane.

4. From the right pane right click **InitialKeyboardIndicators** and from the list click **Modify**.

5. On **Edit String** box in **Value data** field replace existing **2147483648** value (which keeps Num Lock off when system starts) with **2** value (which keeps Num Lock on when computer starts).

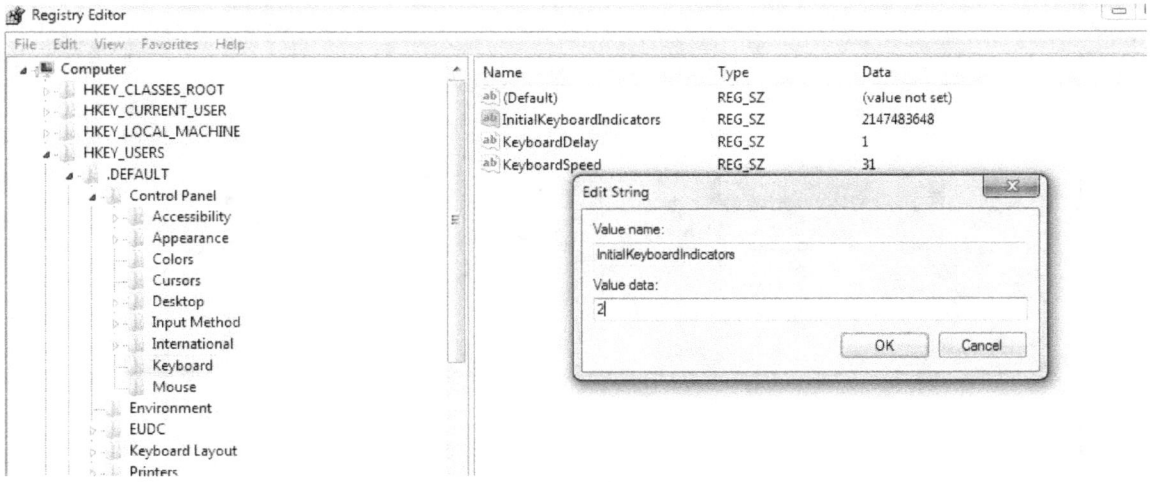

6. Once done, click **Ok** button to save the changes and restart the computer.

Manage Icon Label Texts on Desktop

In legacy versions of Windows operating systems like Microsoft Windows XP, labels of the icons on desktops were not as sharp and easily viewable as they are in Windows 7. This is because Windows 7 has a new feature named Drop Shadows which makes the texts of the labels easily readable. This feature can be enabled or disabled according to the wallpapers of the desktops. By default the feature is enabled and the recommendations are that it should be kept the same way to experience optimum performance. However if you want to disable this feature to get legacy text format of the labels of icons you are required to follow the steps given below:

1. Log on to Windows 7 computer.

2. Click **Start** button and from the available menu right click **Computer**.

3. From the context menu click **Properties**.

4. On the opened window in the left pane click **Advanced system settings** link.

5. On **System Properties** box make sure that you are **Advanced** tab and under **Performance** section click **Settings** button.

6. On **Performance Options** box scroll down to the bottom of the displayed list and uncheck **Use drop shadows for icon labels on the desktop** checkbox to disable the feature.

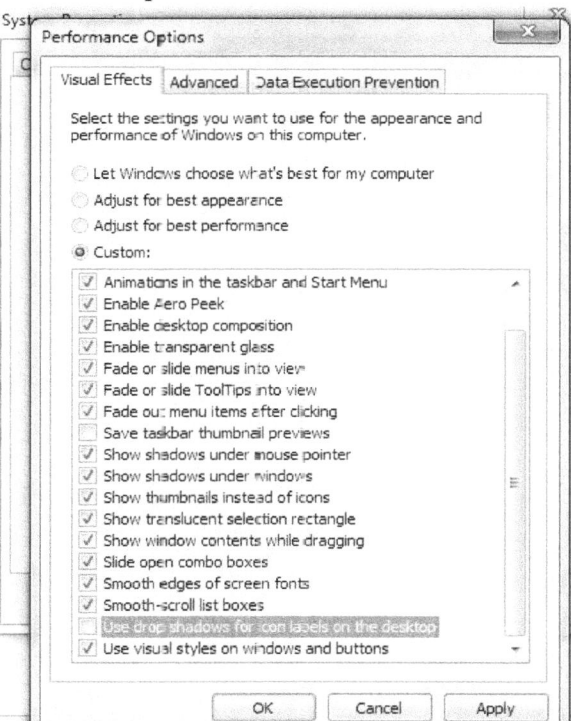

7. Finally click **Ok** buttons on all the opened boxes in Windows to save the changes you have made.

Manage Windows Explorer Search Bar Size

With the release of Windows Vista and Windows 7 in the market many new features are also introduced and one of the best features that have greatly enhanced the performance of the operating system is the quick search bar. Quick search is available at top right corner of any Windows Explorer window and users can type in the name of the desired object to find it on the current location. This option has its own text field in which users can type in the names of the objects which they want Windows 7 to find for them. However many times the names of the objects can be long enough to fit in the entire field and therefore the entire text cannot be fully displayed in it. This may sometimes result in error while typing full text which may further result in undesired searched objects. To eliminate this problem, users can increase the size of the field in order to get the full text displayed while typing. As a Windows 7 user if you want to do so you are required to follow the steps given below:

1. Log on to Windows 7 computer with any account.

2. Browse through, locate and open **Windows Explorer** window of your desired location.

3. Take your mouse pointer to the middle of the Title Bar and Search Bar.

4. You will notice that the mouse pointer has turned to the line with arrows on both sides.

5. Click and drag the mouse to the left to increase the size of search bar and drag it to the right to decrease it.

6. Once convinced with the size, release the mouse button.

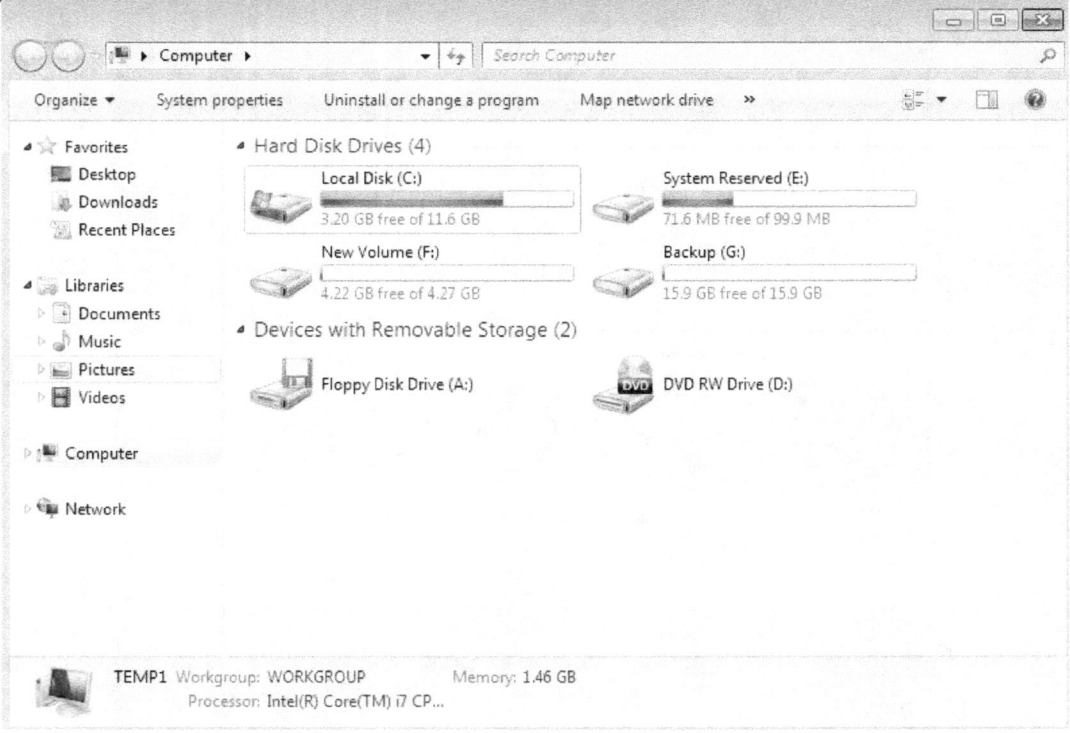

Disable Windows 7 Mobility Center

Mobility Center in Windows 7 is a feature that was introduced in Windows Vista. This is the location where users can customize the settings of their laptop PCs. In other words Mobility Center in Windows 7 serves as a one-stop-shop which allows users to customize almost every configuration related to their laptop PCs which may include adjusting brightness, color schemes, wireless configurations, battery configurations, projector configurations, additional hardware configuration, etc. The important thing to be noticed is that Mobility Center is only available on laptop PCs and by default it is disabled in desktops. However it can be enabled with a single registry tweak. In the same way Mobility Center in Windows 7 can also be disabled easily by customizing the registry settings. Although disabling Mobility Center in laptop PCs is not at all recommended even though if users still want to do so they are required to follow the steps given below:

1. Log on to the computer with the account that has elevated privileges.
2. At the bottom of start menu in search box type **REGEDIT** and press enter key.
3. On the opened **Windows Registry Editor** box from the left pane locate
4. **HKEY_CURRENT_USER\Software\Microsoft\Windows\CurrentVersion\Policies\MobilityCenter.**
5. Right-click anywhere in the right pane and from the menu click **New**.
6. From submenu click **DWORD (32-bit) Value** and rename it to **NoMobilityCenter**.

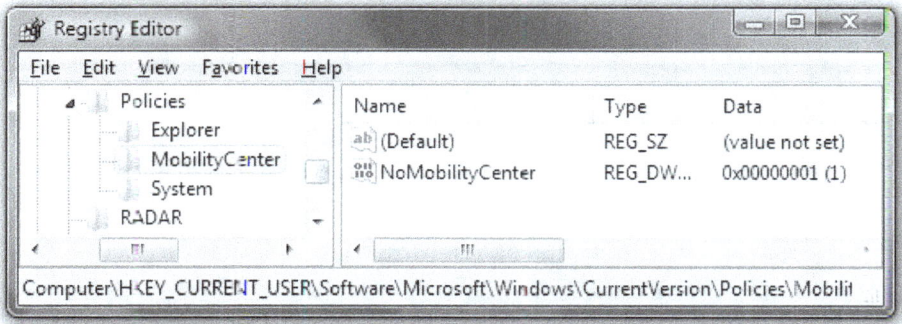

7. Double click on the newly created key and under **Value data** field specify the value as **1**.
8. Click **Ok** buttons on all the boxes and if required restart your computer to allow the changes to take effect.

Disable Windows Media Center

As everyone knows Windows 7 is a complete multimedia operating system which is designed to be used in both home and production environments.Best part that Windows 7 offers is Windows Media Center which is a built-in program that allows users to perform almost all possible multimedia tasks. For example Windows Media Center allows users to view TV, play music, watch movies, view Internet TV, capture TV, etc. In many production environments, however, this utility is not considered as appropriate as it may divert employees' focuses from their works which may affect businesses. Keeping this in mind administrators in many organizations deliberately disable Windows Media Center and as a Windows administrator in such organization if you want to do so you need to follow the steps given below:

1. Log on to Windows 7 computer with the account that has administrative privileges.
2. Click **Start** button and from the menu go to **Control Panel**.
3. On the opened box click **Programs** category link.
4. Click on **Turn Windows features on or off** link under **Programs and Features** category.
5. From the opened box expand **Media Features** and from the available list of features uncheck the check box representing **Windows Media Center**.
6. Click**Yes** button on the confirmation box that appears and finally click **Ok** button to save the changes that you have made.

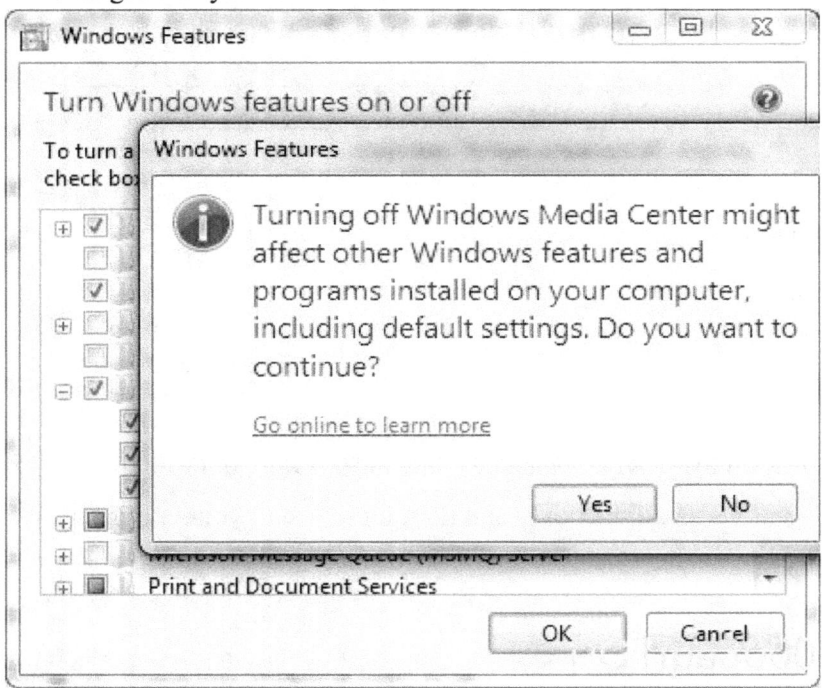

Adjust the Speed of Slide Show

With the release of Microsoft Windows 7 several new features are also introduced in the operating systems and these features are integrated to make the use of Windows 7 as easier and user friendly as possible. One of the main features that make Windows 7 a complete multimedia operating system is that it contains a built-in Slideshow program which can be initiated by pressing Slide show button that is available at the top of every folder that contains images. Because of this feature now users need not to look out for any third-party slideshow application which sometimes might be very expensive and if it is free it is not as efficient as it should be. Best part inSlideshow feature available with Windows 7 is that the speed of the slideshow can also be controlled. As a Windows 7 user if you want to control the speed of slideshow you are required to follow the steps given as below:

1. Log on to Windows 7 computer with any account. This is because enabling slideshow and controlling its speed does not require any elevated privileges.
2. Browse from an navigate toOpen the folder that contains images.
3. From the available options at the top of the folder click **Slide show** to start the slideshow.
4. Once started, right click on the running slideshow and from the available menu click on the appropriate speed as required.

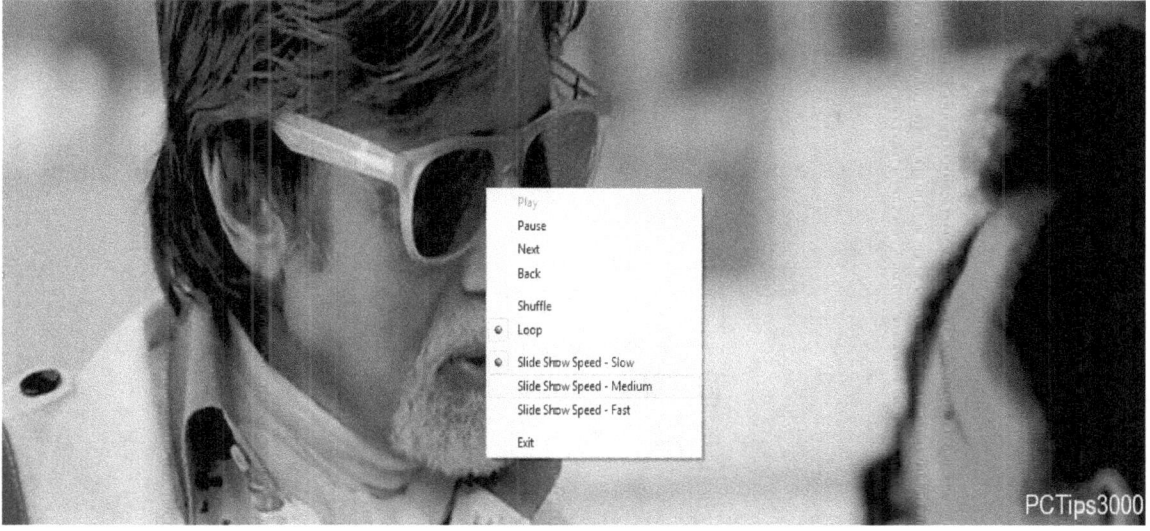

Configure Touchpad of Laptop PCs

In today's laptop PCs era, everyone has one or two laptops and more than 95% of them have Windows 7 installed. Installation of Windows 7 on a laptop PC can be either from vendor's end or users can install the operating systems on their own if they want to upgrade it. Whatsoever the case is, Windows 7 is now taking a lead as far as Windows based operating systems on laptop PCs are concerned. Just like customizations of controls are available in desktop PCs, Windows 7 offers same kinds of controls for laptop computers as well. Case of mouse buttons and configurations of mouse pointers is not left alone in this regard. In other words, touchpad of laptop PCs can be configured in a similar way as mouse settings in desktop computers. Windows 7 is highly flexible while configuring these settings to provide users as much user friendly interface as possible. As a Windows 7 user if you want to configure touchpad settings on laptopsthat are identical to mouse settings of desktop computers you are required to follow the steps given below:

1. Log on to Windows 7 computer with the account on which you want to configure touchpad settings.

2. From the start menu list go to **Control Panel**.

3. From **View by** list in the **Control Panel** window choose **Large icons**.

4. From the now available category click **Mouse**.

5. On **Mouse Properties** box make sure that you are **Buttons** tab.

6. From **Devices** drop-down list choose the name of the touchpad.

7. Configure the appropriate settings as required, for example, **Right-handed** or **Left-handed**, double-clicking speed, etc.

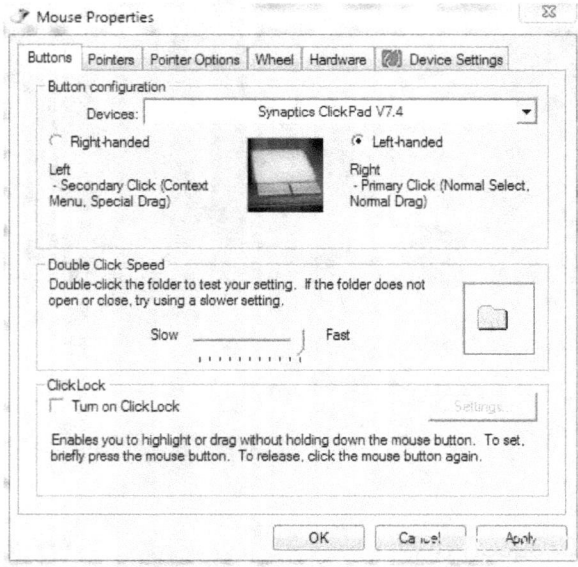

8. Once you are done with the configurations click **Ok** button to save the changes and close all the opened Windows and boxes.

Enter Product Key to Activate Windows 7

Unlike legacy versions of Microsoft Windows operating systems, for example Windows XP or Windows 2000, Windows 7 does not require any product key during installation. This means that even if users do not provide any product key while installing Windows 7 they can still use operating system for 30 days. After the completion of 30 days the operating system stops working and it asks for a valid product key in order to allow users to continue working on Windows 7. This feature is provided to the users so that they can use Windows 7 and can get the feel of it and if they find it useful they can register their copies of Microsoft Windows 7 by entering the product key. Entering product key and activating Windows is a simple process and even a non-technical user can do so by following the steps given as below:

1. Log on to Windows 7 computer with the account that has administrative privileges.
2. Click **Start** button and from the available menu click **Computer**.
3. From the appeared menu click **Properties**.
4. On the opened window under **Protect Activation** click **Change Projects Key**.
5. Follow the on-screen instructions to enter 25 character product key in the specified area and click **Next** button to initiate the activation process.
6. Click **Activate Windows Online Now** to activate the copy of Windows operating system you are running and finally click **Finish** button to complete the process.
7. You can then find the successful activation in Computer's Properties window.

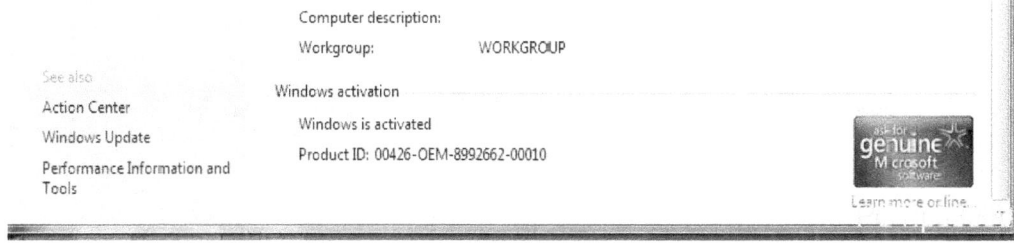

How to Add Recycle Bin to My Computer

Recycle Bin is an important place where all deleted files are stored on a temporary basis. It works as a backup storing point from where deleted files can be easily restored provided they are not permanently removed from the recycle bin itself. Biggest drawback, however, with recycle bin is that it only appears on the desktop screen and because of this, users can only use drag-and-drop feature when they are on the desktop windows. When users are in some other container or folder they need to right click on the object and then they need to select Delete option from the available menu. This limitation can easily be removed by modifying Windows registry. This small modification allows users to have recycle bin in Windows Explorer as well. Since this process requires administrative privileges elevated user account is required to be logged on in order to modify the registry. As a Windows 7 administrator if you want to do so you are required to follow the steps given as below:

1. Log on to Windows 7 computer with the account that has elevated privileges.
2. At the bottom of start menu search box type **REGEDIT** and press enter key.
3. On Windows **Registry Editor** box locate
4. **HKEY_LOCAL_MACHINE\SOFTWARE\Microsoft\Windows\CurrentVersion\Explorer\MyComputer\NameSpace**.
5. Once located, right click anywhere in the right pane and click **New**.
6. From the available submenu click on **Key** and rename it with **{645FF040-5081-101B-9F08-00AA002F954E}**.
7. Close **Registry Editor** and if required restart the computer.

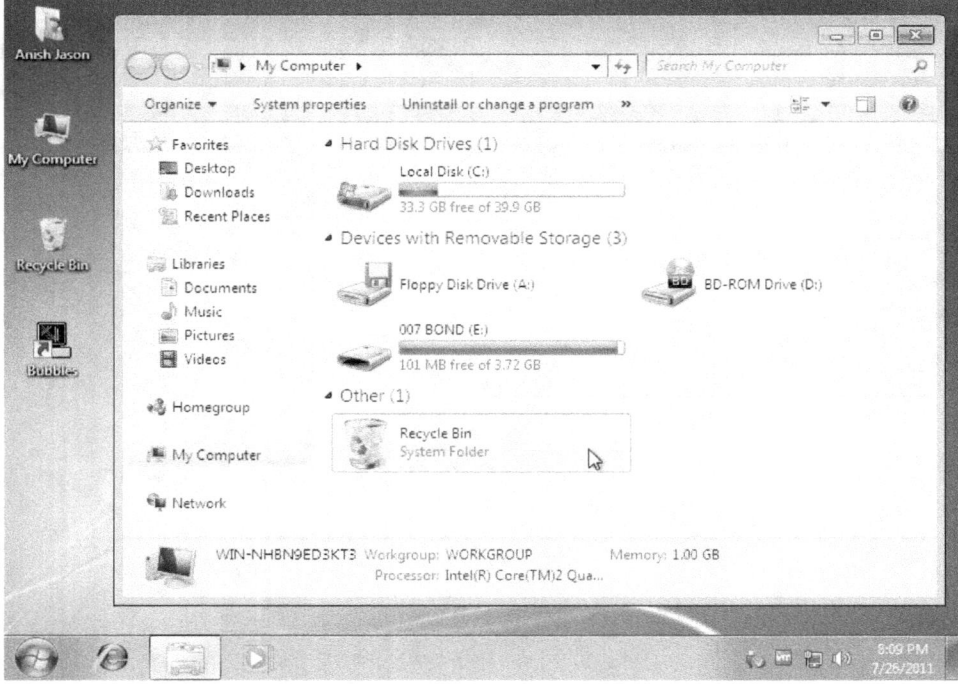

Get More Space on Your Desktop

By default Windows 7 computer displays large icons in the taskbar which increases its size and occupies a decent amount of space on the desktop screen. For people with good eyesight this configuration is quite normal, or rather it is ideal as they can configure the best possible screen resolution supported by their monitors. However users with sight problems may not be able to view the entire desktop screen with large icons in the taskbar. Either they can enable the auto hide feature or alternatively they can reduce the size of the icons that appear in the taskbar. Since this configuration is user specific, users do not have to log on to the computer with administrator account and neither do they require any elevated privileges for this. If you want to reduce the size of the icons in your taskbar you need to follow the steps given below:

1. Log on to your Windows 7 computer with the user account on which you want to reduce the size of the icons of the taskbar.
2. Right click on the taskbar and from the appeared menu click **Properties**.
3. On **Taskbar and Start Menu Properties** box check **Use small icons** checkbox.

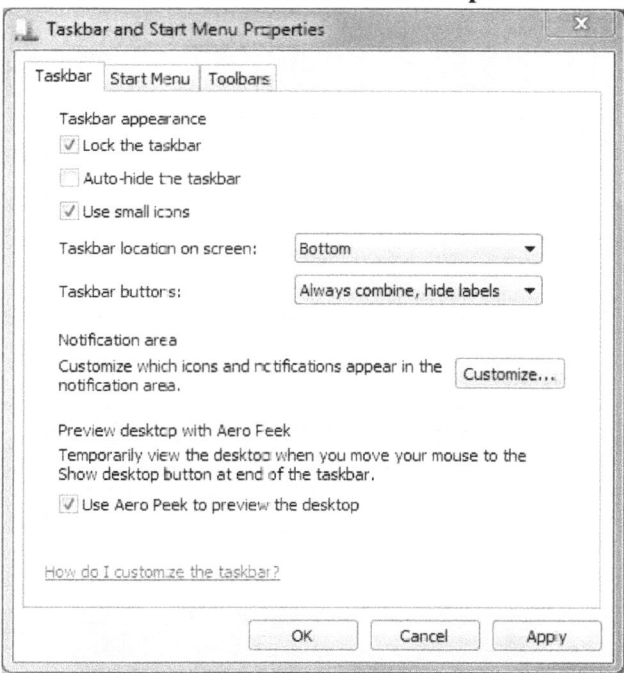

4. You can click **Apply** button to view the effects of the configuration and once you are convinced, you can click **Ok** button to finalize your settings and make them persistent.

Configure Immediate File Deletion

By default every operating system that is installed on a computer makes sure that a user does not delete his data accidentally. To prevent users from doing so, theoperating system asks several questions before it finally deletes the data. Confirmation dialog box that appears every time you are about to delete any data from your computer is a good example for this. Purpose of this message box is to ensure that you are not deleting data accidentally and the deletion is on purpose. Also, once data is deleted it is sent to recycle bin so that it can be restored when required. However some users might find this configuration frustrating and therefore they may want to remove this obstruction and allow Windows 7 to remove the files permanently without sending them to the Recycle Bin. If you want to configure this you need to follow the steps given below:

1. Log on to your Windows 7 computer with the account having administrative privileges.

2. On the desktop right click **Recycle Bin** and from the appeared menu choose **Properties** to click on.

3. On **Recycle Bin Properties** box under **Settings for selected location** section select the radio button that says **Don't move files to the Recycle Bin. Remove files immediately when deleted**.

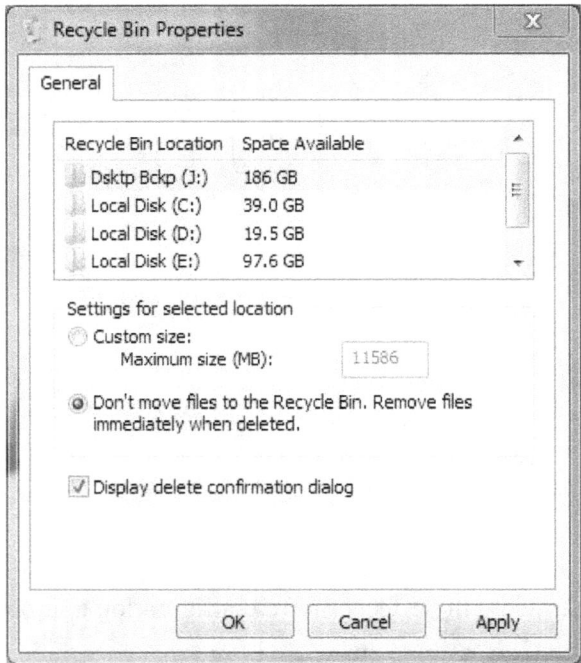

4. Click **Ok** button to confirm your settings once you are convinced with your selection.

Note: The above described configuration is not at all recommended under normal circumstances. You should only do so if there is any specific requirement under special situations.

Connect to the Projector

Windows 7 is designed to serve several purposes. It is almost perfect for everything which includes remote education, home environments, business meetings, etc. To take an example of business meetings there are times when professionals need to connect their laptop PCs, which have Windows 7 installed on them, to the projectors. Windows 7 helps professionals in this regard by making this task even simpler as compared to the earlier versions of Windows. If you want to connect your Windows 7 computer to the projector you need to follow the steps given below:

1. Log on to a Windows 7 computer.
2. Right click on the desktop screen and from the menu click **Screen resolution**.
3. On the appeared window click **Connect to a projector** link and on the appeared box select the appropriate option as per your requirements.

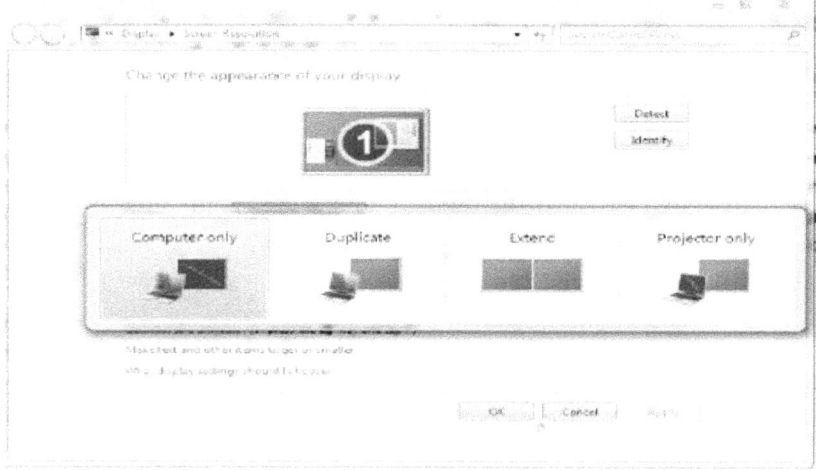

4. Once done, you can close all the windows and enjoy the updated advanced feature of Windows

More Info:

If you want to expedite this task you can use shortcut key combination, which is Windows Key + P. You can reverse the above mentioned process to undo the changes and to get back to the normal configuration of your Windows 7 computer.

Best Practices:

Do not choose the option Projector Only as this may create troubles. You should always Duplicate the display so that you can take complete control of the computer in case of any mishaps.

Prevent Themes from Changing Mouse Pointers

As default nature of Windows 7 operating system, whenever a theme is installed it automatically modifies desktop icons and mouse pointers and cursors in order to provide better look and different ambience to the users. Many users really like to have changed icons and animated cursors and pointers while working on Windows 7 and they enjoy working with them. In some conditions however user may not want to modify their cursors or pointers for various reasons and may want to lookout for a theme that works according to their requirements. Well, now users need not to worry about these matters as Windows 7 itself offers a feature in which users can configure themes so that they may not change cursors or mouse pointers to theme defaults. This feature proves to be quite helpful for almost every user who does not want modifications in the pointers and cursors while applying new themes. As a Windows 7 user if you want to configure this you need to follow the steps given as below:

1. Log on to Windows 7 computer with any account on which you want to configure this and since the configuration is user specific no elevated privileges are required.

2. Right click anywhere on the desktop and from the available context menu click **Personalize**.

3. From the opened window on the left bar click **Change mouse pointers** link.

4. On **Mouse Properties** box uncheck **Allow themes to change mouse pointers** checkbox.

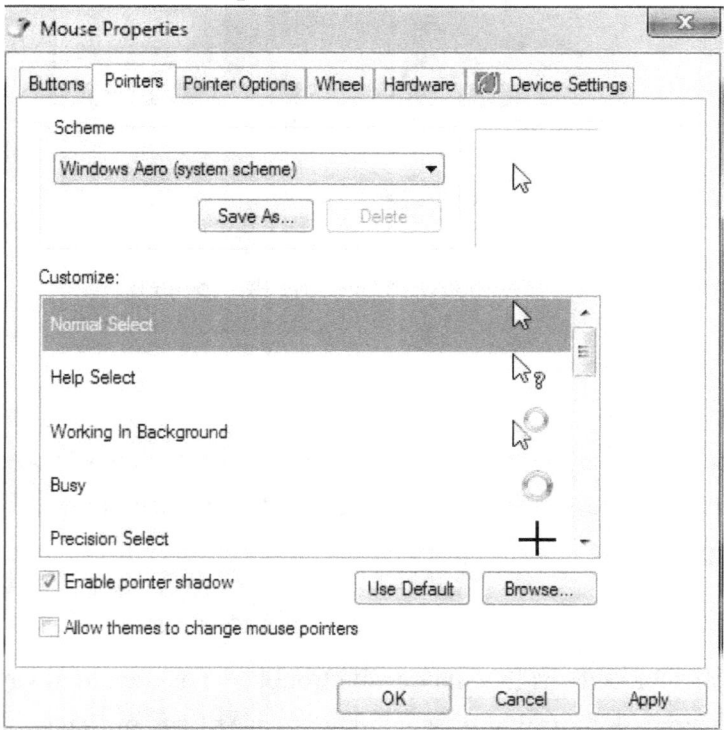

5. Finally click **Ok** button to save the changes you made and close all the opened Windows and boxes.

Prevent Themes from Modifying Icons

In any version of Microsoft operating system, especially in Windows 7, whenever users change themes, icons on desktop screens are also automatically modified to provide better look and enhanced ambience of the screen. This default configuration is handled by the themes and therefore all modifications are done automatically. For home environments and new users of Windows 7 this configuration might be very exciting and users can enjoy colorful and strange icons on the desktops rather than watching same old boring icons. But in production environments, mostly in small-scale organizations, users may still want to implement themes but they do not or may not want to modify desktop icons to maintain the consistency and decorum of the organization at the same time. When this is the case Windows 7 allows administrators or local users to configure the operating system in such a way that even when the themes are applied, icons are still left intact. As a Windows 7 user or administrator if you want to do so you need to follow the steps given as below:

1. Log on to Windows 7 computer with the user account on which you want to configure the settings.

2. Right click anywhere on the desktop screen and from the available context menu click **Personalize**.

3. On the opened window in the left bar click **Change desktop icons** link.

4. On **Desktop Icon Settings** box uncheck **Allow themes to change desktop icons** checkbox.

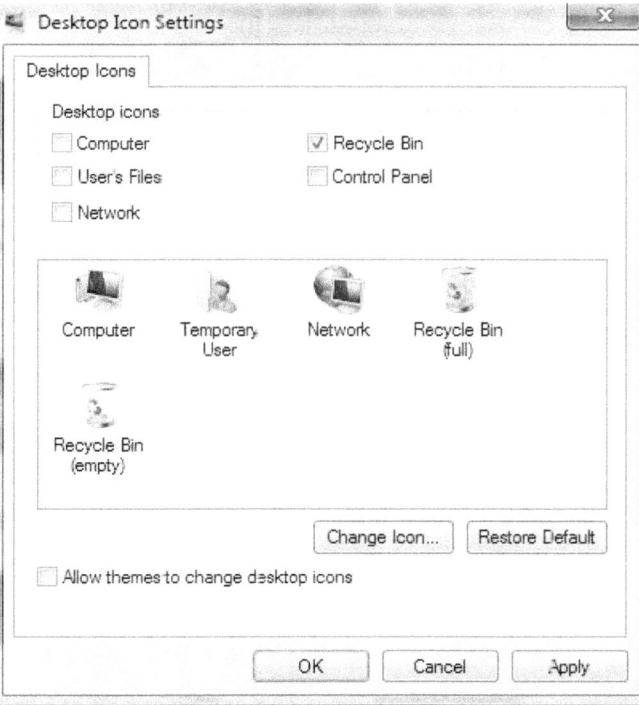

5. Once completed, click **Ok** button to save the changes and close all the opened Windows and boxes.

Increase the Size of Every Object

Because of rich quality display, default nature of Windows 7 is to decrease the size of every object that is displayed on the desktop or any Explorer. If you have decent eyesight you can enjoy this updated feature of Windows 7 up to its full. However for people who have sight problems may find it difficult to view the interfaces of Windows 7 with this kind of display. When this is the case users can increase the size of every object that is displayed on the screen by 25%. Below is the process using which users can do so:

1. Log on to the computer with the account on which you want to increase the display.
2. Right click on the desktop and from the displayed menu click **Screen resolution**.
3. On the opened window click **Make text and other items larger or smaller** link.
4. On **Make it easier to read what's on your screen** window choose **Medium – 125%** radio button and click **Apply** button to accept and confirm your configuration.

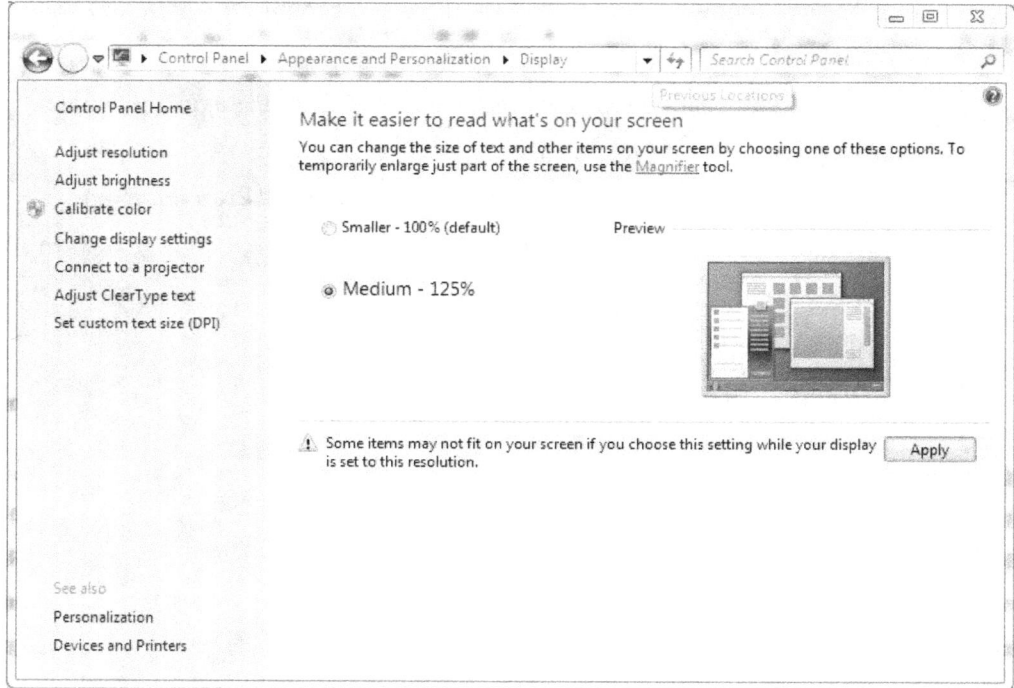

5. Close all opened windows.
6. If you want the changes to take effect you need to log off from the user account and then log back on.

More Info:

If you want to decrease the size you can reverse the process mentioned above.

Enable Screensavers

Many people think that screensavers in any operating system and are present for fun. Whereas there are others who think that screensavers should be, and are, used to protect the data on the screen from being seen by any unauthorized person. But most people don't know that screensavers, in real, are used to save and increase the lives of the monitors. Technical reason behind this is when any image is displayed on a monitor the transistors (in case of TFT monitors) are in use. When screensavers are used most of the area of the monitor displays dark background, hence turning off the transistors. This increases the lives of all the transistors, hence increasing overall lives of monitors. As a normal user you are not expected to know this technical reason however you can enable a screensaver on your Windows 7 computer by following the steps given below:

1. Log on to the Windows 7 computer with the user account on which you want to implement screensaver.

2. On the desktop right click anywhere and from the menu click **Personalize**.

3. On **Change the visuals and sounds on your computer** page click **Screen Saver** link and on the opened box from the drop-down list choose an appropriate screensaver as per your choice.

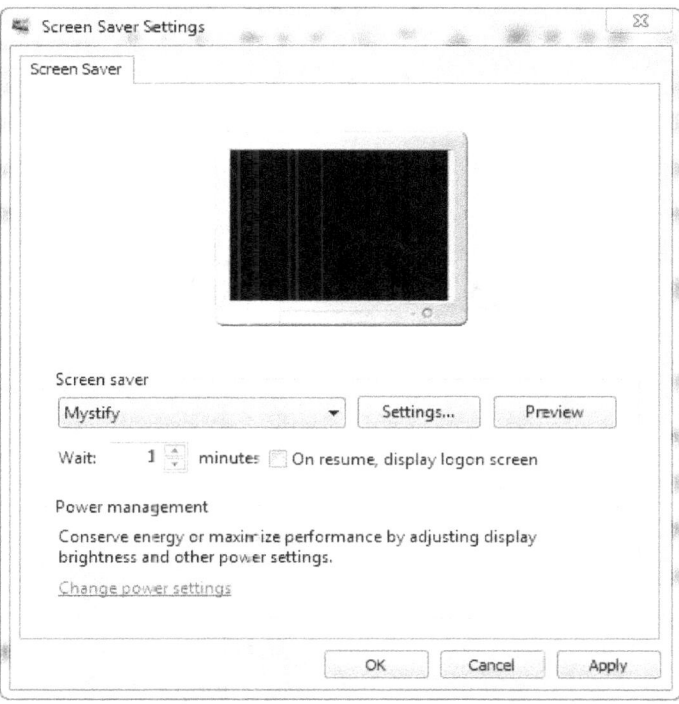

4. Once done, you can either click **Preview** button to see the demo of a screensaver all you can click **Ok** button to apply the changes you have made.

Note: Make sure that you choose the screensaver that has dark background in order to increase the life of your monitor.

Automatically Change Desktop Wallpapers

In earlier days people used third-party software applications such as Web shots to automatically change their desktop wallpapers after a specific period of time. For home users this was fun as they eliminated the chances of getting bored of watching the same desktop background for several days. Third-party software solution helped them a lot but consumed more processing and memory. Microsoft realized the requirements of users in this regard and hence it integrated this feature in Windows 7 operating system. Now, it is just the matter of few clicks and users can configure their Windows 7 computers to change wallpapers automatically. You can do so by following the steps given below:

1. Log on to a Windows 7 computer using the account on which you want to configure the above settings.

2. On the desktop, right click anywhere and from the menu click **Personalize**.

3. On **Change the visuals and sounds on your computer** page click **Desktop Background** link and on **Choose your desktop background** page select multiple wallpaper pictures by pressing Ctrl key when clicking on them.

4. Once the pictures are selected, choose the appropriate duration from the available **Change picture every:** drop-down list.

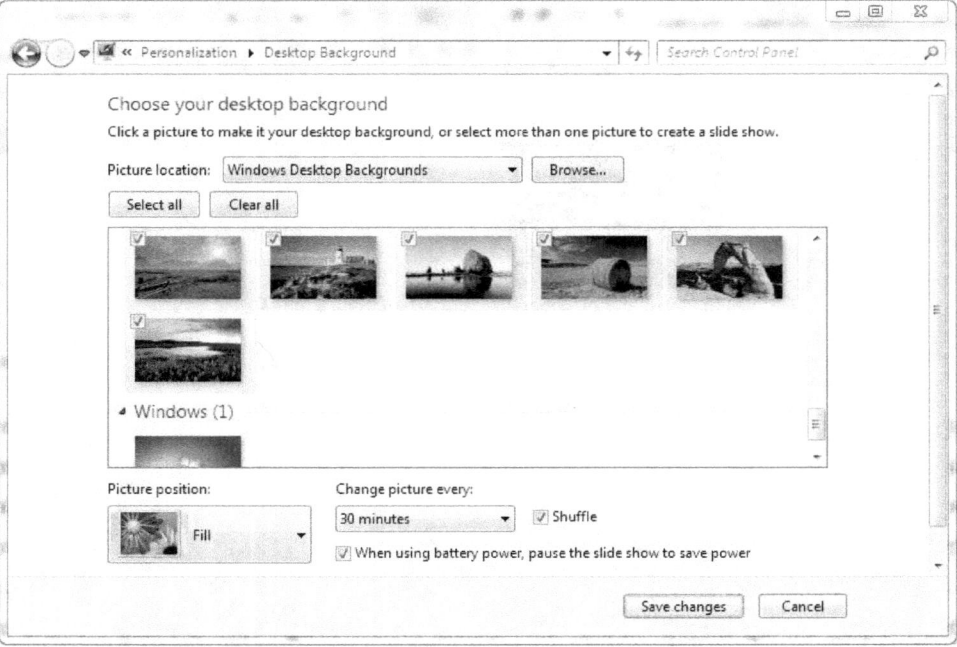

5. Once you are done with your configuration click **Save changes** to make your settings persistent and close all the opened Windows.

Configure Text Display

When working with Windows 7 it is expected that a user has a TFT or an LCD monitor. To increase visibility, Microsoft has designed **Clear Type Text** feature which enables users to see the text clearly as the feature sharpens the fonts. This configuration requires administrative privileges and hence to configure this user must logon with the administrator account on a Windows 7 computer. As an administrator if you want to configure this setting on your computer you need to follow the steps given below:

1. Log on to the computer with administrator account.

2. Right click anywhere on the desktop and click **Personalize**.

3. On **Change the visuals and sounds on your computer** page click **Display** link to go to the next page.

4. On the opened page click **Adjust Clear Type text** link and from the opened window follow the instructions provided on the screen. (Configuration from this screen onwards will totally depend on the user's personal experience and choice. Also from here onwards the wizard will guide you through a simple "Next NextFinish"process.)

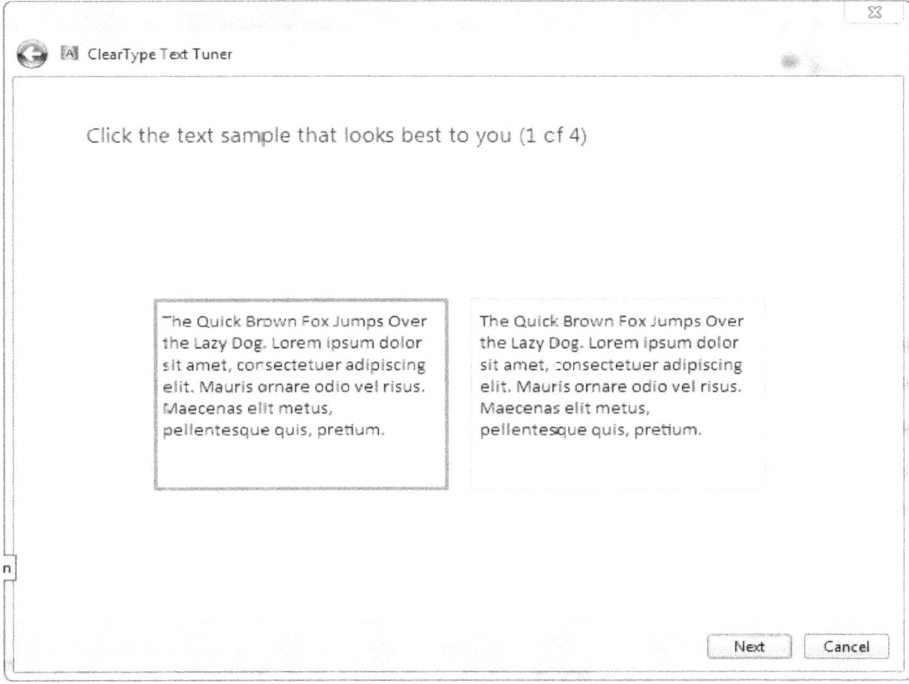

Note: This feature is only valuable when used with either TFT or LCD monitors. Users who still use CRT monitors should disable this feature to get the optimum performance and clearer display. In order to disable this feature you can uncheck Turn on Clear Type checkbox on Make the text on the screen easier to read page.

Manage Aero

When Windows Vista was first introduced it had a unique and great feature known as Aero. This feature used to provide a transparent glassy look to all Windows and other dialog boxes on which users worked. In Windows 7 this technology is improved and users can modify this as per their choices. In other words, users can increase or decrease transparency level of the Windows when working with a Windows 7 computer. Since this transparency level is a user specific configuration, any user is allowed to modify it without any administrative privileges. As a user of a Windows 7 computer you can configure transparency level of Windows and dialog boxes by following the steps given below:

1. Log on to the Windows 7 computer with the user account for which you want to configure transparency level.

2. Right click anywhere on the desktop and click **Personalize**.

3. On the opened page click **Windows Color** link.

4. On **Change the color of your window borders, Start menu, and taskbar** page move the slider left or right to increase or decrease the transparency level as per your choice.

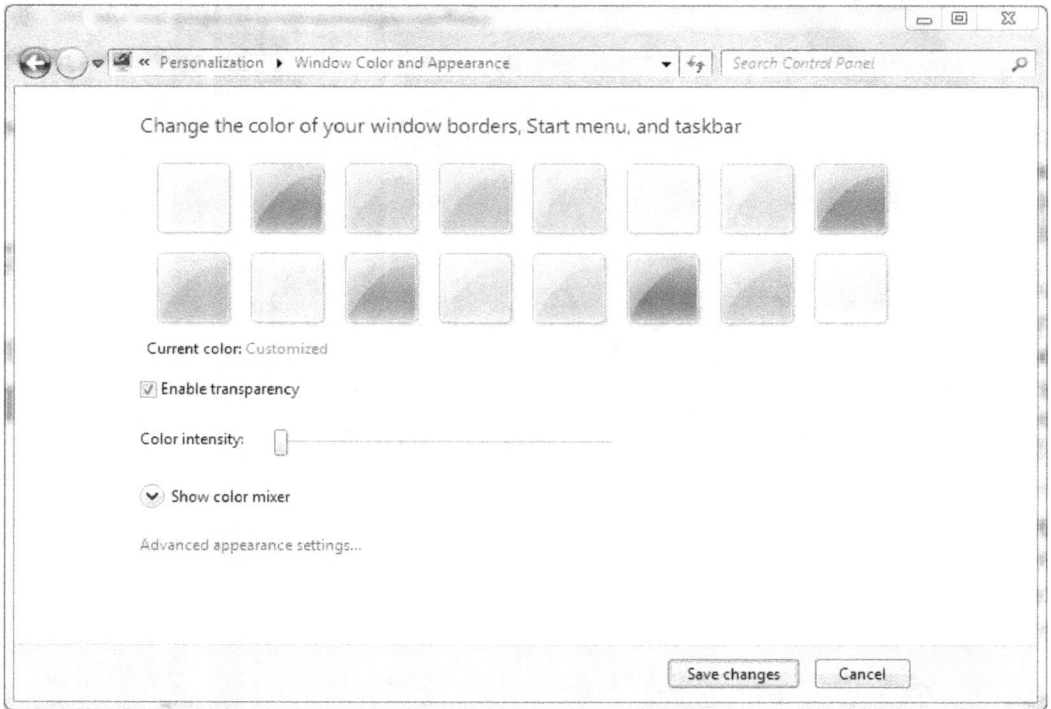

5. Once you are satisfied with your configuration, click **Save changes** button to finalize the changes. (To permanently disable the transparency you can uncheck **Enable transparency** checkbox.)

Change Account Pictures

Microsoft has developed Windows 7 for both homes and production environments. When Windows 7 is used in production environments, where the computers are connected to each other and are used for official purposes, account pictures and desktop backgrounds do not matter much. However when a Windows 7 computer is used in home environments and specifically for multimedia purposes, users may want to change their account pictures, modify desktop backgrounds, etc. If your computer is in your home and you want to change your account picture you need to follow the steps given below:

1. Log on to the computer with user account for which you want to change the picture.
2. Right click on the desktop and from the appeared menu click **Personalize**.
3. On the opened window in the left bar click **Change your account picture** link and on the next window click on appropriate image as per your choice.

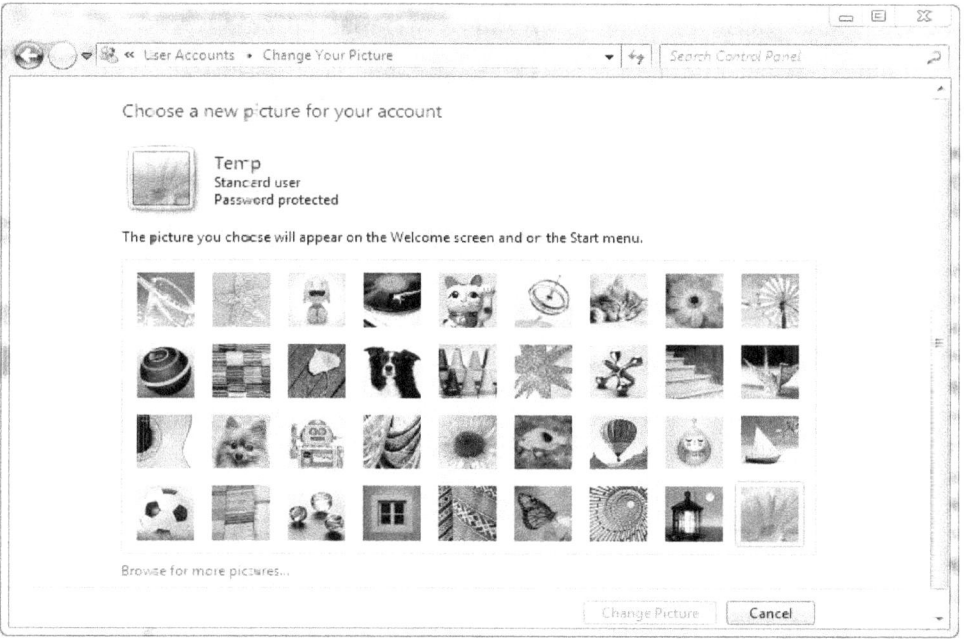

4. Once done, click **Save Picture** button to make the chosen image your default account picture.
5. Close all the opened Windows.

Note: Optionally you can click **Browse for more pictures** link to find other pictures on your computer.

Your account picture can be seen at the top right corner of the start menu. For home users it is recommended to have separate account picture images to identify their accounts at a single glance.

View Hidden Wallpapers

Not many people know that Windows 7 has multiple different themes that can be used according to the locale that is selected while installing the operating system. For example if the locale that is selected during installation says that the PC is from Africa, the theme and the wallpapers for that particular zone will automatically be displayed. Since this configuration is system specific it is not easily visible to every user. However, you can still view hidden wallpapers and apply the themes as per your convenience if you want. Even as a normal user if you want to view secret wallpapers of Windows 7 you need to follow the steps given below:

1. Log on to your Windows 7 computer with the account on which you want to apply the wallpaper from different locale and click **Start** button.

2. From the start menu go to **Computer** to open **Windows Explorer**.

3. Go to the following path: **C:\Windows\Globalization\MCT** where you will find various folders for separate time zones and locales and you need to select any one from them.

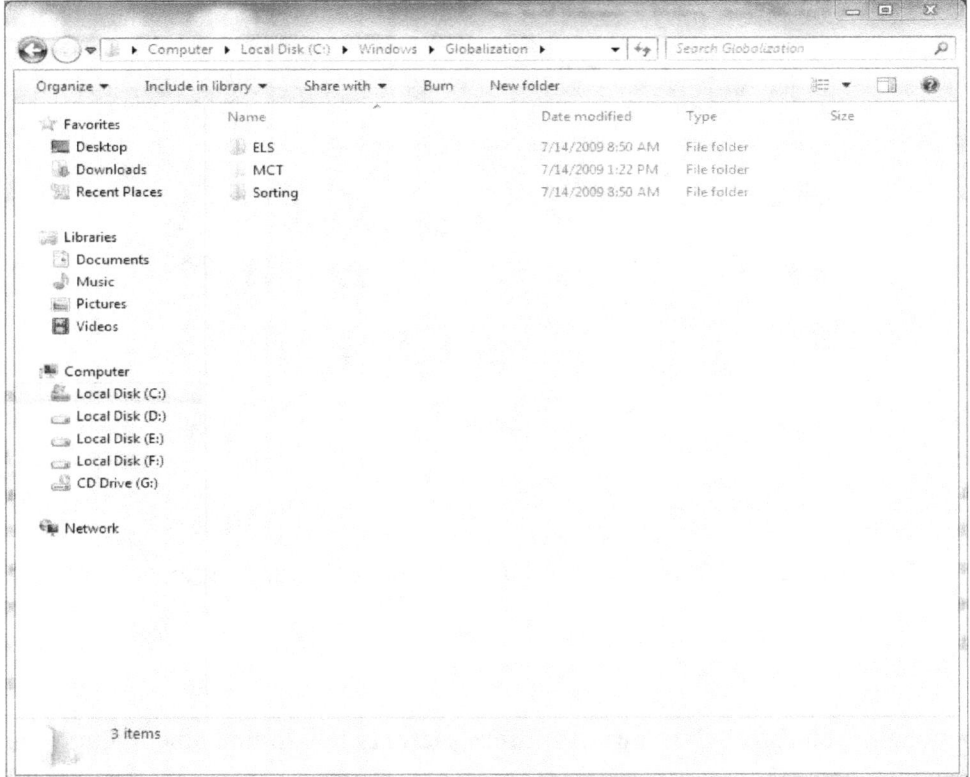

4. Open any folder of your choice and browse through the various subfolders containing different objects in it. The objects may contain theme files, wallpapers, etc.

Note: Since locale specific themes and wallpapers are configured by Windows itself they are hidden by default. In order to access **MCT** folder you need to configure your computer to show all hidden files and folders. Alternatively you type the path directly either in **Run Command** box or in **Search Box**.

Display Recent Programs in Start Menu

Windows 7 has a feature of displaying most frequently used applications in the start menu list. By-default the list contains 10 applications that were recently used by the logged on user. If the display settings of the operating system are customized and the computer is configured to display large icons, entire start menu list may cover up the whole left portion of the desktop screen hence covering all desktop icons behind it. This configuration is not at all harmful by any means but might sometimes be annoying for the users. When this is the case users can customize the number of applications that start menu list can contain at a single given time. If you want to configure your Windows 7 computer as mentioned you are required to follow the steps given as below:

1. Log on to Windows 7 computer with the user account for which you want to customize the number of applications to be displayed in the start menu.

2. Right click **Start** button and click **Properties**.

3. From **Taskbar and Start Menu Properties** box make sure that you are **Start Menu** tab and click **Customized** button.

4. On **Customize Start Menu** box under **Start menu size** section increase or decrease the numbers in front of **Number of recent programs to display** as desired.

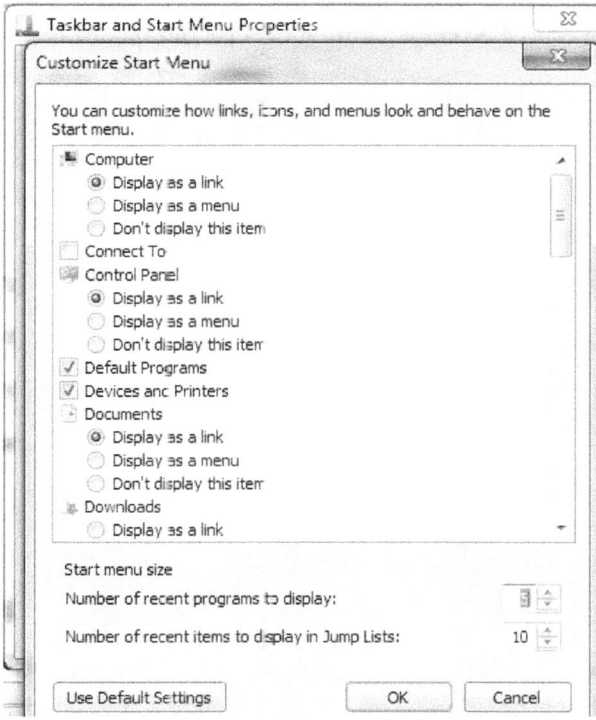

5. Click **Ok** buttons and on all opened boxes to allow the changes to take effect.

Permanently Hide Applications in Start Menu

As a Windows 7 user in both home and productions environments there might be times when you, as a user, do not want to let anybody know which application you use most frequently. Applications can be games or media players. Under normal circumstances and default configurations every application that is frequently used by a user is displayed in start menu list. However with the help of some registry modifications you can permanently hide selected applications from getting displayed in the start menu list. You need to have administrative privileges on the computer in order to do so and the steps involved to accomplish the process are given as below:

1. Log on to Windows 7 computer with any account that has administrative privileges.

2. Click **Start** button and from the available menu in search box type **REGEDIT** and press enter key.

3. On **Registry Editor** Window expand **HKEY_CLASSES_ROOT** and locate and expand **Applications** hive.

4. From the expanded list locate the name of the application which you want to permanently hide **VLC.EXE** in this case.

5. Right click on it and from the available menu point to **New**.

6. From the appeared submenu click **String Value** and type the name of the string value as **NoStartPage**.

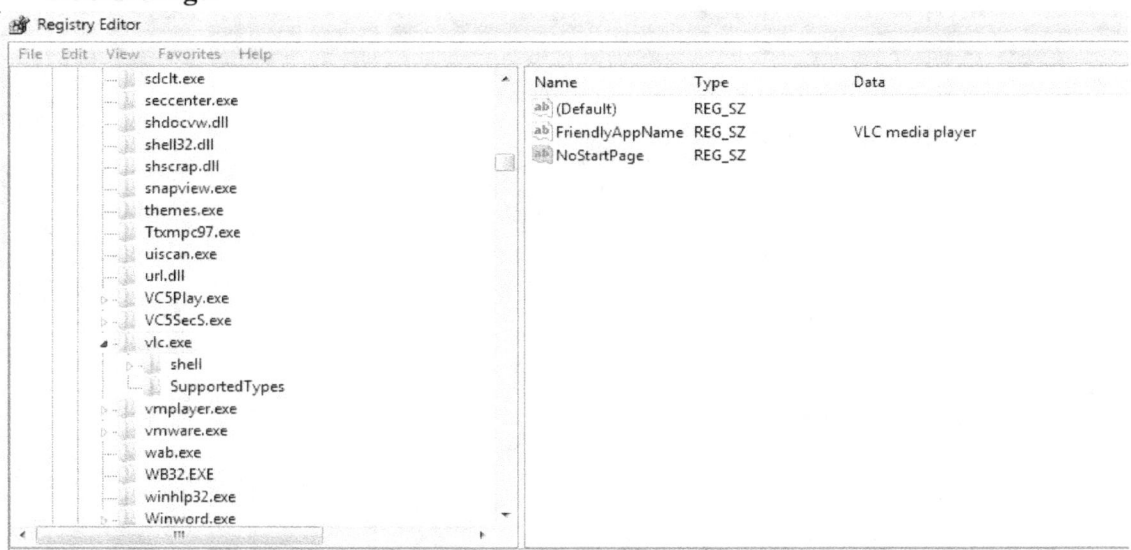

7. Logoff from the account and log back in to allow the changes to take effect.

Change Desktop Wallpaper

As legacy versions of Windows based operating systems, Microsoft Windows 7 also offers the facility of changing the desktop wallpapers as per users will. In other words, users can place desktop wallpapers of their own choices and they are not at all limited to the images which are by default shipped along with Windows 7 operating system. Recommendations, however, are that wallpapers that users choose should be of HD (high-definition) so that the decorum of the operating system is kept intact. Moreover, choosing inappropriate image file may also result in decreased graphics display which further may reduce visual effects of the operating system and hence final output my not be as promising as claimed by Microsoft. Whatsoever the case is, if as a Windows 7 user you want to change desktop wallpaper you are required to follow the steps given as below:

1. Log on to Windows 7 computer with any account as the process does not require any elevated privileges.

2. Right click anywhere on the desktop and from the context menu click on Personalize.

3. From the opened box click **Desktop background** link.

4. On the newly opened box click **Browse** button **Picture location** category

5. On **Browse For Folder** box locate the folder where the desired image is stored and click **Ok** button.

6. Back on the previous page select the desired image that you want to assign as desktop wallpaper and finally click **Save changes** button to save the changes.

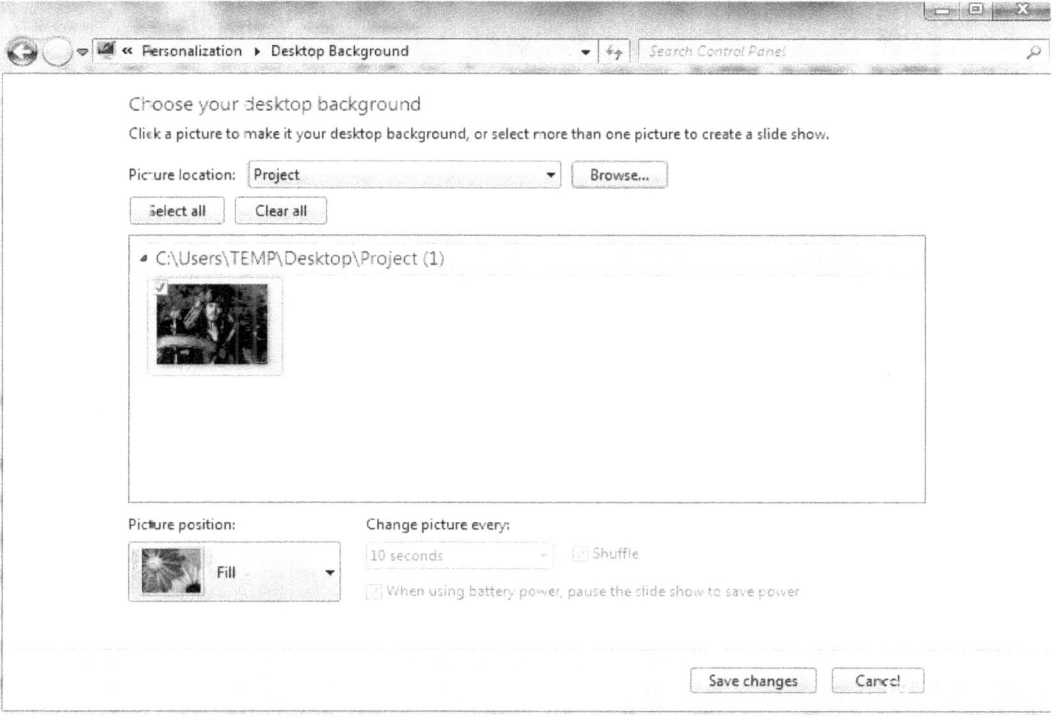

Change the Size of Desktop Icons

With the release of Microsoft Windows 7, the size of the icons on the desktop has also been changed. This modification has disturbed majority of users in a great deal. Hopefully, Microsoft has already pre-estimated these consequences and therefore it has provided the facility of changing the size of the icons as per users' requirements. Although changing the size of the icons was also possible in legacy versions of operating systems but users need to go through several dialog boxes and menus in order to do so. However in Windows 7 the process has become quite simpler and users can change the size of the icons within the blink of their eyes. Although there are several ways to do so in Windows 7 but the easiest way that can be followed by the users in order to change the size of the icons of the desktop is mentioned as below:

1. Log on to Windows 7 computer with the account on which you need to modify the size of desktop icons.

2. Once Windows is booted make sure that you are on the desktop screen and press down and hold **Ctrl** key and scroll the mouse wheel up or down to increase or decrease the size of the icons.

3. Once you are convinced with the size, release the mouse wheel and **Ctrl** key.

Change Logon Background Image

In legacy versions of Microsoft based operating systems users were allowed to change desktop wallpapers and account images according to their choices. Same is the case with Windows 7 but in Windows 7 users can also change logon backgrounds with the help of small registry tweak. The process requires administrative privileges and therefore no standard user can accomplish the task without elevated credentials. As a Windows 7 administrator if you want to modify logon background image you are required to follow the steps given as below:

1. Log on to Windows 7 computer with any account that has elevated privileges.

2. At the bottom of start menu in the search box type **REGEDIT** and press enter key.

3. In **Registry Editor**box navigate to

4. **HKEY_LOCAL_MACHINE\SOFTWARE\Microsoft\Windows\CurrentVersion\Authentication\LogonUI\Background** from the left pane and from the right pane double-click **OEMBackground**. (If it is not present you need to create a new 32-bit DWORD and name it as **OEMBackground**).

5. On the opened box under **Value data** field specify the value as **1** and click **Ok** button.

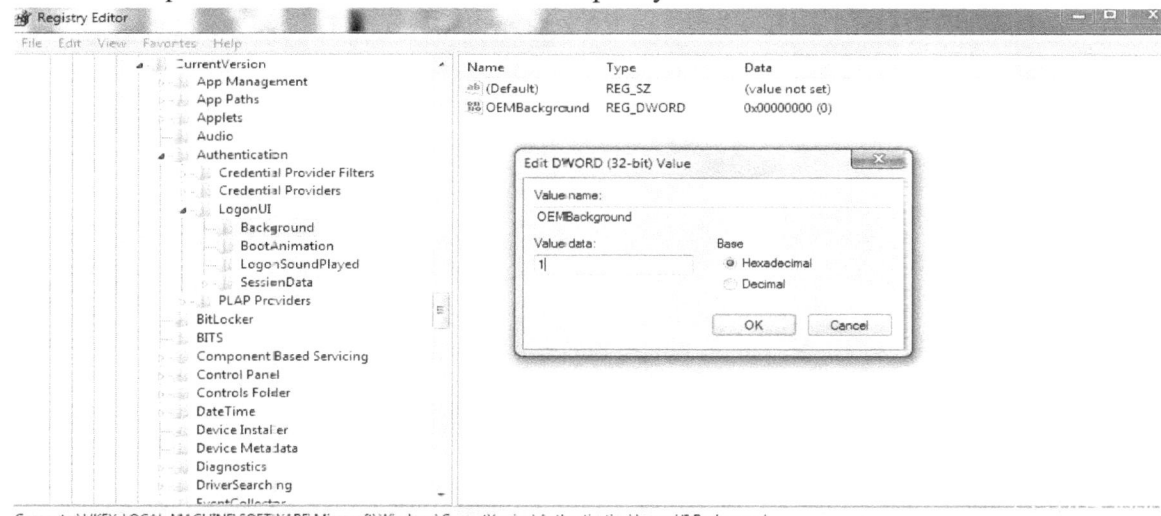

6. Once completed, close **Registry Editor**.

7. Now navigate to **C:\Windows\System32\oobe\info** location and create a new folder named **backgrounds**.

8. Finally copy the desired wallpaper image to this folder and rename it with **backgroundDefault.jpg**.

9. Restart the computer if required.

Enable/Disable Aero Peek to Preview Desktop

In Windows 7 'Show Desktop' icon is not available as it was present in legacy versions of Microsoft based operating systems. Instead, another button, which is almost invisible to users, is provided at the bottom right corner of desktop, that is, at the right most corner of system tray. When Aero Peak feature is enabled, which is the default configuration, the button displays a preview of the desktop screen whenever the mouse is pointed on it. When Aero Peek feature is disabled the button works as the older version of Show Desktop icon which when clicked minimizes all active Windows and displays the desktop. Another feature which is added to this button is that it works on toggle, that is, it displays the desktop by minimizing all Windows when clicked once and restores all the Windows when clicked again. As a Windows 7 user if you want to enable or disable Aero Peek feature to control this button you are required to follow the steps given below:

1. Log on to Windows 7 computer with any account. You can even use standard user account as the process does not require any elevated privileges.

2. Right click at any blank space in the taskbar and from the appeared menu click **Properties**.

3. On **Taskbar and Start Menu Properties** box make sure that you are on **Taskbar** tab.

4. Under **Preview desktop with Aero Peek** section check (to enable) or uncheck (to disable) **Use Aero Peek to preview the desktop** checkbox.

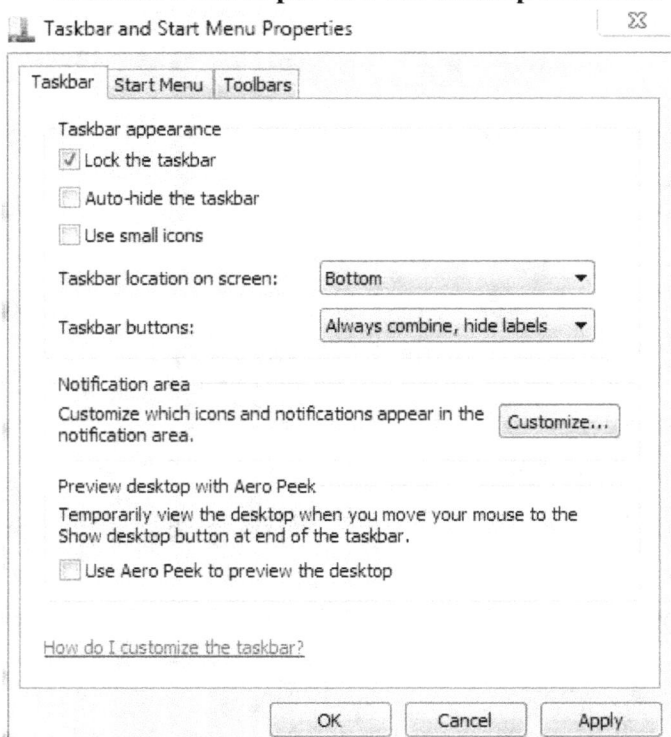

5. Once done, click **Ok** button to save the changes that you have made.

Hide Desktop Icon Text

In Windows 7 whenever an application is installed, in 90% cases shortcut icon of that application is automatically placed on the desktop. All shortcut icons available on the desktop are the links to actual executable files of those applications. Default characteristic of any shortcut icon is that it contains symbol of the application with a small arrow at the bottom left corner of the icon and a text below the symbol displaying its name. 99% users never consider or care to read the name of the application they want to open and they simply recognize it by its official symbol instead. This further means that the text displayed under the icon of the shortcut is just an optional element which, when removed, would not give any negative impact while opening the application. Keeping this in mind if users want to remove the text from the shortcut icon they can do so very easily by following the steps given below:

1. Log on to Windows 7 computer with the user account on whose profile you want to remove the text from the desktop shortcut icons.
2. Right-click on the icon on which you want to disable text and from the available menu click **Rename**.
3. In the editable text box specify any number between **1** and **255** while pressing **Alt** key.
4. Once you are done with it press enter key.

Disable Thumbnail Previews

Windows has provided a feature of thumbnail preview which allows users to get a glance of any image file without even clicking or double-clicking on it. This helps users to locate their desired files easily and quickly without going through all of them one by one. Moreover with this configuration users need not to memorize the names of the files they wish to locate on day-to-day basis as they can directly get the preview of them as soon as they enter the folder in which they are stored. Under normal circumstances and in home and small-scale industries this configuration is quite handy and is mostly not modified at all. However in medium to large scale organizations where computer speeds matter administrators might want to disable this feature as it consumes some processing. Also when this configuration is enabled entire contents of the folders take some time to get fully displayed to the users. Therefore, as a Windows 7 user if you want to disable thumbnail preview feature you are required to follow the steps given below:

1. Log on to Windows 7 computer.

2. From the start menu go to **Computer**.

3. From the opened window click **Organize** from the left corner below the menu bar and from the available list click **Folder and Search Options**.

4. On **Folder Options** box go to **View** tab and from the displayed list check **Always show icons, never thumbnails** checkbox.

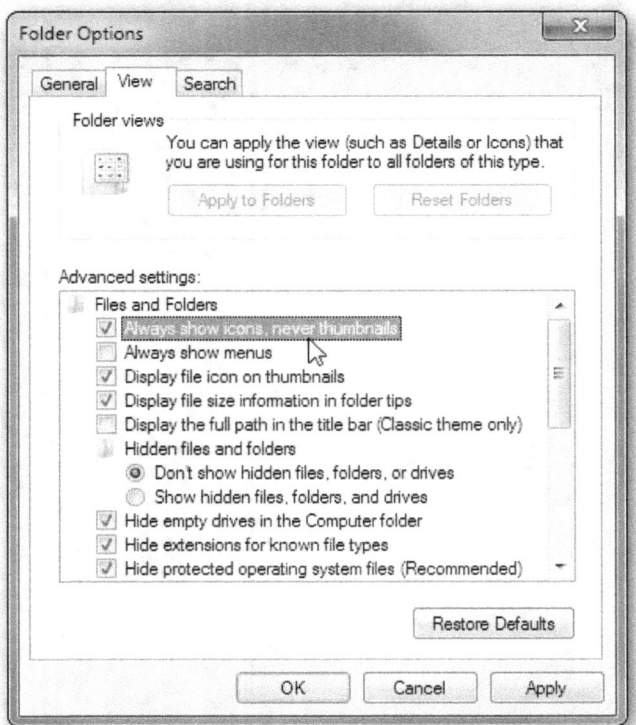

5. Click **Ok** button when done to allow the changes to take effect.

Increase or Decrease Mouse Pointer Speed

As default Microsoft configuration when any of its operating system is installed on a computer, it provides optimum configuration which is best suited for an ideal scenario. Same is the case with mouse pointer speed in Windows 7. By default the speed of the pointer is ideal for every user under normal conditions. However users can increase or decrease pointer speeds of their mice when they move it as per their requirements. Scenarios may include production environments, desktop publishing, etc. Pointer speed configuration is a user specific setting which can be modified by following the steps given below:

1. Log on to the Windows 7 computer with the user account on which you want to manage mouse pointer speed.

2. Right click on the desktop and from the context menu click **Personalize**.

3. On **Change the visuals and sounds on your computer** window in the left side click **Change mouse pointers** link.

4. On **Mouse Properties** box go to **Pointer Options** tab and in **Motion** section move the slider right or left to increase or decrease the pointer speed respectively.

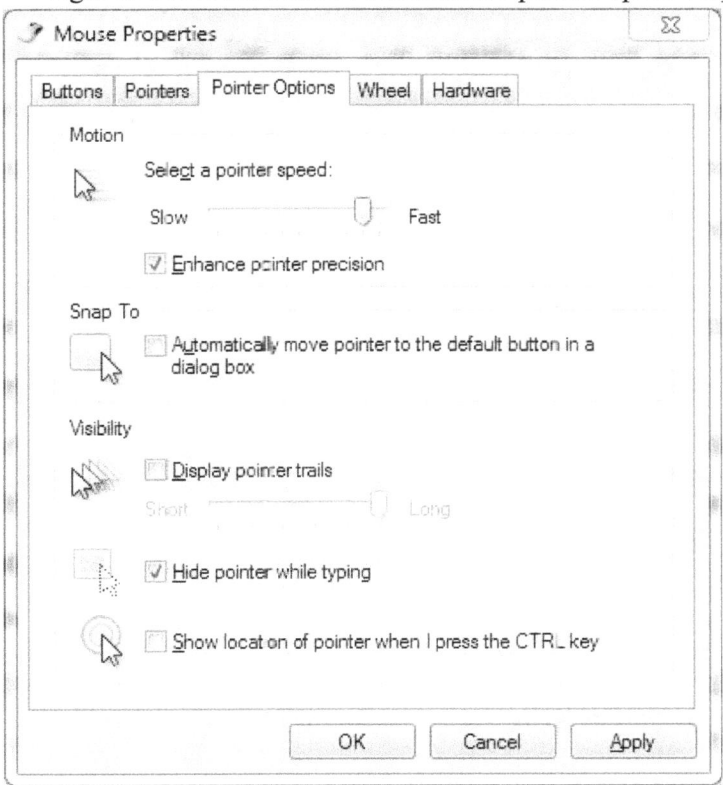

5. Once done, click **Ok** button to accept and confirm your configuration and close all the opened Windows.

Manage Mouse Double-Click Speed

When Windows 7 is installed it senses a normal double-click speed of the mouse. However in the cases where users are physically challenged mouse double-click speed can be increased or decreased as per the requirements. This means that if mouse double-clicking speed is decreased users can increase the time interval between two subsequent mouse clicks. This makes users work with mouse more comfortably. You can increase or decrease mouse double-click speed by following the steps given below:

1. Log on to the computer with the user account on which you want to manage the mouse double-click speed.

2. Right click anywhere on the desktop window and from the context menu click **Personalize**.

3. On **Change the visuals and sounds on your computer** window in the left hand bar click **Change mouse pointers**.

4. On **Mouse Properties** box go to **Buttons** tab and in **Double-click speed** section move the slider left or right to decrease or increase the double-click speed respectively. (If you decrease the speed by moving the slider to the left, users can increase the time interval between two subsequent mouse clicks. The action will reverse when the slider is moved to the right).

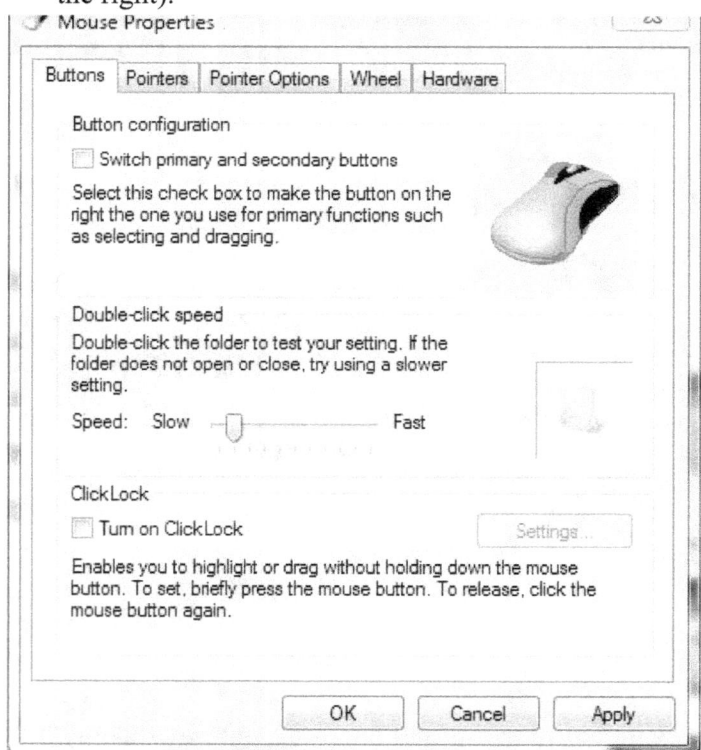

5. Once configured, click **Ok** button to confirm your configuration and close the opened Window.

Increase Mouse Pointer Visibility by Pointer Trails

Microsoft has designed Windows 7 operating system in such a way so that almost everyone can work on it conveniently. It has several features that increase the visibility of objects which helps users easily locate and use them efficiently. Visibility of mouse is among one of these. To increase visibility of mouse pointer and its movements in Windows 7, Microsoft has provided a feature of Pointer Trails which when enabled, adds a trail to the mouse pointer. Benefit of this is whenever a mouse is moved from one location to another it becomes quite easy for users to locate it because of its long trail. You can configure your Windows 7 computer to display mouse pointer trails by following the steps given below:

1. Log on to computer with the user account on which you want to enable mouse pointer trail.
2. Right click anywhere on the desktop and from the menu click **Personalize**.
3. On **Change the visuals and sounds on your computer** window in the left bar click **Change mouse pointers** link.
4. On **Mouse Properties** box go to **Pointer Options** tab and in **Visibility** section and check **Display pointer trails** checkbox.

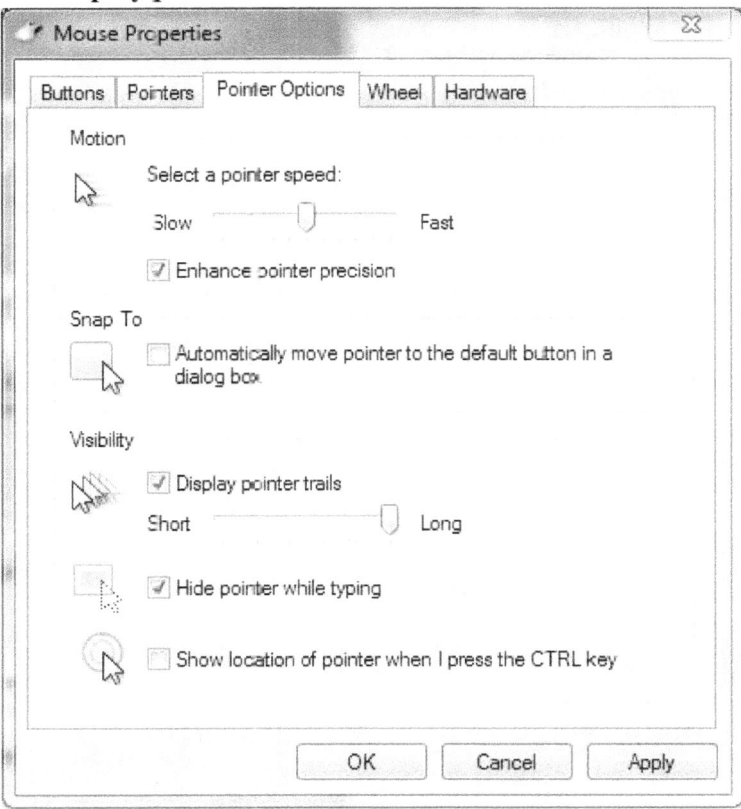

5. Once completed you can click **Ok** to confirm the configuration and close all the Windows.

Move Mouse Pointer to the Default Button

When any dialog box is opened in Windows 7 this indicates that the operating system expects some interaction (input) from the users' end. In most cases users just need to click on any of the available buttons, which may be Ok, Cancel or Help. Whenever any box is opened Windows 7 expects a default value to be chosen by the users and therefore it highlights the default button to help users take decisions easily. As a user you can increase proficiency of this feature by configuring Windows 7 computer to place mouse pointer on the default button whenever any box is popped up. You can do this by following the steps given below:

1. Log on to the Windows 7 computer with the user account on which you want to configure mouse pointer.

2. Right click anywhere on the desktop and from the context menu click **Personalize**.

3. On **Change the visuals and sounds on your computer** window in the left bar click **Change mouse pointers** link.

4. On **Mouse Properties** box go to **Pointer Options** tab and in **Snap To** section and check **Automatically movie pointer to the default button in a dialog box** checkbox.

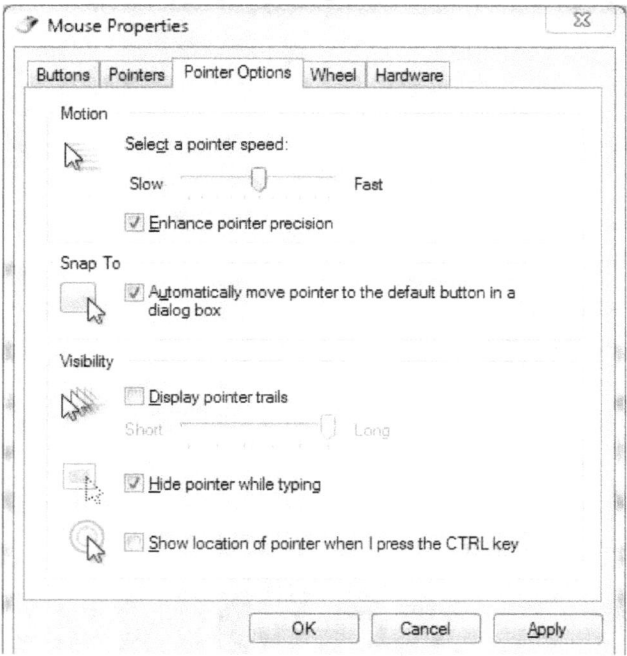

5. Now click **Ok** button to accept and confirm your configuration and close the Window.

Modify Mouse Pointers

By default mouse pointer of Windows 7 computer is small in size to make it well aligned with the ambience the operating system offers. However people who suffer from visibility problems may find it complicated to work with the size of the pointer. When this is the case users can increase the size and/or change its color so that the pointer can become easily visible. Modifying mouse pointers never reduces Windows performance and the customization totally depends upon the ease of the user. You can modify mouse pointers in Windows 7 computer by following the steps given below:

1. Log on to the computer with the account for which you want to modify mouse pointers.
2. Right click on the desktop and from the menu click on Personalize.
3. On the opened page at the bottom left corner choose **Ease of Access Centre** to click on.
4. On the next page click **Make the mouse easier to use** to get the next window.
5. On the appeared page under **Mouse pointers** section choose the appropriate radio button according to your visibility and requirement and click **Apply** button to view the demo.

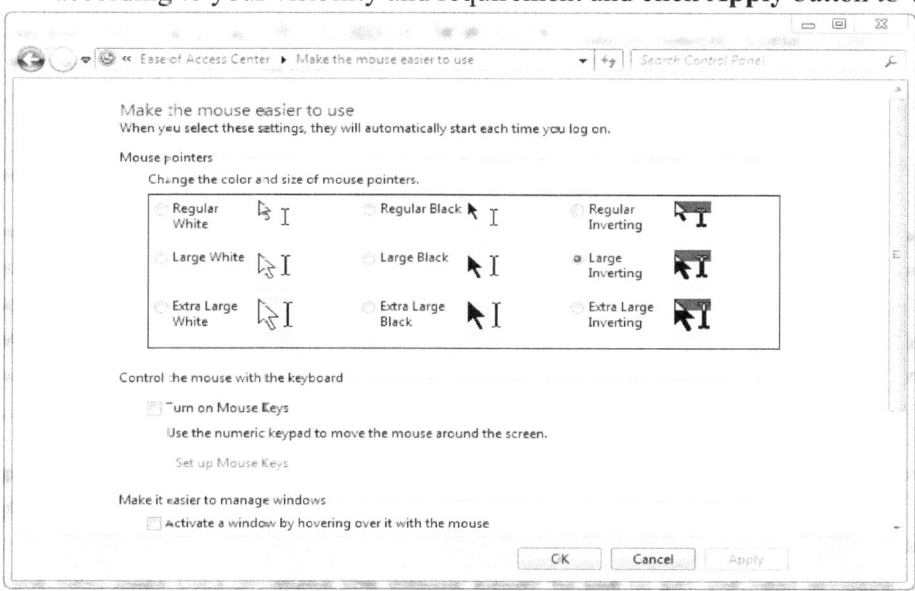

6. Once satisfied with the configuration, click **Ok** button to finalize your settings and close all the opened Windows and pages.

Enable Mouse Keys

Have you ever faced the situation when your mouse stops working and you are then required to remember several key combinations in order to work with Windows 7? Though, experts say that working on computer with keyboard is far easier and quicker than working with mouse. However users nowadays are habitual of using 'mouse and double-click' and they find it hard to use keyboard and even harder to remember thousands of key combinations. In these situations when users do not know important key combinations and their mouse has stopped working, they can enable mouse keys feature available with Windows 7 to use NumPad of their keyboards as mice. You can do so by following the steps given below:

1. Log on to the Windows 7 computer.
2. On the desktop screen right click at any vacant area and from the menu click on Personalize.
3. On the opened window at the bottom of the left corner click **Ease of Access Centre** link.
4. On the appeared page click **Make the mouse easier to use** link and from the next window under **Control the mouse with the keyboard** section check **Turn on Mouse Keys** check-box.

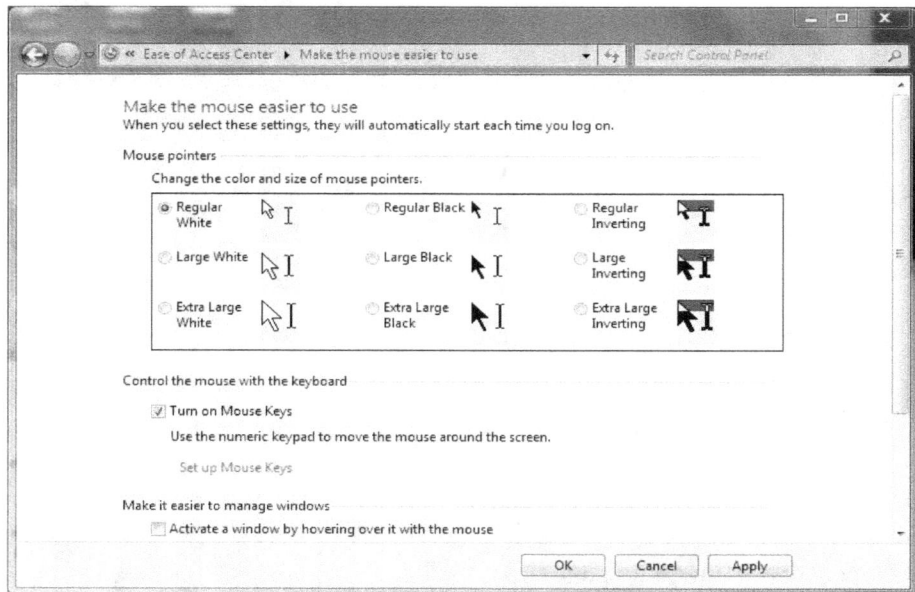

5. Optionally you can click **Set up Mouse Keys** link to fine-tune the settings.
6. Once done, click **Ok** button to finalize the configuration and close all the opened Windows.

Drag Objects without Holding Mouse Button

In Windows 7 when a user wants to move any object he needs to click on that object and while holding the mouse button down he needs to drag it to its destination. This method is quite easy when users need to move objects from one place to another quickly. However, sometimes this process might be quite hectic for users. Also, when the quality of mouse is not up to the mark mouse button automatically gets released in the mid of the process, hence messing up everything. To make things easier for users Windows 7 provides a feature using which you can drag any object from its source to its destination without holding mouse button down. You can configure this by following the steps given below:

1. Log on to the Windows 7 computer using the account on which you want to manage mouse while dragging.

2. Right click on desktop and from the menu click **Personalize**.

3. On **Change the visuals and sounds on your computer** window in the left bar click **Change mouse pointers** link.

4. On **Mouse Properties** box go to **Buttons** tab and in **ClickLock** section check **Turn on ClickLock** check box.

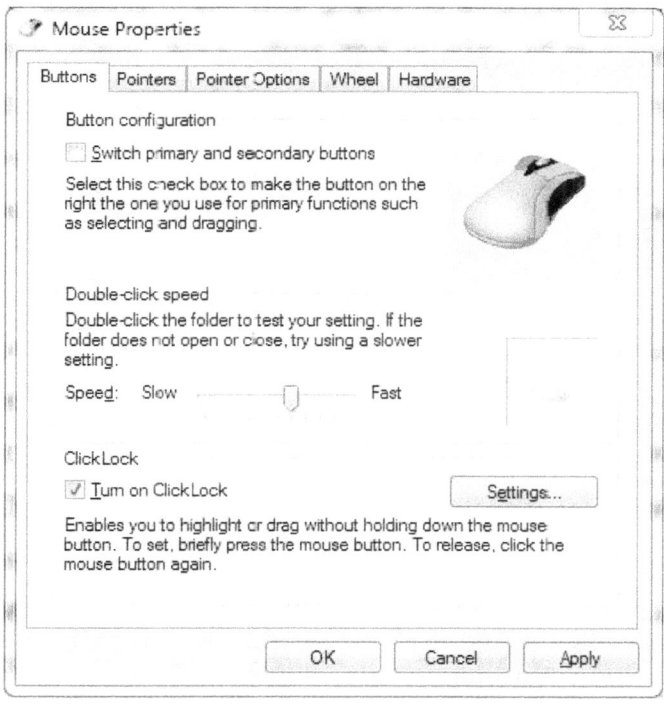

5. Click **Ok** button to accept your configuration and close all Windows.

Once this is configured you can single-click on that object and can move the mouse without holding down the button. To drop the object single click on it once again.

Manage Filter Keys

While typing any text document in any text editor in Windows 7 it is normal that users may sometimes press any key multiple times unintentionally and might end up printing a single character multiple times unwantedly. For professional typists this is a normal error which they make every now and then. This nature of Windows 7 can also be annoying for physically challenged users as they are considered comparatively slow. Microsoft understands this and therefore it has provided Filter Keys feature which, when enabled, ignores multiple key strokes which are unwantedly and unintentionally pressed because of human errors. Filter Keys can easily be enabled by pressing and holding right SHIFT key for 8 seconds. When it is enabled a pop-up box is appeared on the desktop screen of the user asking whether he/she wants to enable Filter Keys. This configuration is developed by Microsoft to provide ease of access to the users however sometimes game lovers may find this annoying and may want to disable it. When this is the case, this feature can easily be disabled by following the steps given below:

1. Log on to Windows 7 computer with the account on which you want to configure the settings.

2. At the bottom of start menu search box type **Change How Your Keyboard Works** and press enter key.

3. On the opened window click **Set up Filter Keys** link.

4. On the new window uncheck **Turn on Filter Keys will right SHIFT key is pressed for 8 seconds** checkbox.

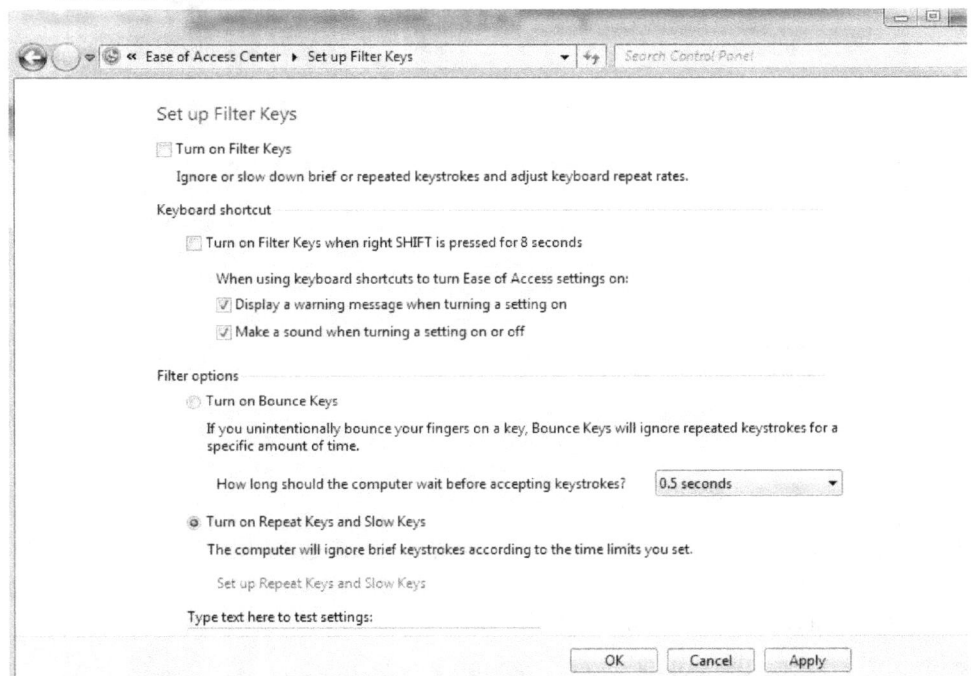

5. Finally click **Ok** button and close all the opened Windows and boxes.

Enable Toggle Keys Notification Sounds

Windows 7 is an operating system which is designed by Microsoft to satisfy every user's needs. This operating system can be used in production environments where there are several machines connected in a local area network and also in home environments where all types of users operate Windows 7 for entertainment purposes. Toggle keys on your keyboard include **Scroll Lock**, **Caps Lock** and **Num Lock**. Sounds for toggle keys can be enabled when usersare physically challenged and are not fast enough to notice frequent changes in the computers. Such users can easily identify when toggle keys are pressed by the notification sounds that the computers make when sounds for toggle keys are enabled. You can enable the above feature on Windows 7 computer by following the steps given below:

1. Log on to the Windows 7 computer.
2. Right click on the desktop screen and from the menu click **Personalize**.
3. From the opened window in the bottom left corner click **Ease of Access Enter** link and on the next page scroll down to the bottom and click **Make the keyboard easier to use** link.
4. On the opened page under **Make it easier to type** section check **Turn on Toggle Keys** checkbox and click **Ok** button to make the settings permanent.

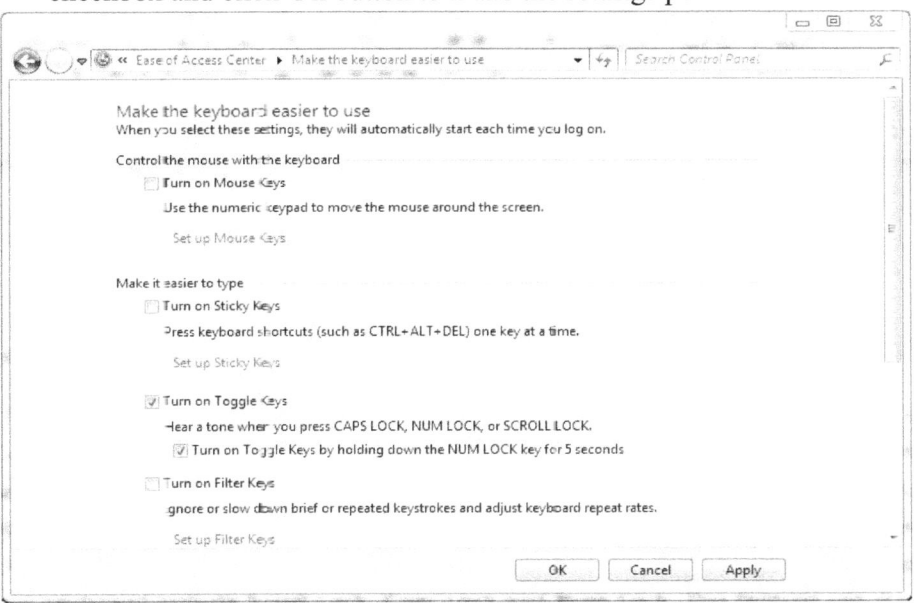

5. Close all opened Windows.

Enable Sticky Keys

In Windows 7 there are many controls which can only be initiated and activated when a combination of keys are pressed. For example when working with Microsoft Word, if a user wants to save his document he needs to press Ctrl+S key to do so. In the same way if a user wants to open **Run Command** box he needs to press Windows+R key to get it done. This key combination feature enables users to use Windows in a simplified manner. However if any user is physically challenged he might find it complicated to press multiple keys at a single given time. When this is the case, a Windows 7 computer can be configured accordingly so that a physically challenged user does not have to press multiple keys in a single go. Instead he can press one key at a time and can get the desired work done. If you want to configure your Windows 7 computer to do so you need to follow the steps given below:

1. Log on to the computer with the account on which you want to configure the above settings.
2. Right click anywhere on the desktop and from the appeared menu click **Personalize**.
3. On the opened window in the left side at the bottom of the bar click **Ease of Access Centre** link.
4. On **Make your computer easier to use** page scroll down to the bottom and click **Make it easier to focus on tasks** link.
5. On the next page under **Make easier to type** section check **Turn on Sticky Keys** checkbox and click **Ok** button to confirm your configuration.

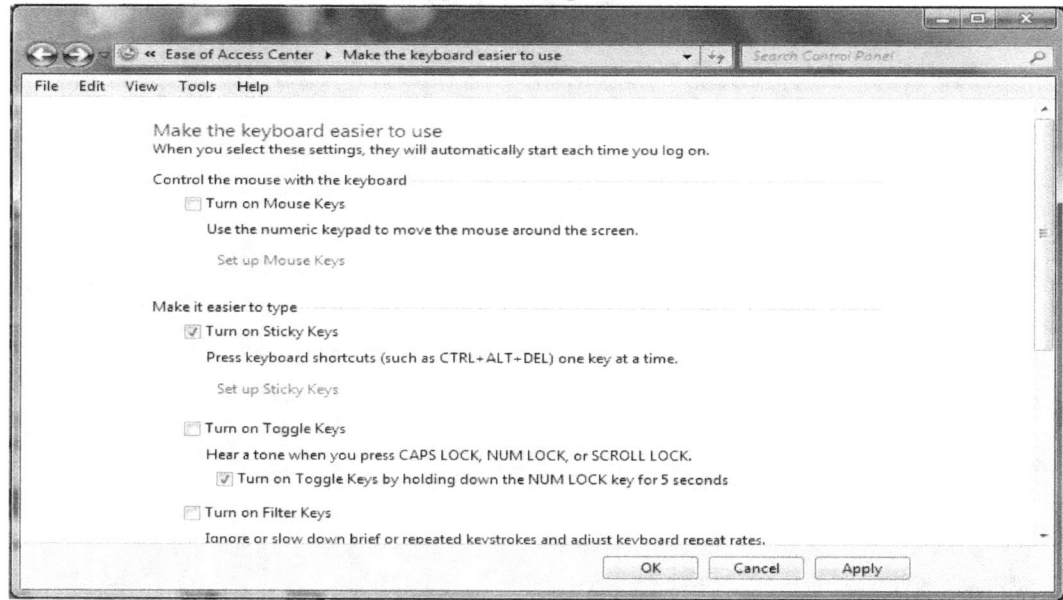

Change Taskbar Location

There can be several reasons because of which you may want to change the default location of your Windows 7 taskbar. Some of them may include: You may not like the default ambience of your Windows 7 desktop screen, you are habitual of using some other operating system and are new to Microsoft platform and you want to adjust the settings to make yourself comfortable with it, you might be using an application that requires more room on your Windows screen and has some valuable controls at the bottom of its interface which you don't want to become unavailable because of the taskbar, etc. In any case you can modify the default location of your Windows 7 taskbar without unlocking it. If you want to change the location of your Windows 7 taskbar you need to follow the steps given below:

1. Log on to the Windows 7 computer with the account for which you want to change the location of the taskbar.

2. On the desktop screen right click on the taskbar and from the menu click **Properties**

3. On **Taskbar and Start Menu Properties** box from the **Taskbar location on screen** drop-down list choose the appropriate location as per your requirement.

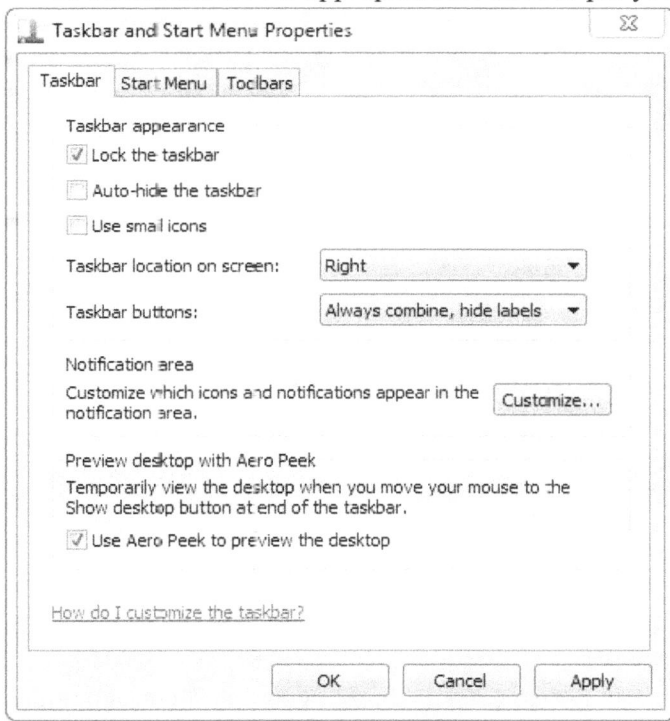

4. To view the demo click **Apply** button and once you are satisfied with the location click **Ok** button to make your settings persistent.

Hide Taskbar Automatically

By default Windows 7 taskbar is static and unchangeable. If you want to resize or change its location you need to unlock it to do so. However, there might be times when users may neither want to resize nor they want to change its location, but they just want to hide it to get a full screen view of any opened window or application. Hiding entire taskbar forever might not be a realistic thing to do and therefore Microsoft has provided auto hide feature for the taskbar. With the help of this feature the taskbar will automatically be hidden when users do not require it. As soon as users take mouse pointer to the bottom of the desktop screens, the taskbar will automatically reappear. If you want to enable auto hide taskbar feature in your Windows 7 computer you need to follow the steps given below:

1. Log on to the computer with the user account on which you want to enable auto hide taskbar feature.

2. Right click on the taskbar and click **Properties**.

3. On the **Taskbar and Start Menu Properties** box check **Auto-hide the taskbar** checkbox.

4. Once done, click **Apply** button to get the demo of your latest configuration and if you are convinced with your modifications click **Ok** button to finalize your settings and make them persistent.

Make Taskbar Adjustable

In Windows 7 taskbar is by default locked and because of this users are unable to modify its size or location. Microsoft has designed this feature so that users can get a static ambience and to protect the configuration from getting disturbed because of mishandling. However in some cases this feature may make users feel suffocated because of its limitation. Microsoft understands this and therefore it offers complete control of this feature to the users. Users can now lock or unlock the taskbar according to their requirements. In other words when the taskbar is unlocked it can be resized or moved to a different location, whereas when it is locked it becomes unchangeable. Since this configuration is user specific, users can adjust their taskbar's nature according to their choices. If you want to unlock your taskbar to be able to modify it you need to follow the steps given below:

1. Log on to the computer with the account for which you want to modify the taskbar.
2. On the desktop screen right click on the taskbar and from the menu click **Properties**.
3. On **Taskbar and Start Menu Properties** box uncheck **Lock the taskbar** checkbox.

4. Click **Ok** button to accept your latest configuration.

You can now resize and/or change the location of your taskbar. Once you are convinced with the modifications you have made you can reverse the above process to lock the taskbar again.

View Labels of Opened Applications

By default Windows 7 combines icons of all opened applications to place them in the taskbar in a managed form. This eliminates the chances of taskbar getting overpopulated when several applications and web browser windows are opened simultaneously. This configuration is quite ideal for the users who are familiar with Windows and the icons of the applications they mostly use. However for new users, who do not have experience to recognize applications by their icons this configuration might be inappropriate. When this is the case users can configure their Windows 7 computer to display full labels of all the opened applications in order to help users recognize what application they are working on. You can configure the above settings by following the steps given below:

1. Log on to the computer with the user account for which you want to enable labels with the icons in the taskbar.

2. On the desktop screen right click on taskbar and from the appeared menu click **Properties**.

3. On **Taskbar and Start Menu Properties** box from **Taskbar buttons** drop-down list choose **Never combine**.

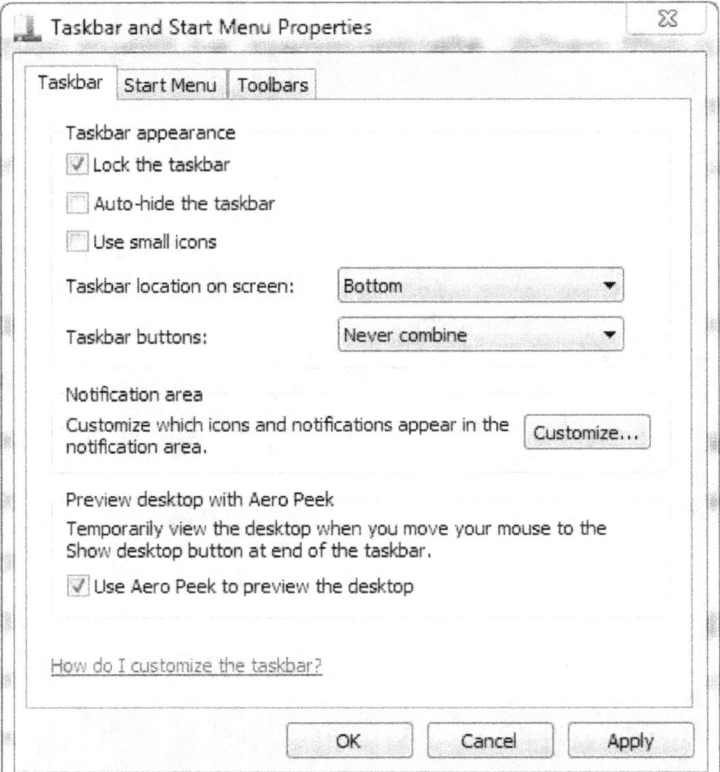

4. You can also view the demo of your configuration by clicking **Apply** button.

5. Once you are satisfied with the modifications you have made click **Ok** button to finalize them and make them persistent.

Display Multiple Clocks in System Tray

When Windows 7 was developed, it was designed keeping in mind that many business class people who are into excessive travelling around the globe will use the operating system. While traveling internationally sometimes it becomes hectic for such people to keep track of time zones and they find the task of changing the times as per the zones quite tiring. Therefore Windows 7 allows such users to place up to 3 clocks in the system tray so that they need not to change time zones of their regular clocks frequently. This process requires administrative privileges on Windows 7 computer and as an administrator of such machine if you want to place up to 3 clocks in the system tray you are required to follow the steps given below:

1. Log on to Windows 7 computer with the account that has administrative privileges.

2. Click the clock available in the system tray and from the appeared pop-up box click **Change date and time settings** link.

3. On **Date and Time** box go to **Additional Clocks** tab and check the checkboxes representing **Show this clock** text.

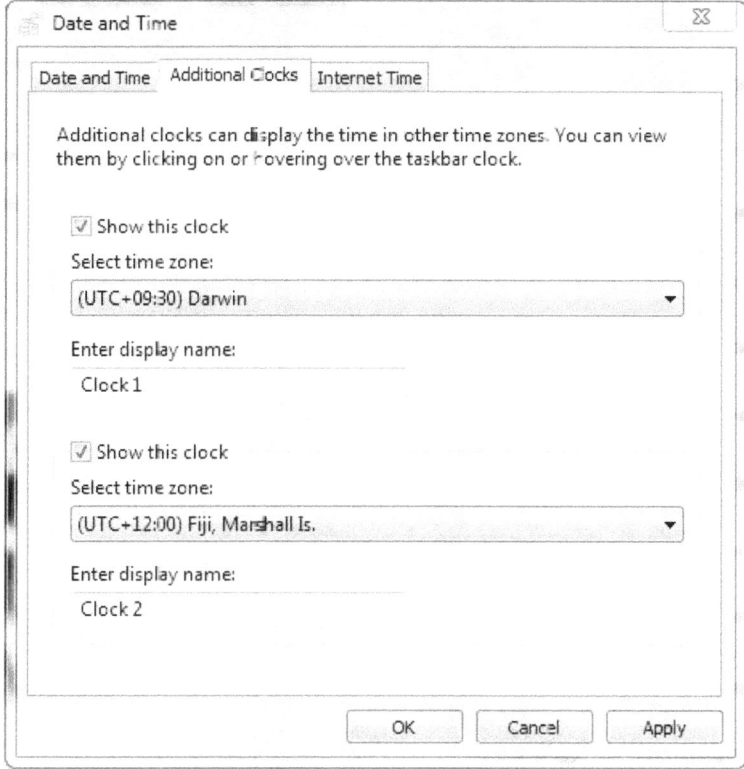

4. Adjust the time zones as desired and optionally you can specify the clock name (which in most cases will be the name of the country to which time zone the clock will be set).

5. Once done, click **Ok** button to save the changes you have made.

Lock or Unlock Taskbar

In early days of Windows 2000 and Windows 98 taskbar was easily adjustable as Windows used to allow users to increase or decrease the size of the taskbar and also allowed them to dock it anywhere on the desktop screen. However this feature was by default disabled with the release of Microsoft Windows XP and onwards operating systems. This means that users are now not allowed to mess around with the taskbar that easily. The reason behind making such modifications in the operating systems is to protect computers from mishandling as according to Microsoft default configurations of operating systems are considered to be the best and most optimized. However many users may still want to play around with the taskbar and as a Windows 7 user you need to unlock the taskbar by following the steps given below:

1. Log on to Windows 7 computer with standard user account.
2. Right click anywhere on taskbar.
3. From the appeared menu click **Lock the taskbar** option and make sure that the check mark in front of it is removed.

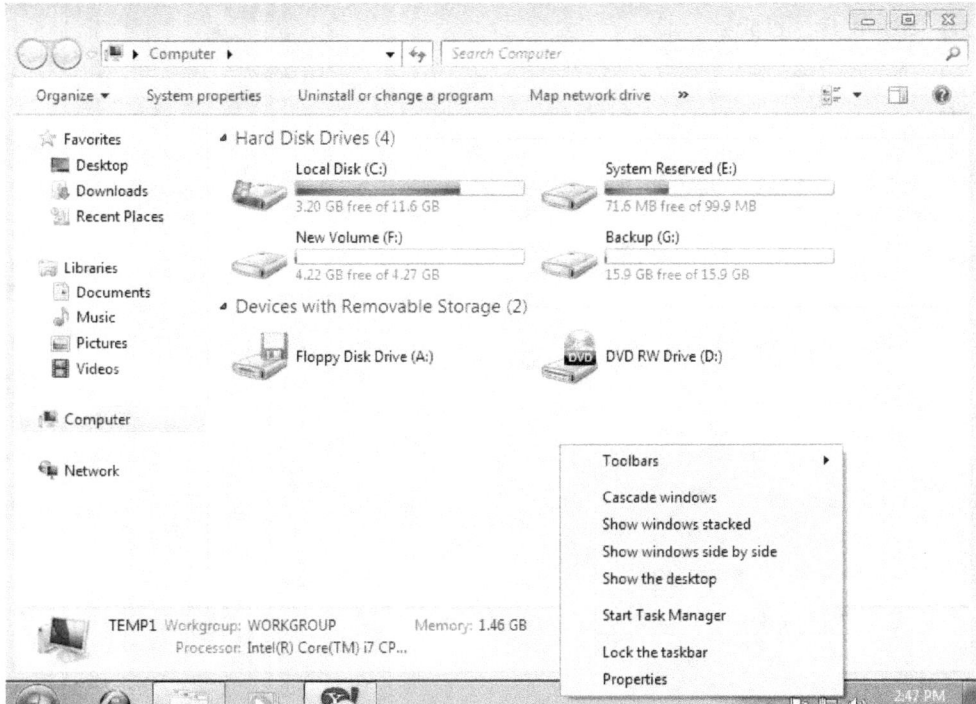

4. This will ensure that your taskbar is now free for adjustments and can be docked anywhere on the desktop.
5. You can repeat steps from **1 to 3** to lock the taskbar again.

Place Desktop Icon on Taskbar

Many times users are required to access desktop objects while working on some other applications on active Windows. Under normal circumstances, when this is the case users are required to minimize all the Windows which are opened on the computer to reach the desktop icons back. This practice is fine enough when there are two or three Windows opened on the computer and just two or three clicks are required to get back to the desktop. Complications occur when a user has opened several Windows at the same time and he needs to access any object from the desktop as in this situation he is required to spend a lot of time minimizing Windows or they can use Aero Peek enabled desktop icon to go directly to the desktop. Windows 7 offers something more than that as well. Users can now place a Desktop icons right on the taskbar and which when clicked displays all the objects on the desktop and users can choose any object by just clicking on it from the list. As a Windows 7 user if you want to place Desktop icon on the taskbar you are required to follow the steps given below:

1. Log on to Windows 7 computer with the account on which you want to place the desktop icon on the taskbar.

2. Right click anywhere on taskbar and from the appeared menu go to **Toolbars**.

3. From the appeared submenu click **Desktop**.

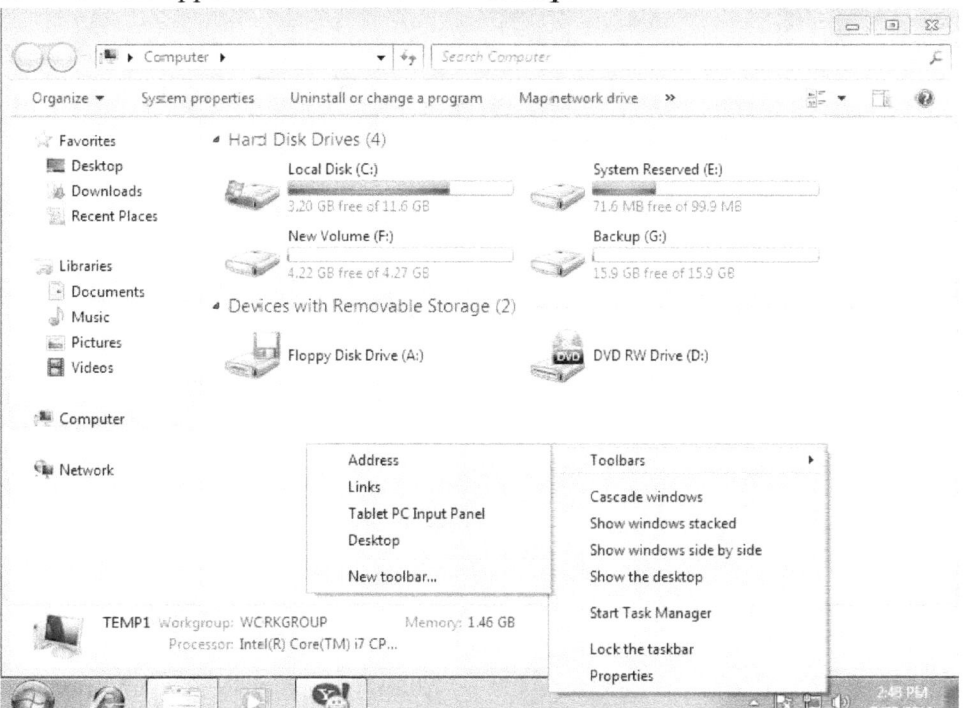

4. You will be displayed with **Desktop** icon in the left side of system tray.

Place Taskbar Anywhere on Desktop Screen

Many Windows 7 users are a bit different and have somewhat indifferent views as far as the interface of the operating system is concerned. Taking this discussion even further it can be said that these users do not feel much comfortable with the default alignments of the objects offered by Microsoft Windows. Such users are required to do a lot of adjustments and modifications after the clean installation of Windows 7 to make the interface according to them. One of the major steps that they take in this regard is that they place their taskbars on either sides of the desktop screen and in some cases they even place it at the top. This can only be done when the taskbar is unlocked by right clicking on the taskbar and clicking on **Lock the taskbar** option. After unlocking the taskbar if you want to place it at left, right or on top of the desktop screen you are required to follow the steps given below:

1. Log on to Windows 7 machine with the user account on which you want to modify the default location.

2. Unlock the taskbar by following the process given above.

3. Once unlocked, click on the taskbar and drag it to the desired location while holding down the left mouse button. Location can be anywhere on the desktop (left, right or top).

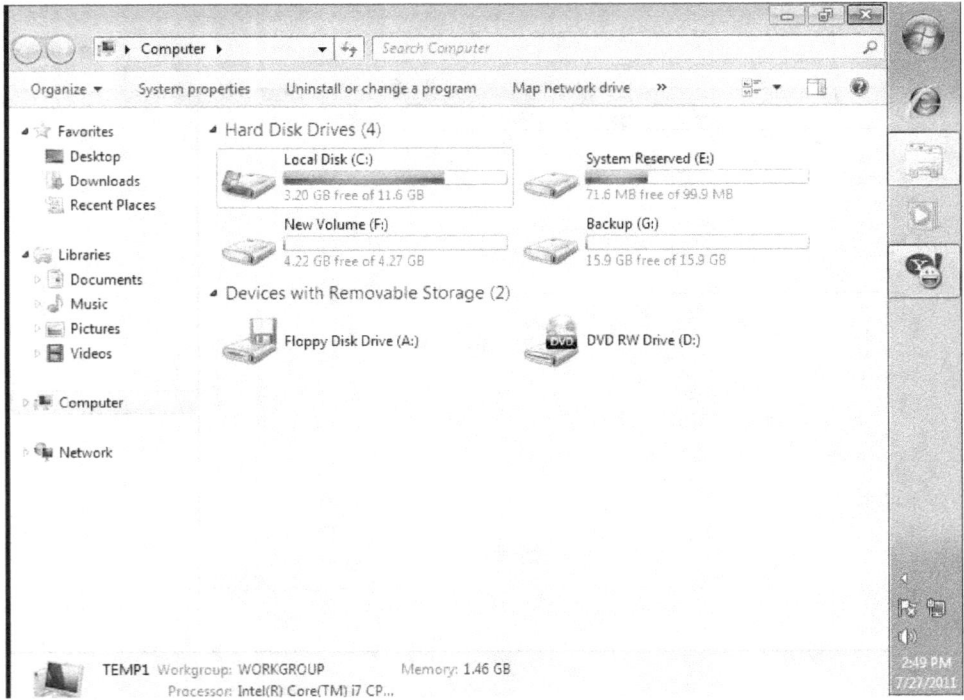

4. Once placed, lock the taskbar again by following the process mentioned above.

Place Recycle Bin in Taskbar

Many Windows 7 home users usually save every downloaded or copied object on the desktops and eventually they overpopulate it and finally end up facing trouble while locating any particular object on the desktop screen. Same is the case with Recycle Bin which can easily be located on the desktop when the desktop is not full of unnecessary items and shortcuts. Since the tendency of users of keeping everything on the desktops cannot easily be changed and therefore Windows 7 allows users to pin the icon of Recycle Bin at the taskbar so that it can easily be located in case users want to retrieve any deleted information from it. As a Windows 7 user if you want to do the same you are required to follow the steps given as below:

1. Log on to Windows 7 computer with the account for which you want to configure the above mentioned settings.

2. Right click anywhere on the desktop and from the context menu go to **New**.

3. From the appeared submenu click **Shortcut**.

4. On the appeared box in **Type the location of the item** field type **%System-Root%\explorer.exe shell:RecycleBinFolder** and click **Next**button.

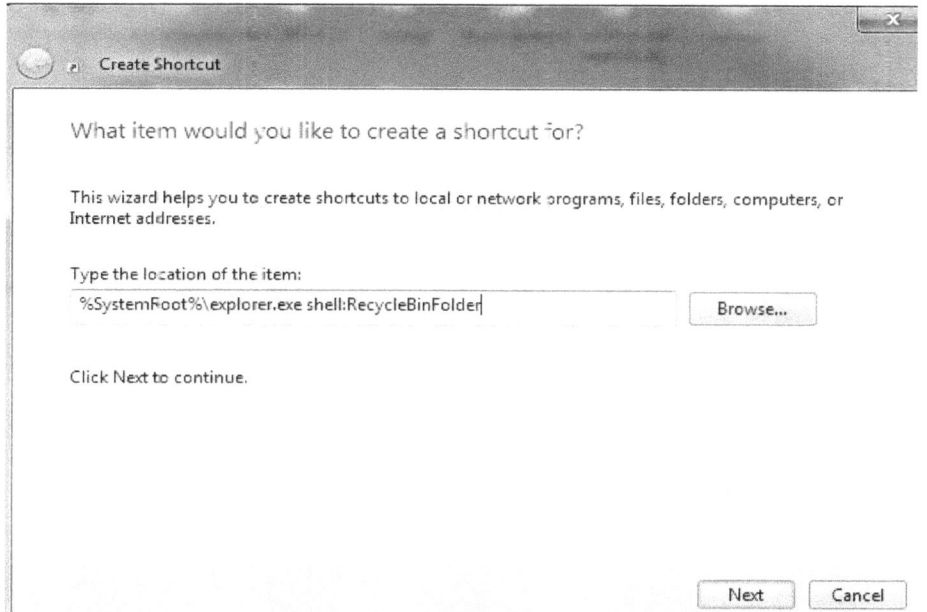

5. On the next page specify the name of the shortcut, for example, **Recycle Bin** and click **Finish** button.

6. You can now drag the newly created shortcut for **Recycle Bin** and drop it in the taskbar to be displayed as another pinned icon.

Change the Taskbar to Work like Vista

Default nature of taskbar in Windows 7 is that it combines all similar Windows in a group which allows users to switch between them easily. This feature is introduced with the release of Microsoft Windows 7 and is unique to the operating system and the entire world of Microsoft windows. Since the feature was integrated in Windows to help out users switching between windows in an easy way users are becoming more familiar while using this. However there are still majority of people who feel themselves comfortable with the taskbar that was introduced in Windows Vista. Nature of Windows Vista taskbar was that it only used to group opened applications when the entire taskbar was populated. This nature of taskbar in Windows Vista can also be configured in Windows 7 if users are more experienced and comfortable with it. As a Windows 7 user if you want to make the taskbar work like Windows Vista you are required to follow the steps given below:

1. Log on to Windows 7 computer with any user account on which you want to configure this.

2. Right click on the taskbar and from the available menu click **Properties**.

3. On **Taskbar and Start Menu Properties** box, make sure that you are on **Taskbar** tab and on **Taskbar buttons** drop-down list choose **Combine when taskbar is full**option.

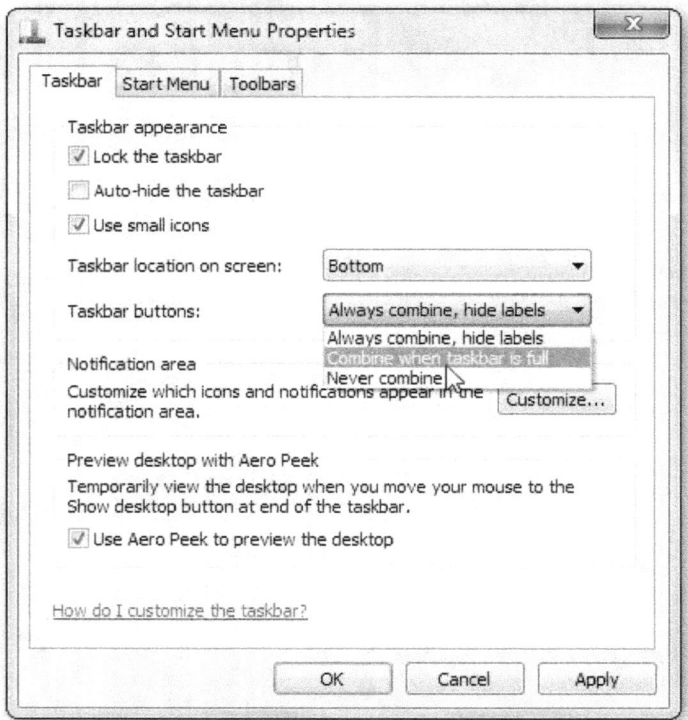

4. Once done, click **Ok** to save the changes that you have made.

Open Desired Window from Taskbar

Even if you have several windows opened in Windows 7 it is commonly understood that you will work only at one application or window at a time. This means that if you are working on one application or window, rest of them will automatically become inactive and in many cases you might prefer minimizing them in order to get some room on the desktop screen for the active application or window. However in some cases you might need to restore any or all of the minimized windows which might sometimes be annoying. Microsoft understands this frustration of the users and therefore it has integrated a feature in Windows 7 using which you can maximize or restore desired window or application right from the keyboard. You want to do so you are required to follow the steps given below:

1. Log on to Windows 7 computer with any account as no elevated privileges are required in this case.

2. Open multiple windows and applications so that they can be seen pinned on the taskbar.

3. If you want to open a specific application from the taskbar you need to count its sequence number from left to right and then you need to press **Windows key** + corresponding number of the application. For example, if the desired application or window is at the fifth place in the taskbar you need to press **Windows key + 5** to maximize or restore that very window.

View Full DOS Path to any Folder

If you are used to the interface of Microsoft Windows 2000 or Windows 98, it is expected that you will never find any problem in locating any object in those operating systems as the entire DOS path is displayed in the title bar. However with the release of Microsoft Windows Vista and above operating systems this feature is disabled and no DOS path is now displayed in the title bar. Instead, just the folder names are displayed there and users can easily navigate through the entire path by clicking on the desired folder available up there. From Microsoft's point of view this feature adds a great advantage to the interface of the operating system as users are now not required to remember the entire path to locate any object and they are not required to click on Back button several times to go to parent folders of any object. However many people do not know that they can still view the entire DOS path without any extra configuration or settings. As a Windows 7 user if you want to view the entire DOS path of any object (precisely a folder) you are required to follow the steps given below:

1. Log on to Windows 7 machine.
2. Browse through, navigate and locate the desired object (folder).
3. Once located and reached, in the title bar, click at the end of the folder names.
4. As you will do so you will be displayed with the full DOS path to that particular folder.

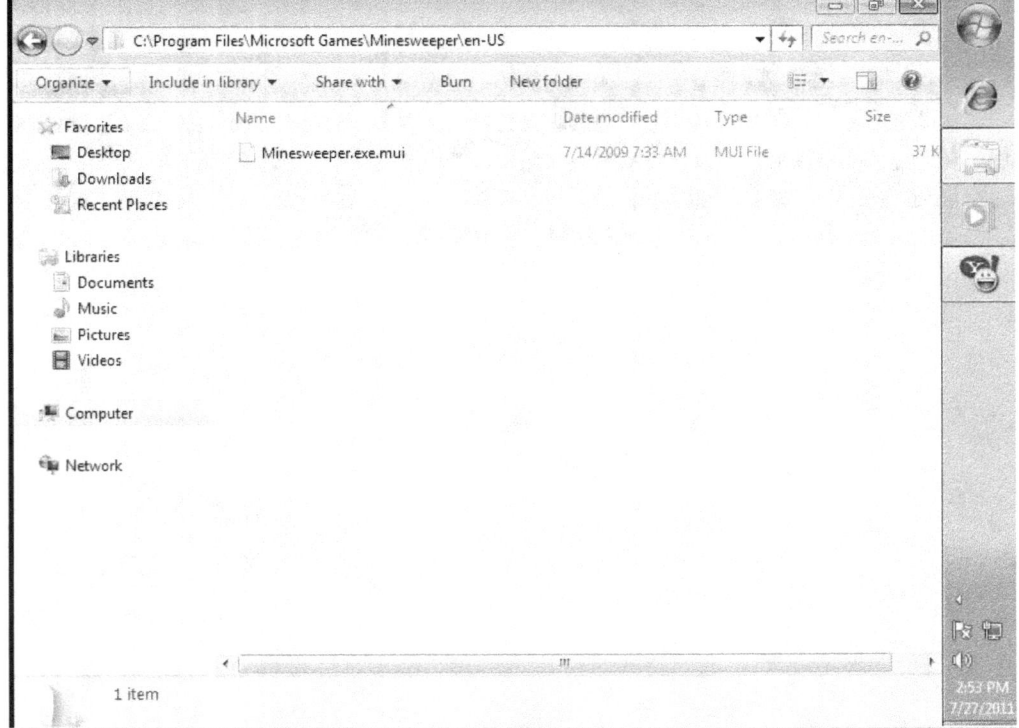

Uninstall/Modify/Repair a Program

Unlike Microsoft Windows XP and Microsoft Windows 2000 operating systems Microsoft Windows 7 now provides feature of uninstalling or modifying programs under Programs and Features section. Entire concept of uninstalling or modifying any application is the same but the location is renamed. Some other major changes that Microsoft has made in this section are that it has provided Uninstall option right at the top of the list so that users can easily use it. Moreover the view of the installed programs is also modified and now it can be viewed even more clearly. When talking about modification of any installed program, not every program can be modified and those which can be modified, process of modification includes clicking the button and selecting the appropriate option from the available application specific list. Example can be of Microsoft Office package which can be modified to add or remove other features and programs in the application. As a Windows 7 administrator if you want to uninstall or modify any program you are required to follow the steps given below:

1. Log on to Windows 7 computer with the account that has administrative privileges.
2. In the start menu click **Control Panel** option.
3. On the opened page click **Uninstall a program** link under **Programs** category.
4. On the appeared window click on the program that you wish to uninstall and click **Uninstall** button. Programs that allow modifications in them will display **Change** button as well when they are clicked in the window.

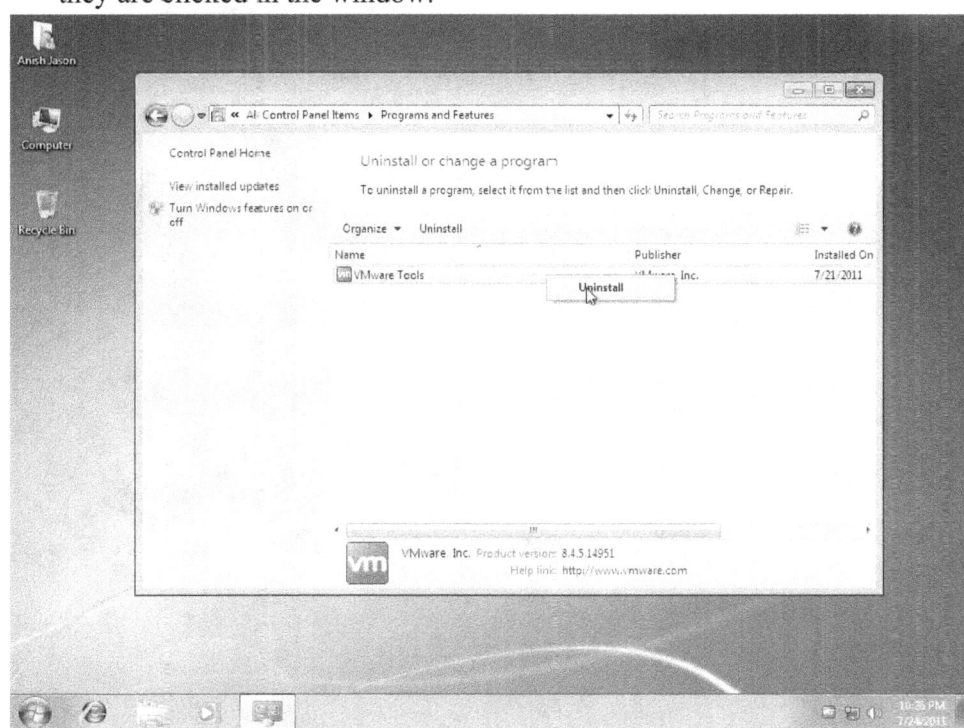

5. Choose the appropriate option and follow the instructions to uninstall or modify the application is required.

Rename Recycle Bin

Since the Graphical User Interface in Microsoft operating systems was released, both professionals and home users love to play with the interface. People mostly love to modify the appearance of the operating system and they love it when they do it off the track. For example, many people change the name of Computer icon available on Windows 7 operating system desktop screen, some of them rename Start button and there are majority of people who still want to rename the recycle bin which is available at the desktop screen of Windows 7 operating system. Renaming Computer icon on the desktop was quite difficult in legacy versions of operating systems offered by Microsoft and required some registry tweaks. However renaming recycle bin in Microsoft Windows 7 is now easier as it offers an option in the context menu which was not available in the older Windows. As a Windows 7 user if you want to rename Recycle Bin for fun you are required to follow the steps given below:

1. Log on to Windows 7 computer with the user account on whose profile you want to rename recycle bin.

2. Click on **Recycle Bin** icon available on the desktop screen.

3. From the menu click **Rename** and type in the new name for the **Recycle Bin**.

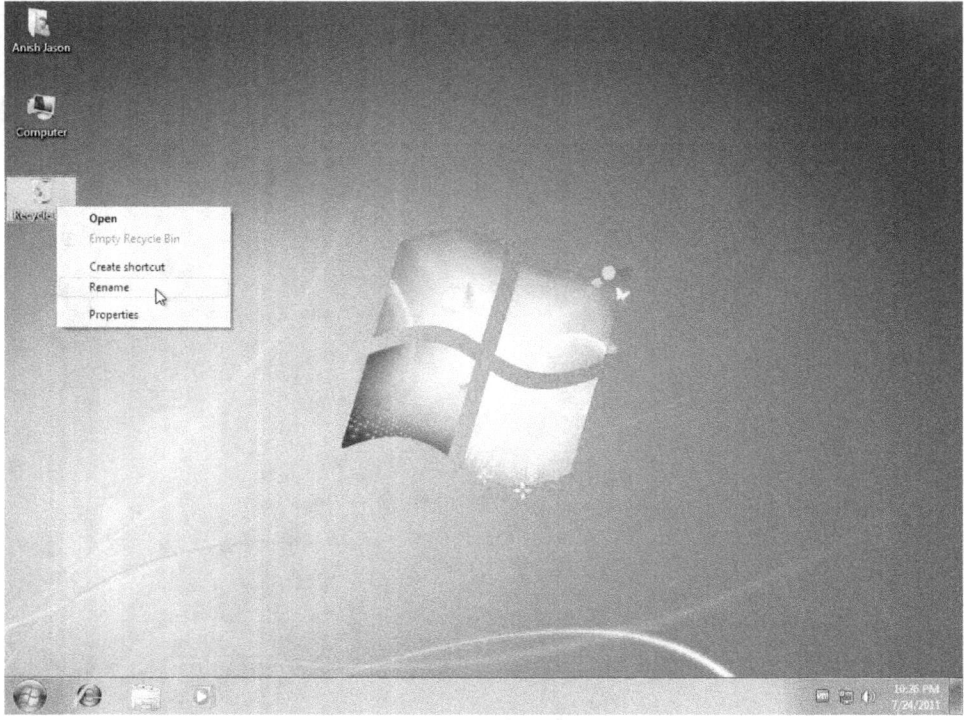

Disable Delete Confirmation Dialog

In every Microsoft operating system Recycle Bin is also available which stores all deleted files on a temporary basis. Recycle bin is capable of storing the deleted files of up to 10% of the entire logical drive space by default. This means that if any logical drive is of 200 GB, any file that is deleted from that logical drive can be stored in the recycle bin provided the file is of up to 20 GB in size. For security reasons and to prevent accidental deletion recycle bin prompts users about the confirmation of deletion of any object. Users need to confirm that they are sure that the object is to be deleted. This default configurations is very essential under normal circumstances however for some users this might be a tedious task to press Yes button every time they are about to delete any object from the computer. This confirmation dialog box can easily be disabled by following the steps given below:

1. Log on to Windows 7 computer.
2. On the desktop screen right click **Recycle Bin** and from the available menu click **Properties**.
3. On **Trash Properties** box uncheck **Display delete confirmation dialog** checkbox and click **Ok** button to save the changes.

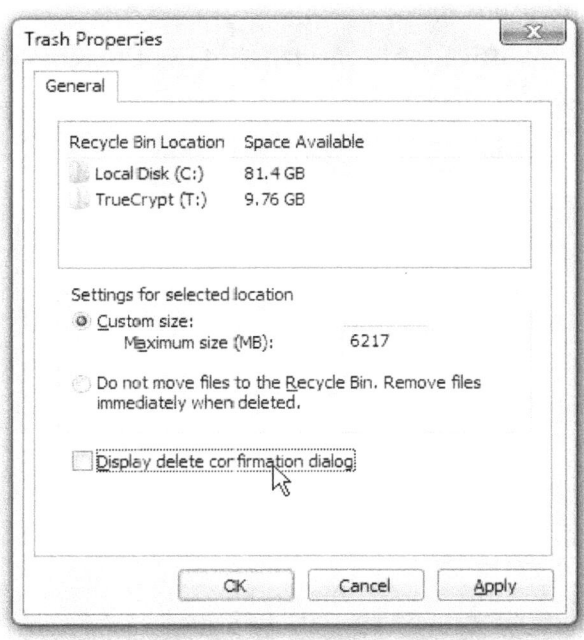

Completely Disable System Tray Icons

In any version of Microsoft Windows operating system, system tray plays an important role by allowing users to identify which applications are active and initialized. Also system tray allows administrators to customize the time and date of the computer which is displayed. As the operating system grows mature and users install several applications on it the items in system tray also increase in numbers hence increasing the size of the space that system tray consumes. This might result in reduced space available for the opened applications on which user might wish to work. Although Windows 7 offers a default feature of hiding all items that are displayed in the system tray and which can be displayed by clicking on the arrow button available next to it. However administrators can still completely disable system tray icons if they find themselves uncomfortable with it. As a Windows 7 administrator if you want to disable system tray icons you are required to follow the steps given as below:

1. Log on to Windows 7 computer with the account that is administrative and elevated privileges.
2. Click **Start** button and at the bottom of start menu in search box type **REGEDIT** and press enter key.
3. On **Windows Registry Editor** box locate
4. **HKEY_CURRENT_USER\Software\Microsoft\Windows\CurrentVersion\Policies\Explorer** from the left pane.
5.
6. In the right pane right click anywhere and click **New**.
7. From the submenu click **DWORD (32-bit) Value** and specify **NoTrayItemsDisplay** as name.

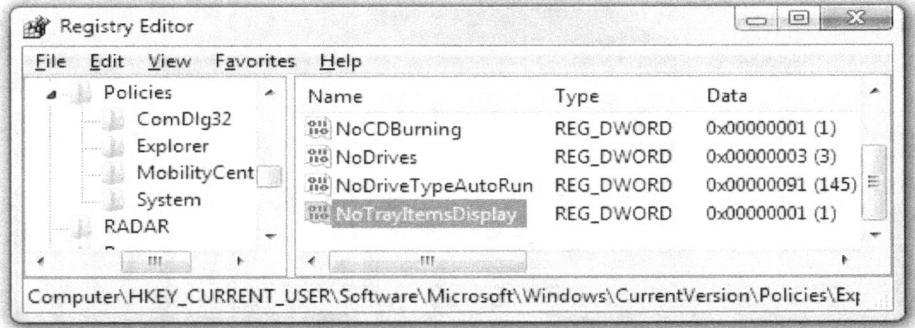

8. Double-click on the newly created key and under **Value data** field give the value as **1**.
9. Once done, click **Ok** button to save the changes and if required restart the computer.

Increase Recycle Bin Capacity

When Windows 7 is installed on a computer it reserves 10% of the space from each drive for recycle bin. This means if drive E: has 50 GB of space in total, Recycle Bin can contain up to 5 GB of data when deleted. If the deleted data from drive E: exceeds 5 GB, the user will be displayed with the message saying that the file cannot be sent to recycle bin because of its large size and if the user wants to delete the file permanently. This default configuration is ideal for almost every scenario, however if administrators want they can increase or decrease the space reserved for Recycle Bin. For example, administrators can increase the reserve space for recycle bin from 10% to 30% to allow it to store larger files. You can do so by following the steps given below:

1. Log on to the computer with administrator account.
2. On the desktop right click **Recycle Bin** and from the menu click **Properties**.
3. On **Recycle Bin Properties** box click to select the desired drive letter for which you want to increase or decrease the reserve space.
4. Under **Settings for selected location** category make sure that **Custom size** radio button is selected and in the available text box specify the amount you want to reserve for recycle bin as per your requirement. (The value you will try should be in the unit of megabytes, for example for 2 GB you need to type 2048).

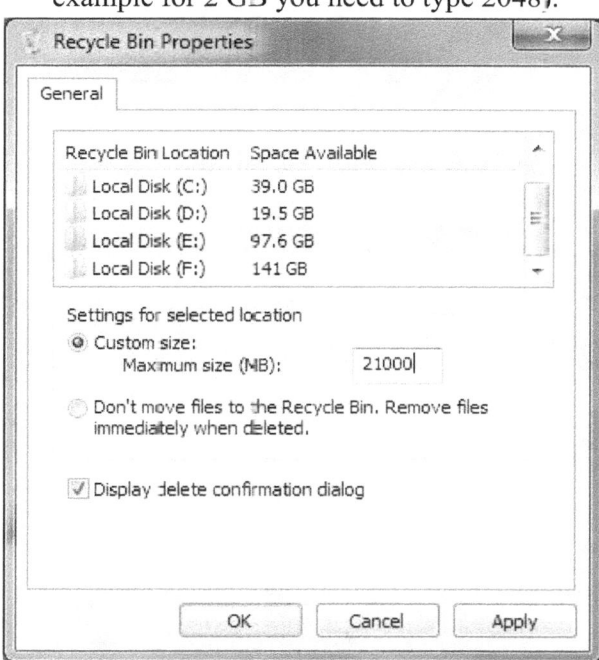

5. Finally click **Ok** button to make your settings permanent.

Installing New Fonts

Installing fonts in almost every operating system developed by Microsoft has proved to be one of the easiest steps involved in customization of the OS as per users' personal requirements. Steps to install new fonts in legacy (older versions of operating systems) included downloading the desired font file from the internet, opening **Fonts** folder either from **Control Panel** or by going to **C:\Windows\Fonts** and copying the newly downloaded font to the directory. Alternatively users could also install the fonts by choosing appropriate option from the **File** menu in **Fonts** folder. However with the introduction of new architecture of Windows Vista and Windows 7, installing a new font is even easier. You can install a new font in Windows 7/Windows Vista by following the steps given below:

1. Log on to the computer with administrator account and download the font from the internet. (You can copy the font from any other location if you have already downloaded).

2. Right click on the copied font and from the appeared menu click **Properties.**

3. From the opened box click **Unblock** button. (If **Unblock** button is not available, you can directly install the font without any hurdles and hassle).

4. To install, right click on the font and from the menu click **Install** button to initiate installation process. Alternatively you can double-click on the font and click **Install** button from the opened file.

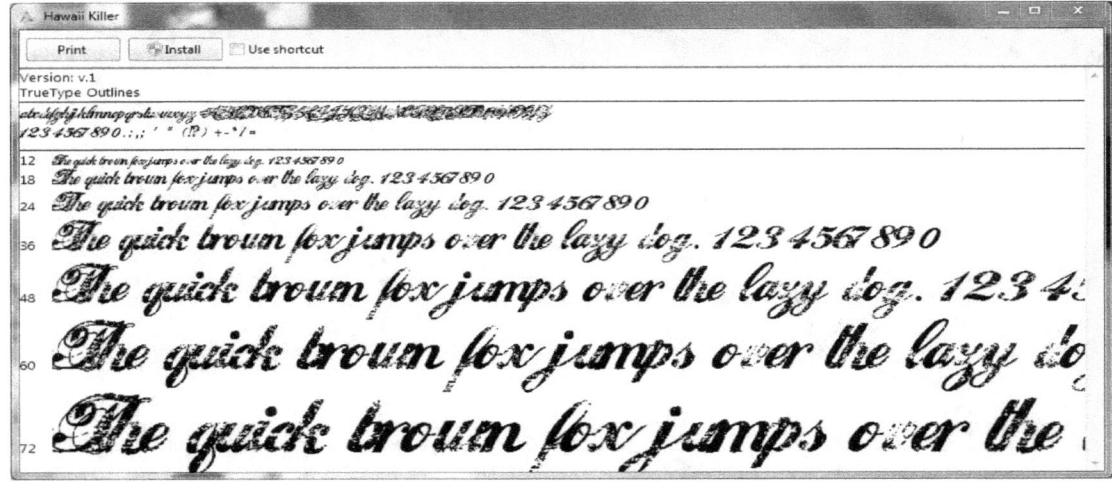

Burn ISO Images

In earlier days if people needed to burn data on the discs they required a third-party application to do so. These third-party applications, even till date, are costly and they require a decent amount of processing speed when they are used. Also, these third-party applications consume a great amount of disk space which many users do not want to spare for any application which is developed just for burning purpose. Microsoft understands this and it has integrated a tool in Windows 7 using which users can burn ISO images without any third-party application. Since ISO images are frequently used nowadays you can now burn them to your DVDs or CDs directly from the Windows 7 interface. As a Windows 7 user you can burn any ISO image to a DVD or CD by following the steps given below:

1. Log on to the Windows 7 computer.
2. Locate the ISO image file that can be present anywhere in your computer.
3. Once found, right click on the ISO image file and from the appeared context menu point your mouse to **Open with** option.
4. From the appeared submenu click **Windows Disk Image Burner** and from the opened box click **Burn** button. Optionally you can check **Verify disc after burning** checkbox before burning to check the integrity of the DVD/CD once it is burned.

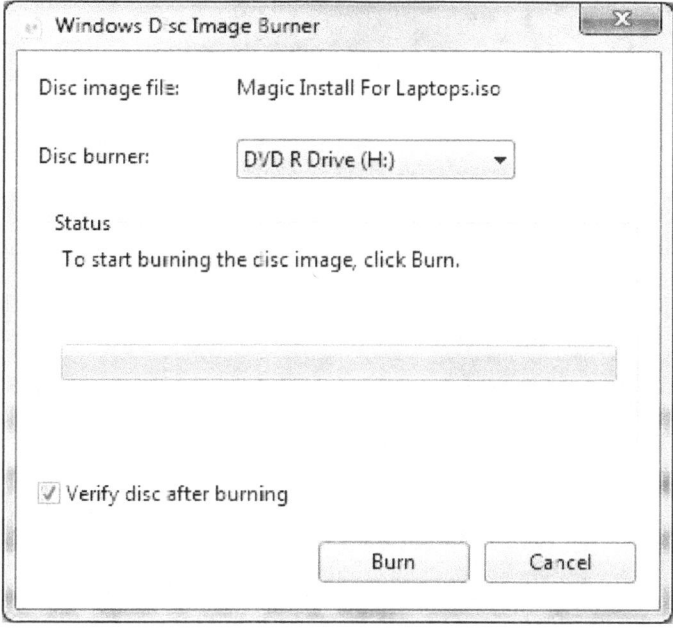

Record DOS Commands Outputs to a File

In many cases where administrators need to keep records of every event that they have fired in Windows 7 they can generate log files to do so. However some events do not allow involved applications to create log files, for example output results of DOS commands, and hence inexperienced administrators stand in the middle of nowhere looking out for some solution. One option can be that administrators can manually document every event and their results. This process can be quite hectic and time taking and many times this practice may end up with several human errors. Taking the above example, as an administrator if you want to maintain accurate transaction records of DOS commands you can capture the results and can forward them to any document file. Process to this is given as below:

1. Log on to Window 7 Computer with any account.

2. Open DOS command prompt by typing **CMD** command in search box at the bottom of start menu.

3. Type the command, output of which you want to record, followed by | (pipe sign) and **Clip** command and press enter key.

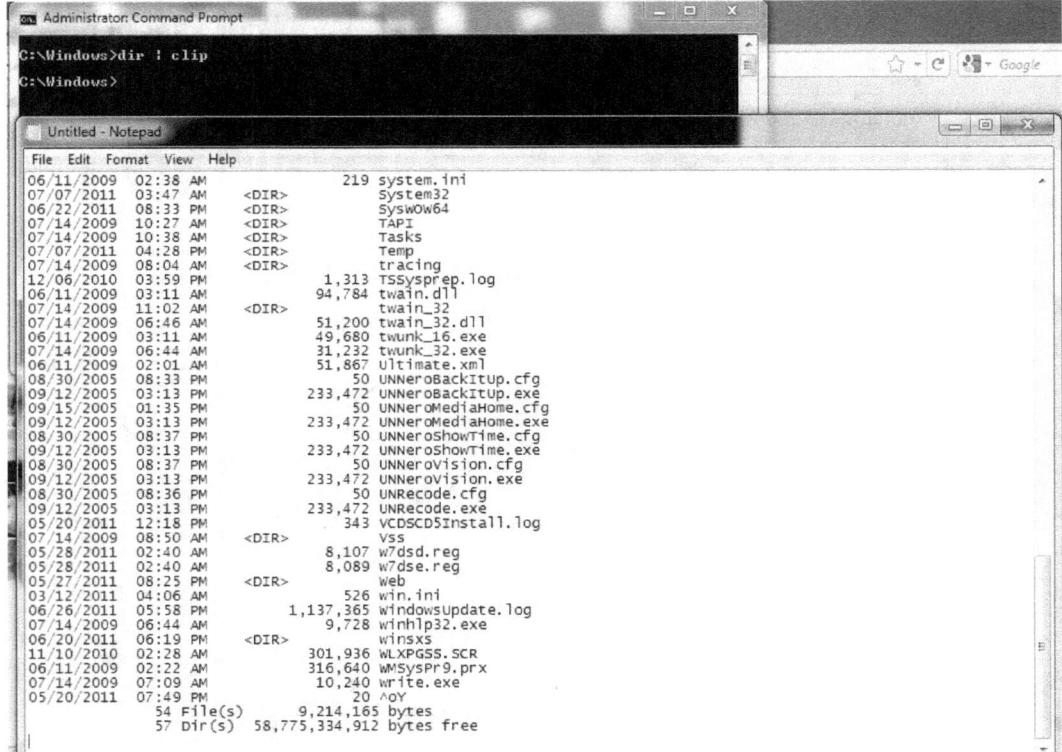

4. This will copy the results to the clipboard of Windows 7.

5. Open any available text editor in your computer, e.g. Notepad, WordPad, MS Word, etc.

6. Press **Ctrl + V** keys to paste the clipboard information on the text editor.

7. Finally save the file with any desired name.

Rename Multiple Files Simultaneously

When Windows 7 is used in home environments it is obvious that people might use their computers to store images and similar types of video files which may contain their family information. When this is the case it becomes essential for users to rename the files in proper numbers so that it becomes easier for them to locate the files whenever they are needed. If there are thousands of files it becomes a very tedious process to rename every file individually. Windows 7, therefore, offers a feature using which you can rename all files in a single go. If you want to do so you are required to follow the steps given below:

1. Log on to Windows 7 computer with any account as the process does not require any elevated privileges.

2. Make sure that all the images for files that you want to rename in a single go are kept in one folder.

3. Go into that folder and press **Ctrl + A** keys to select all the files.

4. Right click on any file and from the appeared menu click **Rename**.

5. Type the new name for the file and press enter key. All files will be renamed with increasing numbers.

Show Full Path to Folders/Files

Although Windows 7 is designed keeping in mind that the operating system will provide as much user-friendly interface as possible, there are still few drawbacks in the operating system which are not much liked by the users as they sometimes hide important information and users need to struggle around to retrieve. Same is the case with finding the exact path to any desired file or folder in Windows 7. When any file is selected or clicked in Windows 7 its entire path is not displayed and as a Windows 7 user if you want to enable this feature you are required to follow the steps given below:

1. Log on to Windows 7 computer with the account for which you want to configure the above mentioned settings.

2. Open **Windows Explorer** and click **Organize** menu.

3. From the available list click **Folders and search options** and **Folder Options** box make sure that you are **General** tab.

4. Under **Navigation pane** section check both **Show all folders** and **Automatically expand to current folder** check boxes.

5. Once done, click **Ok** button to save the changes that you have made.

Unhide Secret Features of Control Panel

There are many Windows 7 users who love to play around with the Control Panel and are also fond of going into every detail of every icon available in it. Since Windows 7 is designed to provide a user-friendly interface to its users many advanced features offered by it are by default hidden and users are required to unhide them manually if they need to access them. Same is the case with options available in Control Panel as many people do not know that it contains up to 260 different features and options available but are not by default visible. As a Windows 7 user if you want to unhide these features in Control Panel you are required to follow the steps given below:

1. Log on to Windows 7 computer with any account on which you want to configure the above settings.

2. Right click anywhere on the desktop and from the available menu go to **New**.

3. From the submenu click **Folder**.

4. Name the folder with any desired name, **Full Control Panel** in this case, followed by ".{ED7BA470-8E54-465E-825C-99712043E01C}" without spaces and quotes so that the entire folder name will look like "**Full Control Panel.{ED7BA470-8E54-465E-825C-99712043E01C}**" (without quotes).

You will notice that the icon of the folder is automatically changed and when you will double-click the icon you will find several new features which are now available and visible in **Control Panel** itself.

Turn Off Windows Explorer Click Sounds

Microsoft has developed Windows in such a way that both professionals can use it and home users and the operating system can be installed in both production and home environments. This means that Windows offers some security features and also provides some multimedia facilities to entertain users such as the notification sounds. Same is the case with Windows 7. While using the operating system at home people may want to hear the notification sounds in order to recognize the effects of their inputs. Example can be the navigation sound of Windows Explorer which can be heard when users open or navigate through it. However in production environments the administrators to maintain the decorum of the office can completely disable these sounds. Process of disabling the sounds is a simple but can only be performed with elevated privileges. As a Windows 7 administrator if you want to disable navigation sounds you are required to follow the steps given below:

1. Log on to Windows 7 computer with any account that has administrative privileges.

2. In the start menu click **Control Panel**.

3. On the opened window click **Appearance and Personalization** category link.

4. On the next page click **Change sound effects** link under **Personalization** category.

5. On the appeared box make sure that you are **Sounds** tab and under **Programs Events** section click **Start Navigation** under **Windows Explorer** category.

6. Now chose **None** option from the drop-down list under **Sounds** section.

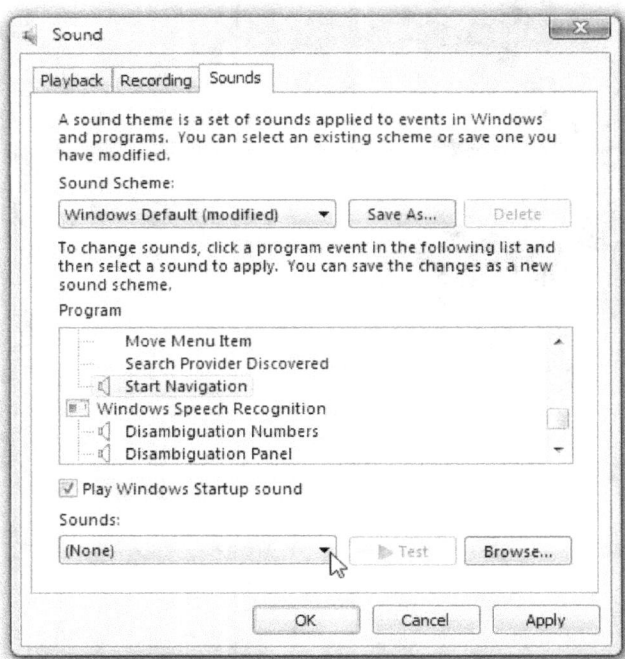

7. Once done, click **Ok** button to save the changes you have made and close all the windows and boxes.

Enable Stereo Mix to Enable Speaker Recording

Many Windows XP users are now habitual of recording any sound that comes out of the speaker so that they can modify it according to their requirements. There are certain third-party applications available in the market that allow users to record the output of the speakers and convert it to MP3 or any other sound format file. No matter what application users use they still require compatible hardware and Stereo Mix feature enabled (which by default is enabled in Windows XP) in order to perform the process success-fully. In Windows 7, however, Stereo Mix option is by default disabled and therefore users need to enable it in order to record any output of the speakers as they used to do in Windows XP. This process requires elevated privileges and therefore as a Windows 7 administrator if you want to enable Stereo Mix to record the output of the speakers you need to follow the steps mentioned as below:

1. Log on to Windows 7 computer with administrator account.
2. From the start menu click **Control Panel**.
3. On the opened window click **Hardware and Sound** category link and from the new win-dow click **Sound** link.
4. On the opened box go to **Recording** tab and right click anywhere in the blank space and from the menu click **Show Disabled Devices**.
5. Right-click on appeared **Stereo Mix** device icon and click **Set as Default Device**.

6. Finally click on **Ok** button to save the changes you made.

Install IIS Service

Microsoft Windows operating systems have been using IIS or Internet Information Services since quite a long time. IIS services allow users to use several applications which can only be installed and used when this service is installed and enabled. Moreover if administrators want to host a single website, IIS services are essential. Since Windows 7 is a client operating system IIS integrated in it can only host maximum of one website at a single given time. Configuration of IIS is beyond the scope of this section however installation process of the service is quite simple. Process of installing IIS on a Windows 7 computer requires elevated privileges and therefore administrator account is required to be used if the services are to be installed. As a Windows 7 administrator if you want to install IIS services you are required to follow the steps given below:

1. Log on to Windows 7 computer with any account that has elevated privileges.

2. Click **Start** button and from the menu click **Control Panel**.

3. On the open window click **Programs** link.

4. On the next window under **Programs and Features** category click **Turn Windows features on or off** link.

5. On **Windows Features** box click on the check box representing **Internet Information Services**. By default all the mandatory services are automatically selected.

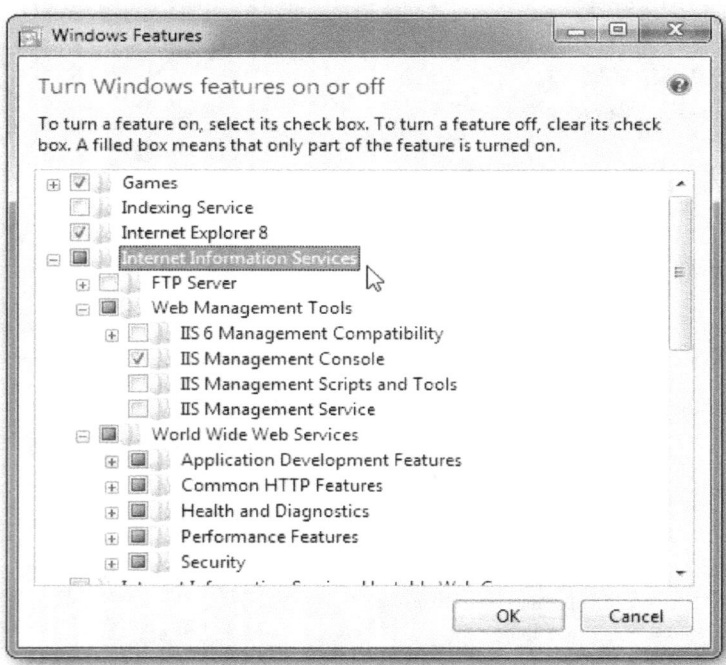

6. Once done, click **Ok** button and close all the open windows.

7. If required restart the computer.

Abort Shutdown Process

There are times when you accidentally click on Shutdown button and after doing so you realize that there was some work, which was yet to be completed, and now you need to restart your computer in order to finish the task. These situations might sometimes be quite frustrating and time-consuming. With the below process you can create a simple desktop button (icon) which, when double-clicked, will abort the shutdown process in case you have initiated it accidentally. To create Abort Shutdown button you need to follow the steps given below:

1. Right-click anywhere on the desktop and from the context menu go to **New**.
2. From the appeared sub-menu click **Shortcut**.
3. On the **Create Shortcut** page type **C:\Windows\system32\shutdown.exe -a** and click **Next** button.
4. On the opened page type **Abort Shutdown** and click **Finish** button.

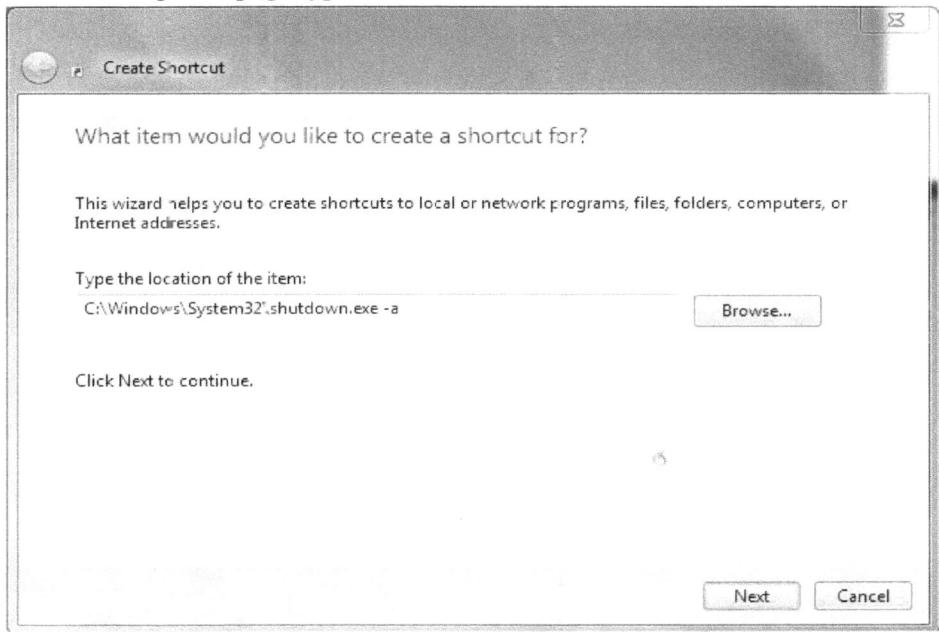

You can try this button by first initializing the process of shutdown and immediately after that double-clicking on the above-created Abort Shortcut button.

Also, the process of shutting down the system can be delayed by typing **C:\Windows\system 32\shutdown.exe -s -t 05**; where **'s'** represents shutdown and **05** specifies the delay time in seconds. This means that when this command is executed shutdown process is delayed by five seconds. Alternatively, you can type **C:\Windows\system32\shutdown.exe -r -t 05** to delay the restart process of your computer by five seconds; where **'r'** represents restart.

Add or Remove Desktop Icons

By-default every user profile has only Recycle Bin available on the desktop. As the time passes by and the operating system gets mature, the desktop screen gets populated with several shortcut icons of the installed software applications but not with the ones that are most commonly used, such as Computer and Documents. When this is the case users can add icons on the desktop on their own manually so that they can easily access them without searching for them at several locations. You can add Windows 7 desktop icons by following the steps given below:

1. Log on to the Windows 7 computer with the account for which you want to add desktop icons.

2. On the desktop right-click anywhere and from the context menu click **Personalize**.

3. On the opened Window in the left pane click **Change desktop icons** link.

4. On **Desktop Icon Settings** box check the check boxes representing the desktop icons in order to configure Windows 7 to display them on the desktop and click **Ok** button to apply the changes that you have made. Optionally you can click **Change Icon** button to change the default icons on the desktop. However, if you install any Windows 7 desktop theme on the computer these icons are changed automatically as an effect of the installed desktop theme.

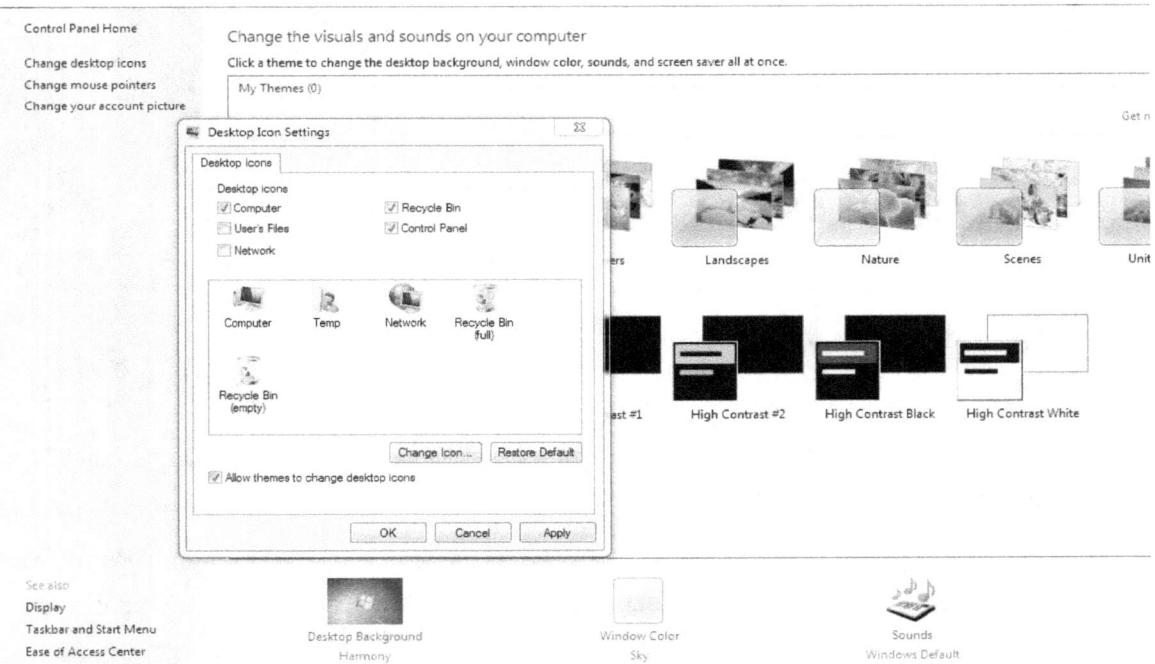

Add or Remove Built-In Games

Sometimes you might want to restrict games so that your kids do not get distracted from their studies. Also, at the same time you would also like to allow them to play some games when they are done and have some free time. Moreover, if your Windows 7 computer is used in an office you would not want your employees to play games during office hours. Using below steps you will be able to enable or disable Windows 7 built-in games at your ease. Along with this, you will also be able to select which games you want users to play on a particular computer, hence disabling rest of them.

Add/Remove Games:

1. Click **Start** button.
2. From the menu click **Control Panel**.
3. Click **Programs** category link.
4. On the next page under **Programs and Features** category click **Turn Windows features on or off**.
5. In **Windows Features** box uncheck **Games** checkbox. This will remove all Windows 7 built-in games from your computer. Alternatively you can expand Games tree by clicking on + (plus sign) next to it to view and check/uncheck each game individually.

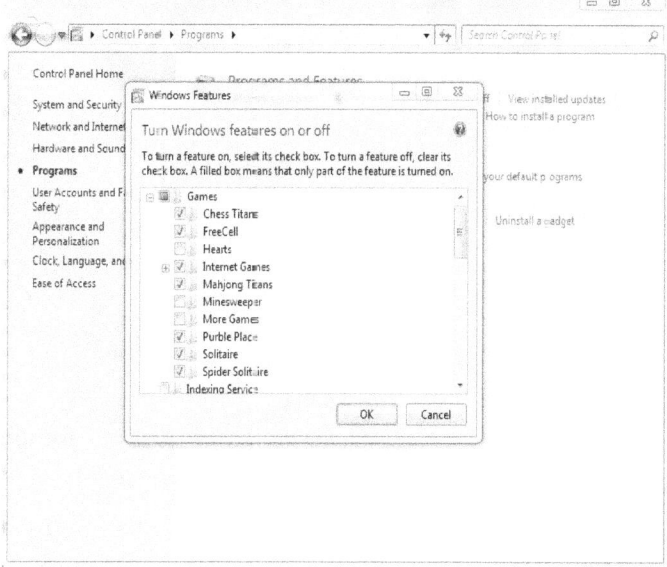

6. Once you have done appropriate modifications you can click **Ok** button to accept and confirm your changes.

Note: This process will add or remove built- games only. If you want to disable other games you need to configure AppLocker or/and Parental Control features offered by Microsoft Windows 7.

Hide Unnecessary Icons to Shrink Notification Area

When Windows 7 is installed, by default it has tidy and neat desktop, which give a soothing ambiance. As you keep on using it on regular basis, you install several applications, which might make your desktop populated and notification area dirty. By following below instructions you can shrink the notification area of your Windows 7 computer so that it may not look overcrowded:

1. Right-click **Taskbar.**

2. Click **Properties.**

3. In the **Taskbar and Start Menu Properties** box under **Notification Area,** frame click **Customize** button.

4. In the opened window, select the visibility behavior of every icon as per your needs.

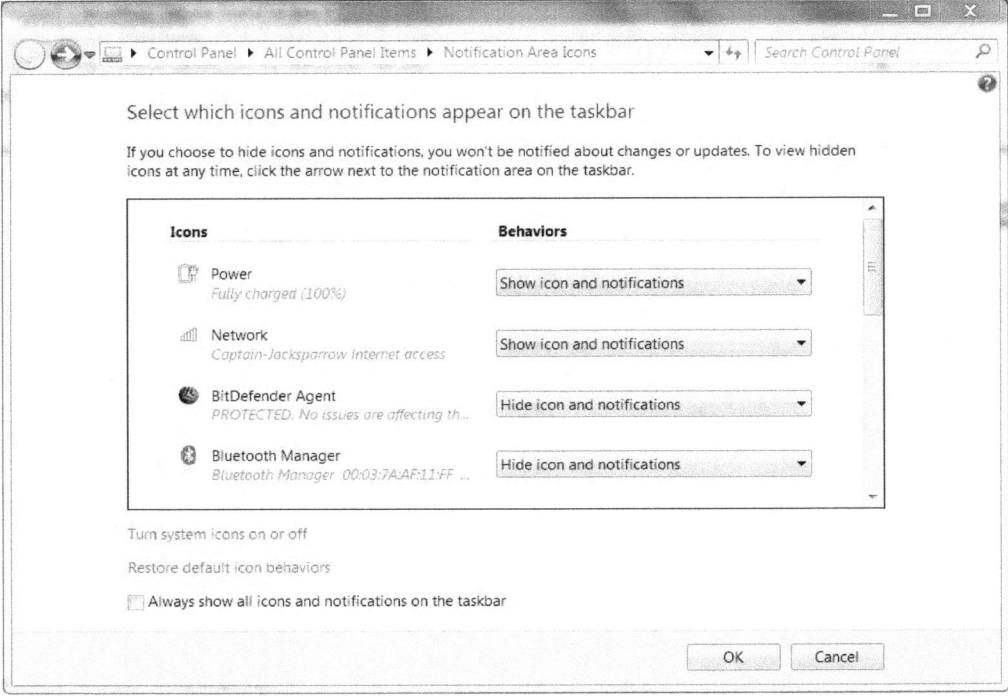

Some recommendations for home users might include: hide icon and notifications for any anti-virus that you have installed, hide icon and notifications for volume, hide icon and notifications for Bluetooth, hide icon and notifications for battery (for laptops), hide icon and notifications for any inactive chat messenger you have. In this way, you can shrink the notification area of your Windows 7 computer and can get back its soothing ambiance even after months of your installation.

If you want to get everything back as before and default, you can click **Restore default** icon behaviors link on the same page. You can also modify the display of clock by clicking **Turn system icons on or off** link on this very page.

Manage Operating System Timeout Duration

Microsoft Windows 7 is not very old in the market and users still feel comfortable while using Windows XP. Considering this many users install multiple operating systems on their computers so that they can use Windows XP for their normal work and can experience the new features offered by the latest operating system, i.e. Windows 7. It is recommended that while going for multiple operating systems on a single machine users must install the older version of operating system first and then they should install the recent version so that both of them can work smoothly. When multiple operating systems are installed on a computer, Windows offers a timeout duration which provides a default time of 30 seconds to the users before which they need to select the operating system they want to use on the computer. If the users run out of time the default operating system selected by the computer automatically boots. Administrators can increase or decrease this timeout duration by following the steps given below:

1. Make sure that you are logged on to Windows 7 computer with administrator account.

2. Click **Start** button and at the bottom of the menu in search box type **MSCONFIG** and press enter key.

3. On the opened box go to **Boot** tab and adjust the desired time out in **Timeout** field.

4. Once done, click **Ok** button to save the changes.

5. Restart your computer to check the effect of the modifications you have made.

Enable Quick Launch Toolbar

People who are familiar with Windows XP and are comfortable with the quick launch toolbar provided with it may sometimes find the absence of the toolbar a bit unconvincing in Windows 7. However many of them do not know that Windows 7 also has quick launch toolbar but it has to be enabled manually. Since the process requires no elevated privileges even a standard user can enable a quick launch toolbar for his personal profile. You can do the same by following the steps given as below:

1. Log on to Windows 7 computer with the user account for which you want to enable quick launch toolbar.

2. Right click anywhere on taskbar and point the mouse to **Toolbars**.

3. From the available submenu click **New toolbar**.

4. On the opened box in **Folder** field type **%userprofile%\AppData\Roaming\Microsoft\Internet Explorer\Quick Launch** and press **Select Folder** button.

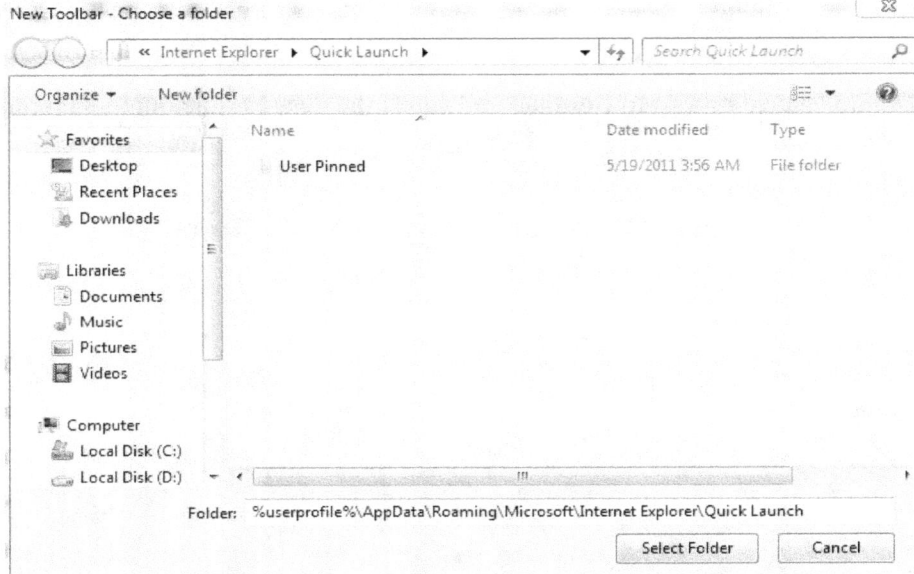

5. A quick launch toolbar will be displayed next to the system tray at the bottom right corner of the desktop.

6. In order to place it in the proper position, that is, at the left side of the taskbar as in legacy operating systems, you need to right click on the taskbar and from the available menu click **Lock the taskbar** to unlock it.

7. You can then shift the quick launch toolbar from right to left corner of the taskbar and again click **Lock the taskbar** in the menu of taskbar to lock it again.

Open Command Prompt for Folder

Even if you are a habitual user of Graphical User Interface, such as Windows 7, you may sometimes need to use command prompt for several reasons. In command prompt you need to type the entire command to locate any particular directory. This process might sometimes be quite annoying for new users as they may not be very comfortable with the command line interface offered by Microsoft Windows platform. Keeping this in mind Microsoft has integrated a new feature in Windows 7 using which users can navigate to the desired folder using Graphical User Interface and then can initiate command prompt right from that very location. You can do so by following the steps given below:

1. Log on to Windows 7 operating system with the desired user account.

2. Open Windows Explorer and navigate and locate to the desired folder for which you want to initiate command prompt.

3. Once located, right click on that folder while pressing down **Shift** key.

4. From the available menu, then, click **Open command window from here**.

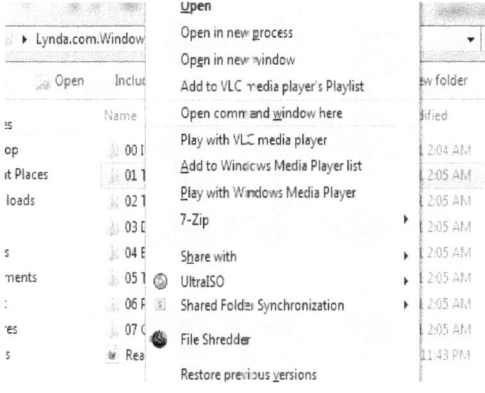

5. You will be displayed with the command window pointing to that particular location.

Note: This process works only with the folders or other containers and is not applicable for any file.

Place Control Panel Menu in Start Menu

As Windows 7 advanced user if you are a frequent visitor of Control Panel you may not want it as a link in the start menu. Instead, you may prefer having a menu of the Control Panel in start menu so that you can choose appropriate icon from the available list and you can eliminate the requirement of going to Control Panel window every time you need to use it. The configuration is user specific and any user can configure the menu for Control Panel. As such user if you want to do so you are required to follow the steps given as below:

1. Log on to Windows 7 computer with the account for which you want to configure **Control Panel** menu.

2. Right click **Start** button and click **Properties**.

3. On **Taskbar and Start Menu Properties** box make sure that you are **Start Menu** tab and click **Customize** button.

4. On **Customize Start Menu** box locate **Control Panel** section and select **Display as a menu** radio button.

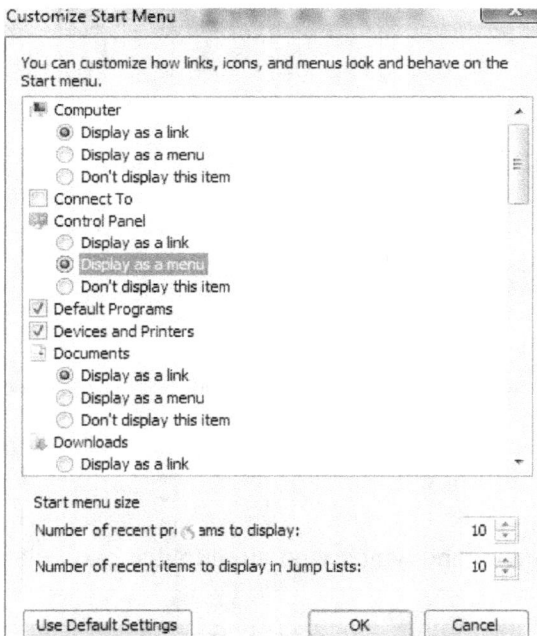

5. Once done, click **Ok** button to save the changes that you have made.

Note: This configuration does not change, add or remove any icon in Control Panel but makes it easier for the users to locate them.

Place Videos Link in Start Menu

In Windows 7 Documents, Pictures and Music links are by default available in start menu. These links prove to be quite handy for the users as they provide direct access to the folders and their contents. Entire list of links available in the menu is considered complete except of one missing link that is of Videos. This link is not by default available in start menu however it can be manually placed by going through a few simple steps. This configuration is user specific and therefore users are not required to have elevated privileges in order to accomplish the task. As a Windows 7 user if you want to place Videos link in the start menu you are required to follow the steps given below:

1. Log on to Windows 7 computer with the user account on which you want to enable Videos link.

2. Right click **Start** button and hit **Properties**.

3. On **Taskbar and Start Menu Properties** box make sure that you are **Start Menu** tab and click on **Customize** button.

4. On **Customize Start Menu** box go to **Videos** section and select **Display as a link** radio button.

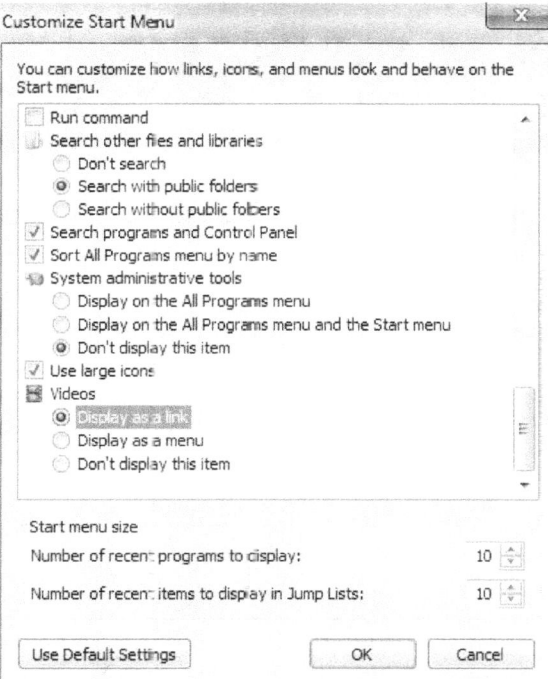

5. Once done, click **Ok** button to save the changes that you have made.

Make Focus on Active Window

As a Windows 7 user it is quite obvious that you might be working on multiple applications in separate windows on a computer very often. As a busy user sometimes you might also get confused as which window you were working on and you might mess up everything and might end up completing your tasks with several errors. A solution to this confusion can be that you can minimize all other inactive windows and keep only active window maximized. This tedious process can be simplified with the help of Windows 7 and as a busy user if you want to do so you are required to follow the steps given below:

1. Log on to Windows 7 computer with any account (standard user account can also work).
2. Open two or three Windows (can be any application window or Windows Explorer).
3. Make the desired window active by clicking on it.
4. To minimize the remaining Windows in a single go press **Windows key** + **Home key**.
5. In order to restore all Windows back to their original state press **Windows key** + **Home key** again.

Note: The above mentioned keys work as toggle to minimize or maximize all the windows except the active ones.

Organize Active Windows on Desktops

While releasing Windows 7 in the market, it seems that Microsoft had only one thing in mind as how to provide the best and the easiest way to operate Windows. Another step which Microsoft took in this regard is to ease the functionality of placing the Windows on the desktop. In legacy operating systems placing opened and active Windows on the desktop was not quite easy and users needed to adjust the size of each window manually in order to place them on the desktop so that they can be viewed easily. However in Windows 7 this arrangement can be done by pressing just two keys simultaneously. No elevated privileges are required in this regard and even standard users can use the process to organize active Windows on their desktops. As such user if you want to do so you are required to follow the steps given below:

1. Log on to Windows 7 computer with any user account.

2. Open one **Windows Explorer** window.

3. Keeping that window active press **Windows key + Left Arrow key** to place window at the left corner of the desktop covering half of the screen.

Optionally you can also open another **Windows Explorer** window and while keeping the new opened window active you can press **Windows key + Right Arrow** key to place the new window in the right side of the desktop covering the remaining half of the desktop screen.

Navigate Through Opened Windows

If you are using Windows 7, it is obvious that you are expecting something new and interesting while working on it. One of the most tedious tasks that many users are bound to do is to navigate through the opened applications or Windows from the taskbar. In legacy days when Windows XP or Windows 2000 was mostly used Alt key + Tab key was used to cycle through the applications or Windows and whenever users were required to make the desired window active they just need to release a keys. Windows 7, however, has much advanced features as compared to the legacy operating systems and these features offer better graphics while users navigate the opened applications in the taskbar. As a Windows 7 user if you want to use this new feature to cycle through opened applications you are required to follow the steps given below:

1. Log on to Windows 7 computer with any account as administrative privileges are not required.

2. Open four or five Windows and applications and keep them minimized in the taskbar.

3. To navigate through the minimized Windows you are required to press **Windows** key + **t**.

4. You can press **Windows** key + **t** multiple times to navigate through all the opened applications or Windows in the taskbar and if you want to make any window active you can press enter key when you reach there.

Note: Windows Aero feature is required to be enabled to follow above mentioned process.

Create Briefcase

In legacy versions of Windows based operating systems like Windows 98 and Windows 2000, Briefcase was the feature that was by default installed during the installation of the operating system. Briefcase was a container that was used to store frequently used files so that users can have instantaneous access to them. Also, Briefcase was used to synchronize computers with other similar devices so that the files can become easily accessible via network. Windows 7 also offers this feature but by default it is disabled. However users can create multiple briefcases so that they can store their important and frequently used files and can also segregate them accordingly. Creation of briefcases in Windows 7 is a simple process and even standard users can create them and no elevated privileges are required to do so. As a Windows 7 user if you want to create a briefcase you need to follow the steps given as below:

1. Log on to Windows 7 computer with any account on which you want to create briefcase.
2. Right click anywhere on the desktop and from the context menu point to **New**.
3. From the appeared submenu click **Briefcase** and specify the name of the newly created **Briefcase** as required and appropriate.

Disable Sticky Keys Popup Dialog

In Windows 7 Sticky Keys is a feature which allows slow users to perform any task that requires pressing multiple keys at a time easily. This means that users need not to press all the keys at the same time, instead they can press single key involved in the combination at a time. This configuration is highly beneficial for physically challenged users as they are not able to use the keyboard as efficiently as normal people do. By default Sticky keys can be enabled by pressing shift key repeatedly for 5 times. This default configuration was designed to help physically challenged users so that they can easily enable the feature but for normal users this configuration might be annoying sometimes, especially while playing games in which repeated key strokes are required. As a game lover if you want to disable this default nature of enabling Sticky Keys you are required to follow the steps given below:

1. Log on to Windows 7 computer with the account on which you want to configure this.

2. At the bottom of start menu in search box type **Change How Your Keyboard Works** and press enter key.

3. On the opened window click **Set up Sticky Keys** link.

4. On **Set up Sticky Keys** page uncheck **Turn on Sticky Keys when SHIFT key is pressed five times** checkbox.

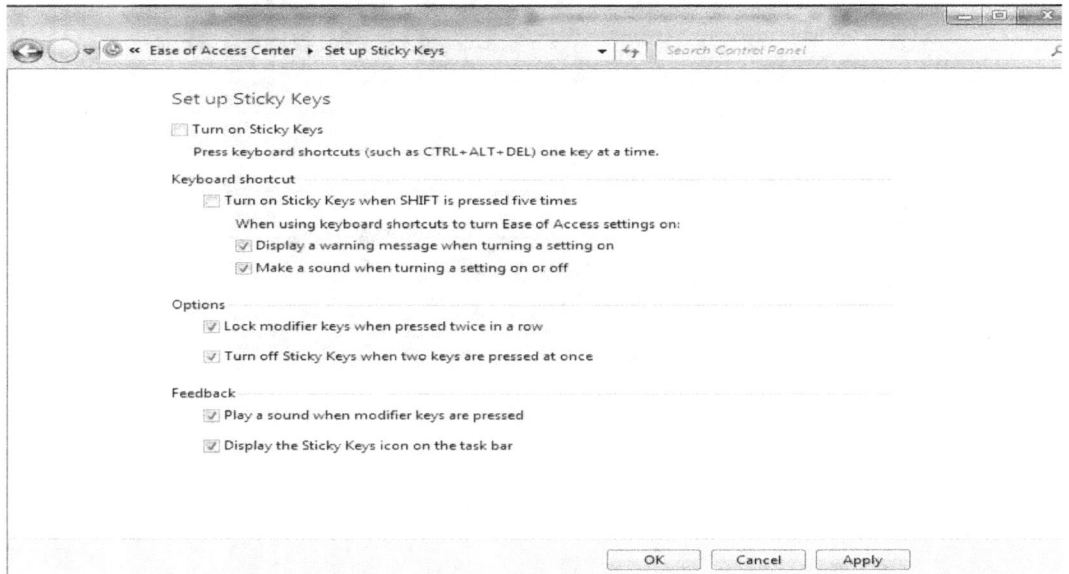

5. Once done, click **Ok** button to save the changes and close all the opened Windows and boxes.

Open Files/Folders with a Single Click

When Windows 7 is installed it offers optimum configuration and settings so that users can easily get familiar and comfortable with the operating system. Also Windows 7 is by default configured to consume least CPU and memory while providing full features to the users at the same time. These default configurations can always be modified according to the users' requirements. This means that users can configure their Windows 7 computers to get enhanced graphics or they can also configure them to consume even less processing and memory and offer enhanced speed. Same is the case with configuring the way of opening and selecting any object (files or folders) which by default is set to click and double-click for selecting and opening respectively. To make Windows interface more comfortable users can configure mouse rollover on any object to select and single click to open it. This configuration is user specific and therefore every user can modify the settings as per the requirements and comforts. As a Windows 7 user if you want to configure this you are required to follow the steps given below:

1. Log on to Windows 7 computer with any account on which you want to configure the settings.

2. From the start menu click **Computer** option and on the **Windows Explorer** click **Organize**.

3. From the available menu click **Folder and Search Options**.

4. On **Folder Options** box make sure that you are on **General** tab and under **Click items as follows** section select **Single-click to open an item (point to select)**radio button.

5. Click **Ok** button when done.

Assign Shortcut Key to Any Application

For any user it sometimes might become quite tedious and hectic to browse through all the shortcuts and menus to open any application. To eliminate this problem many users create shortcuts of the applications on desktop which they can double-click to open them. Even this might sometimes become problematic when there are several icons present on the desktop and it becomes almost impossible for users to locate and double-click on the right one. In these situations as an administrator you can specify shortcut keys (combination of keys) which, when pressed, can initiate desired application. You can do so for any application by following the steps given as below:

1. Log on to Windows 7 computer with any account.

2. Right click on the application for which you want to specify shortcut keys and from the appeared menu click **Properties**.

3. On the opened box make sure that you are **Shortcut** tab.

4. In **Shortcut key** text box specify the shortcut key by pressing **Ctrl** key and any other uniquely identifiable character.

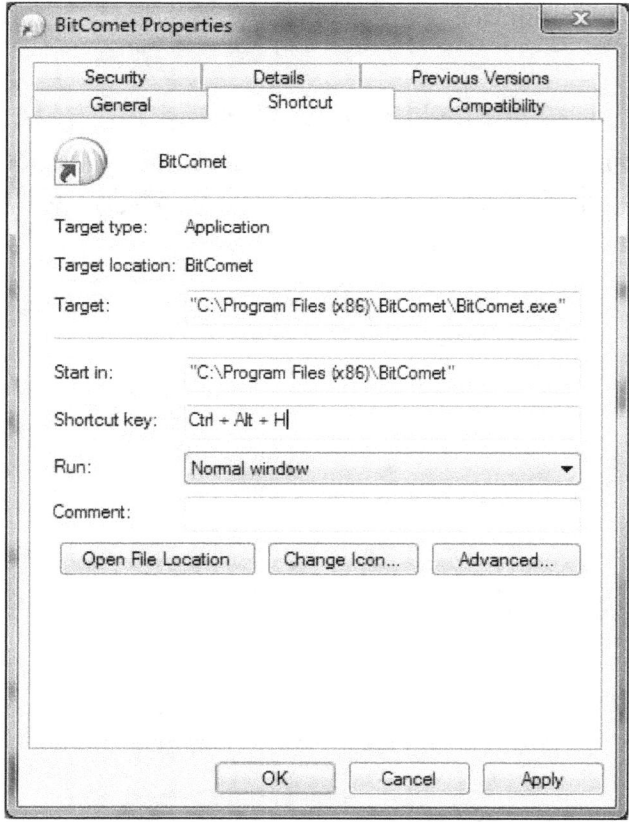

5. Once done, click **Ok** button to save the changes.

Note: You need not to press all three key combinations in order to specify shortcut key. You can simply press either **Ctrl** or **Shift** key and any other character key to assign it as the shortcut to the application.

Calculate Mortgage with Calculator

Although Microsoft Windows 7 contains all the utilities and tools that were also included in legacy versions of operating systems like Microsoft Windows XP. However the fact still remains the same that whenever a newer version of operating system is introduced in the market all the utilities and features are also upgraded and offer much more sophisticated features to make the application more user-friendly and promising for the users. Same is the case with the calculator which is integrated in Windows 7 and now it can be used for several different calculations. In this section calculator will be used to find out the mortgage. As a Windows 7 user if you want to use the built in calculator to find out what will be the monthly installment which is required to be paid for any purchased entity you are required to follow the steps given below:

1. Log on to Windows 7 computer with any account.
2. At the bottom of start menu in search box type **CALC** and press enter key to open calculator.
3. When opened, click **View** menu and from the available list go to **Worksheets**.
4. From the appeared submenu click **Mortgage** to get an extended version of the calculator.
5. From the available drop-down list choose **Monthly payment** and enter the values in their corresponding fields.

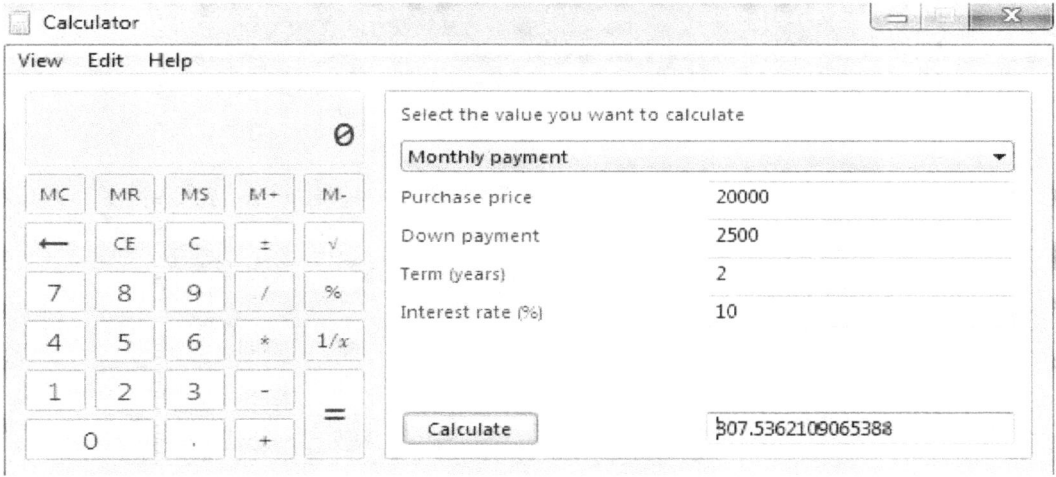

6. In the end, click **Calculate** button to get the results.

Open DOCX Files without MS-Office

One of the biggest challenges with the release of Microsoft Office 2007 and Microsoft Office 2010 is that the default file extensions used by these packages (.DOCX) are not backward compatible and the files with these extensions cannot be used in legacy versions of the application. Because of this very reason users are forced to save the documents created in the above packages in Microsoft Office 97-2003 file formats which used to have the default extension of .DOC. Many people do not know that Windows 7 itself provides the facility to the users using which they can view and edit the documents that have .DOCX file extensions even if they do not have Microsoft Office package (any version) installed on their computers. As a Windows 7 user if you want to view such files you are required to follow the steps given below:

1. Log on to Windows 7 computer with any account and make sure that Microsoft Office 2007/ Microsoft Office 2000 package are not installed on it.

2. Locate the file that has **.DOCX** extension.

3. Right click on the file and from the available menu point the mouse to **Open with** option.

4. From the appeared submenu click **WordPad** to open the document in **WordPad**.

5. You can modify the document as per piece and can save it as well.

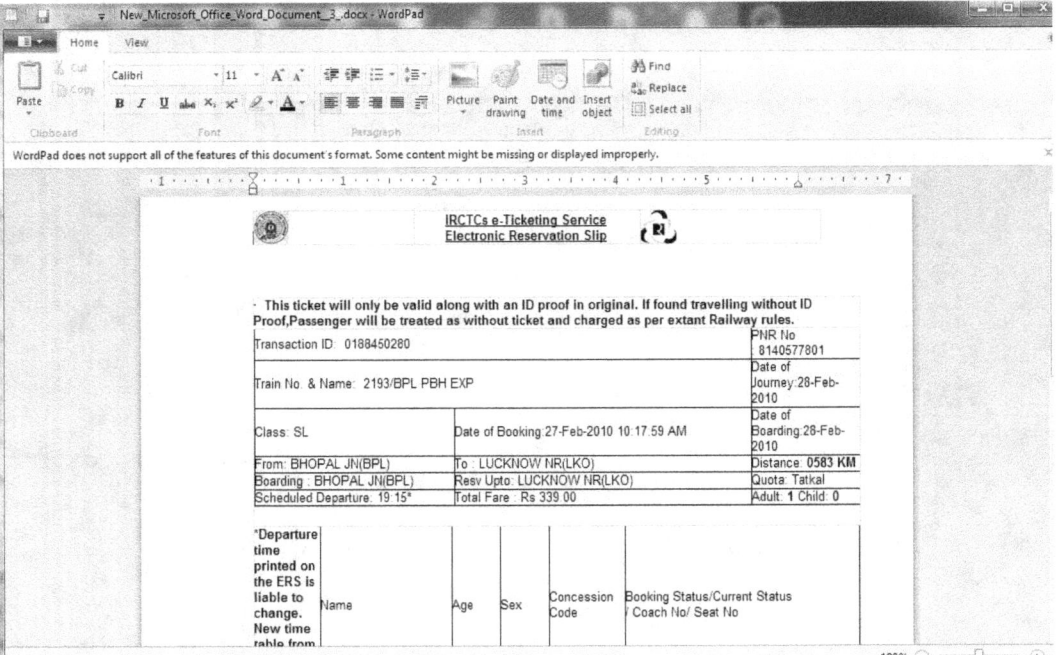

Use Calculator as Unit Converter

Apart from standard calculations, calculator integrated with Windows 7 can perform several different tasks which were not available in the legacy versions of the application in older Microsoft-based operating systems. With the help of new calculator in Windows 7 users can calculate dates, mortgage, vehicle economy, etc. Moreover, the application also offers the facility of unit conversion which can be used to convert several different units to other units accordingly. Unit conversion, practically, has nothing to do with the main interface of the calculator and therefore you need not to enter any digits in the main interface. Instead, when unit conversion feature is enabled in the calculator, its interface is extended and a new input area is displayed to the user. As a Windows 7 user if you want to use the calculator as a unit converter you are required to follow the steps given below:

1. Log on to Windows 7 computer with any account.
2. At the bottom of start menu in search box type **CALC** and press enter key.
3. When the calculator is opened, click **View** menu.
4. From the available list click **Unit conversion** to view the extended interface of the calculator.
5. From the available three drop-down lists choose the appropriate units as desired and then input the number in **From** field that you want to convert.

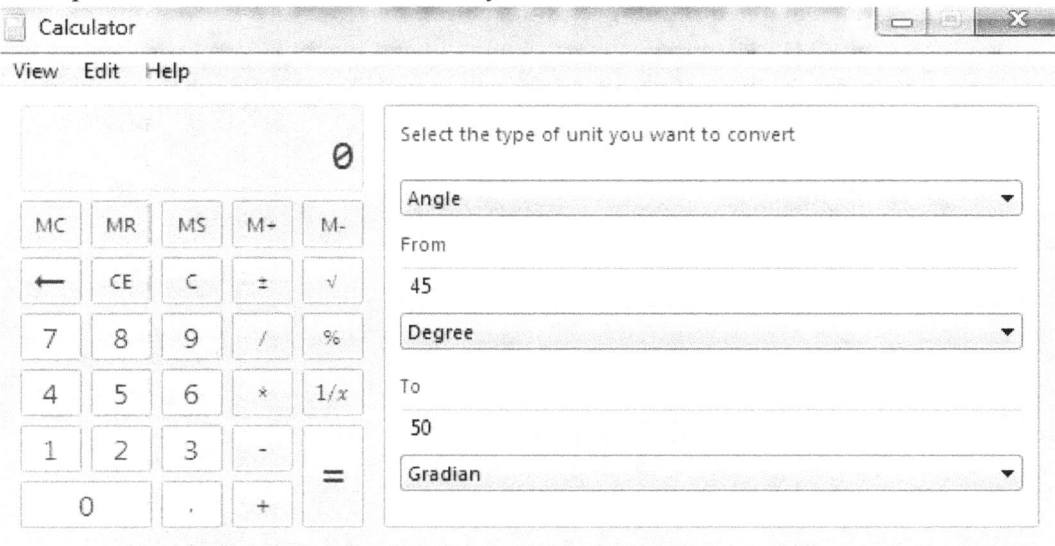

You will be displayed with its converted value in **To** field instantaneously.

Opening Multiple Windows Explorer Windows

While working with Windows 7 there may be times when, as a user, you need to open several Windows Explorer Windows simultaneously. When this is the case, under normal conditions, you need to go to My Computer (Windows XP) or Computer (Windows Vista or Windows 7) icon and double-click on it every time you need to open a new Windows Explorer. However many users do not know that this task can be done easily by using shortcut keys. This method is more useful for the users who are not quite comfortable with the mouse and have good hands on the keyboards. If you are such user and you want to expedite the task of opening multiple Windows Explorer Windows at the same time you are required to follow the steps given below:

1. Log on to Windows 7 computer with any account (no elevated privileges are required).

2. To open a new **Windows Explorer** window press **Windows key** + **E** on the keyboard.

3. To open another **Windows Explorer** window press the above combination again.

Note: By following the above three steps you will notice that you can open several Windows at the same time and that too very quickly.

View Multiple Instances of Application Quickly

One of the most hectic and tedious tasks that Windows 7 users face while using Internet Explorer as a default web browser is that if they have opened multiple instances of the application, it becomes difficult for them to locate the desired one from the available list in the taskbar. Although they can move their mouse pointers to the Internet Explorer icon available in the taskbar and can have a view of all the opened instances, but the view is not clear enough to specify the exact contents of the browser. Windows 7 helps these kinds of users by providing feature of using combination of keyboard and mouse clicks so that users can get the exact preview of all the instances of the web browser and can choose the desired one according to their requirements. As a Windows 7 user if you want to do so you are required to follow the steps given below:

1. Log on to Windows 7 computer with any account.

2. Open multiple instances of **Internet Explorer** by double-clicking on its icon in the taskbar several times.

3. Once opened, just to check, you can take your mouse pointer to its icon and all the opened instances will be displayed as, sort of, thumbnail icons.

4. You can now press and hold **Ctrl key** and click **Internet Explorer** icon in the taskbar with the mouse. Every time you click on the icon the next instance of the browser will be displayed as a preview on the full-screen.

5. You can release **Ctrl** key and stop clicking the mouse once you have reached the desired page to start working on it.

Modify Landing Page of Windows Explorer

When Windows 7 operating system is installed an icon of Windows Explorer is placed in the taskbar by default. When a user clicks on the icon Libraries folder is opened which contains links to Documents, Music, Pictures and Videos locations. Many users do not use these locations to store their files as they might lose them if something bad happens to the computer. In other words it can be understood that this shortcut generally serves no use to the users at all. With the help of small modifications, however, this link can be redirected to Computer location which is opened when Computer link is clicked in start menu. As a Windows 7 user if you want to do so you are required to follow the steps given below:

1. Log on to Windows 7 computer with any account.

2. Click **Start** button and click **All Programs**.

3. From the list click **Accessories** container to expand it and right click **Windows Explorer** icon to display the menu.

4. Click **Properties** and **Windows Explorer Properties** box make sure that you are on **Shortcut** tab.

5. In Target field add **/root,::{20D04FE0-3AEA-1069-A2D8-08002B30309D}** to the already written text so the entire filed would look somewhat like **%windir%\explorer.exe /root,::{20D04FE0-3AEA-1069-A2D8-08002B30309D}**.

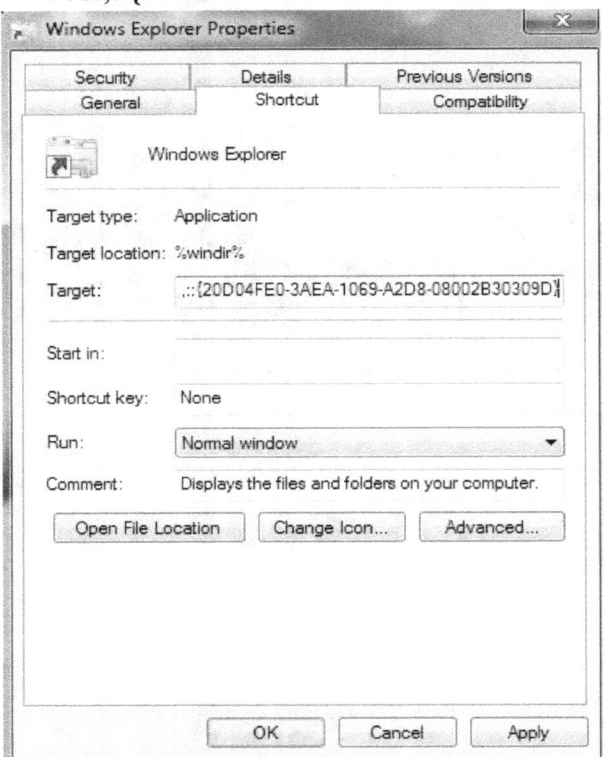

6. Once done, click **Ok** button to save the changes you have made.

7. Click **Windows Explorer** icon in the taskbar to check the configurations.

Surf Internet without Opening Web Browser

When a laptop PC or a desktop is purchased for home use it is expected by the users that they will surf Internet in great deal and therefore they will frequently use a web browser for the purpose. Default web browser in Windows 7 is Internet Explorer 8 and users can also install third party web browsers like Mozilla Firefox for better performances. Whatsoever the case is, every time users need to surf through the Internet they are required to open default browser in order to do so. However many users do not know that they can surf the Internet right from their taskbars by placing Address bar near system tray. As a Windows 7 user if you want to do so you are required to follow the steps given below:

1. Log on to Windows 7 computer with any account on which you want to configure above mentioned settings.
2. Right click on the taskbar and from the appeared menu go to **Properties**.
3. On **Taskbar and Start Menu Properties** box go to **Toolbars** tab.
4. From the available boxes check **Address** checkbox and click **Ok** button to save the changes you have made.

You will be displayed with the address bar at right corner of the taskbar.

Change the Default Save Location

Whenever you create a document or any other file and you want to save it, default location where that file is saved is C:\users\User1, where User1 is the name of a user account in Windows. This means that when User1 tries to save any file it is saved in the above location. As default this configuration is not at all bad. However, if you are regularly connected to Internet there are chances that your computer might get infected with several viruses and that too very frequently. In such cases you need to format and reinstall Windows on your computer after every 3 to 4 months. To save your data you need to copy all your documents from the default location to any other drive every time you want to format your computer. The problem in this case is that if by chance you forget to backup your documents and you accidentally format your system drive all your documents will be lost. Moreover if you save all your data on the system drive there are chances that they would eat up entire disk space earlier than expected.

To prevent this situation you can change the default save location to any other drive where your data can be secured and your system drive still remains free. You can change default save location by following the steps given below:

1. Click **Start** button.

2. In the start menu right click **Documents** and from the context menu select **Properties**.

3. On the Documents Properties page click **Include a folder** button and browse to the different folder at different location where you want to save all your documents and other data files and click **Include Folder** button.

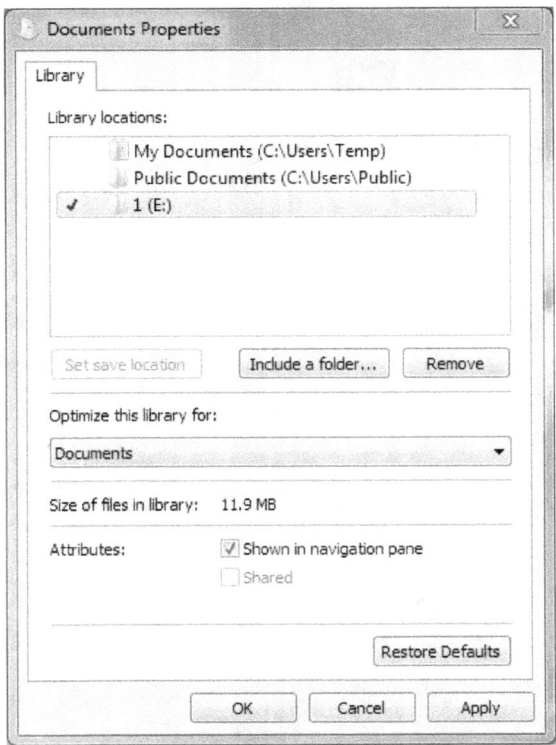

4. Back on the **Documents Properties** page right click on the newly included folder and from the menu select **Set As Default Save Location** and click **Ok** button to accept and confirm your configuration.

PCTIPS 3000

CHAPTER 2
WINDOWS UPDATES

Manage Automatic Updates

Automatic updates are by default enabled. As soon as Windows 7 connects to the Internet Windows 7 Automatic Updates feature communicates with Microsoft update server and looks for recent available updates. As soon as Windows 7 finds new update it downloads and installs them. In production environments where security is a major concern, administrators may not want to modify this default configuration as this setting makes Windows 7 computer secure. However in home environments this configuration might sometimes reduce the processing speed of the computer which might result in decreased performance. Also it is not necessary for home users to download every security update which is available on Microsoft update server. As a home user if you want to receive the notifications of updates and want your Windows 7 computer to ask you before downloading and/or installing any of them you need to follow the steps given below:

1. Log on to the computer with administrator account.

2. Click **Start** button.

3. From the start menu go to **Control Panel** and from the opened window click **System and Security** category link.

4. On the opened page click **Windows Update** category link and on the next page in the left bar click **Change settings** link.

5. On **Choose how Windows can install updates** page on Important updates drop-down list select **Check for updates but let me choose whether to download and install them** and click **Ok** button to accept and confirm your selection.

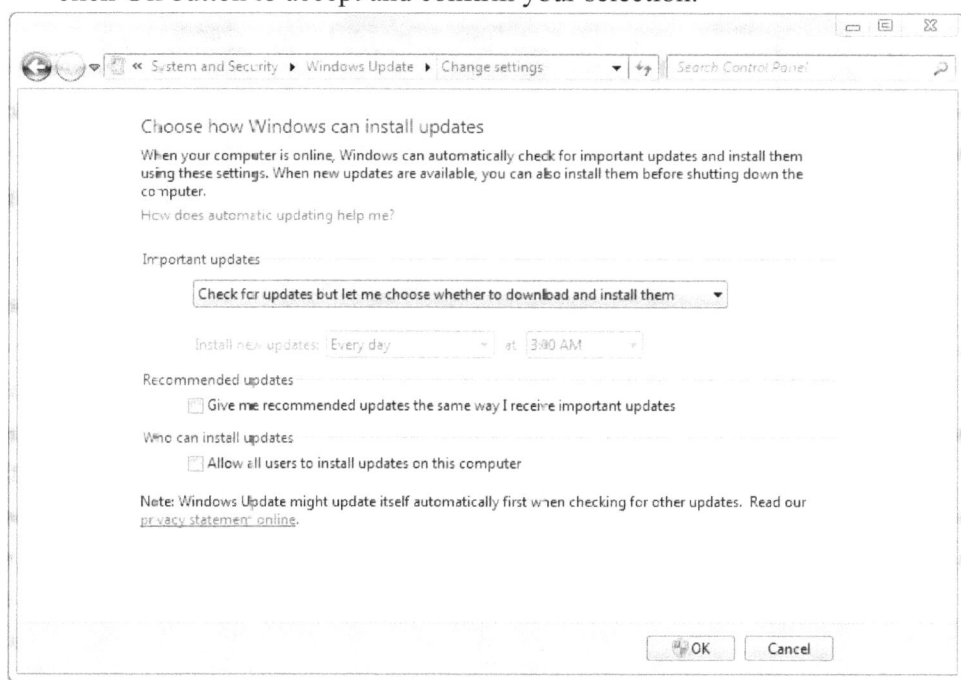

6. Close all opened windows.

Disable Auto Restart after Automatic Updates

In any Windows 7 operating system automatic updates play important role as far as the security of the machine is concerned. No matter if the computer is used for home purpose or in corporate sector it is always recommended that automatic updates feature should be turned on and the operating system must be updated on a regular basis. The consequences, however, are that as soon as the updates are downloaded and installed, computers automatically restart which may create problems to the users who work on it. To eliminate this problem, administrators can modify registry settings so that the computers do not get restarted after the updates are installed. As an administrator if you want to do so you are required to follow the steps given below:

1. Log on to Windows 7 computer with the administrator account and in the search box at the bottom of start menu type **REGEDIT**.

2. As soon as you will press enter key you will be displayed with **Registry Editor** box and you are required to locate **HKEY_LOCAL_MACHINE\SOFTWARE\Polices\Microsoft\Windows**.

3. Right click **Windows** and from the available menu go to **New** and from the appeared submenu click **Key**.

4. Specify the name **WindowsUpdate** to the new key and then right click on it to go to **New** and again click **Key**.

5. Type the name **AU** to the new key and right click on it to go to **New** and then click **DWORD (32-bit Value)**.

6. Specify the name as **NoAutoRebootWithLoggedOnUsers** and when once specified right click it to go to **Modify**.

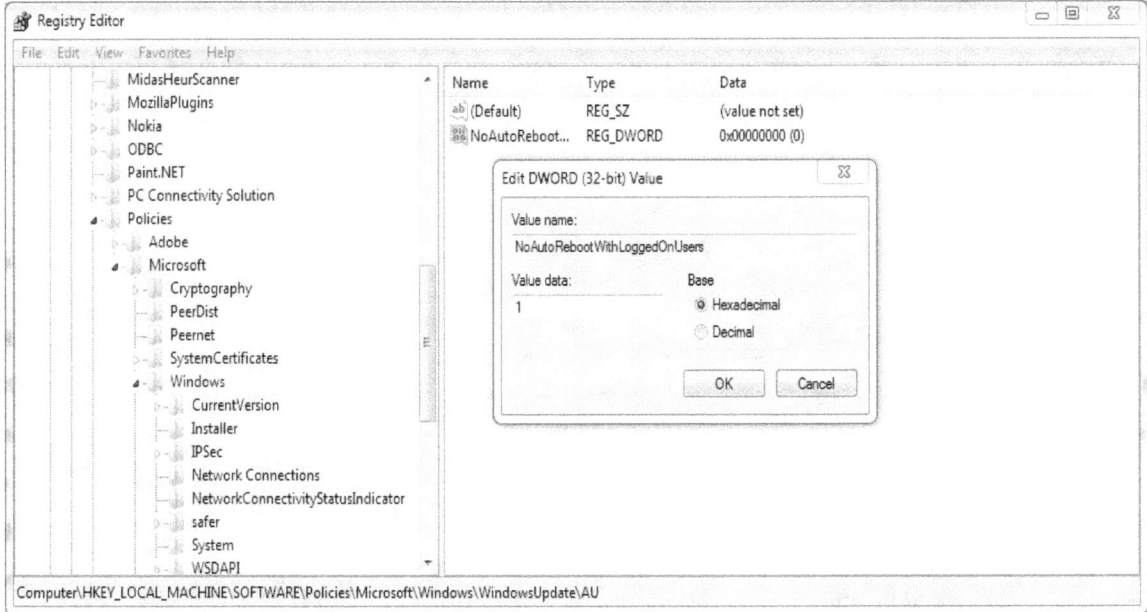

7. On the opened box under **Value data** section type **1** and finally press **Ok** button to save the changes.

8. Restart the computer to make the changes take effect.

PCTIPS 3000

CHAPTER 3

OPTIMIZATION

Use USB Pen Drive as RAM (ReadyBoost)

Windows 7 has a feature called ReadyBoost which enables its users to use their USB pen drives as temporary RAM for their systems. This feature is helpful when because of any reason they need to speed up their systems temporarily. Instructions to do this are given below:

1. Insert a USB flash drive (Pen Drive) in the USB port.
2. Open **Computer** by clicking **Start** button and clicking **Computer**.
3. Right-click the icon of the newly inserted USB flash drive and select **Properties**.
4. In the **Removable Disk Properties** page go to **ReadyBoost** tab.
5. If you want to dedicate the entire space of your flash drive for **ReadyBoost** you can select the radio button that says **Dedicate this device to ReadyBoost**. Alternatively you can dedicate any specified amount of space from the flash drive for **ReadyBoost**. To do this you can select **Use this device** radio button and in the text box you can specify the amount of space from the flash drive that you want Windows 7 to use as RAM.

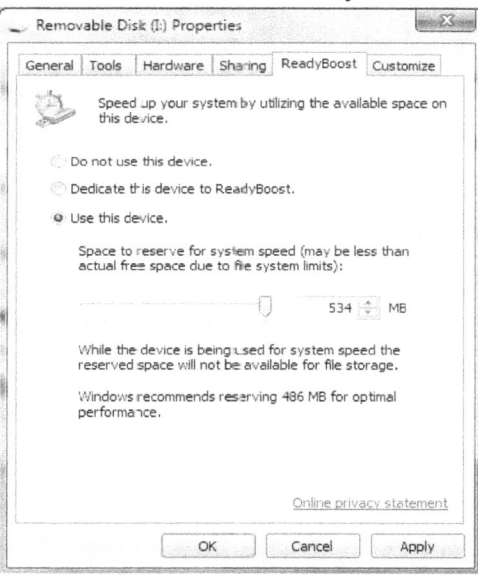

6. Click **Ok** buttons on all Windows to accept and confirm your selections and configurations.

More Info:

When ReadyBoost is enabled a file named ReadyBoost.sfcache is created. This file is compressed and encrypted so that even if anyone steals the USB pen drive, data contained in it cannot be extracted or read.

Recommendations:

Do NOT pull flash drive out of USB Port while it is being used as a ReadyBoost device.

Do NOT save any data files on the flash drive when it is being used as ReadyBoost device.

Increase Virtual Memory

Many times you might have seen that your system starts performing slow. Along with this there might be a notification saying "Low Virtual Memory". This means that the virtual memory of your machine, which is in fact a reserved space in your hard disk that works as a RAM, is getting overloaded and requires some increment. Although, Windows 7 automatically handles this process, however you can manage this manually according to your ease and requirements.

First thing first, the virtual memory of a machine depends directly on the total amount of physical RAM present in your computer. Virtual memory of a computer should be minimum 1.5 times of the RAM present in the computer and can go up to 4 times at the maximum. This means that if you have 1 GB of RAM installed in your Windows 7 computer you can have minimum of 1.5 GB virtual memory and it can be increased up to maximum 4 GB. It should be understood that the more virtual memory your computer has, the faster and efficiently it may work. To increase or manually manage the virtual memory in your Windows 7 computer you need to follow the below steps:

1. Click **Start** button.
2. From the menu right-click **Computer** and select **Properties**.
3. From the **System** window, in the left pane click **Advanced System Settings**.
4. In the **System Properties** box under **Performance** section click **Settings** button.
5. In the **Performance Options** window go to **Advanced** tab.
6. Under **Virtual Memory** section on this tab click **Change** button.
7. In order to make manual changes make sure **Automatically manage page file size for all drives** check box is unchecked.
8. Ensure that **C:** drive is selected.
9. Select **Custom size** radio button and specify the minimum and maximum size of virtual memory according to the physical RAM available in your computer.
10. Click **Set** button.
11. Finally click all **Ok** buttons to accept and confirm your selections.
12. This process will help you in speeding up the boot process of your computer and will also perform efficiently while you are playing high-graphic games.

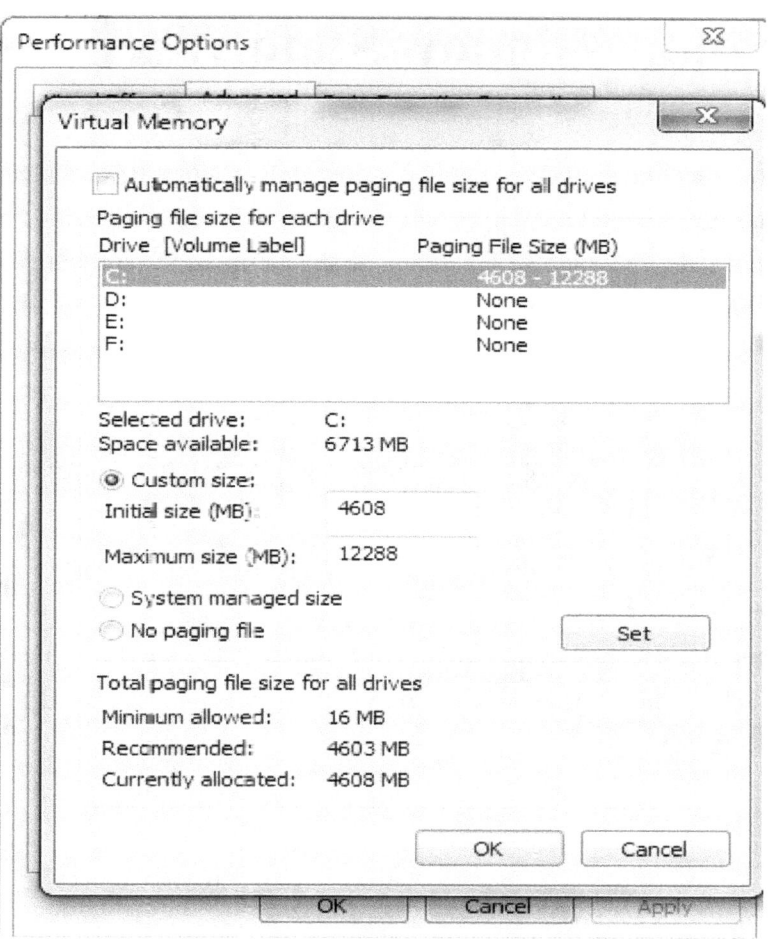

Manage Application Window State When It Starts

In Windows 7 when any application starts its default Window state is Normal. This means that the application will open in default window state when the user initiates it. Some applications run in full screen mode whereas others in normal size window (depending on the nature of the software and screen resolution of the operating system). Users sometimes, however, may want to modify the default window state of the application as per the requirements and/or their personal choices. To modify the default Window state of any application you can follow the steps given below:

1. Log on to your Windows 7 computer on which you want to modify the default Window state of the application when it starts.

2. On the desktop right click on the shortcut of the application and from the appeared menu choose **Properties** to click on.

3. On the **Properties** box make sure that you are **Shortcut** tab and from the drop-down list of **Run:** section on the tab choose the appropriate window state as required.

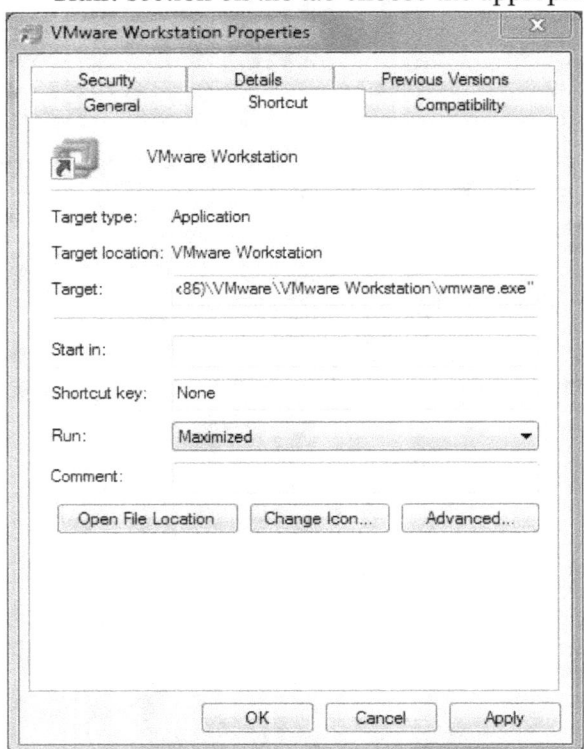

4. Once done, click **Ok** button to make your settings and configuration persistent.

More Info:

Once you are done with the above configuration you can double click the shortcut of the application to get the demo of your recently configured settings. In order to withdraw the settings you can follow the above steps and choose the previously configured option from the drop-down list.

Run Legacy Applications

There are several applications which are developed after the official release of Microsoft Windows 7 operating system and therefore these applications are completely compatible with it. However there are still some of them which are only compatible with the older versions of operating systems developed by Microsoft. These applications are not at all compatible with Windows 7 and therefore they fail to run on it under normal conditions. Since it is very unrealistic to go for a new version of application every time a user installs a latest operating system, Microsoft has integrated Compatibility Mode feature in Windows 7 in order to allow users to run legacy applications while using the latest operating system. You can run any legacy application on a Windows 7 computer by following the steps given below:

1. Log on to the Windows 7 computer.

2. Right click on the shortcut of the application you want to run in compatibility mode and from the appeared menu go to **Properties**.

3. On the **Properties** box go to **Compatibility** tab and under **Compatibility mode** section check **Run this program in compatibility mode for:** checkbox.

4. From the drop-down list choose the appropriate version of operating system for which the application is compatible and optionally you can choose the desired checkboxes under Settings section as per your requirements.

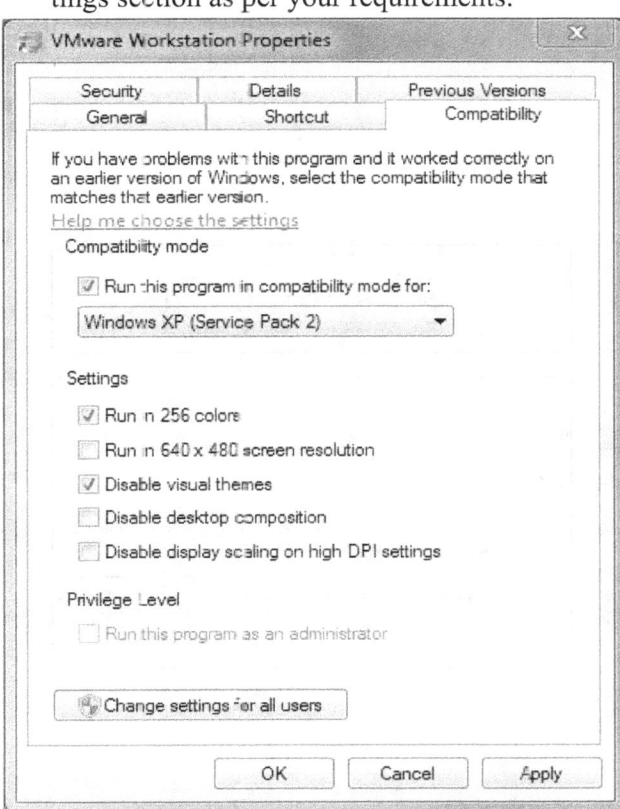

5. Once done, click **Ok** button to make your settings permanent.

Disable Legacy File Creation

Every operating system that is developed by Microsoft has a basic nature of having backward compatibility features in it. This makes even the latest operating system liked by users who use older versions of applications which were fully compatible with the legacy operating systems. With the help of backward compatibility users can install and smoothly run older applications on the latest versions of operating systems for example Windows 7 as it allows applications to create files with legacy naming convention along with latest file names. When older applications are used legacy file names are kept into consideration which used to have 8.3 naming convention. This naming convention means that the file name can contain maximum of eight characters and the extension of the file can be maximum of three characters long separated by a period or dot (.). However in many cases nowadays applications are upgraded by the developers and have been made compatible with Windows 7 and therefore there is no need to use legacy file naming convention (8.3) which normally consumes a decent amount of processing when enabled. When this is the case administrators can disable the creation of legacy files with older naming convention by following the steps given below:

1. Log on to Windows 7 computer with the account that holds administrative rights.
2. Click **Start** button and click **All Programs**.
3. From the appeared list click **Accessories** container.
4. From the available items right click **Command Prompt** and from the menu click **Run as administrator**.
5. On the opened the command window type **FSUTIL BEHAVIOR SET DISABLE8DOT3 1** command to disable the creation of legacy naming convention.

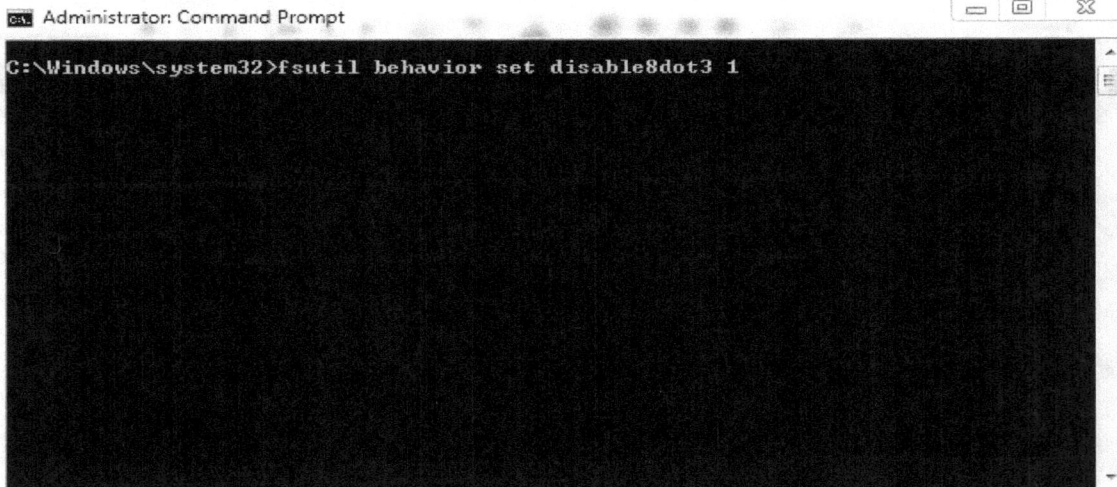

6. Restart the computer to allow the changes to take effect.

Note: To re-enable the above feature type **FSUTIL BEHAVIOR SET DISABLE8DOT3 0** command in the elevated command prompt.

Delete Unused Wireless Network Connection

In many cases it is seen that Windows 7 operating system is installed on a laptop PC and Internet connection is most commonly accessed through wireless connections. Since laptop PCs are mobile computers it is very obvious that users connect their computers to the Internet via several wireless network connections depending on the location they are in and the type of available wireless connection. In these cases sometimes wireless connection icons can overpopulate the area and may also confuse users as which wireless network connection is appropriate to connect at which location. Although Windows 7 is smart enough to connect to only available wireless connection, however if users want they can delete wireless connections from their computers which are not in use. As a Windows 7 user if you want to do this you are required to follow the steps provided as below:

1. Log on to Windows 7 computer with the account that has elevated privileges.
2. At the bottom of start menu in search box type **Network and Sharing Center** and press enter key.
3. On the opened box from the left bar click **Manage wireless networks** link.
4. From the available list of wireless network connections right click on the one which you want to delete and from the available menu click **Remove network**.

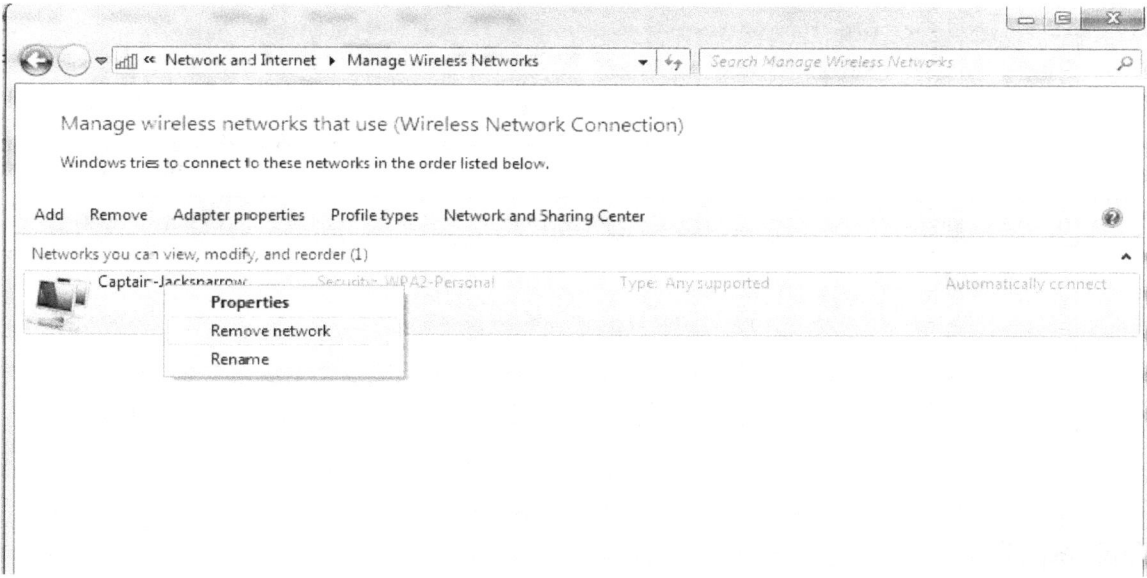

5. On the confirmation box click **Yes** button to finally delete the network connection.

Modify HOSTS File to Run Internet Faster

When Windows 7 computer is connected to the Internet IP address of DNS server provided by ISP is also automatically configured. DNS servers help computers to find out appropriate websites requested by the users. Queries which are sent from client computers to the DNS servers might sometimes take long durations to get resolved. Reason behind this might be that the DNS server gets too busy in serving other client machines. Many administrators in these cases manually specify IP addresses of the websites which are frequently visited by the users. The process involves editing HOSTS file and entering the IP addresses with their respective URLs in the file manually. As a Windows 7 user if you want to do so you are required to follow the steps given below:

1. Log on to Windows 7 computer with administrator account.

2. Go to **C:\Windows\System32\drivers\etc** location and double-click **HOSTS** file.

3. On **Open with** box choose any appropriate text editor (which in most cases is Notepad) and click **Ok** button to open the file.

4. Now you can edit the file by typing in the IP address of the website followed by its URL. (See the picture below to get an example).

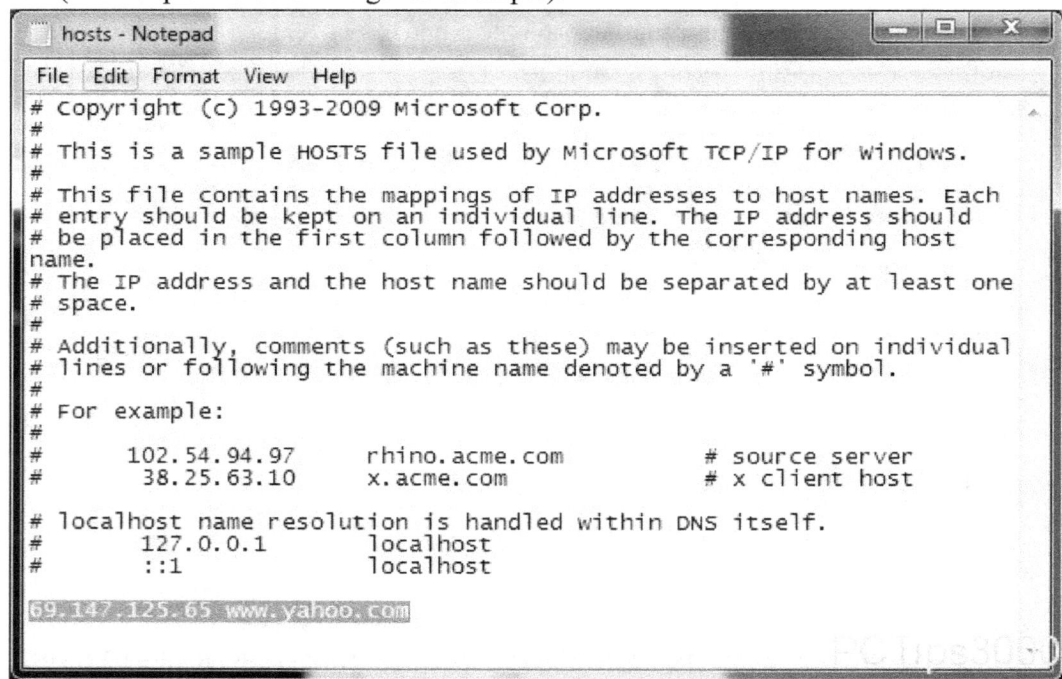

5. Once you are done, save the changes that you have made in the notepad file and close it.

Disable/Enable Lock Workstation Feature

In almost every version of Microsoft Windows operating system whenever Windows + L key is pressed the computer gets locked and users are not able to interact with the operating system. The operating system can only be unlocked by providing the password of the user account which was logged on before it was locked. The computer can also be unlocked by providing the password of the administrator account. In production environments this feature help organizations in great deal as far as security is concerned. However in home environments this feature is not required and therefore can be disabled by the administrators of the computers. Although it is strongly recommended that the feature should NOT be disabled at all but still if users want to play around with the operating system or just want to get familiar with the registry they can follow the steps given below to disable it:

1. Log on to Windows 7 computer with the account that is administrator privileges.

2. Click **Start** button and from the available menu in the search box type **REGEDIT** and press the enter key.

3. On **Registry Editor** window from the left pane locate

4. **HKEY_CURRENT_USER\Software\Microsoft\Windows\CurrentVersion\Policies\System**.

5. On the right pane right-click anywhere in the blank area and click **New** option.

6. From the available options click **DWORD (32-bit) Value** and specify **DisableLockWorkstation** as the new name of the key.

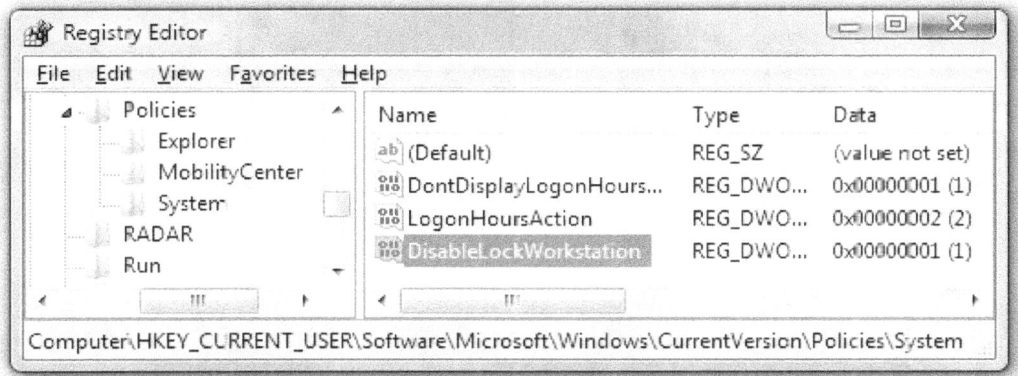

7. Double-click on the newly created key and in **Value data** field specify its value as **1** to disable the feature. (You can re-enable this anytime by specifying the value as **0**).

8. Once done, click **Ok** button and close all the opened boxes.

9. If required, restart your computer.

Enable File or Folder Level Compression

Many people think that only third-party applications such as WinZip or WinRAR are capable of compressing files or folders. But the fact is Windows 7 provides a built-in feature using which files, folders or even whole drives can be compressed up to 17%-20% depending upon the file types. This compression method can be applied on all types of files, folders or drives. However, compression on one side can reduce the size of files or folders hence eating up less hard disk space, on the other hand it may slow down the process of opening files or folders when a user tries to open them. This delay is negligible though.

In order to compress a folder you can follow the below step-by-step instructions:

1. Right-click on the drive, folder or file that you want to compress and from the context menu select **Properties**.

2. In the **Properties** box ensure that you are on **General** tab.

3. Click **Advanced** button.

4. On the **Advanced Attributes** box check Compress contents to save disk space check box and click Ok button to accept and confirm your selection.

5. On the **Properties** box click **Apply** button.

6. On the **Confirm Attribute Changes** box select desired option and click **Ok** button to confirm.

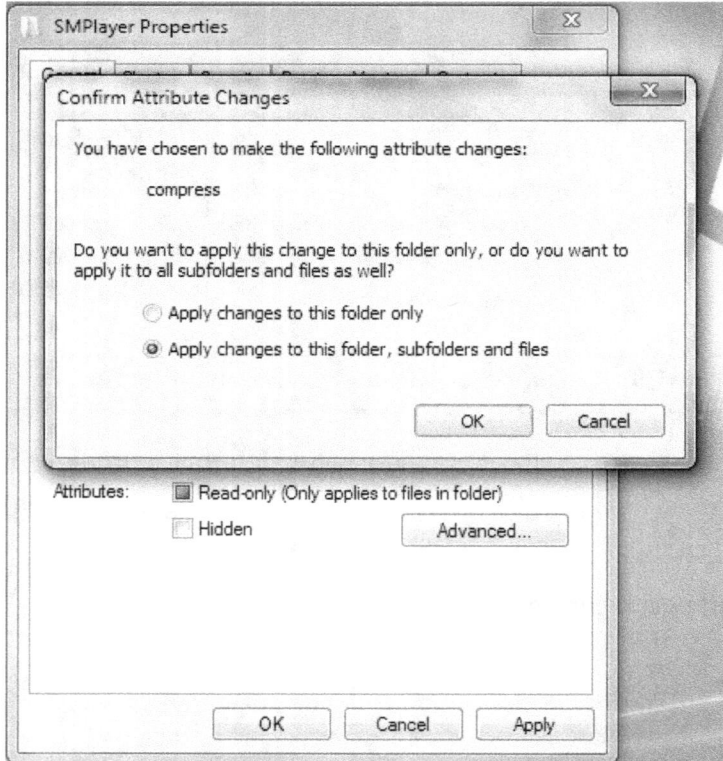

When you see the text color of file or folder is changed to blue, this means that the compression on that folder has been enabled and now the folder is consuming less disk space. You can test this by going to the properties of compressed folder and noticing the folder size. There will be 2 different sizes mentioned for the same folder. Size: xx.xx MB which means the actual size of the folder and Size on disk: xx.xx MB means the space the folder is occupying after compression.

More Info:

When you try to access any compressed file or folder, Windows 7 decompresses it and then opens it for you. Because of this the process of accessing a compressed file or folder is delayed by few microseconds, which of course is negligible. Also, when you close file or folder after you are finished with your work Windows 7 re-compresses it in the background.

System Requirements:

Make sure the drive on which you want to enable compression is formatted with NTFS file system. In almost all cases Windows 7 formats all its drives using NTFS file system only.

PCTIPS 3000

Sort Files According to Date Modified

Whenever files are stored in any folder in Windows 7, they are displayed in alphabetical order to the users. This means that the file name starting with A will appear first and the file name starting with Z will appear at the last. This alphabetical synchronization or arrangement of files in the container makes it easier for the users to locate the required file easily. For home users this configuration is quite well and it does not require any manipulation at all. In production environments, however, there are several files that are modified daily and users may need to find out the files which have been recently modified. When this is the case users can configure the sorting of the files date wise so that they can be located within no time. As a Windows 7 user if you want to sort the files according to the dates on which they were modified you are required to follow the steps provided belo *-+w:

1. Log on to Windows 7 computer with the user account on which you want to enable sorting.
2. Browse through **Windows Explorer** and go to the container that contains files.
3. Right click anywhere in the container and from the context menu go to **Sort by** and from the appeared submenu click **Date modified**.

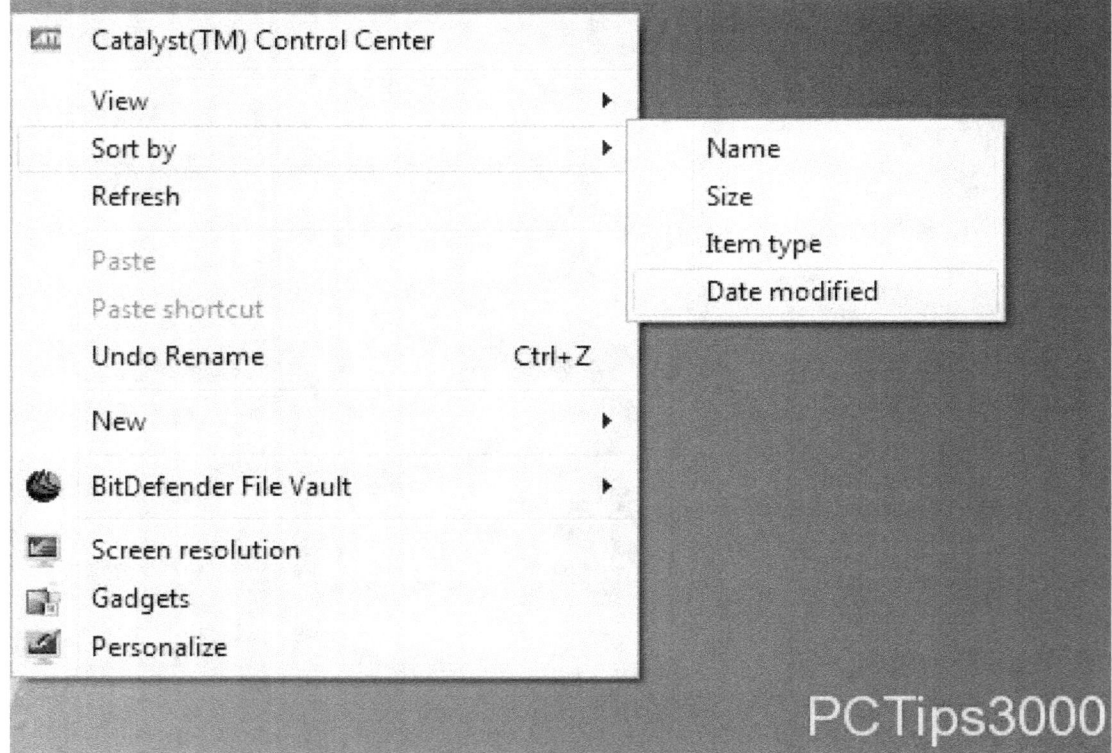

Add Locations for Indexing and Quick Search

With the release of Microsoft Windows 7, search feature is also highly improved and therefore any file or folder which is searched by the user is found almost instantaneously and real-time results are displayed. This is because of indexing feature which is integrated in the operating system and which enables files and folders to be searched even more efficiently. However default indexed locations are only looked for when any object is searched by the user and users can modify and add non-default locations where indexing feature can become applicable to get instantaneous results while they search for any object. As a Windows 7 user if you want to include non-default locations for indexing you are required to follow the steps given as below:

1. Log on to Windows 7 computer with any account for which you want to enable indexing feature on non-default locations.

2. At the bottom of start menu in search box type **Indexing Options** and press enter key.

3. On the opened **Indexing Options** box click **Modify** button.

4. Under **Change selected locations** list check the boxes representing the locations you want to add for indexing.

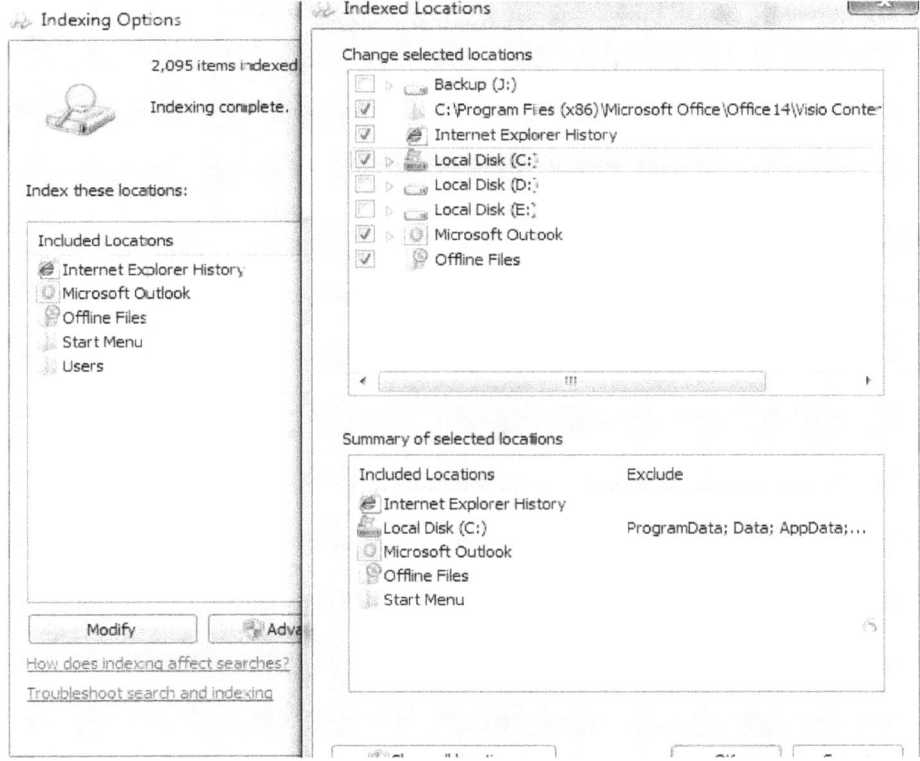

5. Alternatively you can uncheck the boxes representing the locations that you want to exclude from the indexing list.

6. Once done, click **Ok** button to save the changes and click **Close** button on **Indexing Options** box to close it.

Enable Automatic User Logon

Automatic Logon on Windows 7 is a feature which by default is disabled when there are more than one user accounts created on the computer. When there is only one account, Windows 7 automatically enables Automatic Login feature which allows users to log on to the account as soon as the computer starts. This only works when the user account belongs to Administrators group and has no passwords assigned to it. For home users this configuration is quite helpful as it expedites the booting and logon process and displays the users' desktop screen directly. However with some registry modifications administrators can enable Automatic Login feature even with multiple accounts which allows default user to go to the desktop screen without any prior interaction with the operating system even it has been assigned with a password. As an administrator of a Windows 7 computer if you want to configure this you are required to follow the steps given below:

1. Log on to Windows 7 computer with administrator account.

2. At the bottom of start menu in search box type **REGEDIT** command and press enter key.

3. On **Registry Editor** window locate **HKEY_LOCAL_MACHINE\SOFTWARE\Microsoft\Windows NT\CurrentVersion\Winlogon** from the left pane.

4. From the right pane right click **AutoAdminLogon** and from the available menu click **Modify** and set the **Value data** to 1. (If **AutoAdminLogon** entry is not available you are required to create it by right clicking **Winlogon** from left pane and clicking **New > String Value**).

5. Press **Ok** button when done.

6. Follow step 4 to locate or create **DefaultUserName** entry and modify its value to the default username that you want to auto logon when Windows starts.

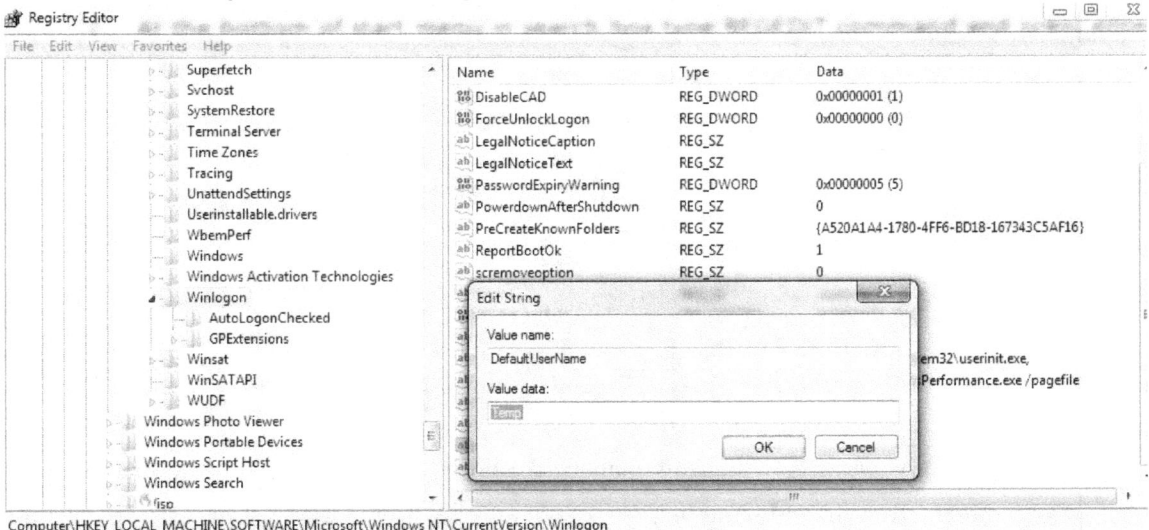

7. Press **Ok** button when done.

8. Follow the step 4 to locate or create **DefaultPassword** entry and modify its value to the default password of that user account.

9. Press **Ok** button to save the changes.

10. Restart your computer to check the results of the new configuration that you have made.

Delete Themes

When Windows 7 is installed on a computer, several default themes are also available for the users so that they can change the ambience of their PCs when desired. This is provided so that the users do not get bored with the same atmosphere every time they log on to their computer systems. Moreover, Windows 7 also offers to create themes. In fact the themes are automatically created when the user chooses any wallpaper other than the default ones provided by Windows 7. In such cases, when users have created several themes the area becomes overpopulated with them which might not tidy and appropriate. Therefore Windows 7 allows users to delete these custom themes in case users want to make some room for the new ones. As a Windows 7 user if you want to delete themes you are required to follow the steps given below:

1. Log on to Windows 7 computer.
2. Click **Start** button and from the available menu click **Control Panel**.
3. From the opened box click **Change the theme** link under **Appearance and Personalization** category.
4. On the opened window right click on the theme that you want to delete under **My Themes** category and click **Delete theme** which is the only option available in the appeared menu.

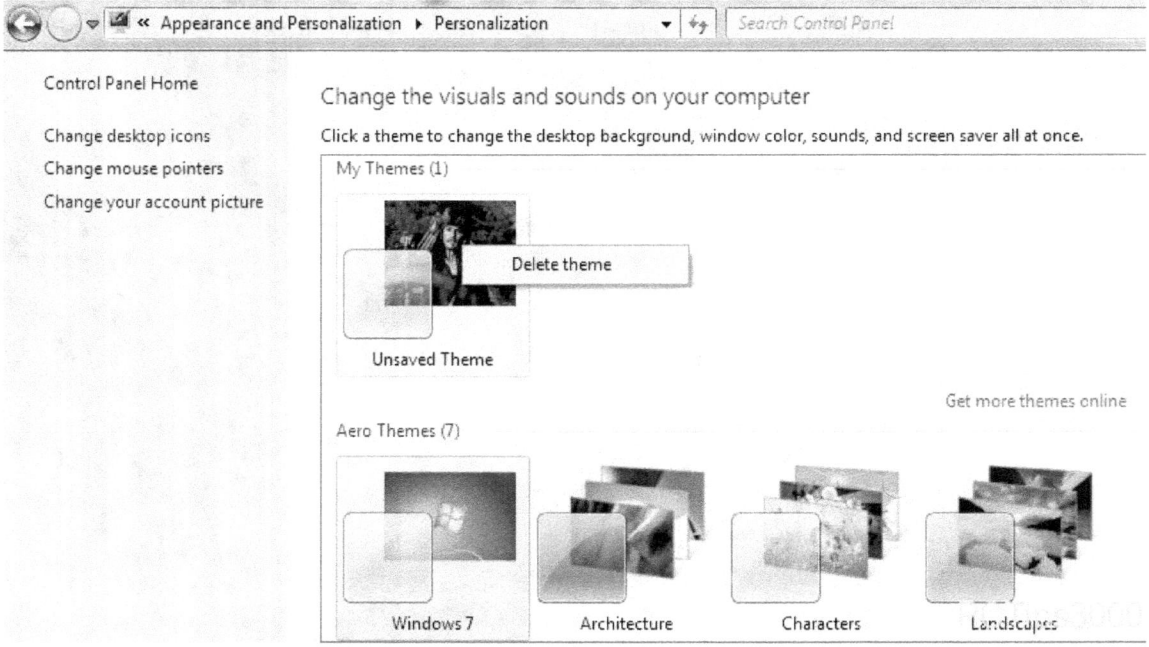

5. Click **Yes** button on the confirmation box to delete the theme.

Keep/Delete User Profiles While Deleting Accounts

With the release of Microsoft Windows 2000 operating systems started maintaining separate user profiles for all user accounts that log on to the computers. This means that if a computer had five different user accounts, five separate profiles were automatically generated on that computer. In Microsoft Windows 2000 and Windows XP these user profiles are stored in C:\Documents and Settings location within the folder that had the name of the user account. In Windows 7 however the location has been changed and now all user profiles are stored in C:\Users directory that contains a folder named as the name of the user account. When a user is deleted from a computer it depends on the administrator whether he wants to keep the profile of the deleted user account or he wants to delete the entire folder that contains his profile. As a Windows 7 administrator if you want to keep or delete user profiles while deleting user account you are required to follow the steps given as below:

1. Log on to Windows 7 computer with administrator account.

2. Click on **Start** button and from the menu click **Control Panel**.

3. From the opened window click **Add** or remove user accounts link under **User Accounts and Family Safety** category.

4. On the next page click on the name of the user which you want to delete and then from the new page click **Delete the account**.

5. On the confirmation window choose the appropriate button named **Delete Files** or **Keep Files** to get the desired output.

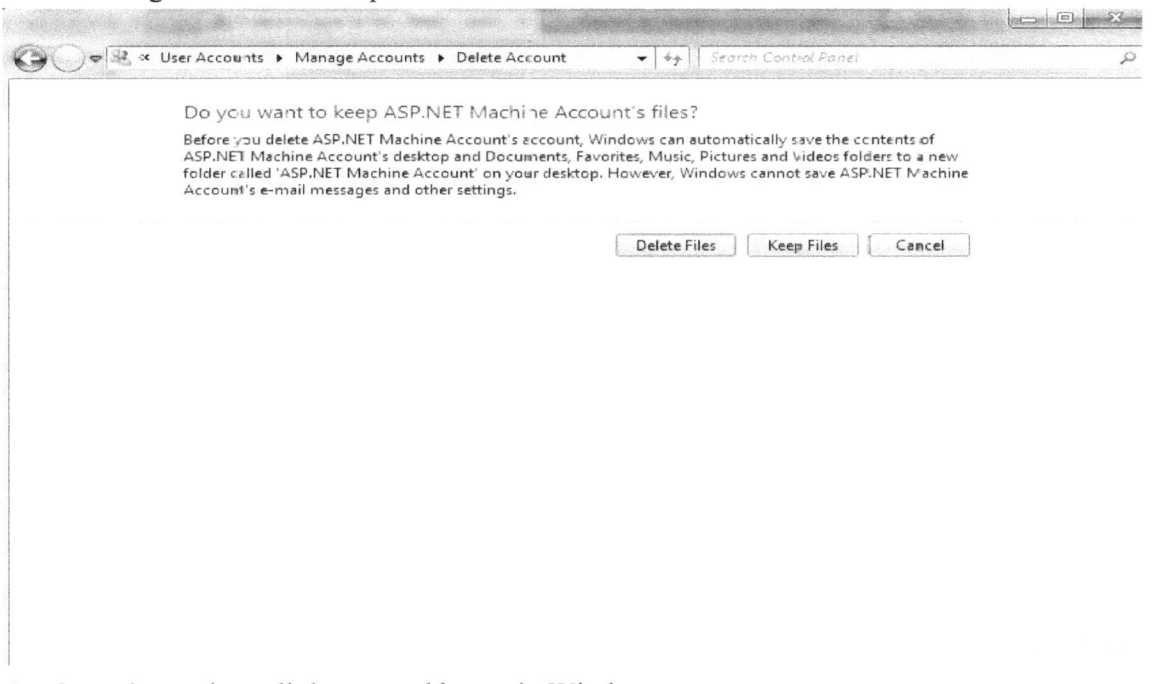

6. Once done, close all the opened boxes in Windows.

Disable Scan and Fix for Removable Drives

As soon as a new removable media is inserted into USB port in a Windows 7 computer, the operating system automatically asks to scan and fix the errors if the media contains any. From security point of view this configuration, which is by default enabled, is quite helpful in production and home environments. However the drawback of this feature is that if the media contains any virus applications they automatically get initiated and infect the computers. Places where strong antivirus applications are installed on computers, users need not to worry about this and they can leave the configuration intact whereas when computers are at home and no strong anti-virus applications are installed sometimes users may want to disable this feature so that the viruses may not harm their computer systems accidentally or unwantedly. As a Windows 7 administrator if you want to disable this feature, you need to modify the services, steps to which are given as below:

1. Log on to Windows 7 computer with the account that has elevated privileges, that is, administrator account.

2. At the bottom of start menu in search box type **SERVICES.MSC** and press enter key.

3. On the opened window double-click **Shell Hardware Detection** service and the opened properties box click **Stop** button in **General** tab.

4. Click **Apply** button and then from the available **Startup type** drop-down list choose **Disabled**.

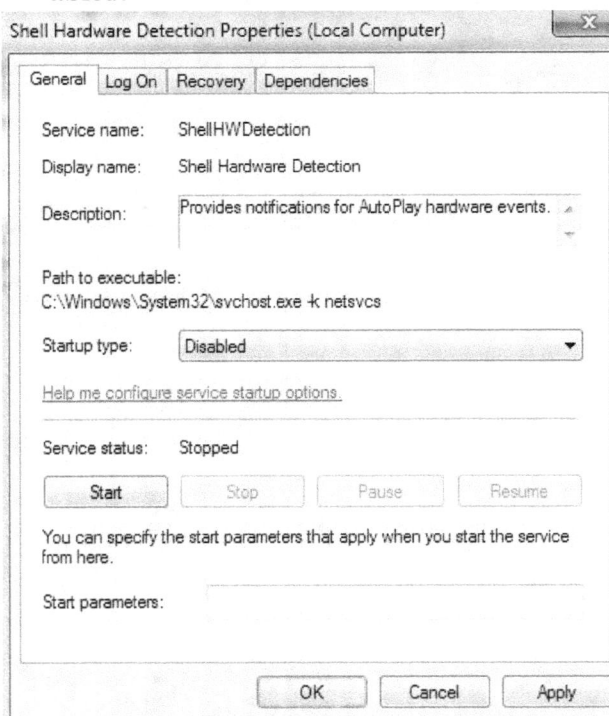

5. Finally click **Ok** button to save the changes you have made and if required, restart your computer.

Manage Operating Systems in Dual Boot Systems

In home environments there are times when users install two operating systems on a single computer in order to run some applications which are only compatible with legacy versions of Windows. When this is the case, the operating system which is installed later becomes the default OS and the default timeout duration that is automatically configured in these situations is 30 seconds. This means that if within 30 seconds a user fails to select any operating system to boot, the default operating system automatically starts. This configuration can be modified as per the requirements and the process to do so is given below:

1. Logon on to Windows 7 computer with administrator account.

2. Click **Start** button.

3. From the start menu right click **Computer** and from the menu select **Properties**.

4. On **View basic information about your computer** page in the left bar click **Advanced system settings** link.

5. On the opened box make sure that you are on **Advanced** tab and under **Startup and Recovery** section click **Settings** button.

6. On **Startup and Recovery** box from **Default operating system** drop-down list choose the appropriate operating system to make it default.

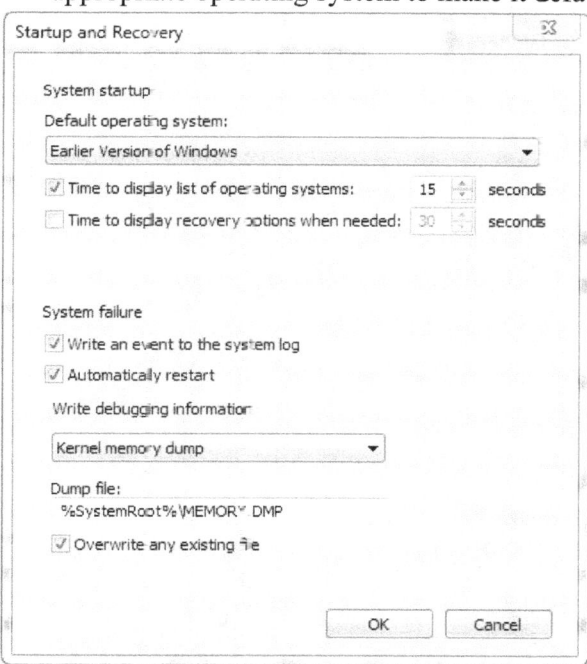

7. On **Time to display list of operating systems** box specify the number of seconds after which the default operating system will automatically start.

8. Once done, click **Ok** button to accept and confirm your configuration and close all opened windows.

Specify System Specific Environmental Variables

System specific environment variables are small keywords which when typed in Run Command box or search box, execute a specific application or open any particular folder to which they are pointed. For example if in search box you type Notepad, a built-in notepad application is executed. In the same way you can add a desired application or folder path to environmental variable list so that it gets executed when you type its name in search box or Run Command box. The only thing you need to do is to edit the environmental variable path and the process to do so is given below:

1. Logon on the Windows 7 computer with administrator account.
2. Click **Start** button.
3. From the start menu right click **Computer** and from the menu select **Properties**.
4. On **View basic information about your computer** page in the left bar click **Advanced system settings** link.
5. On the opened box make sure that you are **Advanced** tab and click **Environment Variables** button.
6. On the opened box under **System variables** list click **Path** variable and click **Edit** button.
7. On **Edit System Variable** box in **Variable value** field at the end of the text add a ";"and include the path of your desired application or folder.

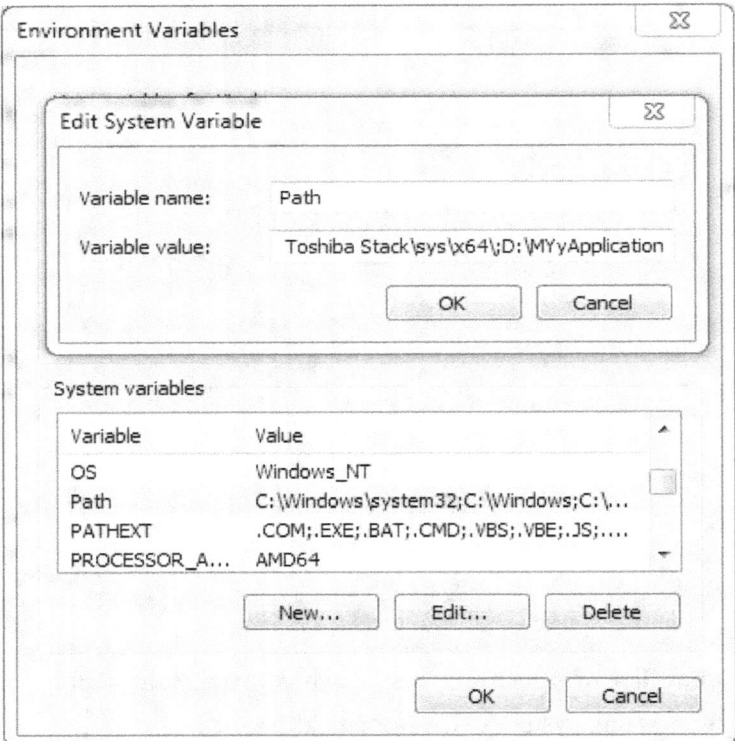

8. Once done, click **Ok** button on all the opened boxes to accept and confirm your configuration and close all windows.

Re-Gain Reduced Audio Volume

Although Windows 7 is developed to work as efficiently as possible but still there are some flaws in the operating system which sometimes may annoy users. These obnoxious behaviors of the operating systems, although, are not actually the flaws but are introduced in them on purpose to ease out the technical aspects whenever any conflicts occur. A good example for this can be reduction in noise which automatically happens all of a sudden. When this happens no matter how high the volume level is increased the noise is still not clearly audible. Technically, this feature is introduced in Windows 7 so that if any other hardware device is detected it is given priority so that users can recognize its presence. But the fact remains the same that in home environments these functions are not at all welcomed by the users and they might want to disable it. As a Windows 7 home user if you want to disable this feature you are required to follow the steps given below

1. Log on to Windows 7 computer.
2. Click **Start** button and from the menu click **Control Panel**.
3. Click **Hardware and Sound** category link.
4. From the available list in next window click **Sound**.
5. On the opened box go to **Communications** tab and select **Do nothing** radio button.

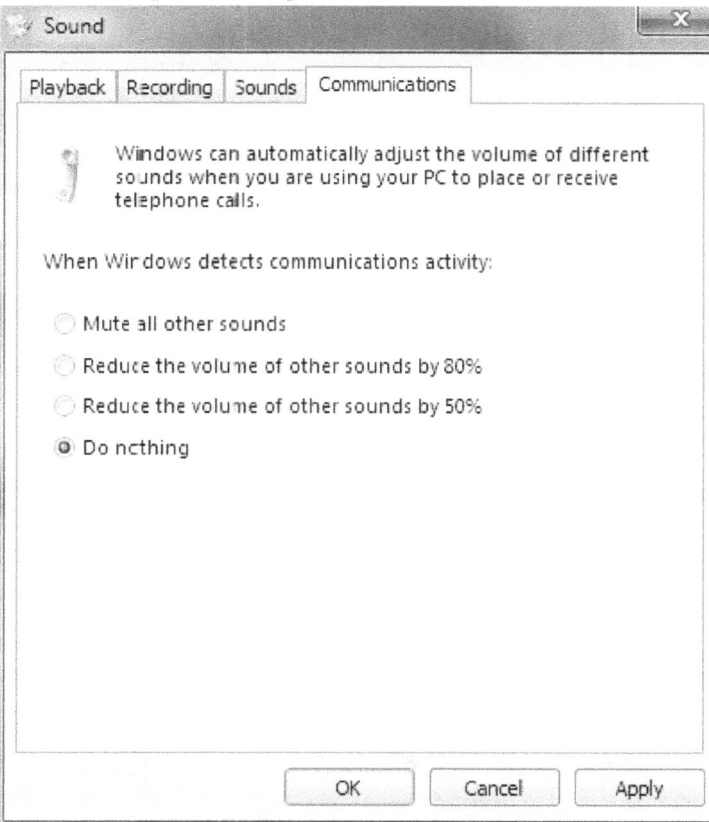

6. Finally click **Ok** button to save the changes you made.

Adjust Volume Mixer for Individual Applications

When it comes to volume settings, Windows 7 offers the most versatile and sophisticated feature with promising facilities. In legacy operating systems by Microsoft whenever any third party application that used audios was configured and volume was adjusted in it, the volume adjustment was reflected globally, that is, the main volume of the computer was adjusted. In Windows 7 users can adjust the volume levels of the computers according to the individual applications. This means that if a user is playing VLC player he can adjust the volume for it individually which will never reflect the global volume settings of the computer. As a Windows 7 user if you want to do so you are required to follow the steps given as below:

1. Log on to Windows 7 computer with any account as the configuration does not require any elevated privileges.
2. Open **VLC** player.
3. Click on speaker icon in system tray and click **Mixer** link.
4. On **Volume Mixer** box adjust the volume bar under VLC icon.
5. You can notice that only VLC volume bar is adjusted and the main volume of the computer is left intact.

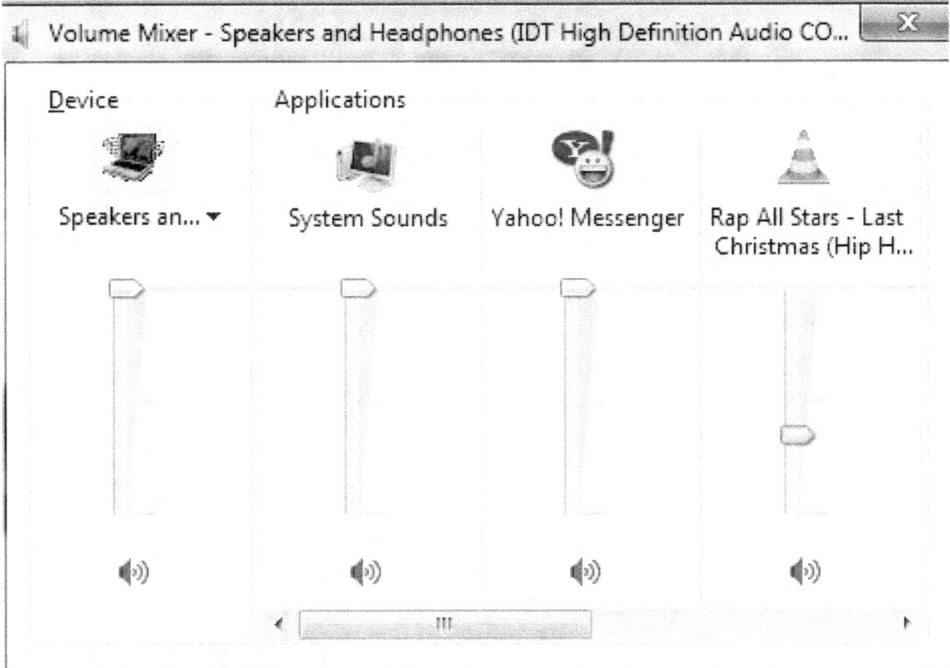

6. Once done, close **Volume Mixer** box.
7. The settings will remain persistent till you change them manually next time.

Disable Windows Defender

Whenever Windows 7 is installed on a bare metal machine, that is, a clean copy of Windows 7 is installed its built-in protection feature named Windows Defender is also automatically installed and initialized. This small program automatically detects any harmful application or malware that may enter into the system and cause harm. Windows Defender works in the background and detects for the harmful applications in real time. Although this application is an integrated program that ships along with Windows 7 its priority is not as high as compared to any full-fledged anti-virus application that users can purchase from the market. Since third-party antivirus applications are precisely developed to protect the computers from harmful and unwanted applications they are considered highly efficient in this regard. Most of these antivirus applications, when installed, automatically disable Windows Defender and if in case they fail to so users disable it manually by following the steps given below:

1. Log on to Windows 7 computer with the account that has elevated privileges.

2. At the bottom of start menu in search box type **SERVICES.MSC** and press enter key.

3. On the opened window double-click **Windows Defender**.

4. On **Windows Defender Properties (Local Computer)** box make sure that you are **General** tab.

5. From the drop-down list available next to **Startup type**, choose **Disabled** and click **Ok** button to save the changes.

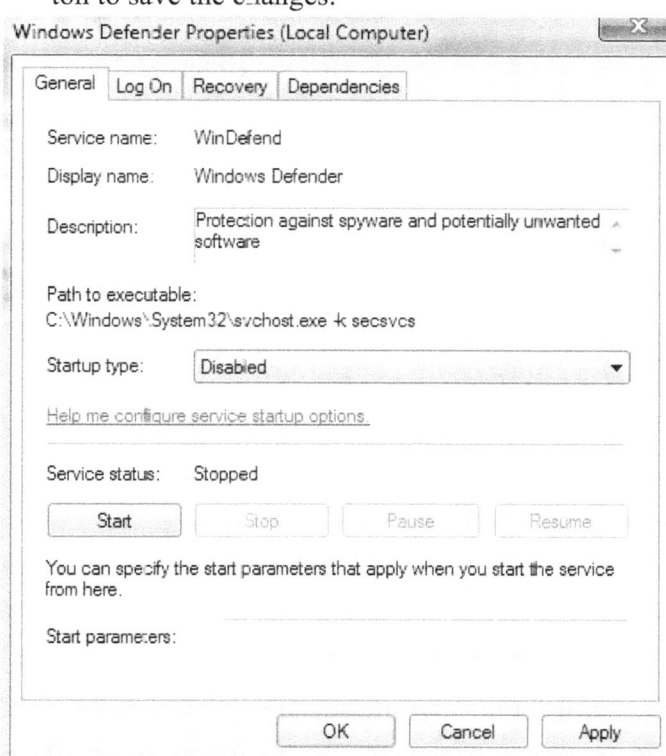

6. If required restart the computer.

Enable and Configure Windows Speech Recognition

Not many people know that Windows 7 can also listen to your voice and can act accordingly. This means that if you have Windows 7 configured properly you don't have to use your keyboard or mouse in order to make Windows do something for you. You can simply give the commands through your microphone and Windows can listen to those commands and can perform the tasks for you. This feature is known as a Windows Speech Recognition which is a built-in feature in Windows 7. To enable and configure this feature you need to follow the instructions given as below:

1. Click **Start** button.
2. From the start menu in the search box type **Windows Speech Recognition** and press the enter key.
3. On the **Welcome to Speech Recognition** page click **Next** button.
4. On **What type of microphone is Microphone?** page select appropriate microphone type and click **Next** button.
5. On the **Set up your microphone** page adjust your microphone as per the instructions and click **Next** button.
6. On the **Adjust the volume of microphone** page speak the text which is highlighted and click **Next** button.

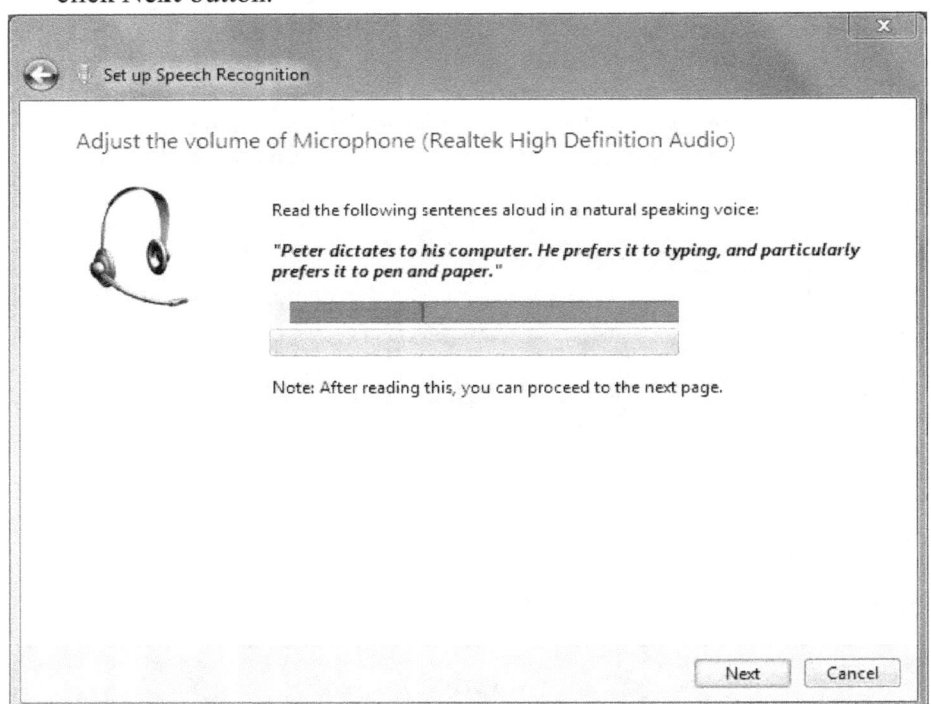

7. On **Your microphone is now set up** confirmation page click **Next** button.
8. On **Improve speech recognition accuracy** page select **Enable document review** radio button and click **Next** button.

9. On **Choose an activation mode** page select **Use voice activation mode** radio button and click **Next** button.

10. On **Print the speech reference card** page click **Next** button.

11. On the **Run Speech Recognition every time I start the computer** page uncheck the **Run Speech Recognition at startup** box if you don't want this feature to start every time your computer starts. Else leave the default setting intact and click **Next** button.

12. On **You can now control this computer by voice** page click **Start Tutorial** button if you want to train your computer to understand your accent. Otherwise you can click **Skip Tutorial** to bypass this part.

And now you have speech recognition feature up and running on your Windows 7 computer.

CHAPTER 4
POWER OPTIONS

Configure Power Button

Many people do not know that they can even configure their power buttons and can make Windows respond accordingly when it is pressed. When your computer is on and Windows is running you can configure your power button as to when it is pressed Windows should either Shut Down, Hibernate, Do Nothing or go to Sleep Mode.

This feature is helpful when a person is in a hurry and wants to shut down or hibernate his computer as soon as possible. Regular process of clicking Start button and then clicking Shut Down button may sometimes be quite irritating and tedious. In order to make power button do all for you, you need to follow the below instructions:

1. Click **Start** button.
2. From the menu go to **Control Panel**.
3. In the **Control Panel** click on **Hardware and Sound** link.
4. From the displayed list and under **Power Options** category click **Change What Power Buttons Do** link.

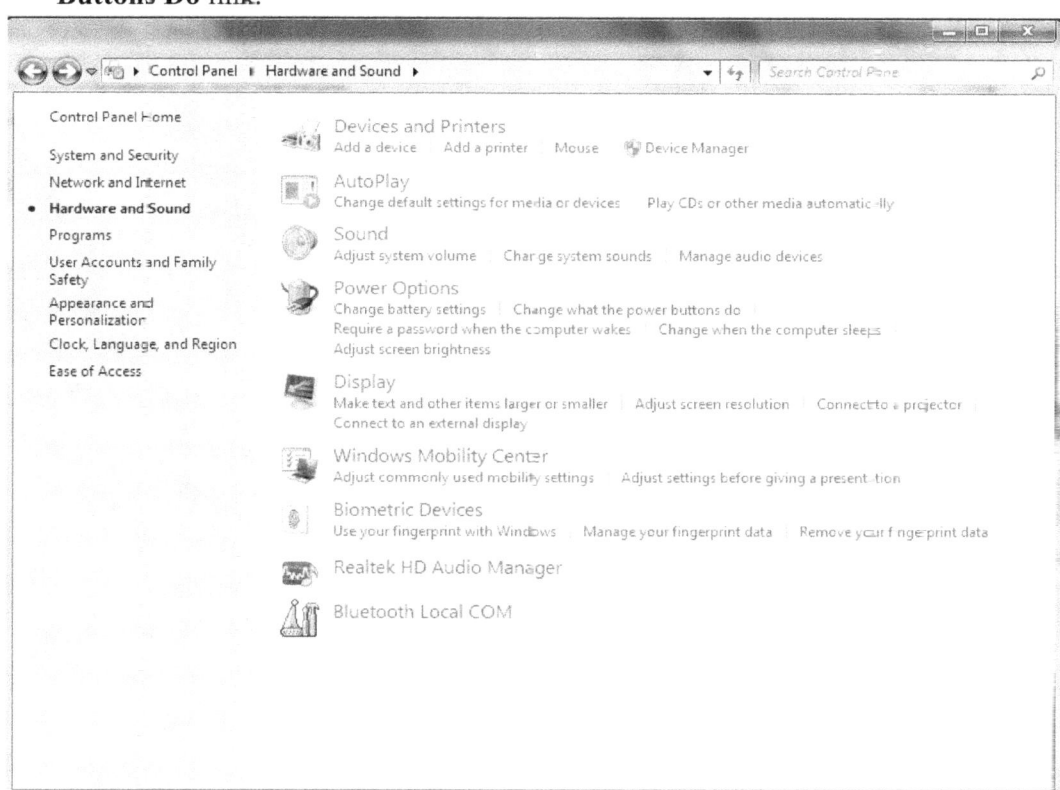

5. From the displayed page find the text which says **When I Press Power Button:** and click the drop-down box opposite to it.

6. Select the appropriate option as desired from the list. In most cases the list may have four options, which are **Do Nothing, Shutdown, Hibernate and Sleep**.

7. After selecting desired option click **Ok** on all the Windows to accept and confirm your selections.

8. Test your current configuration by pressing the power button of your computer.

Manage Power Plan (For Laptop Users)

Windows 7 offers a sophisticated power plan to meet every user's requirement. This feature can be exploited at its full when used on laptop computers. With the help of this feature users can configure their laptop PCs to provide optimum performance. This means that even when there is no power supply available, laptop PCs can be used to provide best possible display and reduced battery consumption at the same time. You can manage power plan computer by following the steps given below:

1. Log on to the Windows 7 computer on which you want to manage power plan. You can log on using any user account as this feature is user specific and is applicable to the user account using which it is configured.

2. Click **Start** button and from the menu click **Control Panel**.

3. On **Control Panel** window click **Hardware and Sound** category link and on the opened window click **Power Options** link.

4. On **Select power plan** page ensure that **Balanced (recommended)** radio button is selected (this is default) and click **Change plan settings** link to manage the plan.

5. On **Change settings for plan: Balanced** page choose appropriate settings and click **Save Changes** button to confirm your configuration. Optionally you can click **Change advanced power settings** link to get additional controls which you can use for more granule configuration.

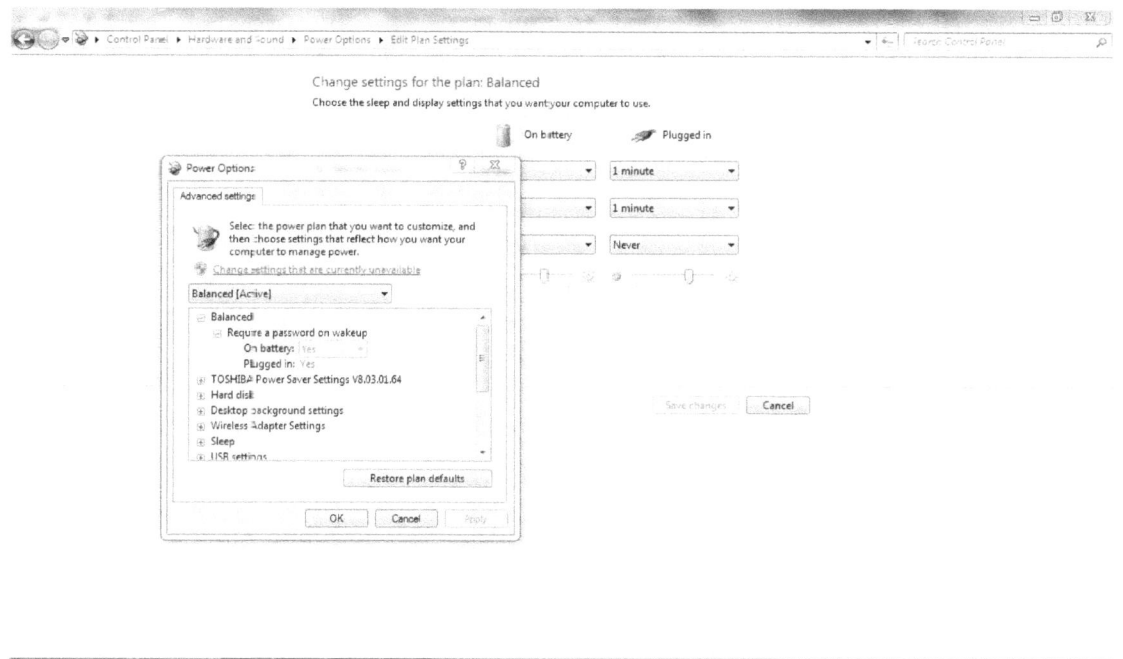

Prevent Windows 7 from Entering Sleep Mode

When Windows 7 operating system is installed on a computer all default settings are automatically applied on it. Along with other default settings one main setting is also applied which allows computers to enter into sleep mode if no user activity is detected by the Windows 7. This configuration is mostly useful for laptop PCs as it is expected that most of them are not directly connected to the power outlets most of the times. This configuration allows laptop PCs to save energy, hence extending the duration of batteries. However in desktop PCs this configuration is not required and therefore users may want to disable this in order to eliminate the requirement of providing passwords every time the computers wake up from sleep mode. As a Windows 7 user if you want to prevent computers from entering into sleep mode you are required to follow the steps given as below:

1. Log on to Windows 7 computer.
2. Click **Start** button and from the menu click **Control Panel**.
3. On the opened window click **Hardware and Sound** category link.
4. On the appeared window click **Power Options**.
5. On **Select a power plan** page click **Change plan settings** under the category of radio button representing the selected power plan.
6. On the next page from the drop-down list in front of **Put the computer on sleep** section choose **Never**.

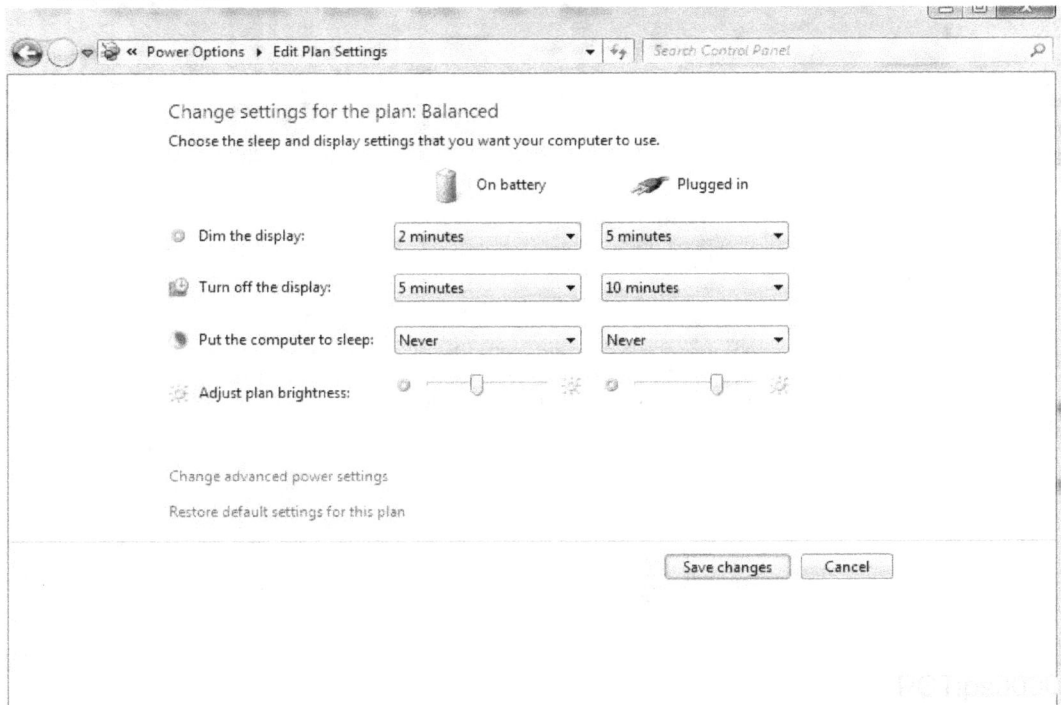

7. Finally click **Save changes** button to save the changes and allow them to take effect.

Prevent Asking for Password on Wake Up

With the release of Microsoft Windows 7, as everyone knows, security measures have been made more efficient in order to make the operating system almost foolproof as far as hacking or spamming is concerned. Same is the case with password protection while waking the computer up from sleep or standby mode. This is default configuration that prevents any malicious user to take a look at the sensitive information of any other user in his absence. This security features is best for production environments and should never be modified under any circumstances. However this feature can be extremely annoying for home users as many of them never like to type passwords because they find it a hurdle. When this is the case administrators of Windows 7 computers can configure their operating systems so they may not ask for passwords whenever systems wake up from standby or sleep modes. As a Windows 7 administrator if you want to configure this you are required to follow the steps given below:

1. Log on to Windows 7 computer with administrator account.

2. At the bottom of start menu in search box type **Power Options** and press enter key.

3. On the opened page in the left bar click **Require a password on wakeup** link.

4. On the new page click **Change settings that are currently unavailable** link.

5. From the enabled options click **Don't require a password** radio button to select.

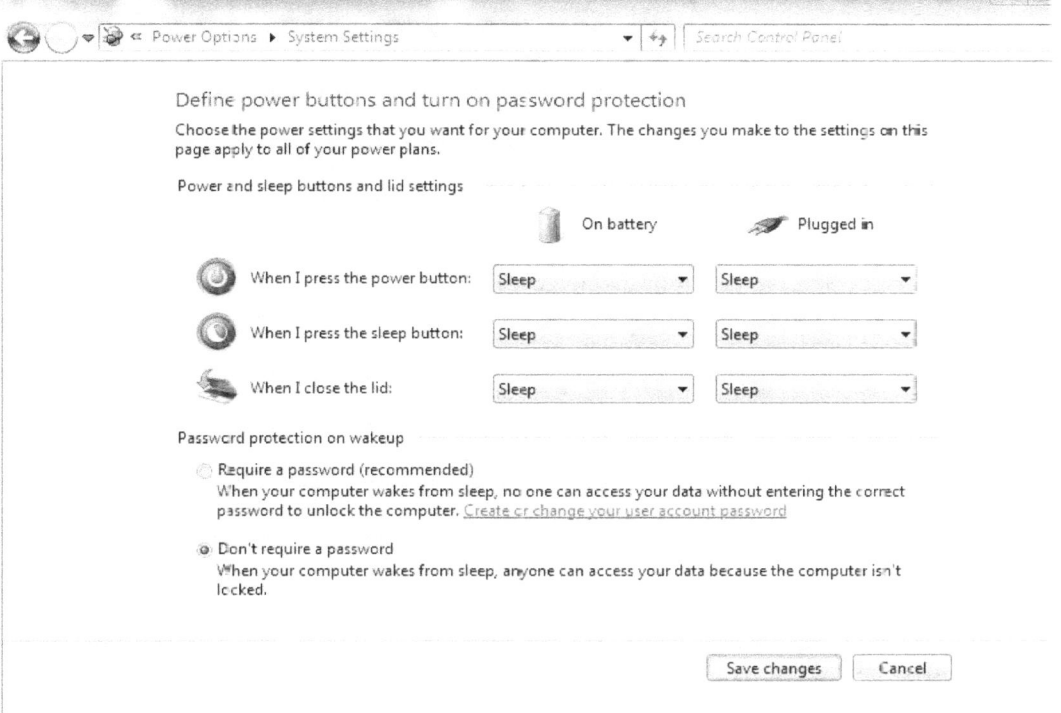

6. Click **Save changes** button to save the changes.

CHAPTER 5
MANAGE ACCOUNTS

Add or Delete User Accounts Using Batch Files

Batch files are considered as one of the best tools to automate processes. They enable administrators to get rid of tedious repeated clicks on same interface several times in a day. For example, if an administrator wants to create 50 user accounts on a computer he has to go to Control Panel and has to go through the user creation wizard for 50 times. This practice might be quite time consuming and boring. However, with help of batch file he can type few commands to create user accounts and can run the file. This would create 50 user accounts within few minutes. Also, if required this batch file can be used to create 50 more users within a fraction of seconds. You can create a batch file to automate the process of user account creation by following the instructions given below:

1. Click **Start** button.

2. At the bottom of start menu in search box type **Notepad** and press enter key.

3. In the notepad type command **NET USER USER1 123 /ADD**, where USER1 is the user name that you want to create and 123 is the password for the user account. If you want to create 50 users at a time you can simply copy the entire command and can paste it 50 times on the same notepad and change the user names as per your requirements like, USER1, USER2, USER3,.. and so on.

4. Once you are done with commands you can save the notepad file with .BAT extension. For example CREATEUSER.BAT. Make sure you specify the file name and extension between " ".

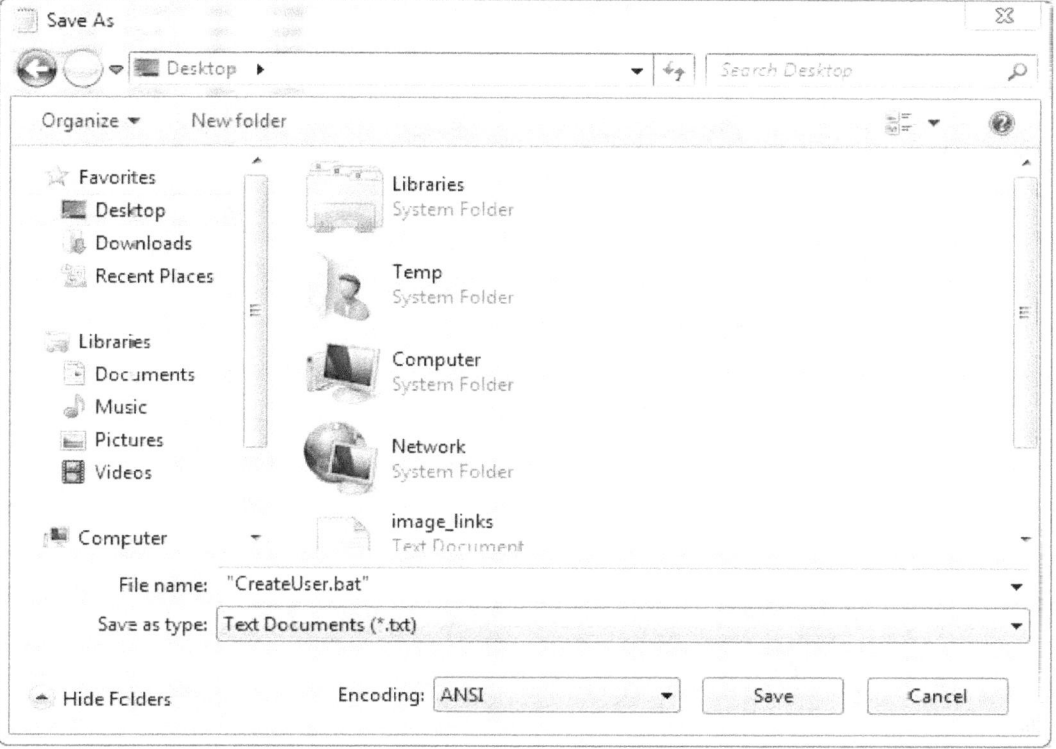

5. To create these 50 users in a single go you just need to right-click on the batch file that you have created and select **Run as Administrator** option. A command window will be popped up for a few seconds and you are done.

6. You can check the created user accounts by going to Control Panel.

7. If you want to delete user accounts you can use the same method but use "/del" instead of "/add" and do not provide password. For example, if you want to delete User1 you can type **NET USER USER1 /DEL**.

Disable a User Account

During exam times, many parents may not want their kids to use computers. However when exams are over they might want to remove this restriction. Moreover, in production environments administrators may sometimes want a user account to become inaccessible even by the owner of that account. In either case administrators can use windows built-in feature of disabling user accounts for indefinite period of time. In order to disable a user account you need to follow the steps given below:

1. Log on to the Windows 7 computer with an administrator's account.
2. Click **Start** button.
3. From the start menu right click **Computer** and from the menu click **Manage**.
4. On **Computer Management** snap-in expand **Local Users and Groups** tree.
5. Click **Users** and from the right pane right click on the name of the user for which you want to enable the restriction.
6. From the opened menu click **Properties**.
7. On **Properties** box make sure that you are on **General** tab and check **Account is disabled** checkbox.

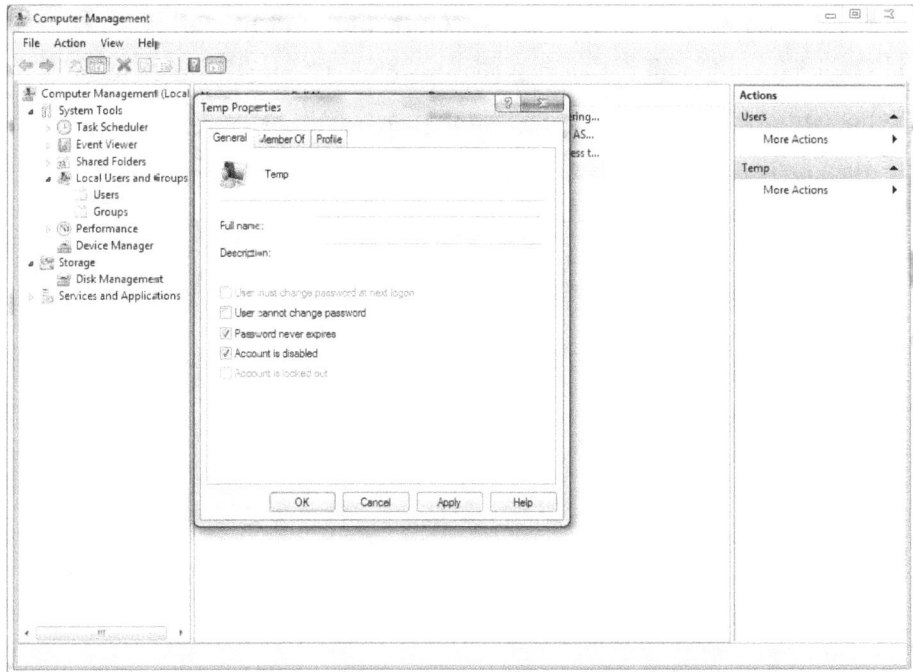

8. Click **Ok** button to accept and confirm your configuration and close **Computer Management** snap-in.

More Info:

If you want to re-enable a disabled user account you can follow all the above steps while unchecking **Account is disabled** checkbox in step 7.

Change Passwords

As everyone knows that no matter what operating system is used passwords play an important role to maintain the security of the information and integrity of the data. When Windows 7 was introduced in the market it was designed to be used by both professionals and home users. When this operating system is used in home environments passwords are not mandatory and users can also live without them. But when it comes to production environments where security of information is a major concern, strong passwords are always recommended. Moreover, Microsoft also recommends that the passwords should also be complex so that they are not easily breakable. It is also recommended that users should frequently change their passwords in order to make their accounts and information stored in them highly secured. In production environments, although almost every user is supposed to log on to the domain account but still if in any case users are logged on locally they can change their passwords on their own by following the steps given:

1. Log on to Windows 7 computer with the user account for which you want to change the password.
2. Click **Start** button and from the menu click **Control Panel**.
3. On the opened window click **User Accounts and Family Safety** category link.
4. On the next window under **User Accounts** click **Change your Windows password** link.
5. On the new window click **Change your password** link.
6. On the opened page populate the fields with appropriate information and click **Change password** button to change the password.

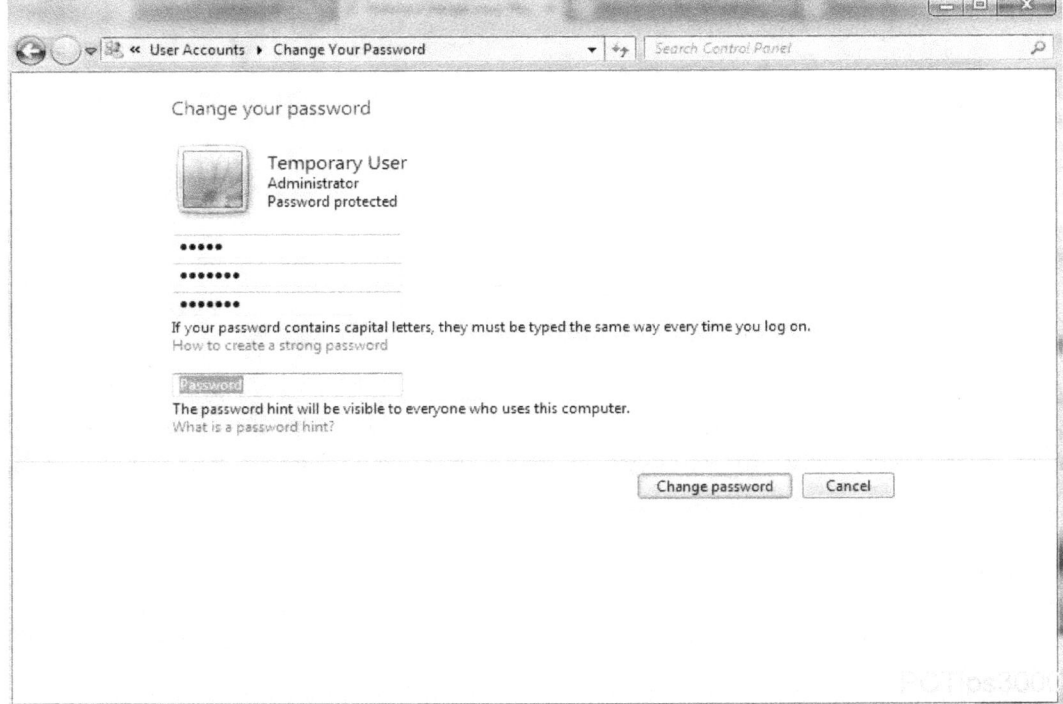

Restrict Users from Changing Passwords

In production environments, for security reasons administrators would want to restrict users from changing their account passwords on their own. No matter what client operating system an organization may use or what type of infrastructure is it working on users should always be restricted from changing their passwords at their will. As an administrator you can configure this setting by following the steps given below:

1. Log on to the Windows 7 computer with an administrator's account.
2. Click **Start** button.
3. From the start menu right click **Computer** and from the menu click **Manage**.
4. On **Computer Management** snap-in expand **Local Users and Groups** tree.
5. Click on **Users** and from the right pane right click on the name of the user for which you want to enable the restriction.
6. From the opened menu click **Properties**.
7. On **Properties** box make sure that you are on **General** tab and check **User cannot change password** checkbox.

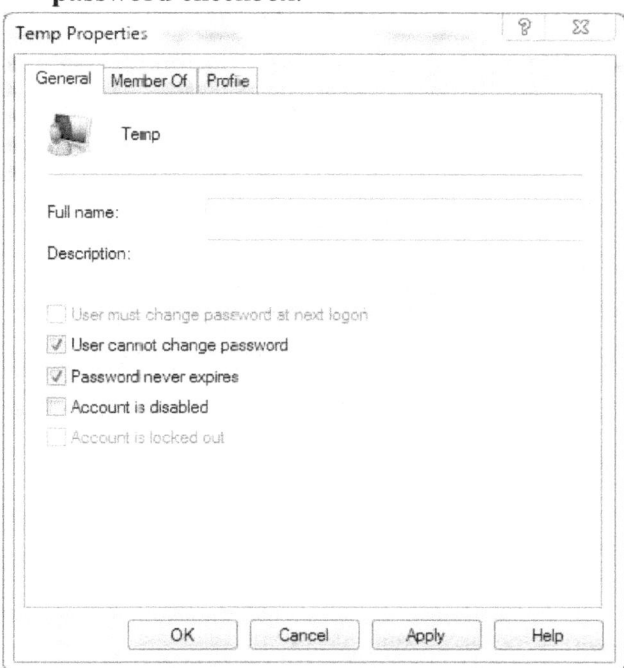

8. Click **Ok** button to accept and confirm your configuration and close **Computer Management** snap-in.

More Info:

If you want to remove this restriction, you need to reverse the above-mentioned process. (Uncheck User cannot change password checkbox).

Create a Password Reset Disk

There are times when you might forget your password if you have not used your computer for a long duration. In this case you can either reset your password using administrator account and/or if your administrator account is blocked too, you need to either format your computer or you need to hack into it in order to get your data back. Resetting your password forcefully using Administrative powers might sometimes block your data forever. This mostly happens when you have enabled drive or folder level encryption.

The best solution for this kind of situation might be a pro-active approach of creating Password Reset Disk. With the help of reset disks you can reset your passwords if you forget them. This disk will straightforwardly provide you with the interface where you can type a new password for your user account.

Process of creating Password Reset Disk is given below:

1. Insert a blank USB pen drive in USB port of your computer. Make sure the device does not contain any important data files in it.
2. Click **Start** button and from the menu select **Control Panel**.
3. In the **Control Panel** window click on **User Accounts and Family Safety** link.
4. In the next window click **User Accounts** link.
5. In the next Window in the left pane click **Create Password Reset Disk** link.
6. In the **Forgotten Password Wizard** welcome page click **Next** button.
7. On **Create a Password Reset Disk** page ensure that **Removable Disk** is selected.
8. Click **Next** button to proceed.On the **Current User Account Password** page type the current password that you use to log in to the computer and press **Next** button.
9. On the next page when you see **Process 100% Complete** click **Next** button.
10. On **Completing the Forgotten Password Wizard** page click **Finish** button to complete the process.

You can check password reset disk by logging off from the currently logged on user and providing wrong password while re-logging. This will give you an error message and will ask if you want to use previously created password reset disk to reset the current password.

Specify the Time at Which a User Can Log On

With Windows 7 you can restrict the time at which a particular user can log onto the computer. This means that if the user is configured to log on to the system only between 7 PM to 9 PM every day he cannot log onto the computer at 5 PM or 8 PM or any other time except the specified one.

To enable this feature below are the steps:

1. Click **Start** button and go to **Control Panel**.

2. From the **User Accounts and Family Safety** category click **Set up Parental Controls for Any User** link.

3. On **Choose a user and set up Parental Controls** page click on the user for which you want to specify time restriction.

4. On **Set up how xxx will use the computer** page under **Parental Controls** section select **On, Enforce Current Settings** radio button.

5. Opposite to **Time Limits** text click **Off** link.

6. On **Control when xxx will use the computer** page drag your mouse to select the denied time. Denied time will be displayed in Blue color. By-default all users are allowed to log on to Windows 7 computers for 24 hours and the allowed hours are represented with White color.

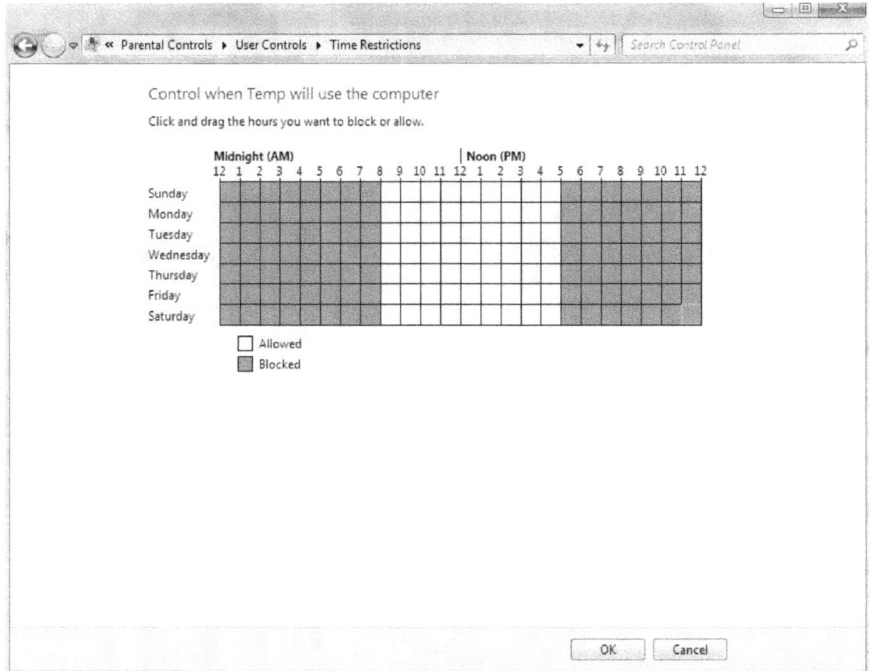

7. Click **Ok** button on each page to accept and confirm your selections.

8. Test the settings by logging on to the computer with the credentials of user account you have just configured.

Disconnect Other Logged On Users

Because of fast user switching feature in Windows 7, administrators can allow other users to log on to the computer without logging off their own accounts. This means that other users can log on to the computer with their accounts without logging off any other already logged on account. This feature enables users to allow other users to use the computer without terminating their own sessions and losing their data. This further allows them to save a lot of time. However in some cases administrators may want to forcefully terminate the session of any logged on user because of various security reasons. As an administrator you can do so by following the steps given below:

1. Log on to the computer with administrator account.
2. Right click on the taskbar and from the appeared menu click **Start Task Manager**.
3. On **Windows Task Manager** box go to **Processes** tab and click **Show processes from all users** button. (This will open elevated Task Manager box).
4. Go to **Users** tab.
5. You will be displayed with the list of user accounts are still logged on but are not currently active. Right click on the user account you want to disconnect and from the appeared menu click **Log off**.

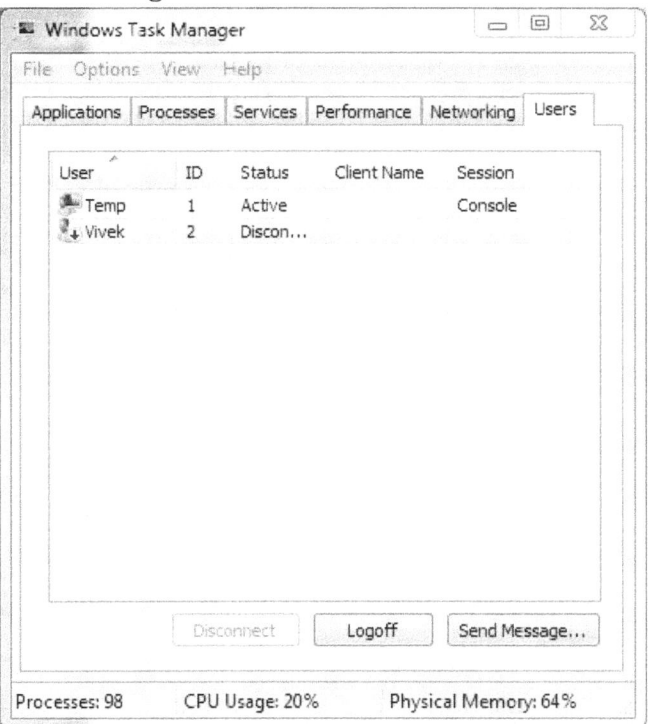

Note: Make sure that you always use elevated task manager box while performing above mentioned task. If not, you will always get Access is denied message while doing so.

Migrate User Accounts

There might be times when you need to transfer your account from one Windows 7 machine to another. The reason behind this might be that you are upgrading your computer and discarding the old one or you just want to install a fresh copy of Microsoft Windows 7 operating system on an existing computer and to secure your account settings you want to remove them temporarily. This task can easily be done using Windows Easy Transfer feature available. To use this feature you need to follow the below steps:

1. Click **Start** button.

2. Go to **All Programs**.

3. From the menu click **Accessories**.

4. Click **System Tools** and select **Windows Easy Transfer**.

5. On **Welcome to Windows Easy Transfer** page click **Next** button.

6. On **What do you want to use to transfer item to your new computer?** page select **An external hard disk or USB flash drive.**

7. On **Which computer you are using now?** page select **This is my old computer.**

8. Wait while Windows 7 verifies the items that can be transferred.

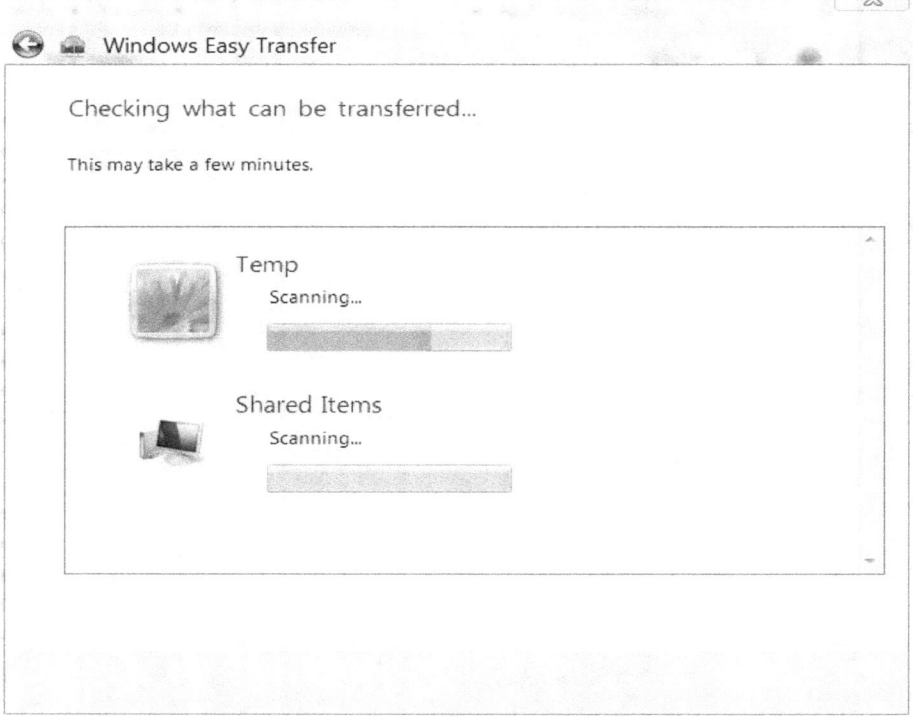

9. On **Choose what to transfer from this computer** page check the boxes of all the accounts/ items you want to transfer and click **Next** button.

10. On the next page if you want you can specify a password to protect the settings, else you may leave it blank and click **Save** button.

11. Specify the location where the file can be saved and click **Save.**

To restore backed up accounts follow the steps 1 to 6 from above instructions and continue with the below instructions:

1. On **Which computer you are using now?** page select **This is my new computer.**
2. On the next window click **Yes** option.
3. From the opened box locate the backed up file by browsing to its location and click **Open** button to restore your accounts.

CHAPTER 6
MANAGING HARDWARE DEVICES

How to Find Drivers for Hardware

Although every computer system that is purchased from the market has its own driver installation disc which contains all drivers to the hardware devices installed on the computer. In cases of laptop PCs restoration discs are provided and if they are not available, facility of creating restoration discs is provided along with the operating systems installed on the laptops. Above mentioned lines are best suited when the scenario is ideal and no mishandling is done with the CDs/DVDs or laptop PCs. But as everybody knows an ideal scenario is very uncommon and is rarely seen in real-world many times users misplace the driver installation discs and in cases of laptops they never care to create restoration discs at all. In such situations it becomes very hard for the engineers or the administrators to find out which device drivers should be installed in order to make the devices on the computers run successfully. Fortunately Microsoft provides the facility to find IDs of 'not-installed' devices and administrators can search out for appropriate drivers according to the IDs easily. As a Windows 7 user if you want to verify hardware IDs to find appropriate drivers you are required to follow the steps given as below:

1. Log on to Windows 7 computer with any account.

2. At the bottom of start menu in search box type **MSINFO32** command and press enter key.

3. On **System Information** page expand **Components** tree from the left pane and from the available list click **Problem Devices**.

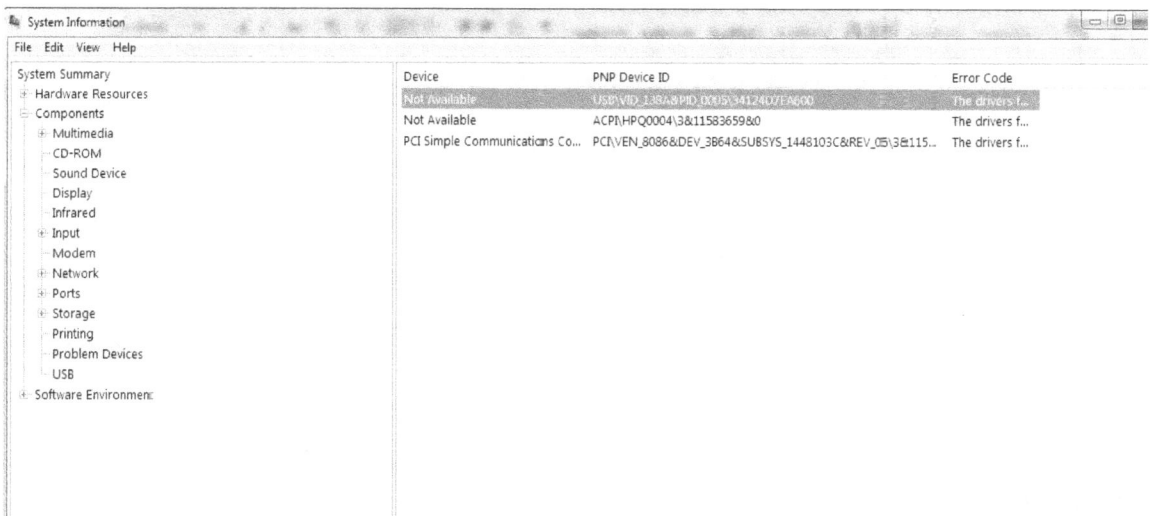

4. In the right pane you will be displayed with the name of the devices and their device IDs which are not installed and administrators can note them and then can search through the Internet for the appropriate drivers associated with those devices.

Scan for Newly Attached Hardware

Windows 7 is although quite sensitive when it comes to detection of new hardware devices. As soon as a user connects a new hardware device to a Windows 7 computer, the operating system automatically detects it and searches for its appropriate drivers within its own driver database. Once it finds a suitable driver for the newly attached device, it automatically installs the driver. However there are times when Windows 7 fails to detect any hardware device attached to the computer. When this is the case administrators can make Windows 7 computer search for the drive manually. As an administrator you can do so by following the steps given below:

1. Log on to the computer with administrator account and click **Start** button.

2. From the start menu right click **Computer** and from the appeared menu click **Manage**.

3. On **Computer Management** snap-in in the left pane click **Device Manager** and from the right pane right click on the name of your computer (which will be at the top of the list).

4. From the menu click **Scan for hardware changes** and follow the instructions on your computer screen.

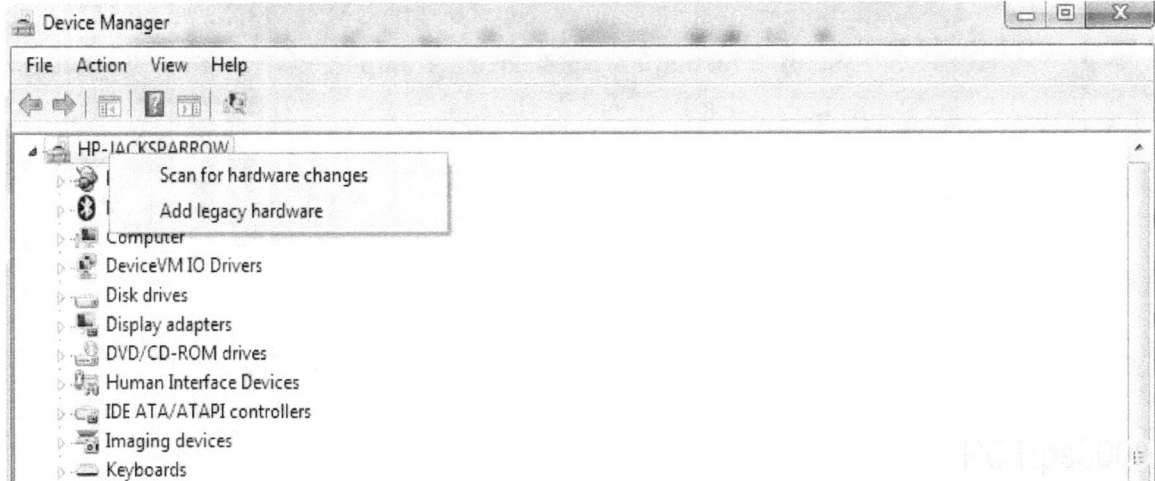

Note: This hardware detection process will only install the drivers that are available in Windows 7 driver database. In case any device driver is not available in the database you need to insert the driver installation disk to complete the device installation process.

Update Device Drivers

Although every device ships along with its driver installation disk that contains latest version of driver which is required by the device to function efficiently. As the time passes by, new drivers are introduced in the market. In these cases it becomes essential for administrators to update device drivers to make devices compatible with the latest versions of operating systems for smooth functionality of the devices. There are many other tools available in the market that can be used to automate driver updating process, but they are only feasible when purchased for production environments. Home users can follow the steps given below to update the drivers manually:

1. Log on to the computer with administrator account.

2. Click **Start** button and from the menu right click **Computer**.

3. From the appeared menu click **Manage**.

4. On **Computer Management** snap-in in the left pane click **Device Manager** and from the right pane expand the category of the device you want to update.

5. From the expanded list of devices right click on the device and from the menu click **Update Driver Software**.

6. On the opened window click **Search automatically for updated drivers software** option and follow the instructions displayed on the screen. (In case you have already downloaded the latest driver on the local hard disk you can choose **Browse my computer for driver software** option).

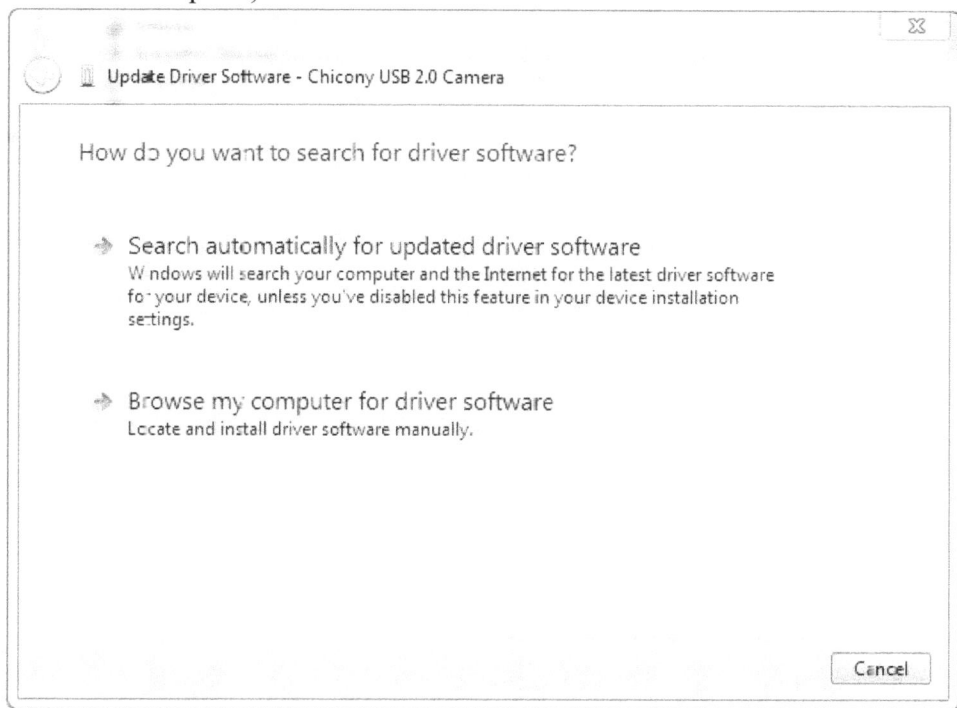

7. Once completed, restart your computer so that the changes may take effect.

Verify Devices and Drivers

There might be times when as a user or administrators of Windows 7 you might need to know about the device drivers that are installed on the computer. The reason behind gathering this information might be that you may want to verify as which devices are available on the computer and how many of them are there without appropriate drivers. If you look around over the Internet there might be several methods to verify the devices and device drivers of computer systems but this section will allow you to verify them through easiest possible steps. Steps involved in this process requires elevated privileges and if you have those privileges available with your account you can follow the steps given below to verify the devices and the installed drivers:

1. Log on to Windows 7 computer with the account that has administrative privileges.

2. Click **Start** button and from the available menu right click **Computer**.

3. From the appeared context menu click **Manage** option.

4. On **Computer Management** snap-in click **Device Manager** from the left pane.

5. You will be displayed with the list of devices specifying the names of their own vendors in the right pane.

6. Sometimes you might also be displayed with some devices with a yellow question mark (**?**) sign next to them which means that the drivers for the devices are not installed.

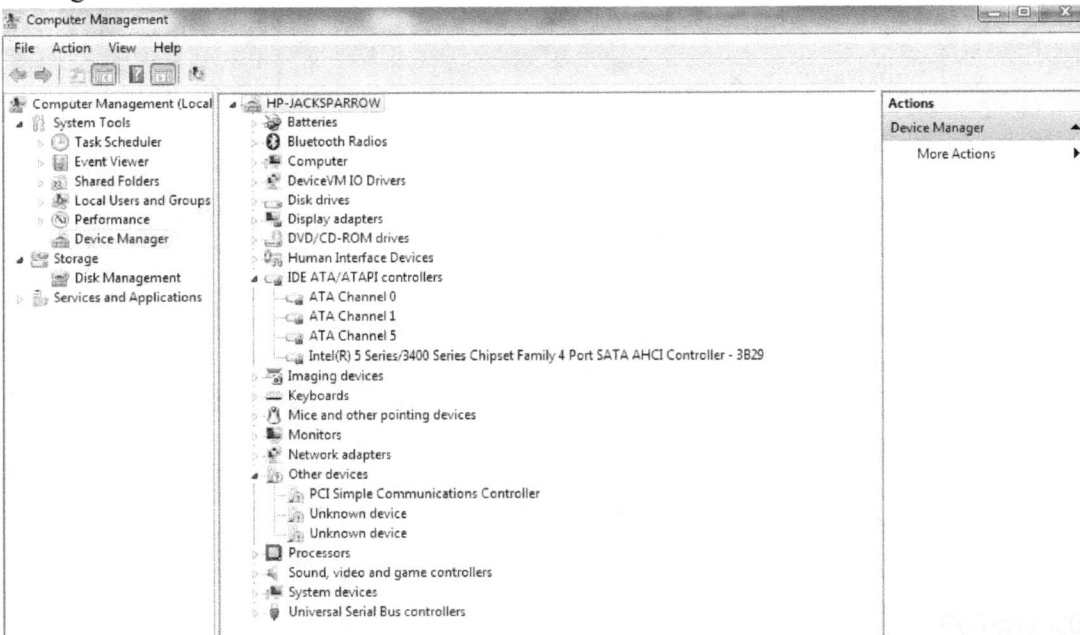

7. You can explore the drivers and devices by right-clicking on them and clicking **Properties** option available in the context menu.

8. Once verified, you can close **Computer Management** snap-in.

Check Which Graphics Card is Installed

For many home users graphics card in desktop computer systems or laptop PCs plays an important role when it comes to high definition movies, advanced games or resource intensive animation applications. This is also a fact that a person who is not technically sound and aware about the hardware of computers is not capable of determining as which graphics card is by default installed on the computer or what graphics card should he/she go for if he/she wishes to buy an additional one. In either case, users need to know how to check the graphics card which is installed on their desktop computer systems or laptop PCs so that they can accordingly judge as what steps should be taken to solve their purpose As a Windows 7 user if you want to determine the vendor and other specifications of the graphics card installed on desktop computer or a laptop PC you are required to follow the steps given as below:

1. Log on to Windows 7 computer.
2. Right click anywhere on the desktop and from the context menu click **Screen resolution**.
3. On the opened window click **Advanced settings** link.
4. On the appeared box make sure that you are **Adapter** tab and under **Adapter Type** section view the name of the vendor of adapter.

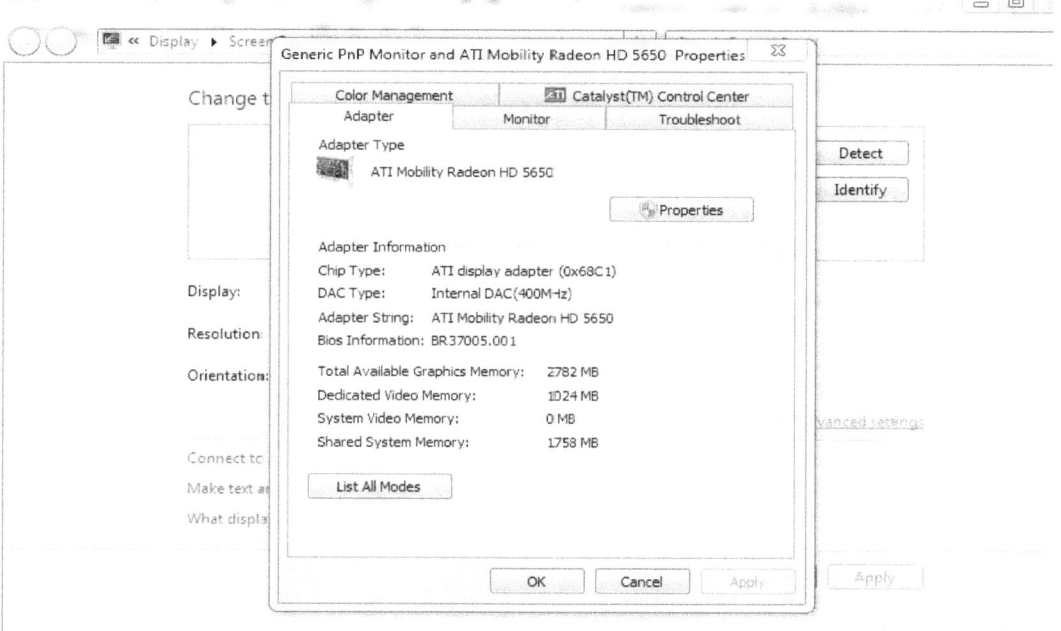

5. Under **Adapter Information** section, go through other specifications of the adapter.
6. Once done, close all the opened boxes and Windows.

Uninstall Hardware Device Driver

In any Microsoft operating system uninstalling any software application is quite simple and users are required to go to Control Panel in order to do so. Moreover, many applications create their own shortcut folders in the start menu and these folders also have Uninstall applications using which users can uninstall those applications from there itself. Problem arises when users want to uninstall any hardware device driver because its uninstallation link is not available under Programs and Features. In such situations they are required to go to Device Manager snap-in and from there they are required to uninstall the desired hardware device. As a Windows 7 administrator if you want to uninstall hardware device driver you are required to follow the steps given as below:

1. Since the process requires elevated privileges, log on to Windows 7 computer with any account that has administrative powers.

2. From the start menu right click **Computer** and from the available context menu click to **Manage**.

3. On **Computer Management** snap-in from the left bar click **Device Manager**.

4. From the right pane right click on the desired hardware device and from the available menu click **Uninstall**.

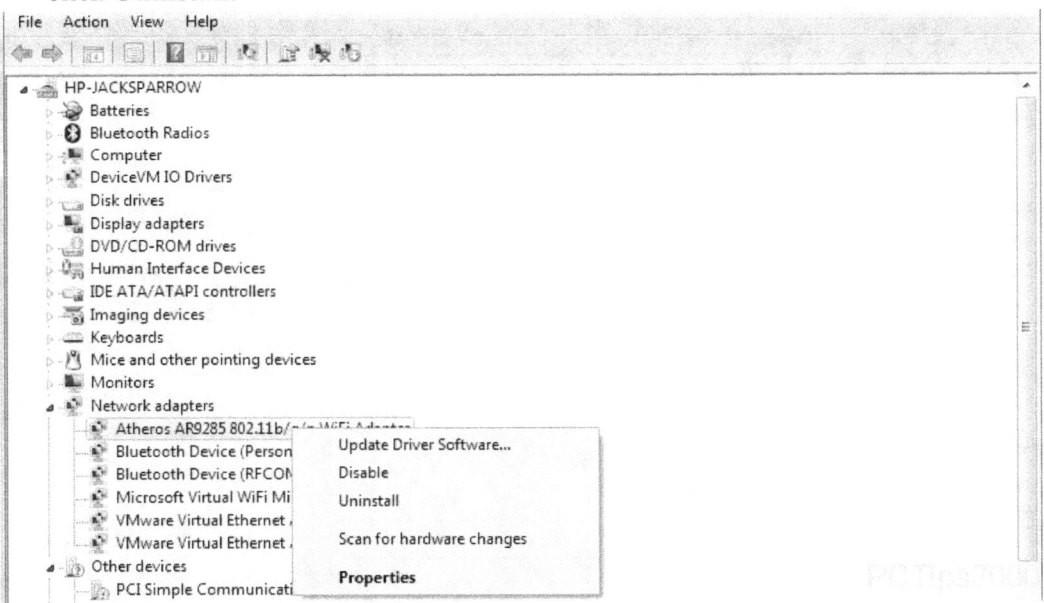

5. Follow the on-screen instructions to complete the uninstallation process.

Disable Hardware Devices

There might be times when you want to disable any hardware device in your computer in order to protect it from misuse. Disabling some hardware devices, like CD/DVD ROM drives or USB ports, on your system also prevents it from getting infected from viruses. If you want to enable or disable any hardware device attached to your computer system you need to follow the steps given below:

1. Log on to the system with administrator account.
2. Click **Start** button.
3. From the start menu right click **Computer** and from the menu click **Manage** button.
4. From the **Computer Management** snap-in from the left pane click **Device Manager**.
5. From the right pane expand the category of the device you want to disable and right-click on the device (DVD/CD-ROM Drives in this example).
6. From the menu click **Disable** to disable the device.

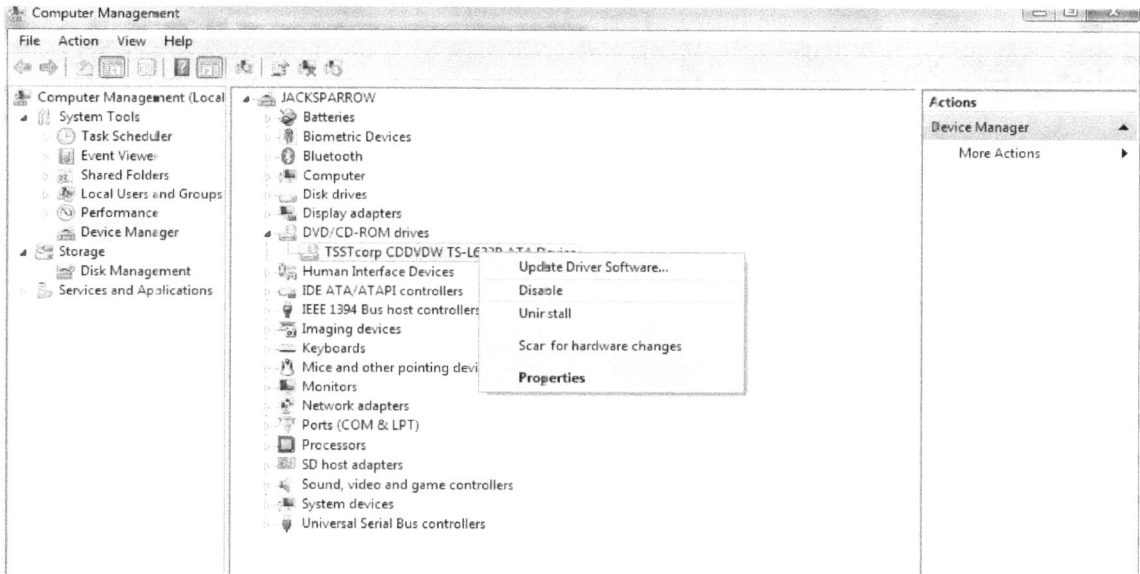

7. Close **Computer Management** snap-in

More Info:

You can reverse the above process to enable the disabled device on your computer.

Best Practices:

In production environments it is always advisable that the above configurations should be managed using Group Policies. If this configuration is required to be done on home computers, users can create batch files to automate the tasks as well.

CHAPTER 7
PRINTERS

Install Virtual Printer

In many cases text editors require printers to be installed on the computer systems so that they can provide appropriate print preview to the users. Moreover many text editors also provide several page sizes only when printers are installed on the computers. In legacy versions of Microsoft operating systems installing virtual printers was an easy task and even home users were able to do so within no time. In Microsoft Windows 7 things are a bit complicated and users need to go through few extra steps in order to install virtual printers so that they can get the same ambience while working with text editors. Virtual printers are usually installed when no physical printers are available and users still need to customize the settings of the text editors. As a Windows 7 administrator if you want to install virtual printer you are required to follow the steps given as below:

1. Log on to Windows 7 computer with administrator account.
2. From start menu right click **Computer** and from the context menu click **Manage**.
3. On **Computer Management** snap-in from the left pane click **Device Manager**.
4. From the right pane right click on the name of the computer that is displayed at the top of the list and from the available menu click **Add legacy hardware**.
5. On the appeared screen click **Next** button and on the next window choose **Install the hardware that I manually select from a list (Advanced)** radio button and click **Next** button.
6. From the available list of hardware devices on the next window click **Printers** and click **Next** button.
7. On **Choose a printer port** page click **Next** button and on **Install the printer driver** window choose the appropriate vendor of the printer from the left pane and from the right pane choose the desired model of the printer.

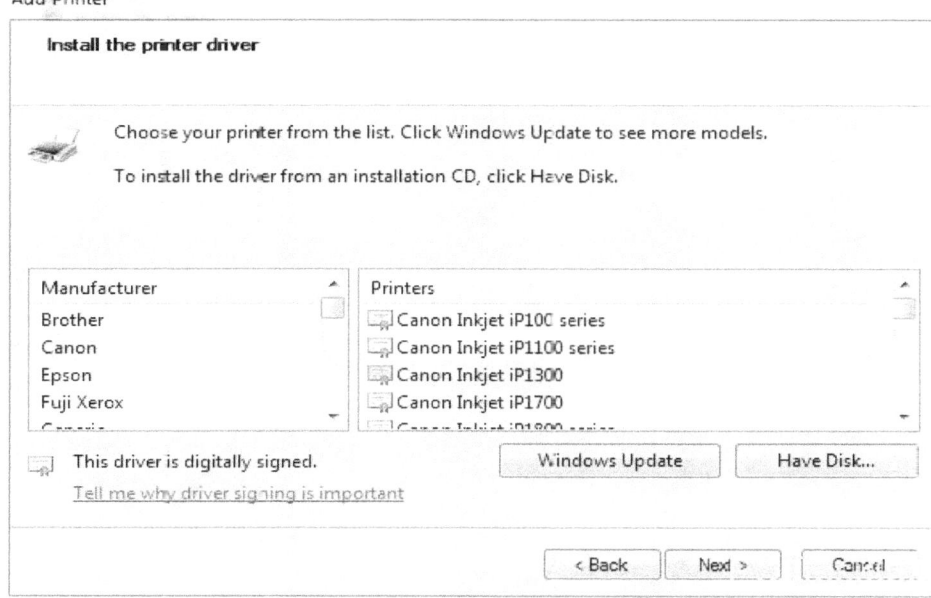

8. Click **Next** button and on the next page click **Next** button as well to start the installation process.

9. On **Printer Sharing** page choose the appropriate radio button as required and click **Next** button.

10. On final page click **Finish** button to complete the installation process.

Manage Printer Availability

When a printer is installed by default it is available for all users for 24 hours a day. This means that users can use the printer any time they want as far as the printer is powered on and attached to the computer or network. For home environments this configuration might be quite ideal however in complex network scenarios or in production environments administrators may want to restrict users from using a shared printer during odd hours. Administrators can do so by making the printers available at specific time after which the printer will become unavailable for the users. This configuration can be done by following the steps given below:

1. Log on to the computer with administrator account.
2. Click **Start** button.
3. From the start menu go to **Devices and Printers**.
4. From the opened window right click on the icon of the printer for which you want to specify time availability and from the menu click **Printer Properties**.
5. On the **Properties** page go to **Advanced** tab and select **Available from** radio button.
6. In the two text boxes specify the time duration between which you want to make this printer available and click **Ok** button to confirm you selection. Users will only be able to use this printer during specified hours.

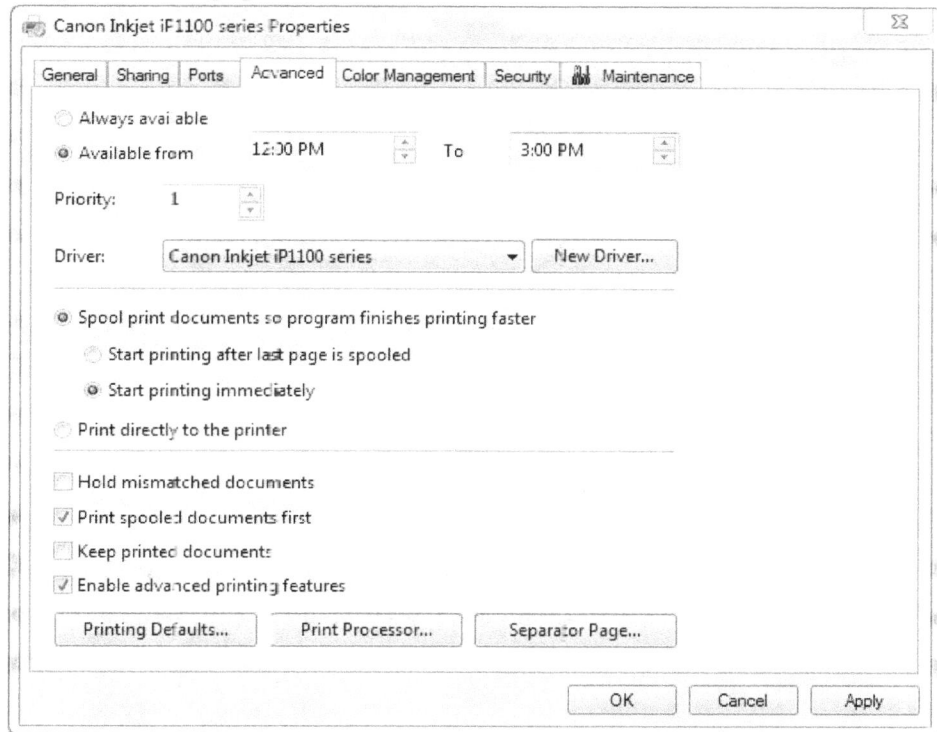

7. Close the opened window.

Share a Locally Installed Printer

Printers are essential almost everywhere. Whether you are at home or in office, without a printer your computer system is always incomplete. Where there are multiple computers in a premises, office or home, it is feasible to have one printer and share it among all. This makes the setup cost effective and comfortable to use. You can share a local printer which is physically attached to your computer by following the steps given below:

1. Log on to the computer with administrator account.

2. Click **Start** button.

3. From the start menu go to **Devices and Printers**.

4. From the opened window right click on the icon of the printer that you want to share and from the menu click **Printer Properties**.

5. On the **Properties** page go to **Sharing** tab and check **Share this printer** checkbox.

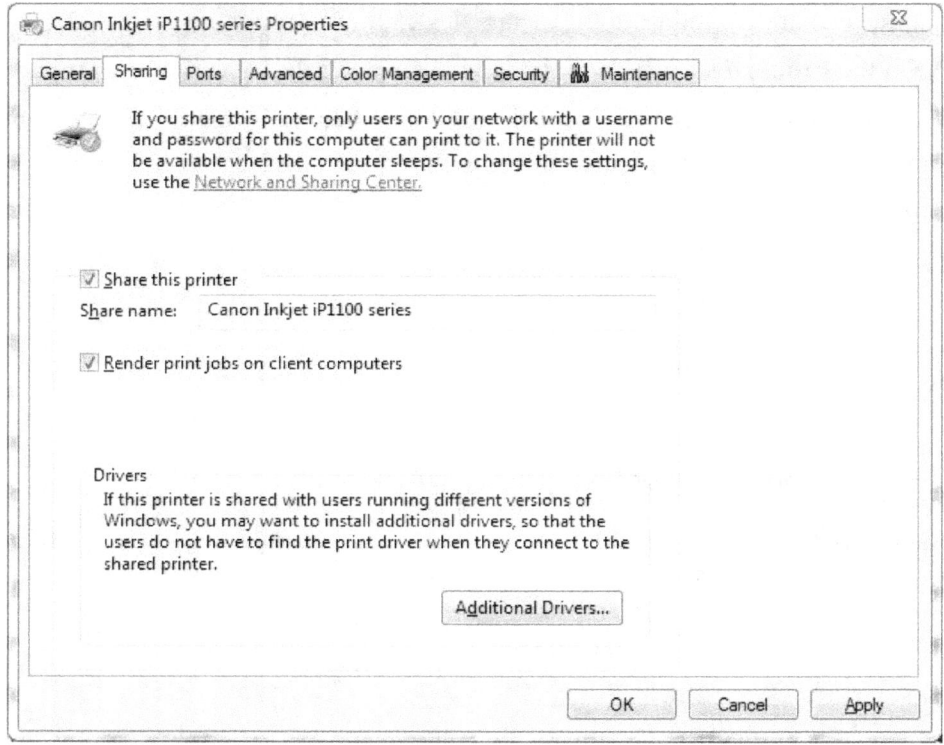

If required change the share name of printer to make it easier for users to locate and click Ok button to accept and confirm your settings and close the window. If your network setup has multi-platform environment or contains different flavors of windows you can click Additional Drivers button and from the opened box check the boxes representing the flavors to make the printer accessible by those operating systems as well.

Manage Printer Security Using NTFS Permissions

When a printer is shared on the network it becomes vulnerable to the risks. Risks for the printers might not include theft or hacking but misuse. This means that if printing permissions are granted to everyone, anyone can misuse the printer by sending personal or unofficial print commands to it. Even in home environments where there are one or two users who share a common printer which is physically attached to a local computer, security of the printer is still required in order to reduce the chances of misuse. As an administrator you can secure your printer by assigning NTFS permissions and by specifying which user gets what permissions on the printer. To do so you need to follow the steps given below:

1. Log on to the computer with administrator account.

2. Click **Start** button.

3. From the start menu go to **Devices and Printers**.

4. From the opened window right click on the icon of the printer on which you want to enable security and from the menu click **Printer Properties**.

5. On the **Properties** page go to Security tab.

6. Click **Everyone** group under **Group or user names** list and click **Remove** button to remove permissions **Everyone** group.

7. You can then add the desired groups or users by clicking **Add** button and from the opened search box typing the name of the group or user.

8. Once the user or group is added to the list you can specify its NTFS permissions from the **Permissions** list and click **Ok** button to accept your configuration.

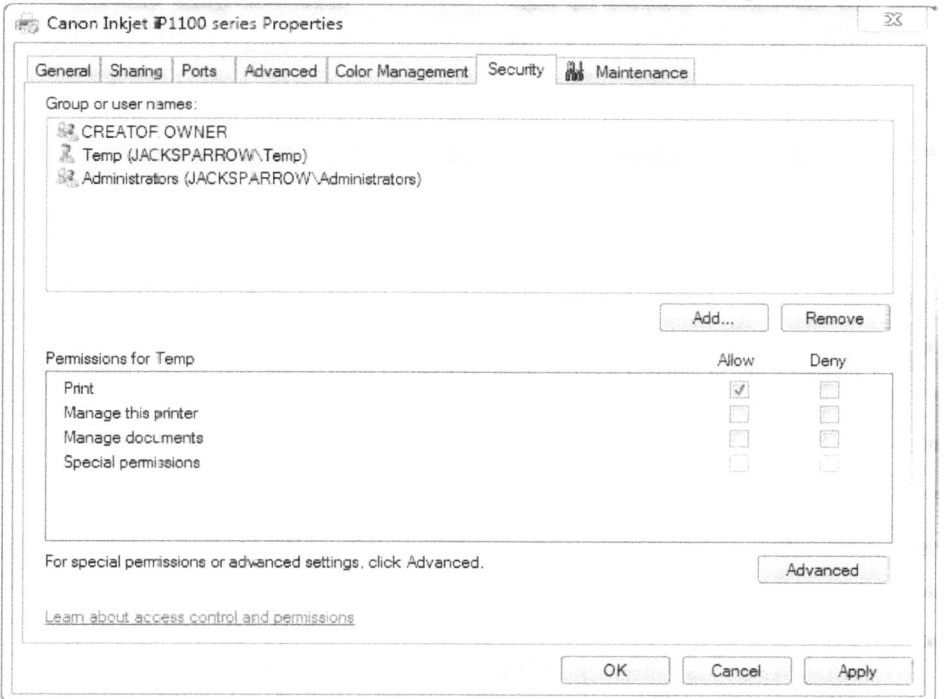

More Info:

By default **Everyone** group gets Print permissions. This means that all users and/or groups are allowed to use to printer to print their documents.

Best Practices:

As an administrator you should reserve Manage this printer permission for yourself and should assign only Print permissions to the groups or user accounts.

Enable Printer Pooling

When a Windows 7 computer is attached to a network where there are multiple printers of same vendor and make, administrators can configure printer pooling to load balance the usage of the printers. With help of printer pooling feature documents are automatically redirected to the next available printer if the first printer is busy in printing other documents. The limitation, however, with printer pooling feature is that all the printers which are to be pooled together need to be from the same vendor and of same model. As an administrator you can enable printer pooling by following the steps given below:

1. Log on to the computer with administrator account.
2. Click **Start** button.
3. From the start menu go to **Devices and Printers**.
4. From the opened window right click on the icon of the printer on which you want to enable pooling and from the menu click **Printer Properties**.
5. On the **Properties** page go to **Ports** tab and check **Enable printer pooling** checkbox.

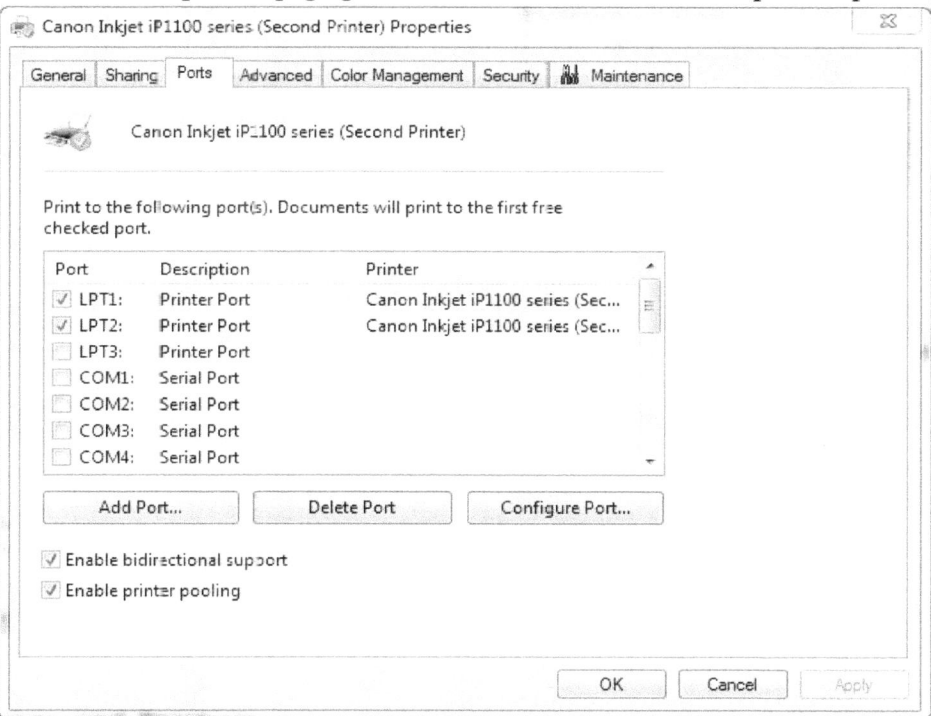

6. Once done, from the ports list check the checkbox representing the port on which second printer is installed and click **Apply** button to allow the computer to update new settings. Both the printers will then be mapped to a single port.
7. Click **Ok** button to accept and confirm your selection and close the Window.

More Info:

You need to follow the above process for all the printers on which you want to enable printer pooling.

Note: Printer pooling can only be enabled when there are two or more printers attached to the network and are of same make and model.

Disable Printer Spooling

Printer spooling is the feature which ensures that the documents which are to be printed get buffered in the temporary memory so that users can close the documents right after they have given the print command to the printer. This process saves a lot of time of the users as they can start working with some other work as soon as they have sent print command. Where spooling safes a lot of time of the users it also occupies some space on the local hard drive. Generally spooling is not the feature to be messed with, however if administrators still want to disable this feature to increase the printing process or to save disk space they can follow the steps given below:

1. Log on to the computer with administrator account.
2. Click **Start** button.
3. From the start menu go to **Devices and Printers**.
4. From the opened window right click on the icon of the printer on which you want to disable spooling and from the menu click **Printer Properties**.
5. On the Properties page go to **Advanced** tab and select **Print directly to the printer** radio button.

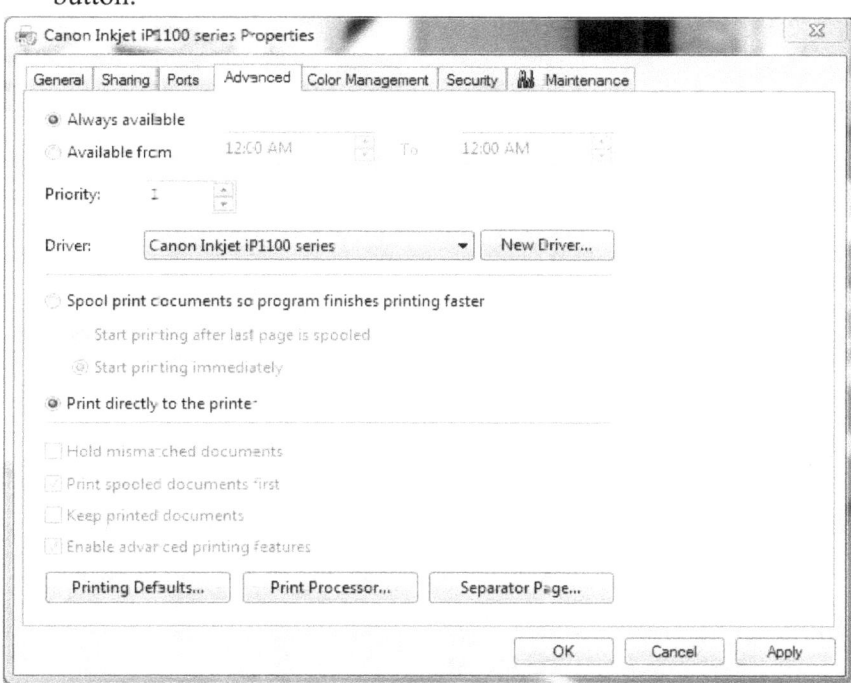

6. Click **Ok** button to accept and confirm your selection and close the Window.

More Info:

When spooling is disabled users are required to keep the documents open till they are not completely printed. If they close the document in the middle of printing process, document printing process will not be completed, hence ending up with incomplete printed document.

CHAPTER 8
DISK MANAGEMENT

Create Partitions in Microsoft Windows 7

During the installation of Microsoft Windows 7 it is recommended that the entire disk space must be allocated as the system drive in order to allow the operating system function smoothly and efficiently. This recommendation however is only followed in production environments where storage capacity is not a major issue. When talking about home environments, it is unlikely that home users might go for multiple storage devices and therefore many times they create multiple partitions in single hard disk drive and install Windows operating system on the very first drive that they create. The volume (partition) on which Microsoft Windows 7 is installed is technically known as system drive and is considered sensitive location that must be protected as efficiently as possible.

Whatsoever the case may be, home users must know how to create new volumes in hard disk drives in Windows 7 in case they have not done so while installing the OS. Creating volumes in a hard disk drive requires unallocated space in the drive and administrative privileges on the computer. In case the hard disk drive does not have unallocated space volumes cannot be created whatsoever.

In order to create volumes on a local hard disk drive in Microsoft Windows 7 operating system administrators must follow the steps given as below:

1. Log on to Windows 7 computer with any account that has administrative privileges.
2. Click **Start** and from the menu right click **Computer.**
3. From the context menu click **Manage** to open **Computer Management** snap-in.
4. On the opened snap-in from the left pane expand **Storage** category and click to select **Disk Management.**
5. From the right pane right click on the unallocated space on the target hard disk drive and from the context menu click **New Simple Volume.**
6. On **Welcome to the New Simple Volume Wizard** window click **Next.**
7. On **Specify Volume Size** window specify the size of the volume in megabytes in the available field and click **Next.**
8. On **Assign Drive Letter or Path** window leave everything as default and click **Next.**
9. On **Format Partition** window leave everything as default and click **Next.**
10. On **Completing the New Simple Volume Wizard** window click **Finish** to close the wizard and start new simple volume creation process.

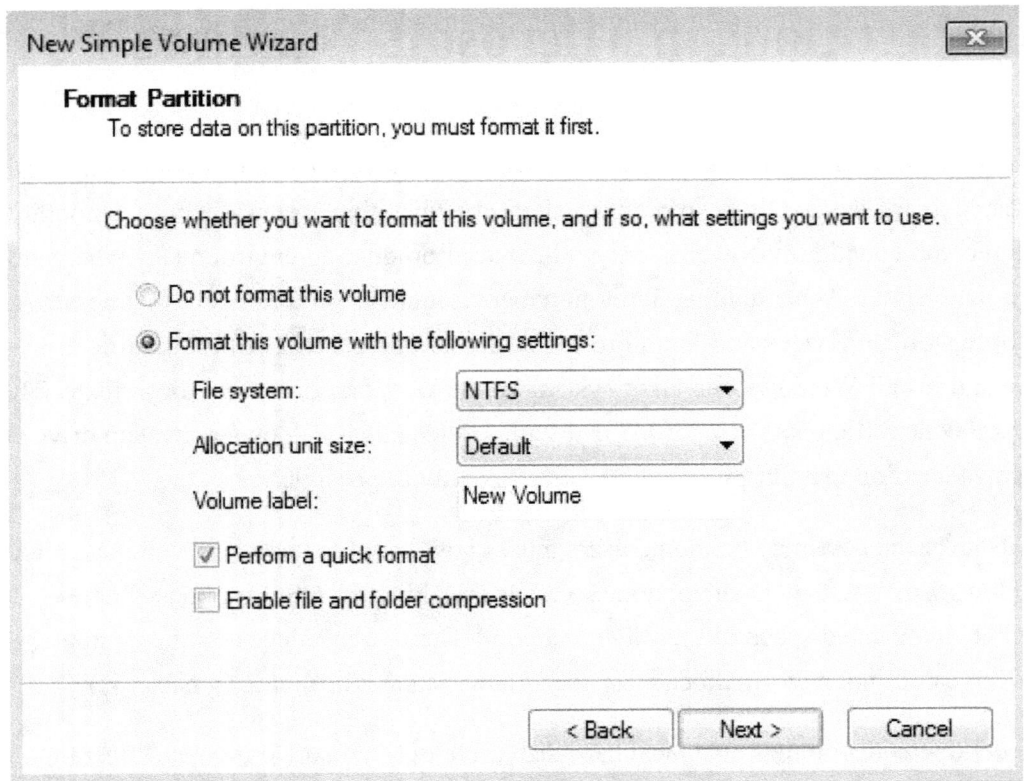

Change Drive Letter of Fixed or Removable Drive

There might be times when you need to change the drive letter of a partition in your computer. The situations might include non-sequenced drive letters, irrelevant drive letter assignment due to any reason, etc. Below are the steps using which you can assign, change or remove a drive letter on your Windows 7 computer.

1. Click **Start** button.
2. From the start menu right click **Computer** and click **Manage**.
3. From the **Computer Management** snap-in in the left pane select **Disk Management**.
4. From the right pane right click on the partition for which you want to change the drive letter and select **Change Drive Letter and Paths** button.
5. On the opened box click **Change** button.
6. From the **Change Drive Letter or Path** box select appropriate character from the drop-down list opposite to **Assign the following drive letter** radio button.

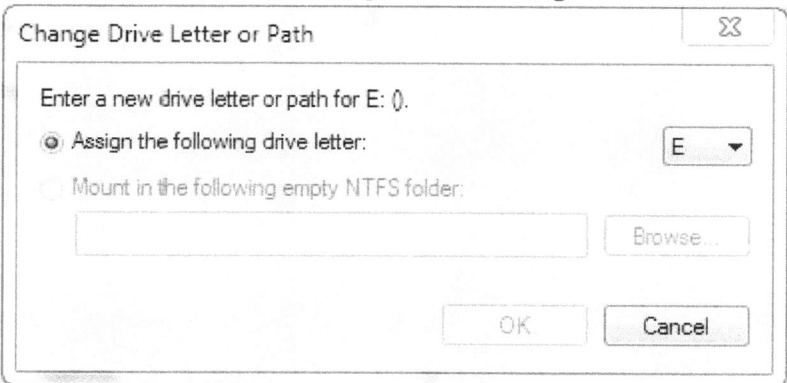

7. Click **Ok** button on all windows to accept and confirm you configuration.

Versatility

By following the above process you can also modify the letters assigned to CD/DVD ROM Drives, USB Flash Drives, etc.

Limitations

You cannot change drive letters of System Drives or boot partitions using this method.

Best Practices

If you are installing Windows on a bare metal machine (new hard disk with no Operating System installed on it) you should create only one partition of the size of your choice and leave rest of the hard disk space unallocated. After Windows is installed you can change the default CD/DVD drive letter from D: to something else. After this you should start creating other partitions on your hard disk drive. If you have executed this in a planned way you will notice that after you have created all the partitions your drive letter assigned to CD/DVD drive comes in the last. (For example C:, D: and E:, for primary partition and logical drives and F: for CD/DVD drive).

Manage Quota on Drives

Disk Quota is the feature using which you can restrict other users to use more than specified amount of space on a particular drive. This means that if you have drive D: on your computer with the maximum available space of 250 GB you can restrict users from using the full space and can limit their usage up to 5 GB or 10 GB per user. Once quota limit is applied, no user will be able to use more than the specified disk space whatsoever. Process to apply disk quota is quite simple and the steps are as below:

1. Click **Start** button and select **Computer**.

2. From the opened window select the drive on which you want to specify quota limit.

3. Right click on the drive and click **Properties**.

4. From the **Properties** dialog box of that drive go to **Quota** tab.

5. To enable quota feature click **Show Quota Settings** button.

6. From **Quota Settings** dialog box check the check box which says **Enable Quota Management**.

7. Select the other check box which says **Deny Disk Space to Users Exceeding Quota Limit**.

8. To enable default quota limit for every user on the computer select the radio button which says **Limit Disk Space To:** and specify the maximum space you want to assign for all the users on that particular drive. You can also specify warning level which will start prompting the user if exceeds the specified warning limit.

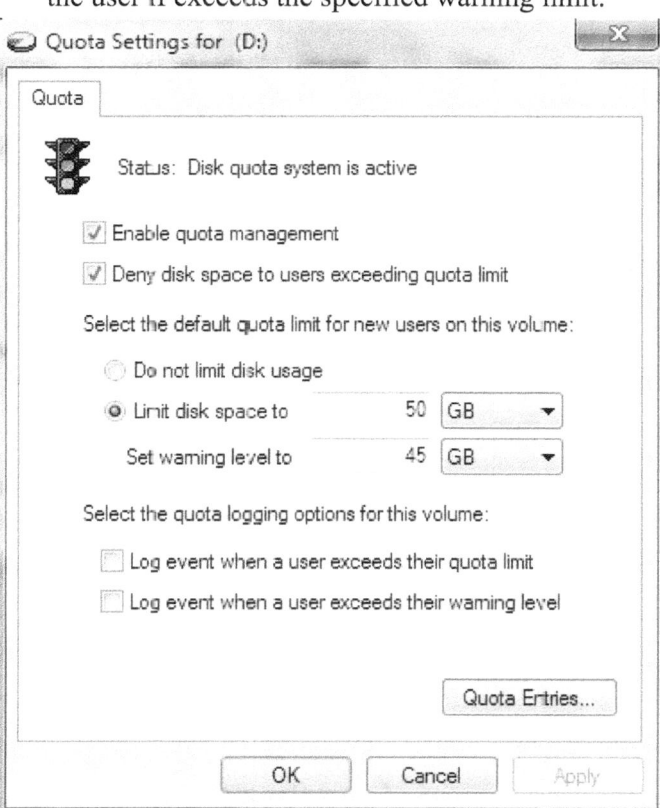

9. Click **Apply** button and click **Ok** button in the confirmation box that appears next.

10. Ensure that the **Status** changes to **Disk Quotas Are Enabled**.

Alternatively, you can click **Quota Entry** button and from the next window click **Quota** and from the drop down list select **New Quota Entry** in order to select a specific user and assign separate quota limit for him.

Create and Use Virtual Hard Disk

Windows 7 has a brand new feature of creating Virtual Hard Disk (VHD) that was not available with any other versions of Windows operating systems earlier. This feature also allows you to attach this VHD file and use it as a data storage device. Moreover, sometimes in local computers or in complex network configurations these VHDs are used to install a full-fledged Windows 7 operating system which then become quite handy for the administrators to deploy it at remote locations, such as branch offices, etc. This means that with Windows 7 in VHD, they can copy the VHD file to their USB flash drives or can burn the entire VHD file on a single DVD and can parcel it to any branch office. Alternatively, administrators can also use VHD files to take backup of a baseline operating system which can be restored in case of disasters. To create VHD files and attach them to your Windows 7 computer you need to follow the instructions given below:

1. Click **Start** button.

2. From start menu right-click **Computer** and click **Manage**.

3. In the **Computer Management,** snap-in from the left pane right-click **Disk Management** and select **Create VHD**.

4. In **Create and Attach Virtual Hard Disk,** box browse to the location where you want to store this VHD file.

5. In the **Virtual Hard Disk Size** text box, specify the amount of space you want to assign for your Virtual Hard Disk and select the unit from the drop down list. (Recommended is GB)

6. Leave everything else as default and click on button.

7. When the process will be completed you will find another hard disk attached in **Disk Management** snap-in as shown in the snapshot below:

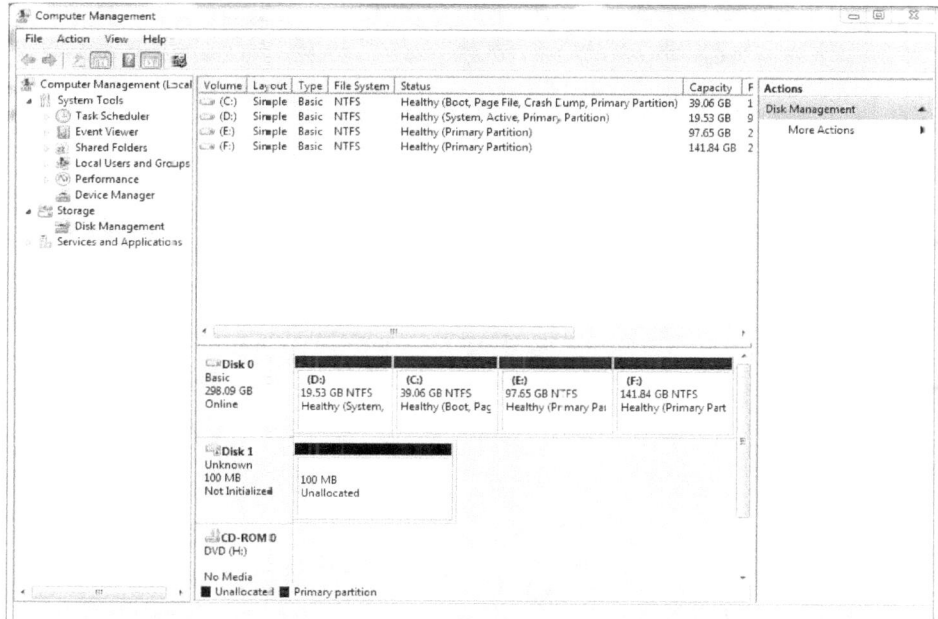

8. However, this disk is not usable at present. To use this disk you need to initialize it by right clicking on it and selecting **Initialize Disk**.

9. Now, from **Initialize Disk** box ensure that the checkbox opposite to your current Virtual Hard Disk is selected. Leave everything else as default and click **Ok** button.

10. Once completed you can use this Virtual Hard Disk as any other physical hard disk drive attached to your computer.

11. If you want to detach this VHD, you can do so by right clicking on the attached VHD and selecting Detach VHD.

Install Windows 7 on Virtual Hard Disk (VHD) File

If you are an administrator in an office or you are a simple home user of Windows 7 it is always a real pain in the neck if it gets corrupt and you come to know that you need to reinstall the operating system to bring it back up and running as before. To ease out this problem various tools are available in the market that are capable of taking backup of the entire hard disk or a particular partition in the form of image. This image can be used to restore your computer quickly and easily whenever it starts behaving abnormally and obnoxiously.

However, another even simpler method to do this is that administrators can install entire Windows 7 operating system on a Virtual Hard Disk and can save the VHD file at a secure location. This VHD file would then work as a backup of Windows 7 operating system. Process of creating and attaching VHD file and installing Windows 7 on it is given below:

1. On a new computer (in which no operating system is installed) insert Windows 7 installation DVD and start the computer from DVD ROM.
2. During the process of installation at the first screen, that appears select appropriate language, time zone and currency and click **Next** button.
3. On the next window, click **Repair Your Computer** link.
4. On **System Recovery Options,** box select **Use recovery tools that can help fix problems starting Windows. Select an operating system to repair** radio button and click **Next** button.
5. On **System Recovery Tools,** page click on **Command Prompt** link.
6. In the **Administrator: x:\windows\system32\cmd.exe** command window type **DISKPART** and press enter.
7. On the DISKPART prompt type **SELECT DISK 0** (assuming that you have single unpartitioned hard disk attached to your computer) and press enter.
8. On the DISKPART prompt type **CREATE PARTITION PRIMARY SIZE=20000** where 20000 is the size in megabytes of the first primary partition of your physical hard disk drive and press enter key. Minimum size should be 10 GB and recommended is 80 GB-100 GB. Alternatively, you can type the command without "SIZE=20000" to assign entire disk space to a single partition.
9. You will be displayed with the message saying creation was successful.
10. On the DISKPART prompt type **FORMAT** and press enter key. (In case any error message appears , type **SELECT VOLUME 1**)
11. Once formatting is successfully completed you need to type **ASSIGN LETTER C:** and press enter key. (In case any error message appears, type **SELECT VOLUME 1**)

12. To create a virtual hard disk file and to store it on C: drive type **CREATE VDISK FILE="C:\VIRTDISK.VHD" MAXIMUM=15000** where VIRTDISK is the name of virtual hard disk file and 15000 is the maximum size of the virtual hard disk and press enter key. (Note that the size of virtual hard disk should not be more that total size of the partition in physical hard disk where virtual hard disk is stored. For example, if while creating partition on physical hard disk you chose 20 GB than your total size of virtual hard disk can only be less than or equal to 20GB)

13. To attach virtual hard disk type **SELECT VDISK FILE="C:\VIRTDISK.VHD"** and press enter key.

14. Then type **ATTACH VDISK** and press enter key.

15. Type **EXIT** to come out of DISKPART and again type **EXIT** to close command window and finally click on close button on the top right corner of the window.

16. You can now continue with the installation of Windows 7 in regular way. When you will reach where Windows asks for the drive where you want to install Windows 7 you will find two hard disk drives attached namely Disk 0, which is the physical hard disk drive, and Disk 1, which will be the virtual hard disk drive that you have created just now.

17. Select Disk 1 and follow the instructions on the screen to install Windows 7 on virtual hard disk drive.

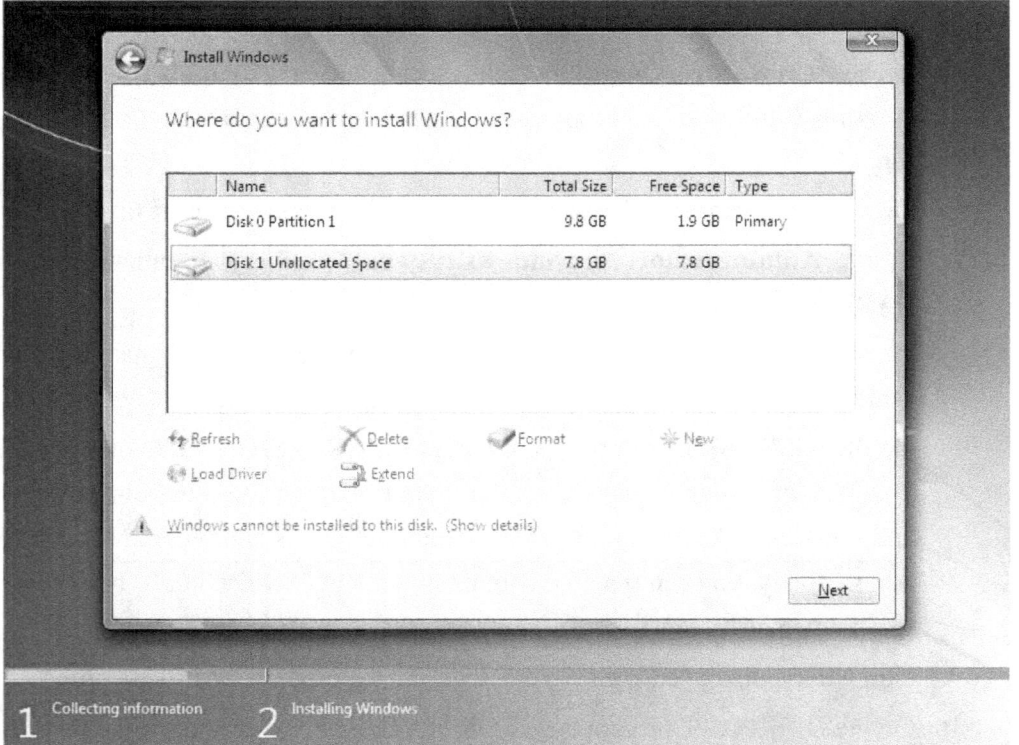

With help of above method, you will be able to backup and restore your Windows 7 quite easily and with minimal overhead. In addition, the method can be used to transfer a preconfigured copy of Windows 7 to any remote location, probably a branch office.

CHAPTER 9
SECURITY

Hide or Unhide Files and Folders

For security reasons it is always recommended that you hide files and folders that contain sensitive data. Hiding a file or folder on your computer will add an extra layer of security as it doesn't allow anyone to view the contents of that object. Hidden files or folders can still be viewed however any unauthorized person will need to provide some extra clicks to the computer in order to fetch them. You can hide files or folders on a Windows 7 computer by following the steps given below:

1. Right click on the file or folder which you want to hide and click **Properties**.

2. On the **Properties** box under **Attributes** section check **Hidden** checkbox to hide the folder of file and click **Ok** button.

3. On **Confirm Attribute Changes** box select appropriate radio button as per the needs (recommended is **Apply changes to this folder, subfolders and files** option) and click **Ok** button to confirm your configuration. Note: This box will only be displayed when you are setting attributes of a folder. In case you are following the process to hide a file, **Confirm Attribute Changes** box will not be displayed

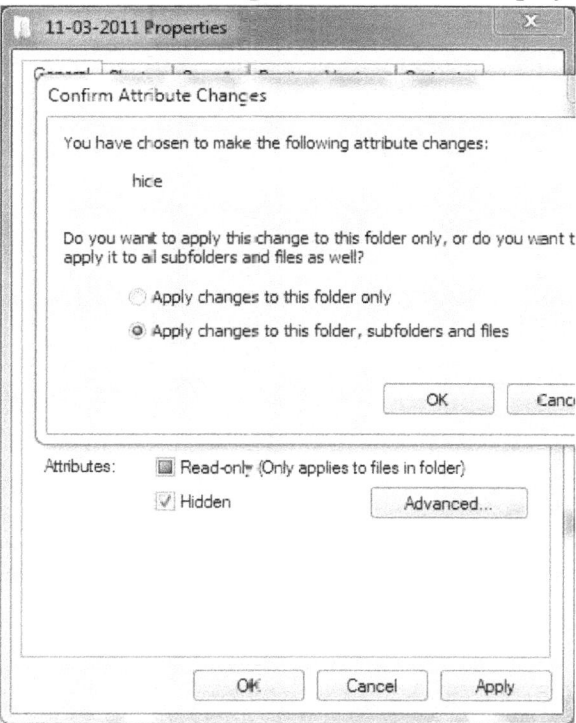

More Info:

In order to unhide any file or folder, first you need to configure your machine to show hidden files and folders. Once done, you can follow above steps to reverse the process.

Alternatively you can use command window to set attributes for any file or folder through commands.

View Hidden Files or Folders

Many users hide folders or files on their computers for security purposes and after some time they forget where they had stored them. Since files or folders are hidden they are not visible, hence making search process complicated for the users. You can view hidden files or folders on a Windows 7 computer by following the steps given below:

1. Log on to the computer with any user account. (Feature of viewing hidden files or folders is user specific and will only be applicable for the user account using which it is configured.)

2. Click **Start** button.

3. From the start menu click **Computer**.

4. On the opened window from the menu bar click **Organize** and from the drop-down menu click **Folder and search options**.

5. On **Folder Options** box go to **View** tab.

6. Under **Hidden files and folders** category select **Show hidden files, folders and drives** radio button and click **Ok** button. Optionally you can uncheck **Hide protected operating system files (Recommended)** check box to view Windows 7 system files. (This configuration is not recommended though).

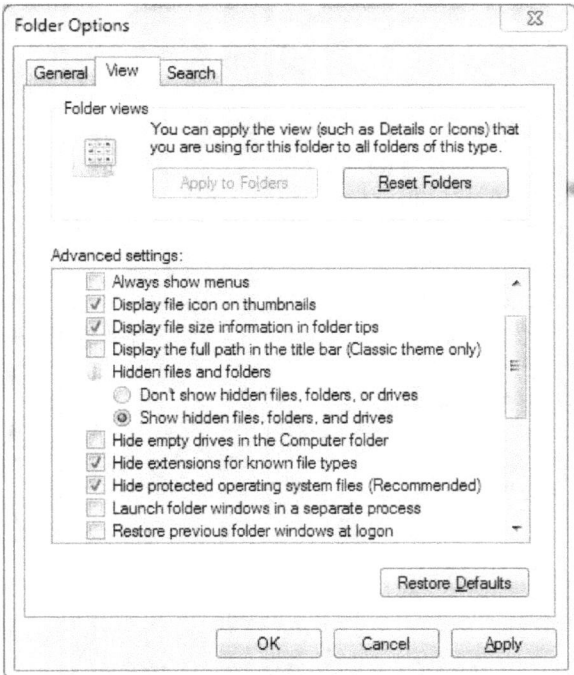

More Info:

You can reverse the above-mentioned process if you don't want hidden files to be viewed by anyone.

View Effective NTFS Permissions

In offices and production environments where there are several groups containing thousands of users, administrators need to keep track of all NTFS permissions that they have assigned. When the scenario is gigantic and has numerous configurations it becomes next to impossible for administrators to view effective NTFS permissions that are applied on any particular user or group. Microsoft understands this and has offered a promising feature called Effective Permissions to help administrators in this regard. With help of this feature administrators can browse through the name of any user or group to view the actual set of permissions which are applied on that particular object. If you want to view effective permissions for any user or group on a folder or file you need to follow the steps given below:

1. Log on to your Windows 7 computer with the account that has administrative or equivalent powers.

2. Right click on the folder for which you want to view the effective permissions and from the appeared menu click **Properties**.

3. On the **Properties** box go to **Security** tab and click **Advanced** button.

4. On **Advanced Security Settings** box go to **Effective Permissions** tab.

5. Click **Browse** button to locate the name of the user or group for which you want to view the effective permissions and once found click **Ok** button to get the desired results.

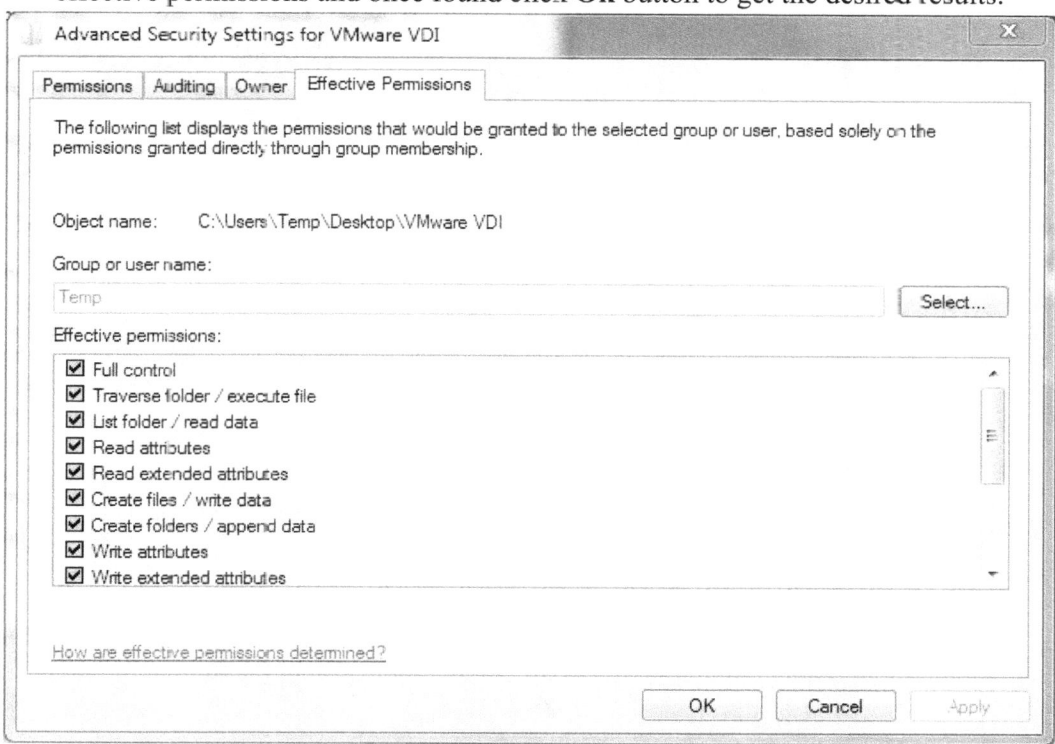

6. Once viewed, you can close the opened boxes and Windows to get back to the main screen.

Enable Object Access Auditing

For security purposes many organizations enable auditing feature in their scenarios. With the help of auditing you can regularly monitor the usage of any file or folder available on the computer. For example, if auditing is enabled on Accounts folder, you can view the names of the users who have tried to access the object. Auditing can be enabled for both Successful and Failed access attempts depending on the requirements of the organization. Successful auditing logs every successful access attempt that was made by the user on the specified file or folder whereas Failed auditing logs the records of all the failed attempts which were made to access the object. Every logged (recorded) transaction contains time at which the attempt was made and the name of the user who was logged on when the event actually took place. You can enable auditing on any file or folder by following the steps given below:

1. Log on to the computer with the account having administrative or equivalent privileges.

2. Locate the folder or file for which you want to enable auditing and right click on it.

3. From the appeared menu go to **Properties** and from the opened box go to **Security** tab.

4. Click **Advanced** button and from the **Advanced Security Settings** box go to **Auditing** tab.

5. If required click **Continue** button to enable the editable box.

6. Click **Add** button to add the users and/or groups for which you want to enable auditing on this folder or file. Once found, click **Ok** button to get another box called **Auditing Entry**.

7. In the new box check the **Full Control** boxes for **Successful, Failed** or both auditing events as per your requirements and click **Ok** button to add the user or group in the list.

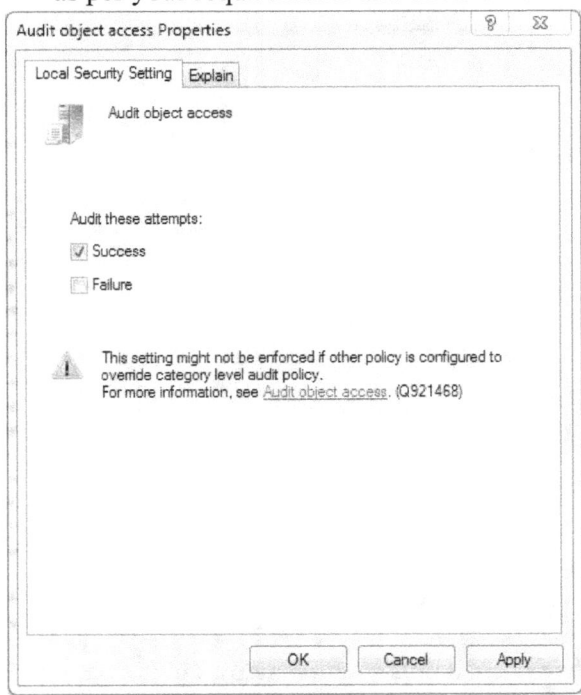

8. Once done, click **Ok** button to confirm your settings.

More Info:

You can view the logged (recorded) auditing information from the **Event Viewer** snap-in which can be found in **Computer Management. (Start > Run > COMPMGMT.MSC)**.

Note: You need to enable Object Access auditing policy from group policies in order to enable Windows 7 start recording the events.

Security Without Anti-Virus

Virus is a common problem that everyone faces while using computer and internet. It makes system slow to the extent that after some time it becomes mandatory to remove the operating system and re-install Windows right from the scratch.

To eliminate this tedious process and to protect Windows from getting corrupt every now-and-then almost everyone uses Anti-Virus programs which are quite expensive and require regular updates from the internet.

This section will tell how to secure Windows using some of its built-in features, hence eliminating the need of any Anti-Virus program.

In order to do so, two user accounts are required, i.e. one with administrative privileges and the second one with limited access. First user account with administrative privileges is created by default when Windows 7 is installed. To create a standard user account, follow the steps below:

1. Click **Start** and click **Control Panel**.
2. Under **User Accounts and Family Safety** category click **Add or Remove User Accounts** link.
3. From the opened window click **Create a New Account**.
4. In the next window type the name of new user account. (E.g. Vivek Nayyar)
5. Make sure that **Standard User** is selected in the available radio buttons.

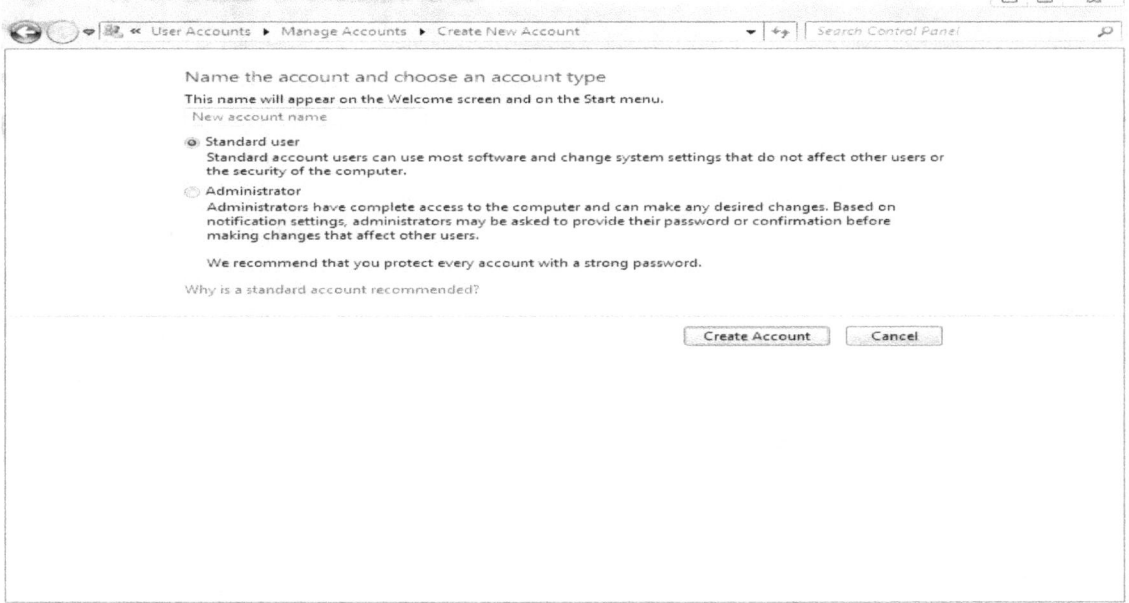

6. Click **Create Account** button to complete account creation process.
7. To assign password to the account click on the icon of newly created account.

8. From the next window click **Create a Password** link.
9. On **Create Password for xxx Account** window, type and confirm the desired password. Also type some hint to the password in **Type Password Hint** box.
10. Click **Create Password** button to create password.

Once the standard user account is created, it should be used on regular basis for daily tasks. Because this user account has least privileges, no virus program can automatically get placed on C: drive or any other secured location like Program Files, System32, etc. This can be tested by logging on to the computer with standard user account and trying to create a new file on C:. The access will be denied, thus making the system secured from almost all kinds of virus programs without using any Anti-Virus software.

PCTIPS 3000

Enable File or Folder Level Encryption

Encryption is the process using which you can secure your files or folders without using any third-party application or hiding the folder or file using Windows integrated features. To enable encryption on Windows 7 computer you can follow the instructions given below:

1. Right-click on the drive, folder or file that you want to encrypt and from the context menu select **Properties**.

2. In the **Properties** box ensure that you are on **General** tab.

3. Click **Advanced** button.

4. On the **Advanced Attributes** box check **Encrypt contents to secure data** check box and click **Ok** button to accept and confirm your selection.

5. On the **Properties** box click **Apply** button.

6. On the **Confirm Attribute Changes** box select desired option and click **Ok** button to confirm.

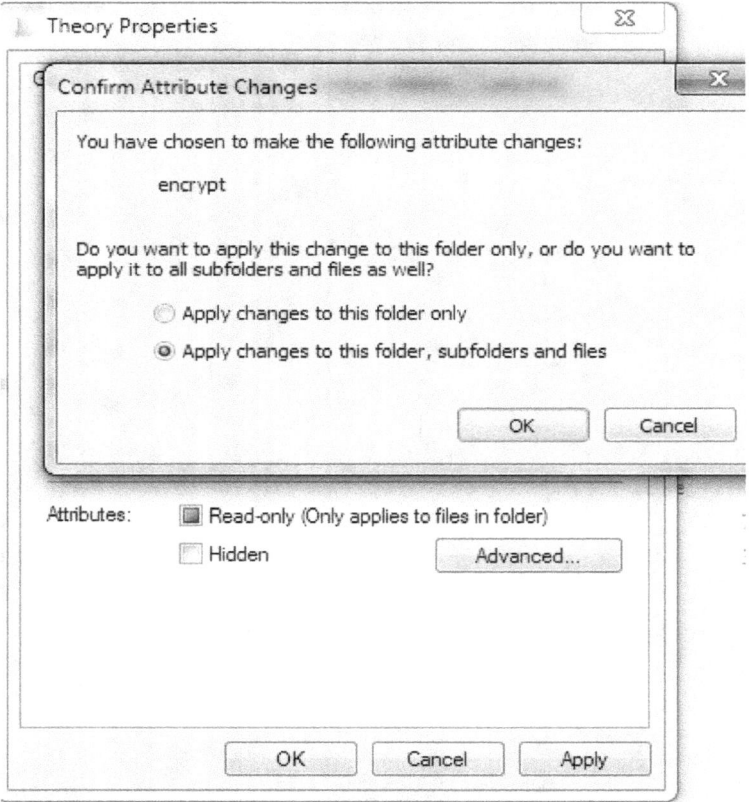

When you see the text color of file or folder is changed to green, this means that the encryption has been enabled and now your data is secured. You can test this by logging on to the computer using different user account and trying to access the encrypted file or folder. You will see the message telling you that your access to the encrypted file or folder is denied.

More Info:

Encryption uses algorithm to generate an encryption key which is used to encrypt your data. As soon as you encrypt your file or folder you will be notified by Windows 7 that you should back up your encryption key. This is because if because of any reason you lose your password and if the administrator of the computer resets it, the encryption key would be modified, hence making your data unreadable for you. Whereas if you backup your encryption key and if even you lose your password and the password is reset by the administrator you can restore your encryption key from the backup and can decrypt your encrypted data thus making it readable again as before.

System Requirements:

Make sure the drive on which you want to enable encryption is formatted with NTFS file system. In almost all cases Windows 7 formats all its drives using NTFS file system only.

Restrict Windows Games for any User

Disabling or removing games from Windows 7 computer prevents all users from playing them. However, there might be cases when you want to allow one person to play a particular game and restrict the same game for another person at the same time. When this is the case you can configure Parental Control feature to get desired results. By following the steps given below you can configure Parental Control to restrict a user from playing games:

1. Click **Start** button.

2. From the start menu click **Control Panel**.

3. In the opened window under **User Accounts and Family Safety** category click **Setup parental controls for any user** link.

4. On the next page click on the user account on which you want to apply restriction. Alternatively you can create a new user account by clicking **Create a new user account** link on the same page.

5. On the appeared page under **Parental Controls** category select **On, enforce current settings** radio button.

6. Under **Windows Setting** category, click **Games** link.

7. In the opened page under **Block (or Allow) any game on your computer by name** category click **Block or Allow specific games** link.

8. On the next page, select the radio button under **Always block** column for the game that you want to restrict from this user. You can see the status of that game change to **Can not play** instantaneously.

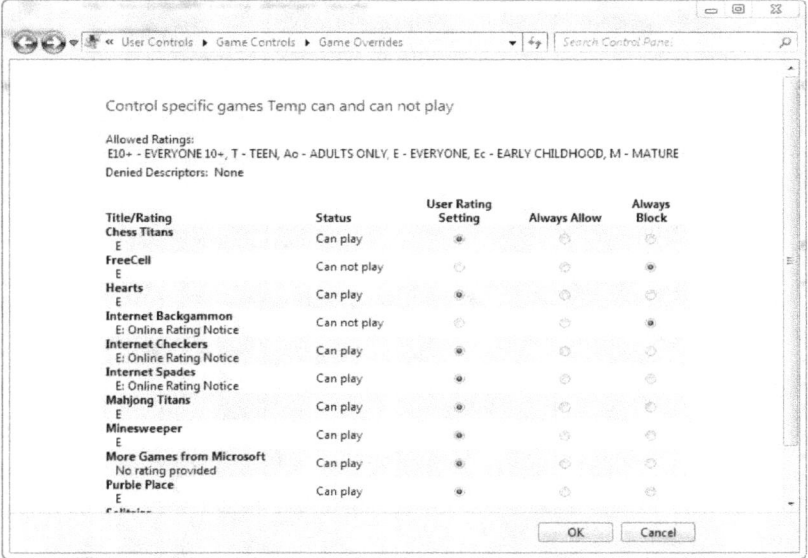

9. Click **Ok** button on all the windows to accept and confirm your selection and close **Control Panel**. If necessary, restart your computer.

Restrict a User from Playing Rated Games

Almost every game that is developed has a specific rating tag on it, for example, Adults Only, Teens, 10+, etc. With the help of Parental Control feature you can allow a user to play only games with specific rating. This means that if a person is 13 years of age you can allow him to play 10+ rated games. In the same way if a person is 21 years of age you can allow him to play Adults Only rated games on your computer. The process of this configuration is as below:

1. Click **Start** button.

2. From the start menu click **Control Panel**.

3. In the opened window under **User Accounts and Family Safety** category click **Setup parental controls for any user** link.

4. On the next page click on the user account on which you want to apply restriction. Alternatively you can create a new user account by clicking **Create a new user account** link on the same page.

5. On the appeared page under **Parental Controls** category select **On, enforce current settings** radio button.

6. Under **Windows Setting** category click **Games** link.

7. In the opened page under **Block (or Allow) games by rating and content types** category click **Set game ratings** link.

8. On the opened page you can specify games of what rating would be appropriate for this user to play. In the below screenshot you will find that Temp user is a teenager and therefore **Teen** rating is configured for him.

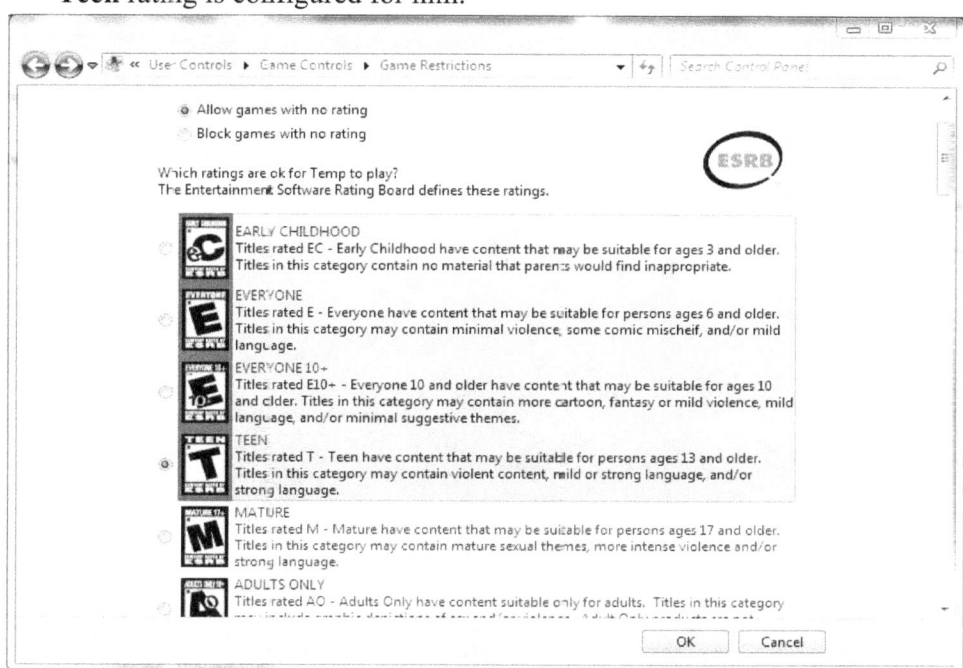

9. Once you're done with the appropriate configurations you can click **Ok** button on all windows to accept and confirm your settings.

10. Finally close **Control Panel** window and if required restart your computer.

Restrict Users from Using Specific Application

Many times, you would not want any person or kids to use a particular application installed on your computer. Prior to Windows 7 people were not able to prevent users from using any application and to do so they used to uninstall the application and re-install it whenever they needed it. However, with the help of Parental Control feature you can now restrict a user from using applications hence allowing him to use only applications that you permit. The process of restricting users on a Windows 7 computer is given below:

1. Click **Start** button.

2. From the start menu, click **Control Panel**.

3. In the opened window under **User Accounts and Family Safety** category click **Setup parental controls for any user** link.

4. On the next page click on the user account on which you want to apply restriction. Alternatively you can create a new user account by clicking **Create a new user account** link on the same page.

5. On the appeared page under **Parental Controls** category select **On, enforce current settings** radio button.

6. On the right side of the page click **Off** link in front of **Program Limits**.

7. On the **Which programs can Temp use?** page select **Temp can only use the programs I allow** radio button. (Temp is the user account name)

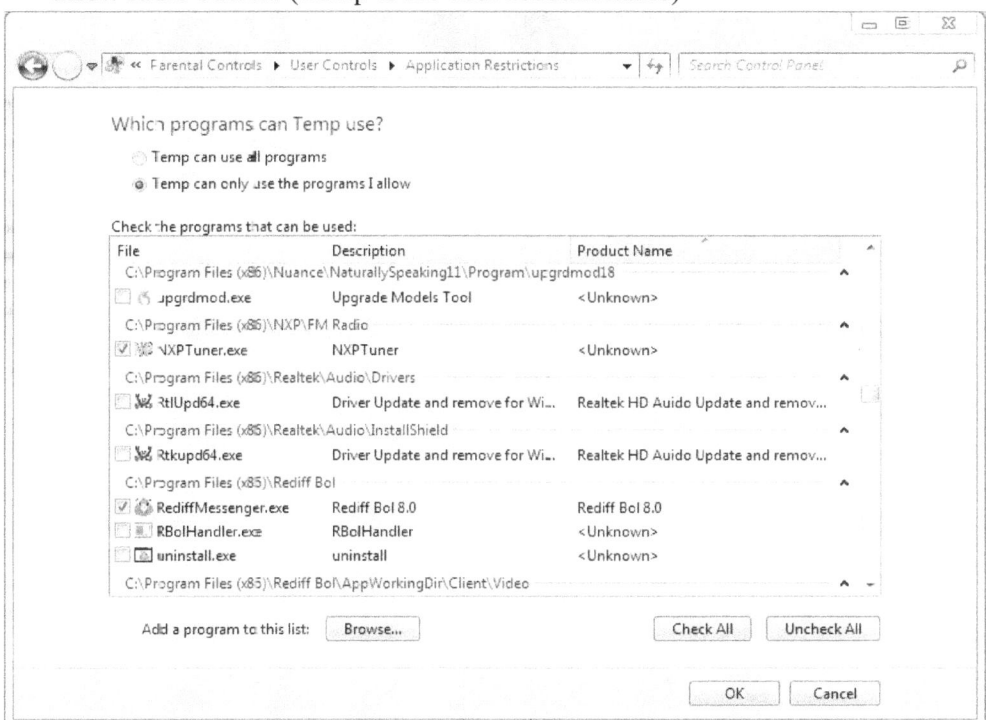

8. From the displayed list check the name of the programs that Temp user can use. All other programs will automatically become unavailable for this user. If you could not find any application in the list you can browse it by clicking on Browse button at the bottom of the page.

9. Once you are done with your configuration, you can click **Ok** button to accept and confirm your selection.

Manage Data Execution Prevention Feature

Data Execution Prevention is the feature which prevents malicious applications from getting loaded into the memory and corrupting system files. By default this feature is turned on in order to make the computer system securer. However in some cases the users may install third-party applications, codes of which are not readable by Microsoft Windows. When this is the case Data Execution Prevention feature stops those applications to run, hence preventing users from using that particular application even if it is safe to use. To eliminate this problem, administrators may want DEP to overlook the codes of these applications and allow them to get executed. Administrators can easily do this by following the steps given below:

1. Logon on the Windows 7 computer with administrator account.

2. Click **Start** button.

3. From the start menu right click **Computer** and from the menu select **Properties**.

4. On **View basic information about your computer** page in the left bar click **Advanced system settings** link.

5. On the opened box make sure that you are on **Advanced** tab and under **Performance** section click **Settings** button.

6. On **Performance Options** page go to **Data Execution Prevention** tab and select **Turn on DEP for all programs and services except those I select** radio button.

7. Click **Add** button to add the program or programs that you find incompatible with DEP to create an exception list and click **Ok** button.

8. Close all opened Windows.

Encrypt Drives with BitLocker

After you have configured your computer to enable BitLocker without TPM support, now you need to enable BitLocker Drive Encryption on the drive that has operating system installed on it. This drive is also known as System Drive. To enable BitLocker on system drive you need to follow the instructions below:

1. Click **Start** button.
2. From the menu click **Control Panel**.
3. On **Control Panel** window select **System and Security** link.
4. In the right pane click **BitLocker Drive Encryption** link.
5. In the opened window click **Turn on the Locker** link opposite to **C:**.
6. In **Set BitLocker startup preferences** click **Require a startup key at every startup** link.
7. On the next page Windows 7 will ask you to insert a blank USB flash drive where it can store the key. This USB drive will be required every time your computer starts.
8. On **How do you want to store your recovery key?** page click **Save the recovery key to a USB flash drive** link.

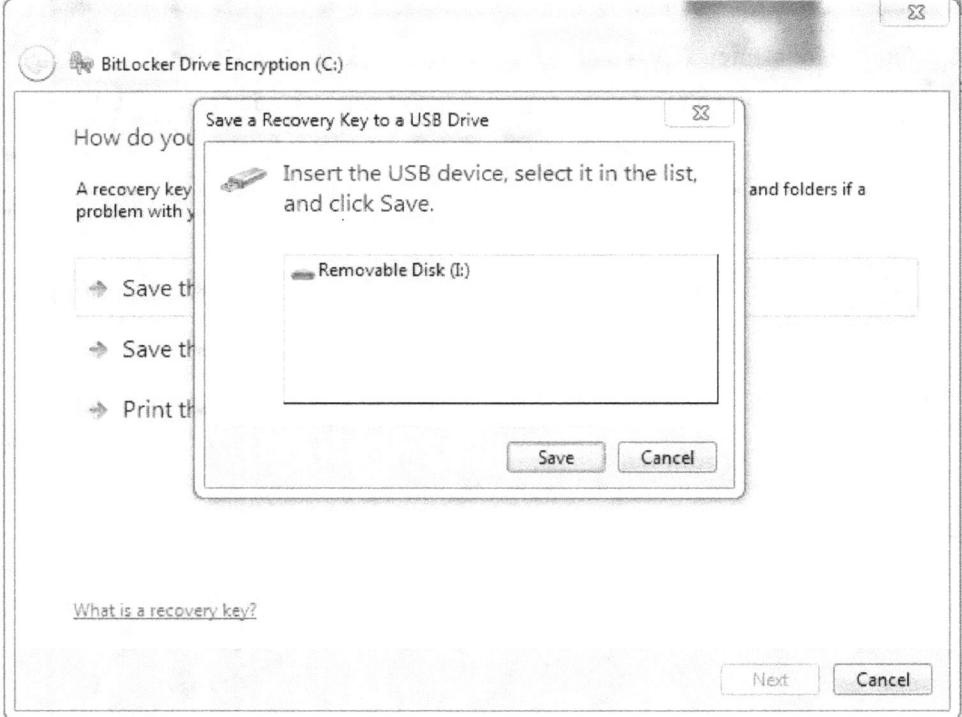

9. On **Save a Recovery Key to a USB Drive** box ensure that USB flash drive that you inserted is selected and click **Save** button.
10. On the previous page click **Next**.
11. On the confirmation box click **Continue** button to start encryption process.

You can test this configuration by restarting your computer and setting and allowing it to read contents from USB drive at startup.

BitLocker is mostly used for security purposes when you need to encrypt the entire hard disk drive. This allows a person to add an extra layer of security to the desktop or laptop PCs. When this type of drive encryption is enabled, even if a thief steals the laptop or desktop he will still not be able to read or extract any information without the PIN and the USB flash drive which is required at every startup.

PCTIPS 3000

How to Enable or Disable Windows Firewall

For those who don't know, Windows Firewall is a built-in application that ships along with Windows and protects your computer from any malicious attacks. When a person tries to enter your computer, it is firewall that prevents him from doing so. In other words Windows Firewall works as an efficient gatekeeper for the computer that prevents any unknown application or a known application from untrusted source to enter your system until and unless you have specifically allowed it. In medium or large-scale organizations where security is a major concern, administrators usually rely on third-party firewall solutions and most of them prefer dedicated hardware firewalls, whereas in homes or small-scale industries Windows Firewall works just fine. It is always recommended that you should NOT turn off the firewall whatsoever the case is. However for testing purposes if you want to disable Windows Firewall you need to follow the steps given below:

1. Log on to the computer using administrator account.

2. Click **Start** button.

3. From the start menu go to **Control Panel** and from the opened window click **System and Security** category link.

4. On next page click **Windows Firewall** category link and on next page from the left bar click **Turn Windows Firewall on or off**.

5. On **Customize settings for each type of network** page under **Home of work (private) network location settings** select **Turn off Windows Firewall (not recommended)** radio button.

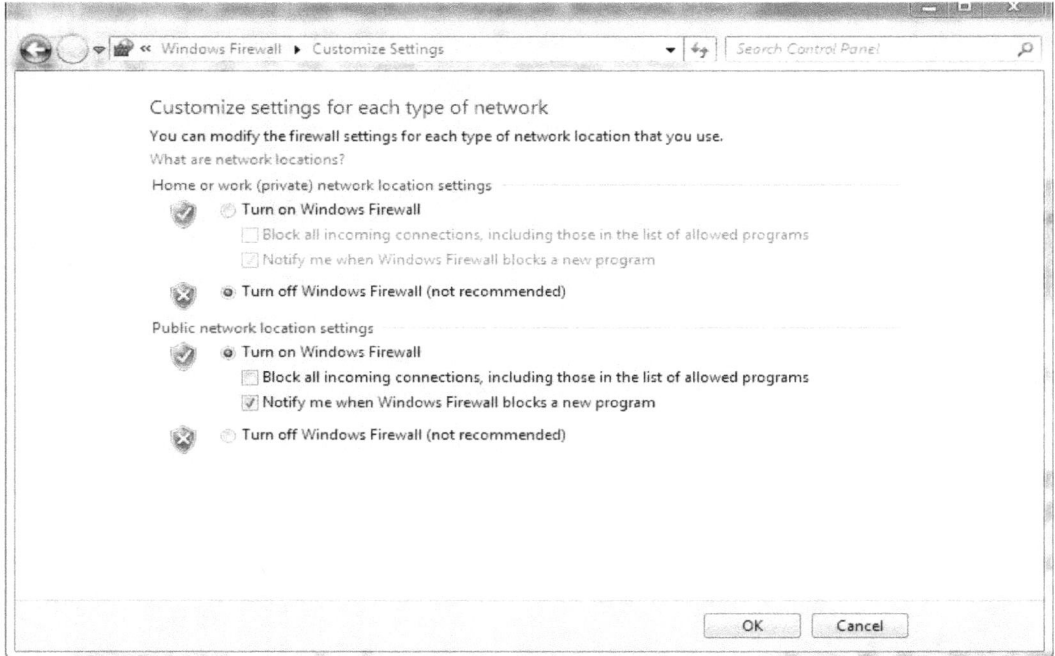

6. Once done, click **Ok** button to accept your configuration and close all windows.

Manage Windows Firewall Exception List

When a program is installed on a Windows 7 computer, Windows firewall exception rule is automatically created for it. Windows firewall exception list is a list of programs which can pass through Windows Firewall without any restrictions. This means that whenever a computer is connected to the Internet programs listed in the exception list of Windows Firewall can send or receive data from other computers unrestrictedly. Since the process is automated, administrators need not to configure such settings manually. However if because of any reason Windows Firewall fails to create an exception rule for any program administrators can do so manually by following the steps given below:

1. Log on to the computer using administrator account.

2. Click **Start** button.

3. From the start menu go to **Control Panel** and from the opened window click **System and Security** category link.

4. On next page click **Windows Firewall** category link and on next page from the left bar click **Allow a program or feature through Windows Firewall** link.

5. On **Allow programs to communicate through Windows Firewall** page click **Allow another program** button.

6. On **Add a Program** box browse through and locate the program that you want to allow to communicate through Windows Firewall.

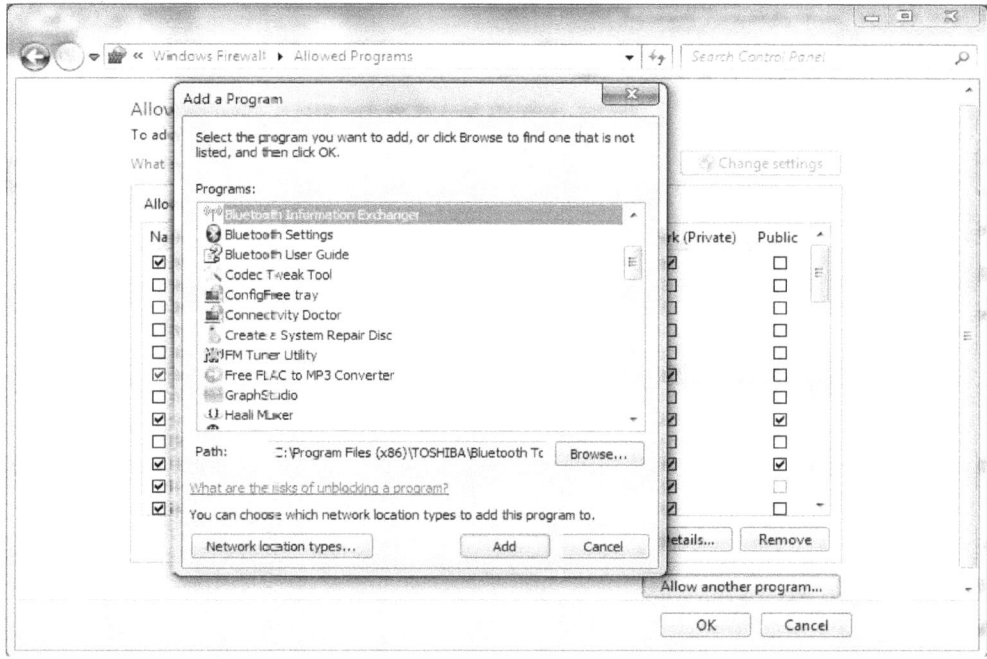

7. Once done, click **Add** button and back on previous page click **Ok** button to accept and confirm your configuration.

8. Close all opened Windows.

CHAPTER 10

MANAGING INTERNET EXPLORER 8

Make Internet Explorer Default Web Browser

Microsoft Internet Explorer 8 is a web browser that ships along with Microsoft Windows 7 itself. When Windows 7 is installed on a computer the default web browser is Internet Explorer which serves its purpose at its best. However many times users might prefer any third-party web browser application for example Mozilla Firefox or Opera because of their flexible features. Whenever any third-party web browser application is installed on a computer, it automatically becomes the default web browser and if it does not, it prompts the user if he wants to make the newly installed web browser the default. Under certain circumstances user might say no but in most cases users accept the default configuration and allow third-party web browser to become the default. After sometime, that is, because of some reasons, user might realize that Internet Explorer is required to be the default web browser in order to open some webpages and pop-ups. When this is the case users must manually make Internet Explorer the default web browser and as a Windows 7 user if you want to do so you need to follow the steps given as below:

1. Log on to Windows 7 computer.

2. From the quick launch toolbar in the taskbar click **Internet Explorer** icon to open it.

3. Click **Tools** menu and from the list click **Internet Options**.

4. On the opened box go to **Programs** tab and under **Default web browser** section click **Make Default** button.

5. To get the notification if **Internet Explorer** is not default web browser you need to check **Tell me if Internet Explorer is not the default web browser** checkbox.

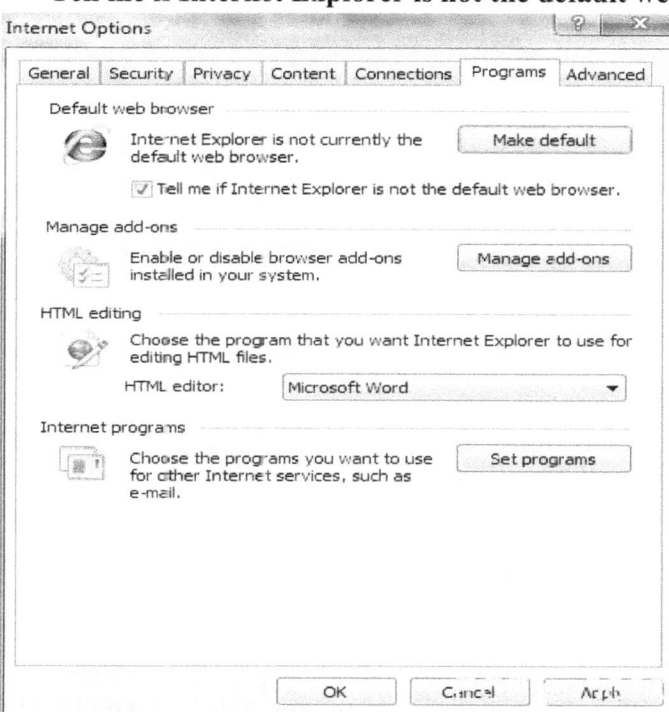

6. Once and click Ok button and close all the opened boxes in Windows to save the changes.

Set Default Homepage Internet Explorer

When Windows 7 is installed, default homepage that Internet Explorer has is MSN.com. Many times this might not be appropriate for many users and they may want to change this setting and set the homepage of their own choices. Changing default homepage might also become handy when it comes to saving Internet bandwidth. This is because if users set the default homepage of their own choices they can directly view their desired information. On the hand if the default MSN.com page is left unchanged, users may need to switch to the desired homepage manually, hence consuming more time and band-width. To eliminate this trouble, you can change the default homepage of Internet Explorer by following the steps given below:

1. Log on to the computer with the user account on which you want to modify the default Homepage.

2. Click **Start** button.

3. From the start menu go to **All Programs** and from the opened list click **Internet Explorer**.

4. On the **Internet Explorer** click **Tools** menu and from the drop-down menu click **Internet Options**.

5. On **Internet Options** box, make sure that you are **General** tab and under **Home page** text box type the name of the webpage, which you want to make default on Internet Explorer.

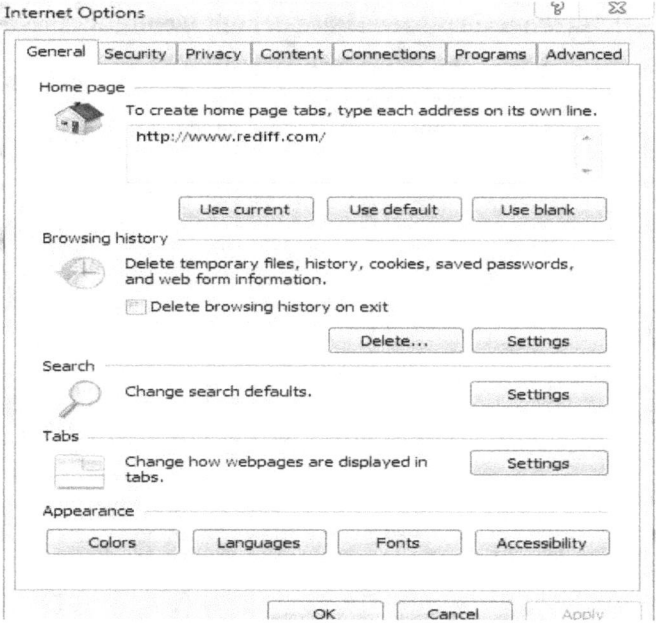

6. Once done, click **Ok** button to accept and confirm your configuration.

More Info:

If you want to restore previous settings, you can click **Use default** button on **General** tab to do so. Also, if you want to use a blank page as the default Internet Explorer setting you can click **Use blank** button.

Privacy Settings in IE 8

Privacy Settings give you the authority to prevent your computers from unwanted viruses, spams and cookies. There are many sites over net that your computer must not ever visit, but just in case if it does then you should know your privacy settings. These settings give you options to stay away from those entities that can damage and harm your system. There are levels of privacy settings; starting from "Accept All Cookies" (this means that you have decreased the privacy level to the lowest) up to "Block All Cookies" (which means that you have increased the privacy level to the highest). If you are not familiar with Privacy Setting then you can start with the Medium level and if that doesn't work you can always increase your level. You can also add different sites to either "Block" (if u don't trust the sites) or "Allow" (if you fully trust the sites) categories. To change your privacy settings follow these steps,

1. Log on to Windows 7 computer with any account.
2. Click **Start** button then click to **Control Panel**.
3. Open **Internet Options**.
4. Go to **Privacy tab**.

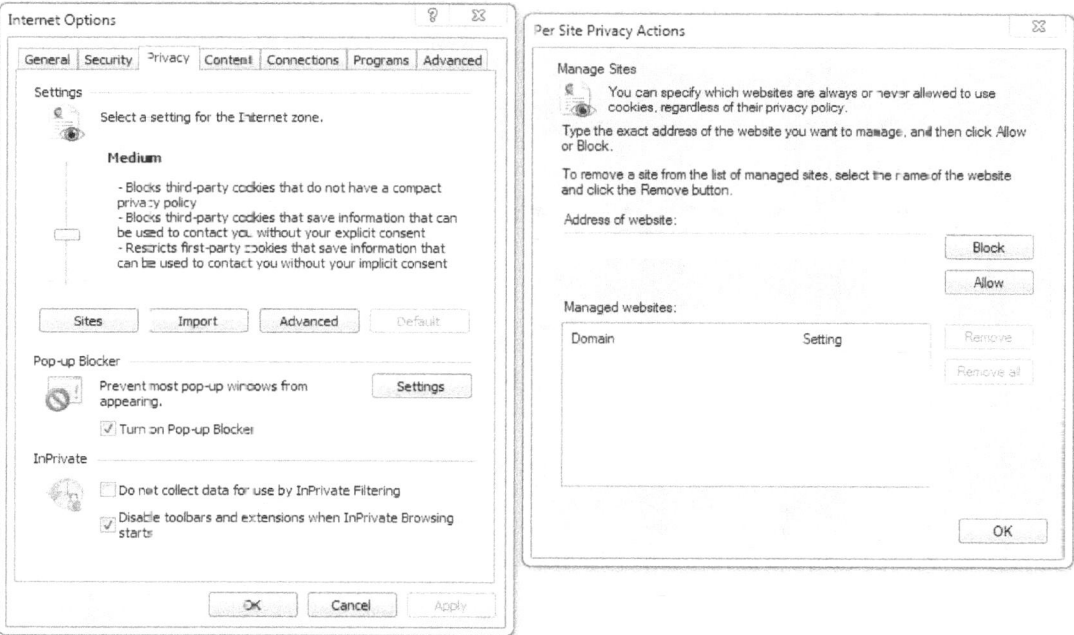

5. Under this you change your privacy levels.
6. Click '**Sites**' button to add sites to either '**Allow**' or '**Block**' sections.

Adding Sites to the Trusted Zone

Users of Internet Explorer in Windows 7 can assign all websites to any one of the four security zones: Internet, Local Intranet, Trusted Sites, or Restricted Sites. The zone to which a website is assigned specifies the security settings that are applied on it when the user opens site. You can specify the websites that you need to assign Restricted, Trusted or Intranet Zones. Security level of websites can be controlled by adding them to the desired zones. For example, if you have a list of websites that you visit and you completely trust those sites you need to add those sites to the Trusted Sites zone. This zone contains Web sites that you trust that they come from safe means and you can download any data from these sites and that data cannot harm or damage your computer. By default, there are no web sites added to this zone. Below are the steps to add websites to the Trusted Sites zone.

1. Log on to Windows 7 computer with any account.
2. Click **Start** button then click to **Control Panel**.
3. Open **Internet Options**.
4. Go to **Security** tab
5. Under this tab you will find four different zones.
6. Click **Trusted Sites** icon
7. Under this, click **Sites** button

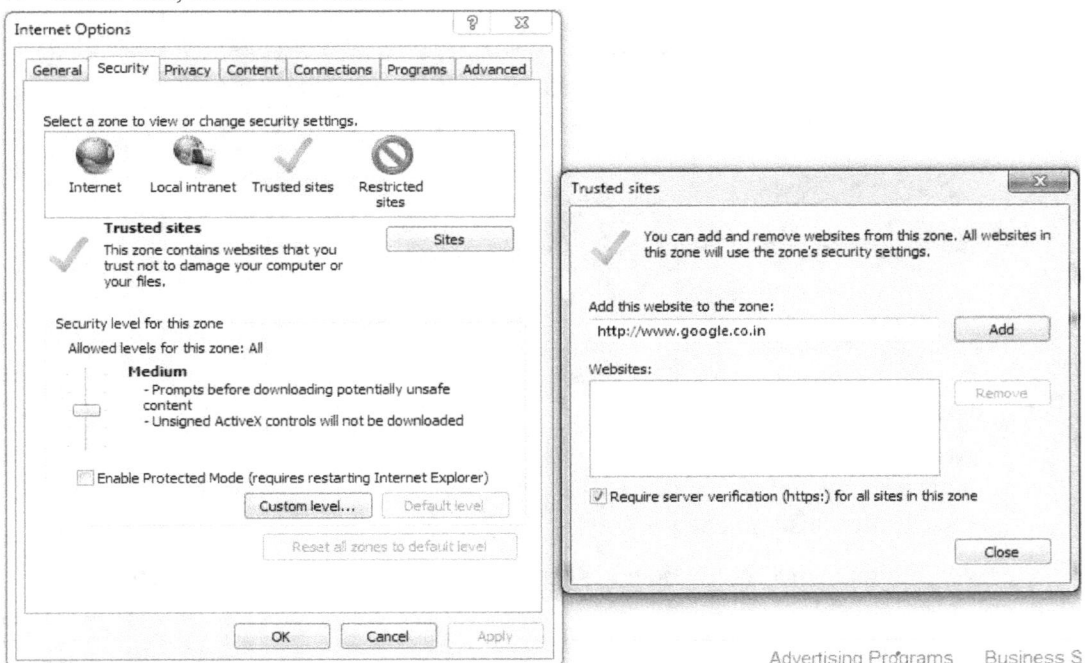

8. Finally add your trusted sites to this zone.

Note: Adding a large amount of sites to this Zone in Windows 7 may decrease efficiency of some applications.

Adding Sites to the Restricted Zone

The Restricted Sites zone contains Web sites that are not trusted by your organization or you or are not on your local intranet. By default the security level for Restricted Zone is High. This zone contains websites that cannot be trusted when opened and are not considered safe for downloading any file. In other words adding websites to this zone means that you are not supposed to download any data from this site, as they might harm or damage your computer. For example, if you add a site in this zone and when that site is opened Internet Explorer warns you. Therefore you can use this zone to cause Internet Explorer to alert you from unsafe content to download or to prevent that content from downloading.

This zone contains web sites that you do not trust. By default, there are no Web sites that are assigned to the Restricted Sites zone, and the security level is set to High. To add sites to this zone follow these steps,

1. Log on to Windows 7 computer with any account.
2. Click **Start** button then go to **Control Panel**.
3. Double-click **Internet Options** to open it.
4. Go to **Security** tab.
5. Under this tab you will find four different zones.
6. Click **Restricted Sites** icon.
7. Under this, click **Sites** button.

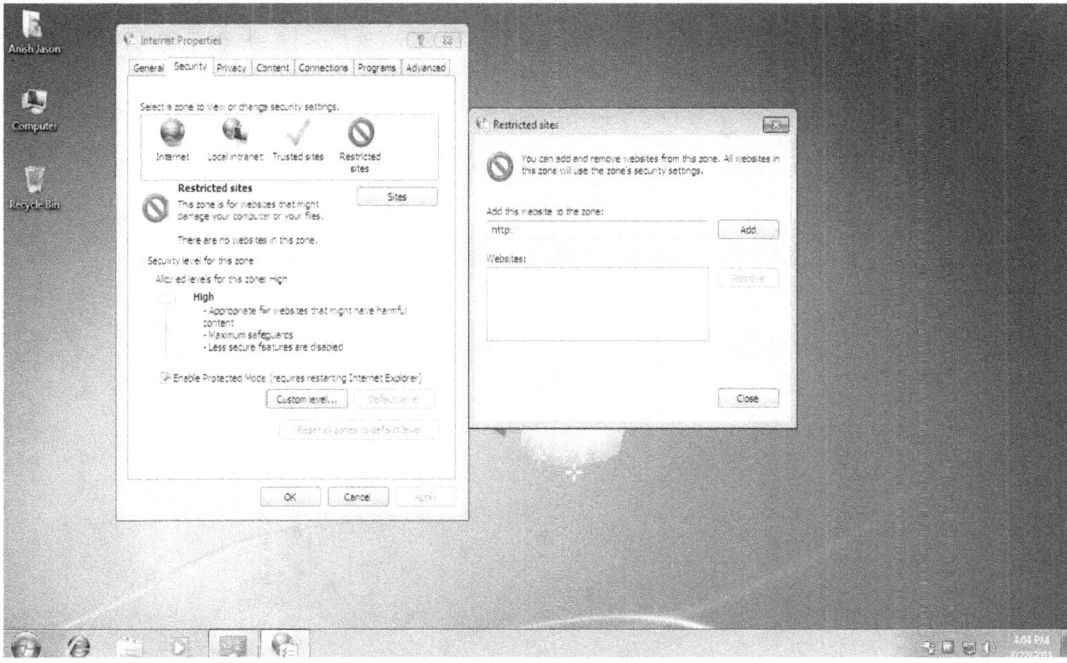

8. Finally add desired URLs of the sites to this zone.

Tabbed Browsing Settings in IE 8

With the installation of Windows 7, Internet Explorer 8 is also installed and can be used as the default web browser to navigate through several websites. The new feature in Internet Explorer 8 is that it allows tabbed browsing which means that users are not required to open multiple instances of the application for every website they want to visit. On the contrary, a single instance of Internet Explorer is now capable of opening multiple webpages in tabbed form. Technically, this increases the performance of the computer by utilizing laser processing of CPU. Although this feature is very helpful for all types of users however in some cases users may not want this facility to be enabled for several security and personal reasons. Keeping this in mind Microsoft has also included the feature of disabling this tabbed browsing as per users' requirements. As a Windows 7 user if you want to disable tabbed browsing in Internet Explorer 8 you are required to follow the steps given as below:

1. Log on to the computer on which Windows 7 and Internet Explorer 8 is installed.

2. Click **Start** button and from the menu click **Control Panel**.

3. In the open window click **Network and Internet** and on the next window click **Internet Options** link.

4. On **Internet Properties** box, make sure that you are on **General** tab and under **Tabs** section click **Settings**.

5. On **Tabbed Browsing Settings** box uncheck **Enable Tabbed Browsing (requires restarting Internet Explorer)** check box to disable tabbed browsing.

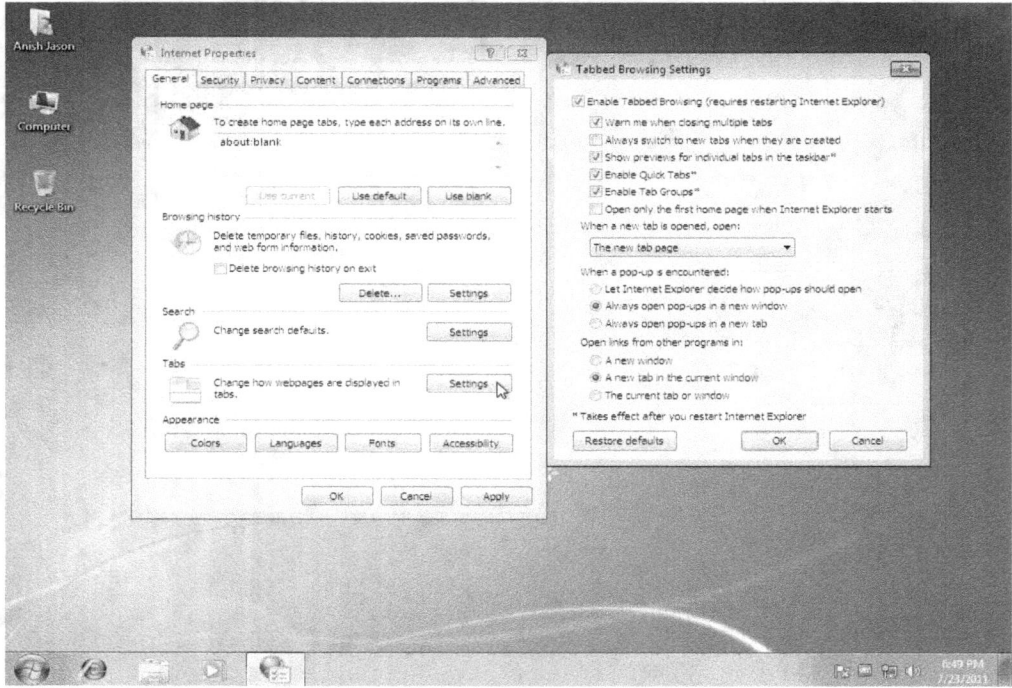

6. Once done, click **Ok** buttons on all the opened boxes to allow the changes to take effect.

Manage Cookie Handling

Cookies are small text files which are stored in the users' local profiles to make surfing easier. However default nature of Windows is that it blocks all third-party cookies for security reasons. Not all third-party cookies are malicious and therefore many times users need to modify the default configuration in order to make web surfing smoother. This manual manipulation is known as cookie handling. You can modify the default configuration of cookies, for better Web surfing performance and make Windows prompt whenever third-party cookies try to enter your computer, by following the steps given below:

1. Log on to the computer.

2. Click **Start** button.

3. From the start menu go to **All Programs** and from the opened list click **Internet Explorer**.

4. On the **Internet Explorer** click **Tools** menu and from the drop-down menu click **Internet Options**.

5. On **Internet Options** box go to **Privacy** tab and click **Advanced** button.

6. On **Advanced Privacy Settings** box check **Override automatic cookie handling** check box and from enabled radio buttons under **Third-party Cookies** column select **Prompt** radio button.

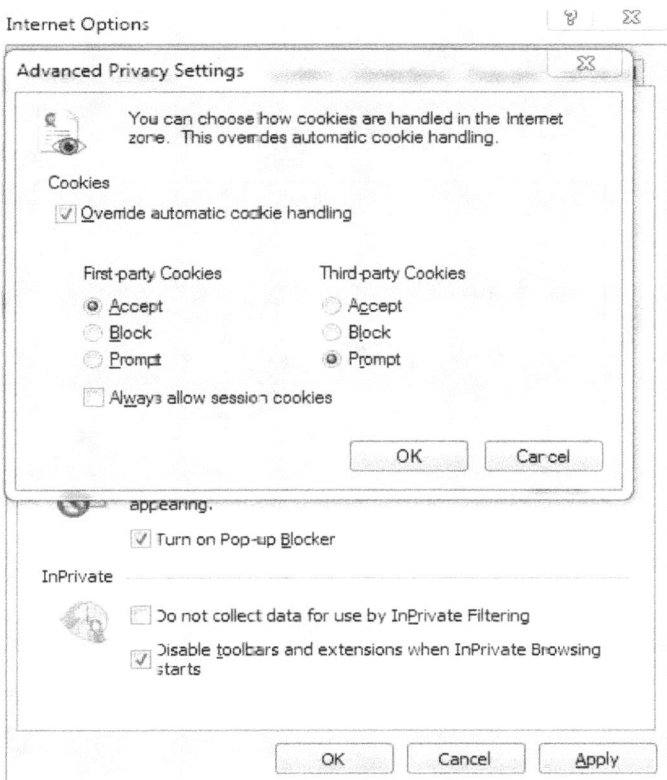

7. Once done, click **Ok** button on all opened boxes to accept and confirm your configuration. If necessary, logoff and re-logon to allow the changes to take effect.

Changing the Appearance of IE 8

As default nature of Internet Explorer in Windows 7, it allows the operating system to take care of the color schemes and the languages in it. This means that whenever any website is visited using Internet Explorer 8 the appearance of the website is adjusted according to the color scheme and appearance offered by the Windows itself. In normal situations and in both production and home environments where everything goes normally, this default configuration serves the purpose at its best. Since the default color scheme and appearance of the Internet Explorer is very common, majority of users are used to it and they find this configuration user friendly. However in some critical conditions where this configuration is not liked or recommended by the users or organizations, it can be changed accordingly. As a Windows 7 user or administrator if you want to change the color scheme of the Internet Explorer 8 you are required to follow the steps given below:

1. Log on to Windows 7 computer with any user or administrator account.

2. Click **Start** button and from the appeared menu click **Control Panel** option.

3. On the open window click **Network and Internet** link.

4. On the next window click **Internet Options**.

5. On **Internet Properties** box, make sure that you are on **General** tab and under **Appearance** section click **Colors**.

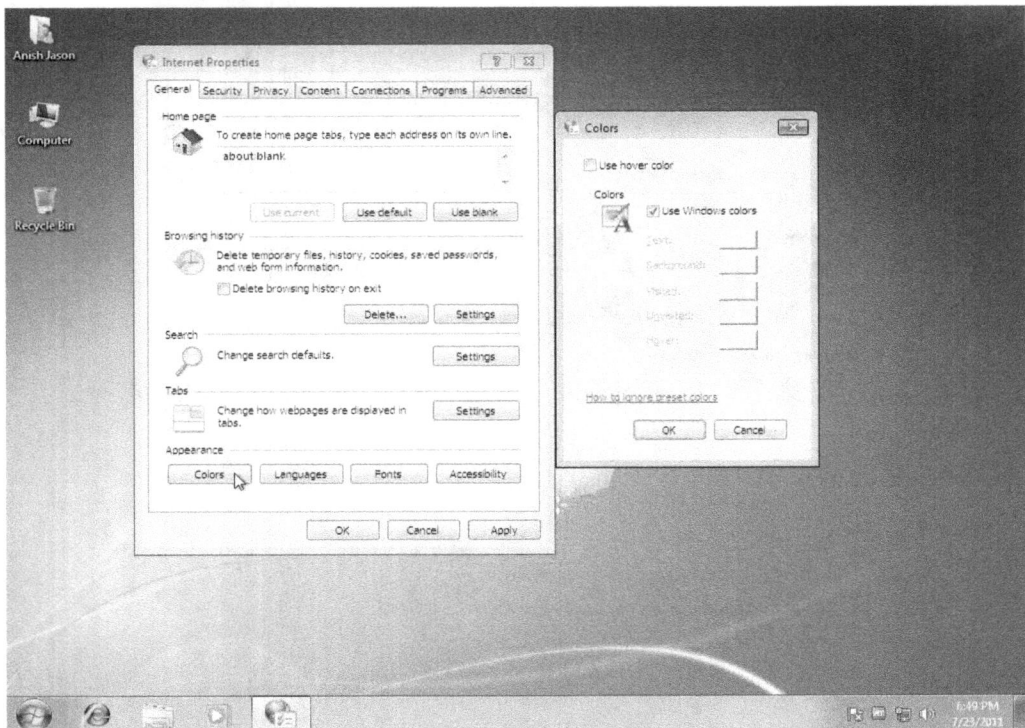

6. On the opened new box choose the appropriate settings as desired and click **Ok** buttons on all the boxes to save the changes.

AutoComplete in Internet Explorer 8

AutoComplete feature offered by Internet Explorer in Windows 7 allows users to automatically populate essential fields with appropriate information which is required by the website. With the help of this feature users can save a lot of time which they would otherwise have spent by typing in the information in the fields. Although, there are several third-party applications available in the market which solve the same purpose but, logically speaking, why to spend extra dollars when the same purpose is being solved free of cost? Since this feature is integrated in the application, it cannot be expected to work as efficiently as those which are precisely developed for the purpose however the basic tasks can still be performed like populating appropriate fields with the respective values automatically, encrypting the passwords, etc. This AutoComplete feature in Internet Explorer can be customized and/or enabled or disabled as per the requirements. As a Windows 7 user if you want to customize or enable or disable AutoComplete feature in Internet Explorer 8 you are required to follow the steps given as below:

1. Log on to Windows 7 computer with a user account for which you want to modify the settings for **AutoComplete** feature.
2. Click **Start** button and from the list click **Control Panel** option.
3. On the opened page click **Network and Internet** link.
4. On the next page click **Internet Options** link.
5. On **Internet Properties** box go to **Content** tab.
6. Click **Settings** button under **AutoComplete** section.

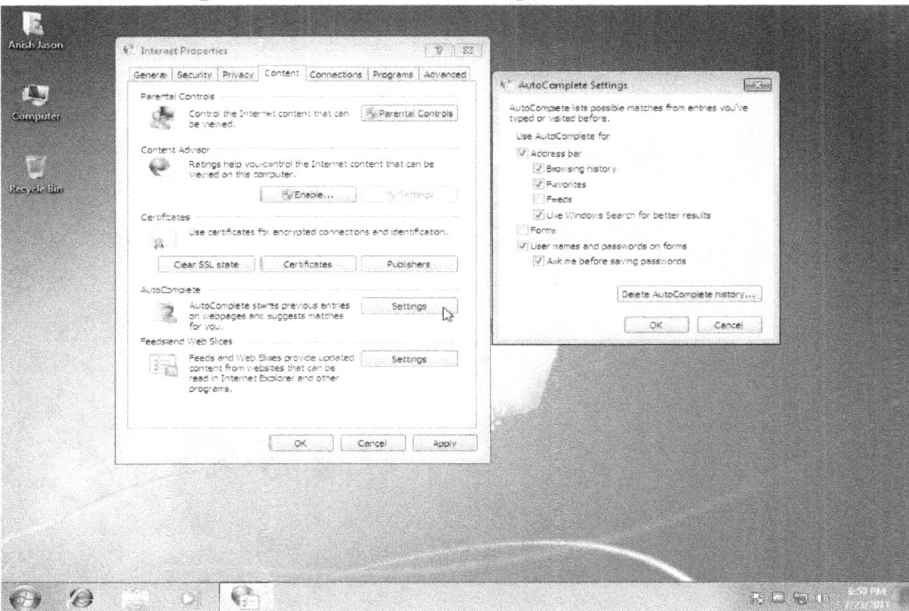

7. Make appropriate changes as required. Alternatively you can uncheck all the checkboxes to completely disable the feature.
8. Once done, click **Ok** buttons on the opened boxes to allow the changes to take effect.

Managing Content Advisor

Content advisor in Windows 7 is a unique feature that prevents your kids from visiting the sites that they are not supposed to. Example contents may include nudity, violence, porn, etc. This problem is not only faced by the parents who want to protect their children from porn sites but can also make a computer vulnerable to risks in production environments. In Windows 7 Internet Explorer 8 handles this through Content Advisor. When Content Advisor finds the user going to a restricted page, it issues a warning. As default nature Content Advisor is capable of blocking web pages which are considered unrated as it cannot identify as which page should be allowed. When you go to an unrated page, you will be presented with a dialog saying you cannot view the page. You can restrict the websites you think should not visit and also you can categorize them as desired. You can also delete sites from this list.

Turning Content Advisor off can be done by clicking the Disable button and specifying the password. To manage this, follow the steps below:

1. Log on to Windows 7 computer.
2. Click **Start** button then click **Control Panel**.
3. Open **Internet Options**.
4. Go to **Content** tab.
5. Under **Content Advisor** section click **Enable** button.

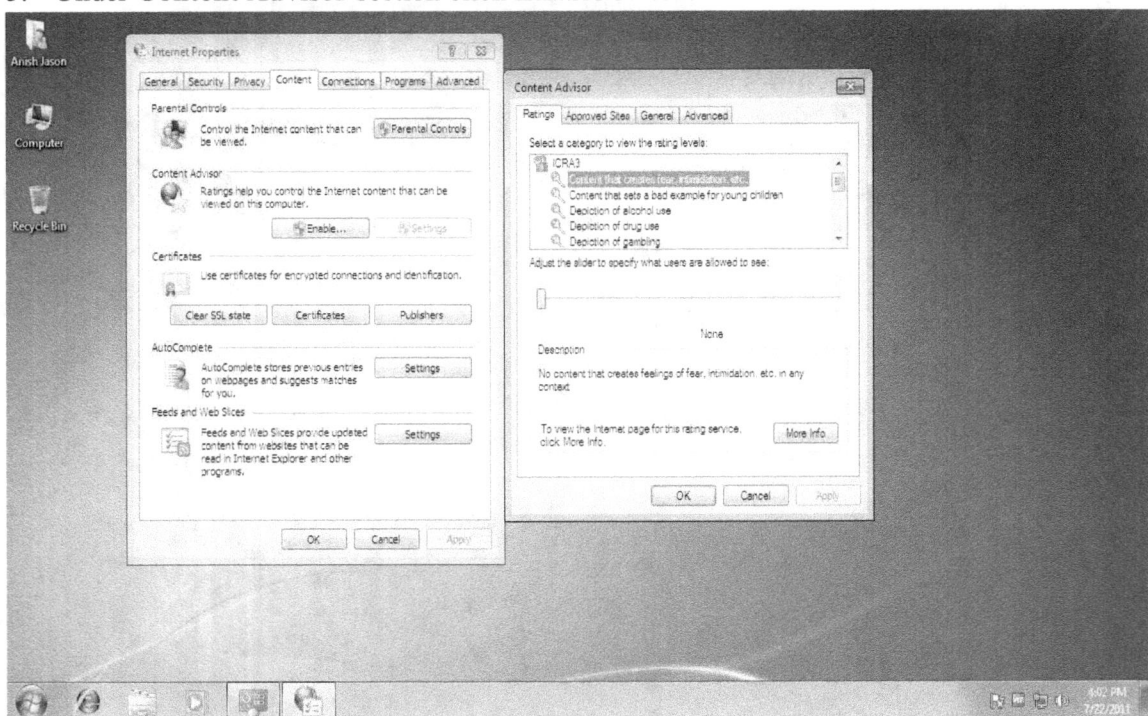

Now you can manage content advisor as per your choice.

Manage Pop-Up Blocker

Pop-up blocker is designed to eliminate the irritation that is created when unnecessary windows are popped up while you are surfing the Internet. Microsoft did this for the noble cause however in some cases pop-up blocker might become a real pain in the neck, as there are few websites, which allow users to interact through pop-up windows only. When this is the case users need to disable pop-up blocker in order to use the pop-up window initiated by those particular sites. With the advanced feature in Internet Explorer, users can now create an exception list to specify the sites from which pop-up windows should be allowed. You can manage this nature of pop-up blocker and create pop-up exception list by following the steps given below:

1. Log on to the computer.

2. Click **Start** button.

3. From the start menu go to **All Programs** and from the opened list click **Internet Explorer**.

4. On the **Internet Explorer** click **Tools** menu and from the drop-down menu click **Internet Options**.

5. On **Internet Options** box go to **Privacy** tab under **Pop-up Blocker** section click **Settings** button.

6. On **Pop-up Blocker Settings** box in **Address of website to allow** text box type the URL of the website for which you want to create exception and click **Add** button.

7. Once done, click **Close** button and then **Ok** button on all opened boxes to accept and confirm your configuration. If necessary, logoff and re-logon to allow the changes to take effect.

HTML Editing in IE 8

When Windows 7 is installed, by default Internet Explorer 8 is also installed along with it. This web browser allows users to navigate through several websites and normally the application functions just like any other normal web browser. A unique feature that is offered by this application, though, is that users can edit the HTML codes of the websites which are opened in Internet Explorer 8. With the help of this feature users can see the pages of their choices in the default text editor which is Notepad. Under normal circumstances this configuration works perfectly fine and no changes are required. However in production environments or for some advanced users this configuration might not be appropriate and users may want to change the default text editor from Notepad to any other editor like Microsoft Word. This enables users to save the webpages in full or they can also save a particular part of the page by editing the HTML codes of the opened website in Internet Explorer. As a Windows 7 user if you want to change the default text editor in Internet Explorer 8 you are required to follow the steps given below:

1. Log on to Windows 7 computer with any account as the process does not require any elevated privileges.
2. Click **Start** button and from the available menu click **Control Panel**.
3. From the opened window click **Network and Internet** and in the next window click **Internet Options**.
4. On **Internet Properties** box go to **Programs** tab and under **HTML editing** section choose the desired text editor from the available drop-down list.

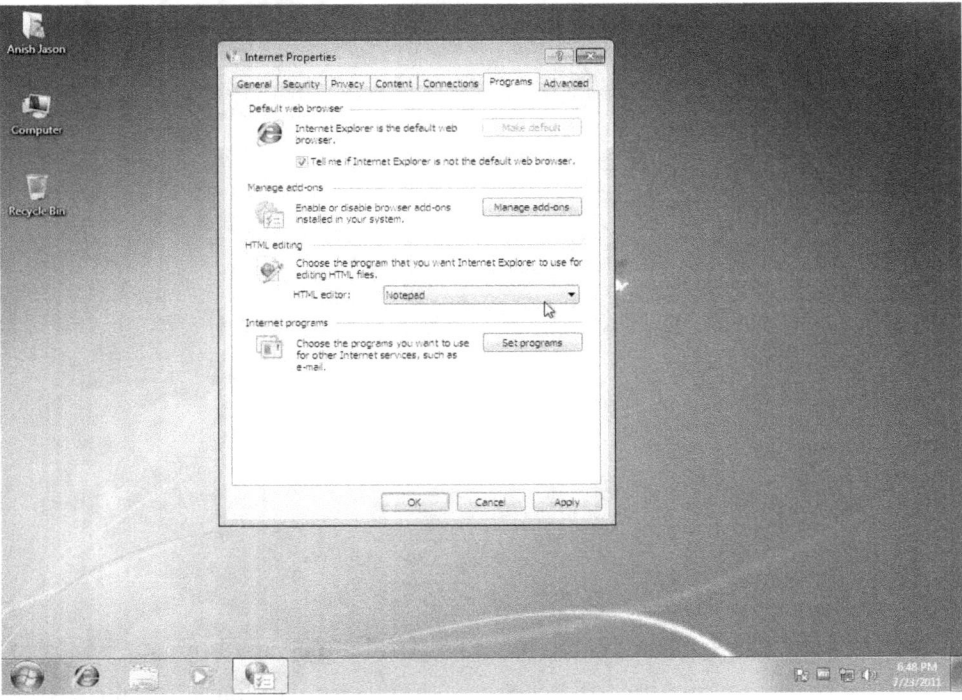

5. Once done, click **Ok** button to save the changes you have made.

Enable JavaScript in Internet Explorer 8

JavaScript in Windows 7 allows several irritating pop-ups to come up on the screen unwantedly. More-over, along with these pop-ups many harmful scripts are also downloaded on the unprotected computer systems and can harm sensitive data almost instantaneously. However, there might be times when users are required to allow pop-ups on purpose because some educational and commercial sites offer some online forms and other promising features through pop-up and/or JavaScript only. When this is the case, users need to enable JavaScript in there web browsers in order to allow these pop-ups so that additional features of the sites can be used. As a Windows 7 user if you want to enable JavaScript in Internet Explorer 8 to allow several additional features (at your own risk of course) you need to follow the steps given as below:

1. Log on to Windows 7 computer.
2. Click **Start** button and from the menu click **Control Panel**.
3. On the opened page click on **Network and Internet** category link and from the next page click **Internet Options**.
4. On **Internet Properties** box go to **Security** tab and click **Custom level** button.
5. On the opened box under **Scripting** section click **Enabled** radio button under **Active script-ing** option.

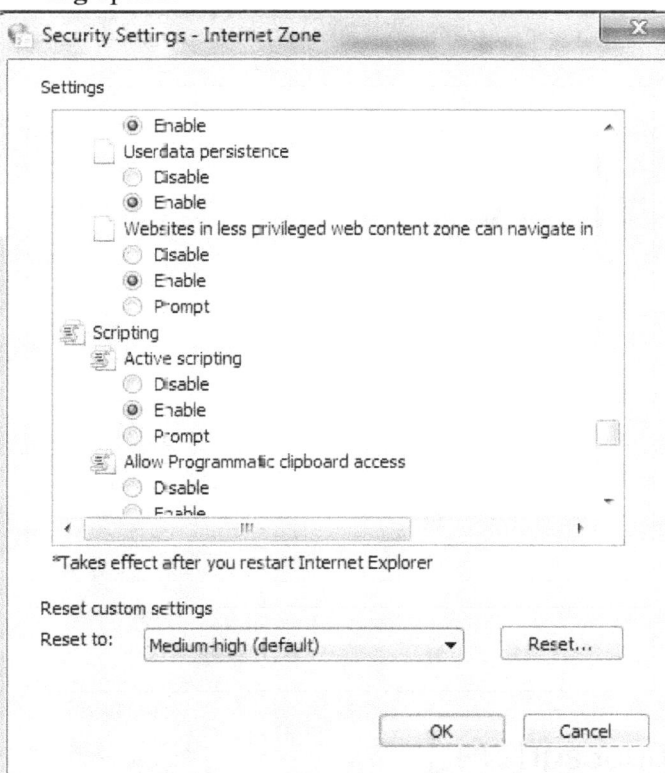

6. Once done, click **Ok** buttons on all the opened boxes and windows.

Feeds and Web Slices

When talking about Web Slices Microsoft Internet Explorer offers a feature using which users can subscribe them for a particular section of the web page. The section of the web page that is specified by the user needs to be updated on a regular basis and when this mandatory requirement is fulfilled, the section becomes eligible to be used as Web Slices by the users. When users subscribe for Web Slices regular updates for that particular section of the page are automatically popped up making a notification noise so that users can be notified about the updates. This feature can be used for news updates, weather reports, share market updates, etc. Many users use these Web Slices to receive automatic updates about the contents of their interests like latest movie releases, etc. The process of utilizing the feature of Web Slices is simple and is user specific. This means that no elevated privileges are required and the configuration can be set on a per user basis. As Windows 7 user if you want to use Web Slices you are required to follow the steps given below:

1. Log on to Windows 7 computer with any account on which you want to configure Web Slices.

2. Click **Start** button and from the menu click **Control Panel** option.

3. From the opened page click **Network and Internet**.

4. Click **Internet Options** link on the next page.

5. On **Internet Properties** dialog box go to **Content** tab and click **Settings** button under **Feeds and Web Slices**.

6. On **Feeds and Web Slices Settings** box make appropriate adjustments and click **Ok** buttons on all the boxes to allow the changes to take effect.

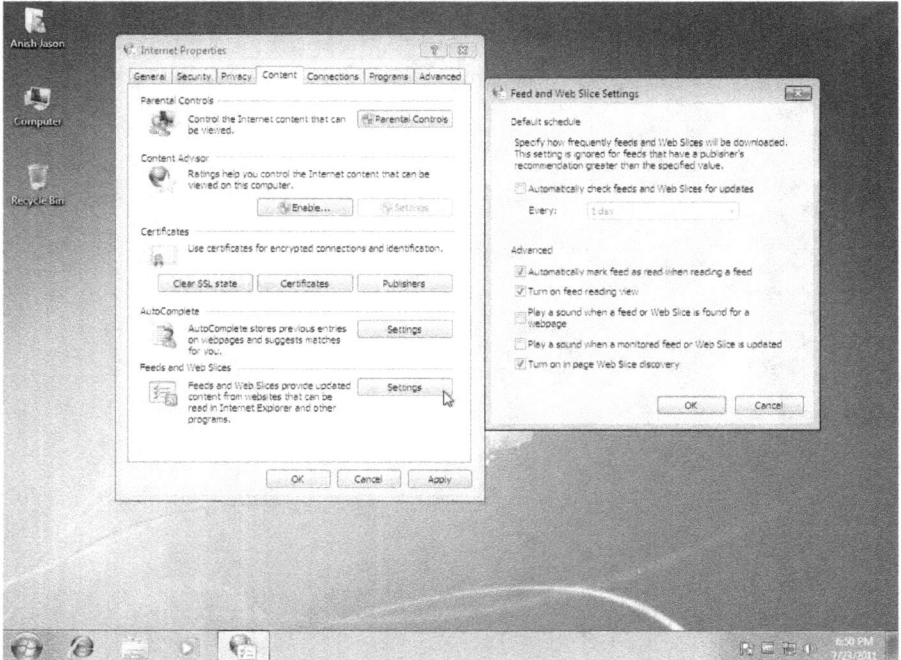

Managing Add-ons in IE 8

Add-ons in Internet Explorer in Windows 7 allow users to enable some additional features in the application. These features may include search bars offered by various search engines, for example, Yahoo, Google, Bing, etc. Moreover, some accelerators like Maps, E-Mails, Translate, etc. can also be installed in the form of add-ons in Internet Explorer 8 in Windows 7. Toolbar extensions and ActiveX controls add-ons can also be installed in Internet Explorer offered by Windows 7 operating system. Also several add-ons can be installed in the web browser, however there is still a limit as the more the add-ons are installed the reduced performance users will experience. The best part is that add-ons can be enabled or disabled as per the requirements and they are not required to be permanently uninstalled if they are not required. Any Windows 7 user can manage these add-ons according to the requirements and can customize their availability as desired. As a Windows 7 user if you want to manage these add-ons you are required to follow the steps given below:

1. Log on to Windows 7 computer with the user account in which you want to manage add-ons.

2. Click **Start** to and from the available list click **Control Panel**.

3. From the opened page click **Network and Internet** link and from the appeared page click **Internet Options**.

4. On **Internet Properties** box go to **Programs** tab and under **Manage add-ons** section click **Manage Add-ons** button to add or remove the add-ons.

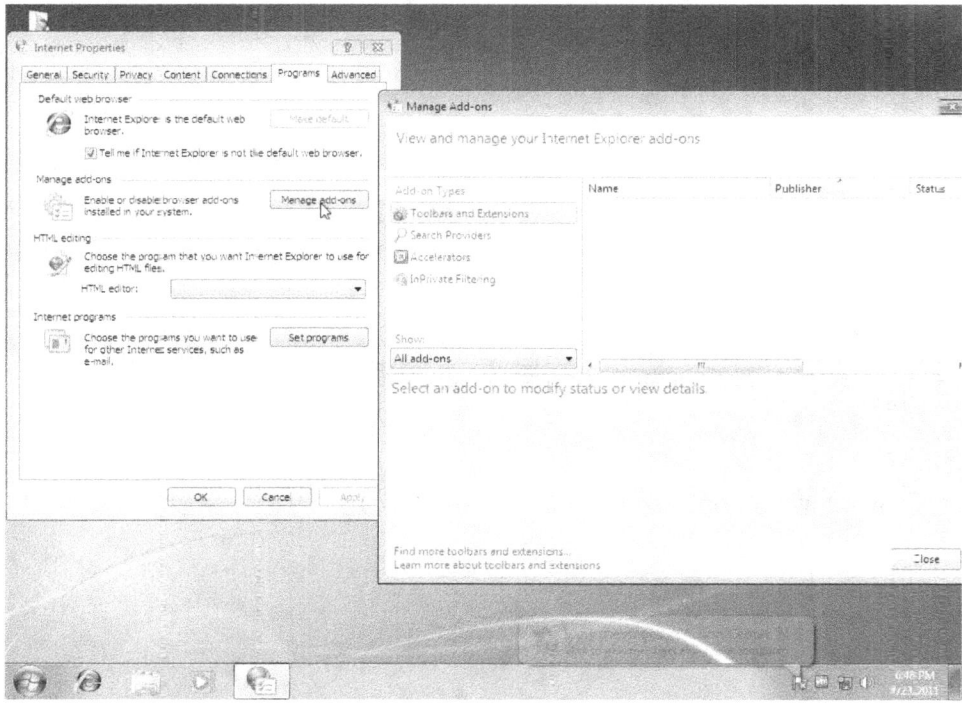

5. Once done, click **Ok** buttons on all the opened boxes to save the changes you have made.

Clearing History of Internet Explorer 8

We visit thousands of sites through different browsers and those browsers keep on saving history of what we had visited. Sometimes it is good that if we want to know the visited sites we can go there again but there are many people who don't want anyone or anybody to know about the pages they have viewed. Suppose you have visit a secured banking site which you don't want anyone to know about. What you can do is that you can delete all your records and tracks so that no one can ever find which site you visited earlier. Clearing browser history is a simple method for deleting Internet Explorer history states. These histories provide users better and faster surfing experience. Many people know from where to delete browser history and for those who don't know but want to delete the history they can follow these steps,

1. Log on to Windows 7 computer with any account.
2. Click **Start** button and then click **Control Panel**.
3. Open **Internet Options**.
4. Go to **General** tab.
5. Under Browsing history section click **Delete** button.

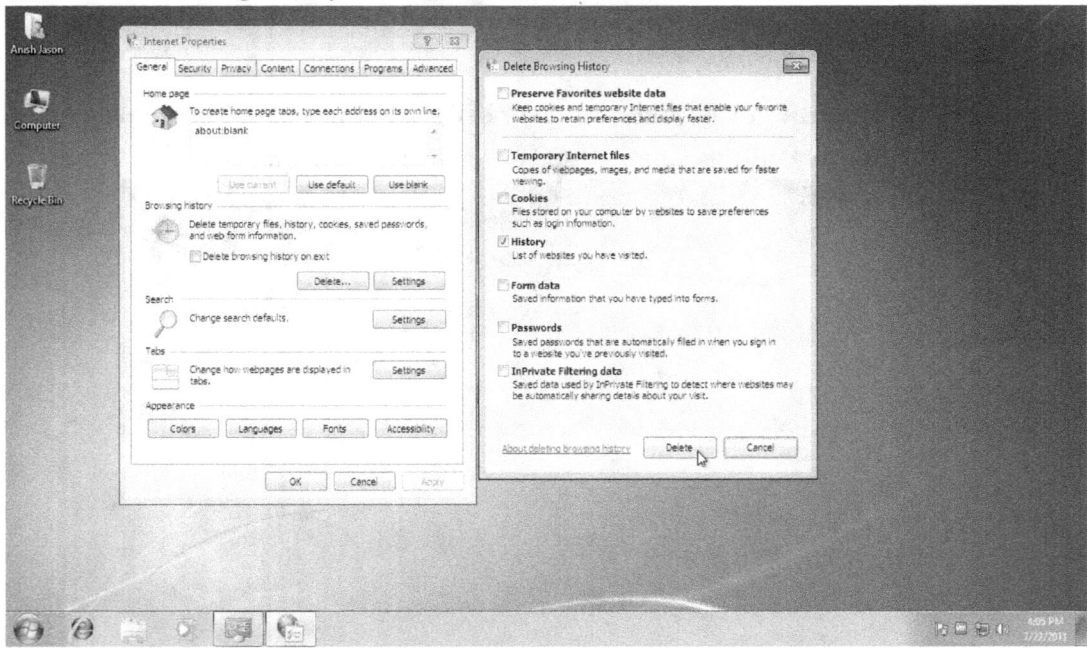

6. A window will open and in this window check **History** checkbox and click **Delete** button.

Delete Single Internet Explorer History Entry

When Windows 7 was released, Internet Explorer 8 was also integrated in the operating system and was shipped along with it. Unlike the features offered by older versions of Internet Explorer, IE 8 offers several new features that prove to be quite helpful and secured as far as privacy of the computer and individual user account is concerned. In home environments basic privacy measure that users seek is how to erase history of recently visited sites. There are several options which can be used to accomplish the task however almost all of them are capable of deleting entire history of Internet Explorer address bar. With the help of Internet Explorer 8 now users can delete even a single address bar history by following the steps given below:

1. Log on to Windows 7 computer with the account from which you want to erase a single address bar history of Internet Explorer.

2. Open **Internet Explorer** by clicking on its icon either on the quick launch toolbar or from start menu.

3. On **Internet Explorer** window click on the triangle at the end of the address bar to view the list of recently visited sites.

4. Take the mouse pointer to the name of the site you wish to delete and click on the red **X** button at the right most corner of the address.

Delete Stored Passwords in Internet Explorer

By default Internet Explorer prompts users to store their usernames and passwords to make their surfing and authentication process to the sites easier. For home users this configuration is ideal, or in fact considered as the best setting. However in production environments or at the places where a single computer is shared among several users, such as Internet cafes, this feature should NOT be used for various security reasons. You can erase stored passwords and other browsing history from Internet Explorer in a Windows 7 computer by following the steps given below:

1. Log on to the computer.

2. Click **Start** button.

3. From the start menu go to **All Programs** and from the opened list click **Internet Explorer**.

4. On the **Internet Explorer** click **Tools** menu and from the drop-down menu click **Internet Options**.

5. On **Internet Options** box make sure that you are on **General** tab and under **Browsing History** section click **Delete** button.

6. On **Delete Browsing History** box check all the available checkboxes and click **Delete** button.

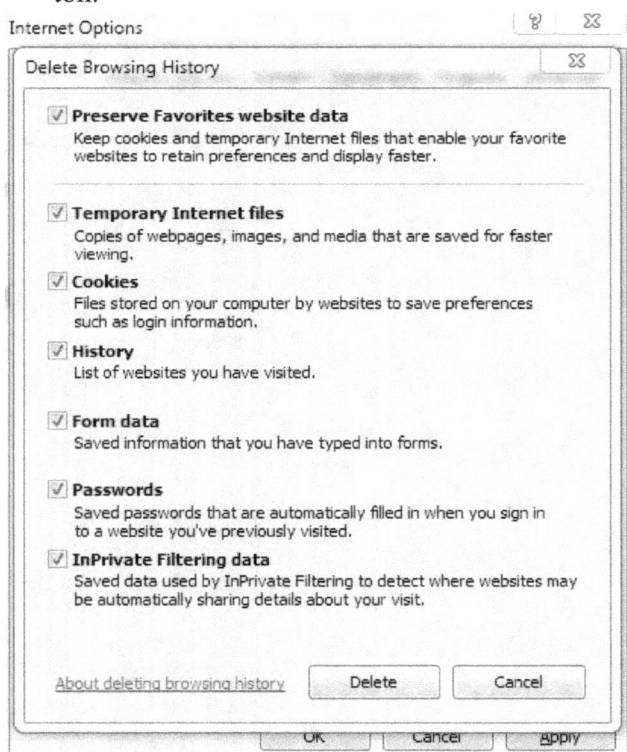

7. Once done, click **Ok** button on all opened boxes and Windows to accept and confirm your configuration. If necessary, logoff and re-logon to allow the changes to take effect.

Remove Internet Explorer 8

With the installation of Microsoft Windows 7, Internet Explorer 8 is also automatically installed on the computer. For home users and in any small-scale industry this built-in default web browser serves the purpose at its best however in many production environments and medium to large scale industries many administrators prefer any third-party browser to exploit the features offered by them fully. Moreover in such cases administrators may also want to uninstall the default built-in Internet Explorer 8 from Windows 7 because of several security reasons. When this is the case, after installing any third-party web browser application on Windows 7 computer if administrators want to uninstall Internet Explorer 8 they need to follow the steps given as below:

1. Log on to Windows 7 computer with any account that has elevated privileges.
2. Click **Start** button and from the available menu click **Control Panel**.
3. On the opened window click **Programs**.
4. On the next page click **Turn Windows features on or off** link under **Programs and Features** category.
5. On **Windows Features** box uncheck **Internet Explorer 8** checkbox and on the confirmation box click **Yes** button to continue the process.

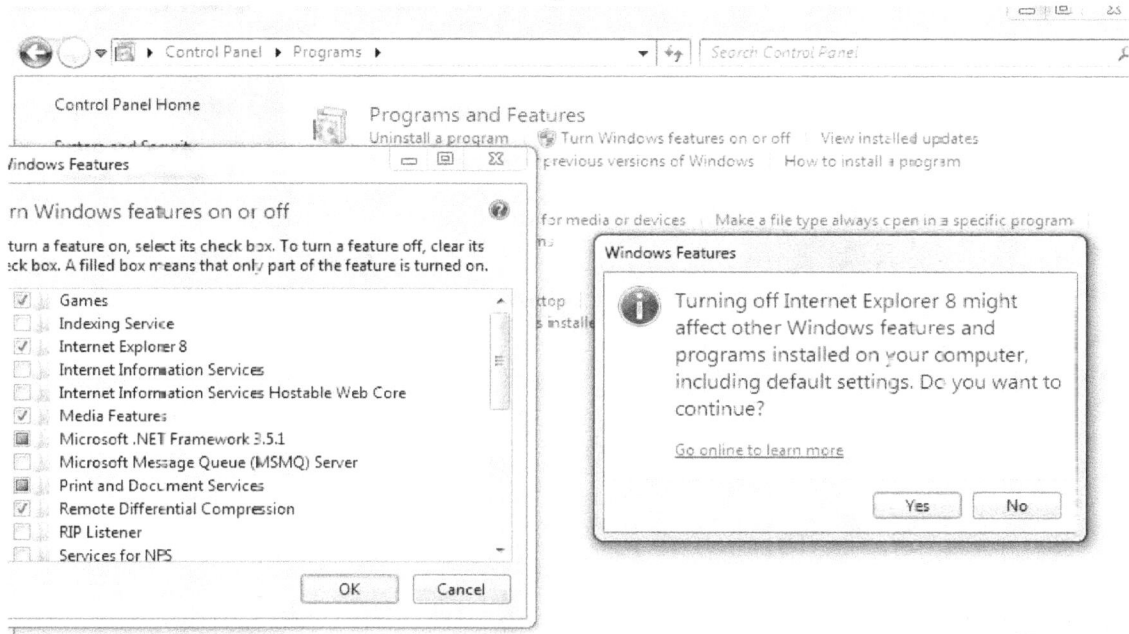

6. Once done, close all the Windows and boxes and if required restart the computer.

CHAPTER 11

NETWORKING

Provide Static IP Address on a LAN Card

By default all LAN cards (including Microsoft Loopback Adapter) are configured to obtain IP addresses automatically, that is from DHCP server. However, in some cases where DHCP server is not available you need to provide an IP address to the LAN card on your computer manually. Same is the case with Microsoft Loopback Adapter in which you need to provide a static IP address in order to enable it to communicate with virtual LAN card present on the virtual machine. Process of providing static IP address on physical machine is identical to that of virtual machine. Below are the steps using which you will be able to provide a static IP address to any LAN card available on your computer. However, the example below is focused on specifying static IP address to the Microsoft Loopback Adapter.

1. Click **Start** button.
2. At the bottom of the start menu in the search box type **NCPA.CPL** command and press Enter key.
3. On the **Network Connections** window right click on the icon of the LAN card which says **Microsoft Loopback Adapter** and from the context menu select **Properties**.
4. On the **Local Area Connection Properties** box select **Internet Protocol Version 4 (TCP/IPv4)** and click on **Properties** button.
5. On the **Internet Protocol Version 4 (TCP/IPv4) Properties** box select **Use the following IP address** radio button and provide the IP address of any range in front of **IP Address** text box. For this example let it be 192.168.0.1.
6. Provide subnet mask 255.255.255.0 in the **Subnet mask** text box and click **Ok** button on all windows to accept and confirm your configuration.

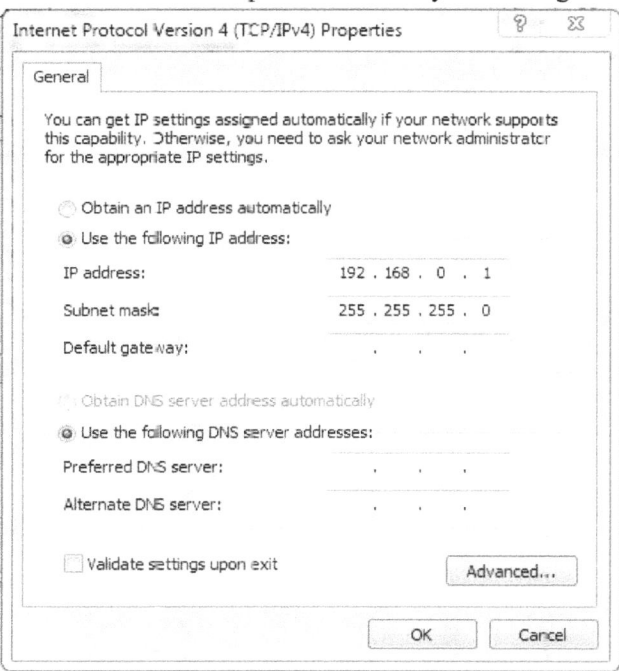

Virtual Machine Settings:

Once you are done, you need to follow the same process to provide static IP address on virtual machine. IP address should be different though. For example, on virtual machine you can define 192.168.0.2 as IP Address and 255.255.255.0 as Subnet Mask to enable communication between physical and virtual machines.

Assign More than One IP Address to a NIC

You can assign multiple IP addresses to a single LAN card. This feature allows you to connect to multiple network segments using single NIC, however at the cost of chances of bottlenecks. This means that if a LAN card has multiple IP addresses it will send or receive more packets thus facing congestion during transfer process. This type of setup can still be useful in small scenarios where there are separate network segments but the total scale of network is not quite large. In order to provide multiple IP addresses to a single LAN card you need to follow the below steps:

1. Click **Start** button.
2. At the bottom of the menu in the search box type **NCPA.CPL** and press enter key.
3. On **Network Connections** page right click on the NIC on which you want to assign multiple IP addresses and click **Properties.**
4. In the **Local Area Properties** box from the list select **Internet Protocol Version 4(TCP/IPv4)** and click **Properties** button.
5. On **Internet Protocol Version 4(TCP/IPv4) Properties** page click **Advanced** button.
6. In **Advance TCP/IP Settings** page ensure that you are on the **IP Settings** tab and click **Add** button.
7. On **TCP/IP Address** page type the IP address and its subnet mask and click **Add** button.

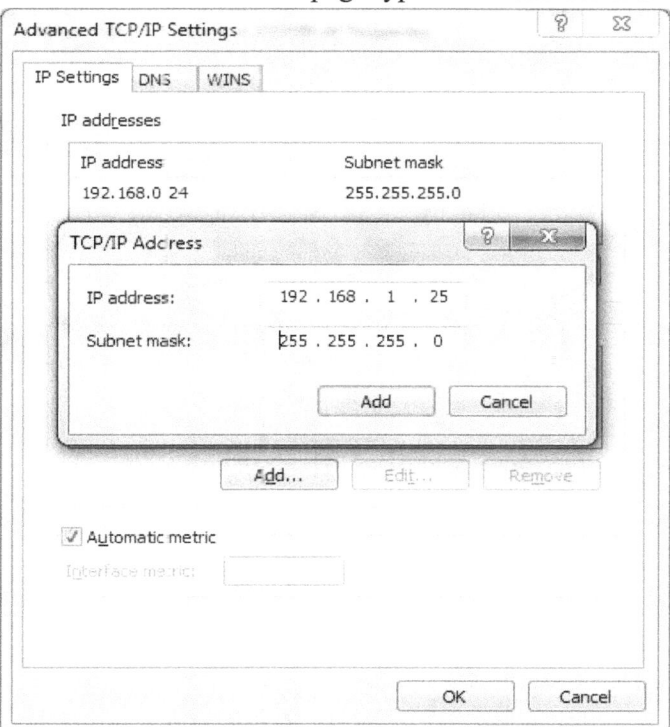

8. Click Ok button on all windows to accept and confirm your selections. Alternatively you can repeat Steps 6 and 7 every time you need to assign IP address to the NIC.

Assign More Than Two DNS Server Addresses

There are times when your Windows 7 computer is connected to a network infrastructure where you have more than two DNS servers. A simple network scenario may be a network setup with two local DNS servers and one DNS server of ISP. In this type of setup sometimes you might want to assign three DNS servers to your Windows 7 computer to get optimum performance. You can do so by following the below steps:

1. Click **Start** button.

2. At the bottom of the menu in the search box type **NCPA.CPL** and press enter key.

3. On **Network Connections** page right click on the NIC on which you want to assign multiple DNS addresses and click **Properties.**

4. In the **Local Area Properties** box from the list select **Internet Protocol Version 4(TCP/IPv4)** and click **Properties** button.

5. On **Internet Protocol Version 4(TCP/IPv4) Properties** page click **Advanced** button.

6. In **Advance TCP/IP Settings** page click **DNS** tab and click **Add** button.

7. On **TCP/IP DNS Server** box type the address of additional DNS server and click **Add** button.

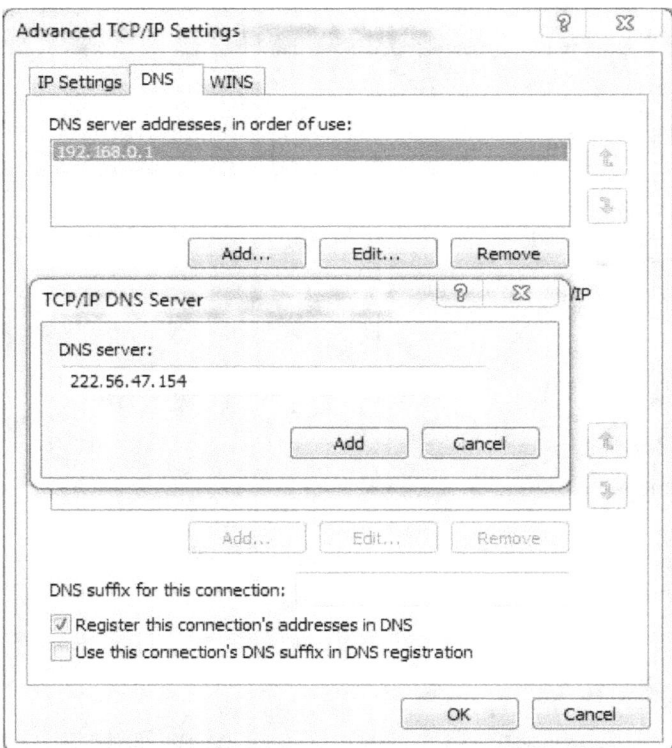

8. Click **Ok** button on all the windows to accept and confirm your selection/configuration. Alternatively you can repeat Steps 6 and 7 multiple times if you want to add multiple DNS server addresses.

Real World Scenario Tip:

While defining multiple DNS servers which include IP addresses of both local and ISP's DNS server make sure that you assign local DNS server address as Preferred DNS server and ISP's DNS server as an Alternate or Additional DNS server. If you assign ISP's DNS server as Preferred DNS you would experience extremely slow communication between the computers connected within a local area network.

Find Assigned IP Address

In any version of Microsoft operating system IP address is a dotted decimal 32-bit number which contains four octets. This IP address is supported by its respective subnet mask which allows administrators to specify as how many computers can be connected together in a particular subnet. In small network environments administrators specify IP addresses manually but in large network environments these IP addresses are dynamically assigned to the client computers by DHCP servers. In later cases sometimes it becomes very hectic for normal users to identify their own IP addresses which may be asked by the administrators who might be working at any distant geographical location. By following the steps given below users can easily identify the IP addresses that are assigned to the computers which further may help administrators to diagnose and rectify the problems.

1. Log on to Windows 7 computer with any account as this process does not require elevated privileges.

2. At the bottom of start menu in search box type **CMD** and press enter key.

3. On the open command window type **IPCONFIG** command and hit enter key to know the IP address that is assigned to the computer. Alternatively you can also type **IPCONFIG /ALL** command to view the entire configurations of network adapters available on the computer.

Assign Static/Dynamic IP Address Using Batch File

IP addresses can be assigned to a Windows 7 computer instantaneously using batch files. This means that you need to create appropriate batch files in order to assign static or dynamic IP addresses to the computer. Below are the steps using which you will be able to create a batch file with .bat extension which, when executed, will assign a specified IP address to the machine. Also you will learn to create another batch file which will configure your Windows 7 computer to obtain IP address automatically from a DHCP server.

1. Click **Start** button.

2. At the bottom of start menu search box type **NOTEPAD** and press **Enter** key.

3. In the notepad type **NETSH INTERFACE IPV4 SET ADDRESS "Local Area Connection" STATIC 192.168.0.2 255.255.255.0 192.168.0.1** command where 192.168.0.2 is the static IP address, 255.255.255.0 is the subnet mask and 192.168.0.1 is the default gateway for the computer. IP address given above is just an example and you can use any IP address as per your choice.

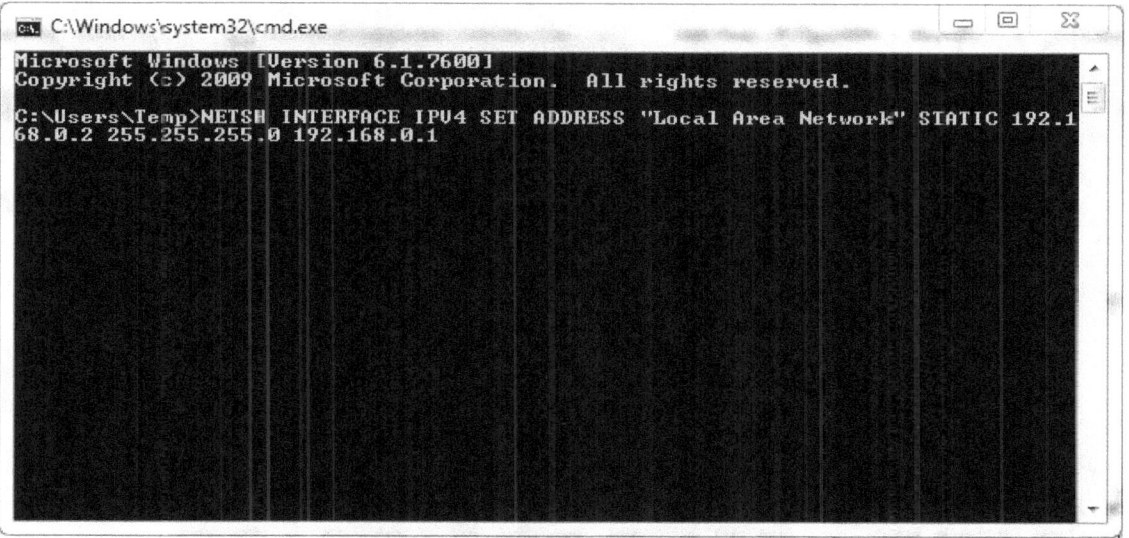

4. Once you are done, you need to save this notepad file with .bat extension. To do so press **CTRL+S** keys together and from the opened box specify the name of the file with .bat extension between double quotes. For example, "IPCH.BAT"

5. To run this file you need to right click on it and from the context menu select **Run as Administrator**.

6. To configure your Windows 7 computer to obtain IP address automatically from DHCP server you need to create another batch file containing **NETSH INTERFACE IPV4 SET ADDRESS NAME="Local Area Connection" SOURCE=DHCP** command.

Best Practices:

You can use this batch file to assign IP address easily and quickly. In case you want to change IP address you can modify this .bat file by right-clicking on it and selecting Edit from the context menu that appears. This practice will save you couple of clicks and lots of time.

Provide an Alternative IP Address to NICs

When Windows 7 is installed by default it is configured to obtain IP address automatically, that is from the DHCP server which can be present anywhere in the network. This default configuration is quite helpful for the administrators as they need not to move to every computer and type the IP addresses manually. However there may be times when DHCP server becomes unavailable because of any reason and in these cases computers may get self-generated IP addresses from Automatic Private IP Addressing (APIPA) feature of the operating system which has the default IP range of 169.254.0.0 with the subnet mask of 255.255.0.0. Addresses of this range might not be suitable for the computers used in production environments as with this IP address scheme they cannot communicate with the servers which might be assigned with different range of, most commonly static, IP addresses. In order to avoid this situation, administrators can provide alternative IP addresses to the computers which can be used by them in case of unavailability of DHCP server. As an administrator in such scenario if you want to assign an alternative IP address to the computer you are required to follow the steps given below:

1. Log on to Windows 7 computer with administrator account.
2. In search box at the bottom of start menu type **NCPA.CPL** command and press enter key.
3. Right click on the network interface card that is connected to the network and from the available menu click **Properties**.
4. On the opened box double-click **Internet Protocol Version 4 (TCP/IPv4)** from the available list.
5. On the appeared box go to **Alternate Configuration** tab.
6. Click **User configured** radio button to select and populate the desired fields with appropriate values.

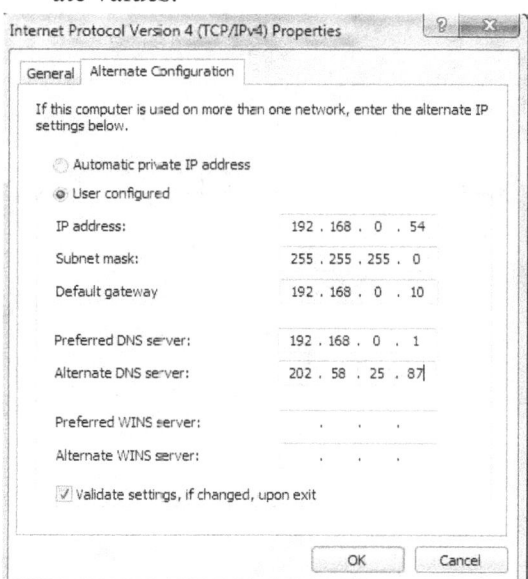

7. Once done, click Ok buttons on all the opened boxes to allow the changes to take effect.

Release and Renew IP Address

Whether Windows 7 computer is kept in home or production environment, it is very common that the operating system gets an IP address through DHCP server. In production networks DHCP server can be a dedicated computer which is precisely configured to serve the purpose whereas in homes Internet modem connected to a computer works as a DHCP server to the local computers. Internet modem connected to the computer works as DHCP server and provides an IP address automatically to it which helps computer to connect to the Internet easily. Since this IP address is dynamically assigned to the computer there are times when users experience connectivity problems. When this is the case users can release the IP address, which means that the computers will not have any IP address and the one which is assigned will be surrendered back to the DHCP server. After releasing the IP address they can request for a new one from the DHCP server which technically is known as renewing the IP address. As a Windows 7 user if you want to do so you are required to follow the steps given as below:

1. Log on to the Windows 7 computer with the account that has elevated privileges.
2. Click **Start** button and then click **All Programs**.
3. From the available list click on accessories container and right click **Command Prompt** to get the menu.
4. From the available options click **Run as administrator** and click **Yes** button on **User Account Control** confirmation box.
5. On the opened command window type **IPCONFIG /RELEASE** (to release the already assigned IP address) and then type **IPCONFIG /RENEW** (to request for a new IP address from DHCP server).

6. Close command window once you are done.

Network Discovery and File and Printer Sharing

In home or production environments when two PCs are required to connect with each other, it is essential that both the computers must be discoverable on the network. This helps remote users to locate the PCs and access shared files or folders remotely. By default Windows 7 computers are not discoverable on the network due to security reasons and this feature needs to be manually enabled when the PCs are connected. As an administrator you can make your Windows 7 computers discoverable on the network by following the steps given below:

1. Log on to the computer with administrator account.

2. Click **Start** button.

3. From the start menu go to **Control Panel** and from the opened window click **Network and Internet** category link.

4. The opened page click **Network and Sharing Centre** category link and on **View your basic network information and set up connections** page in the left bar click **Change advance sharing settings** link.

5. On **Change sharing options for different network profiles** page under **Network discovery section** select **Turn on network discovery** radio button and under **File and printer sharing section** select **Turn on file and printer sharing** radio button

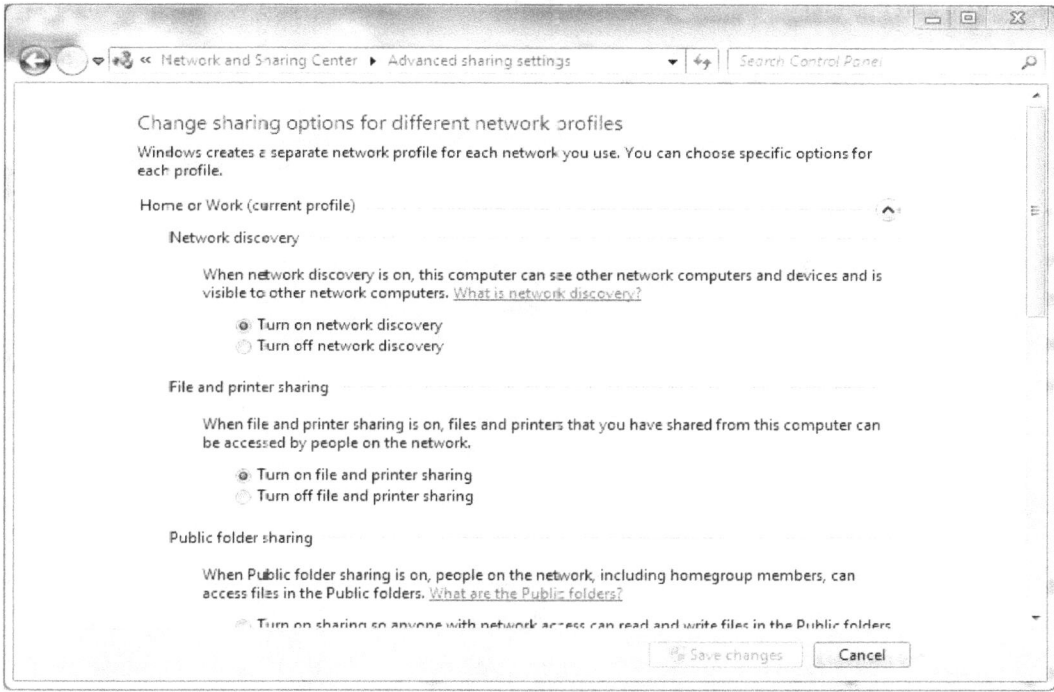

6. Once done, click Ok button to accept and confirm your selection and close the window.

Enable Internet Connection Sharing (ICS)

In Small Office/Home Office (SOHO) scenarios or in homes where more than two or more computers are present it becomes mandatory to share a common Internet connection between all. Many people think that this task is complicated and should be performed only by a certified professional. But in many cases this is not true at all. Sharing an Internet connection between 2 to 3 computers is quite easy and does not require a highly qualified professional to do so. However, there are few prerequisites which are to be met before you can configure Internet Connection Sharing on your Windows 7 computer. Below is the list of them:

Prerequisites:

- If you are trying to share your Internet connection between more than two computers you should have an Ethernet switch or hub.
- You should have at least two network interface cards present on your computer. One connected to the Internet and other connected to either other computer directly or to an Ethernet switch or hub.
- You should have Ethernet cable of appropriate length. If you are using wireless medium you should have appropriate Wireless Access Point (WAP).

Once you have collected and connected all the above devices you can follow the steps given below to configure ICS on your Windows 7 computer.

1. Click **Start** button.
2. At the bottom of start menu in the search box type **NCPA.CPL** and press enter key.
3. On the **Network Connections** page right click on the LAN card which is connected to the Internet and from the context menu select **Properties**.
4. In the **Local Area Connection Properties** box go to **Sharing** tab.
5. Under **Internet Connection Sharing** category select **Allow other network users to connect through this computer's Internet connection** radio button to enable ICS and click **Ok** button to accept and confirm your selection.

Best Practices:

To avoid confusion, always rename the LAN cards by right clicking on them and selecting **Rename** option from the context menu. LAN card which is connected to the Internet should be renamed as **INTERNET** or **PUBLIC** and the other one which is connected to local area network should be renamed as **PRIVATE** or **LOCAL AREA NETWORK**.

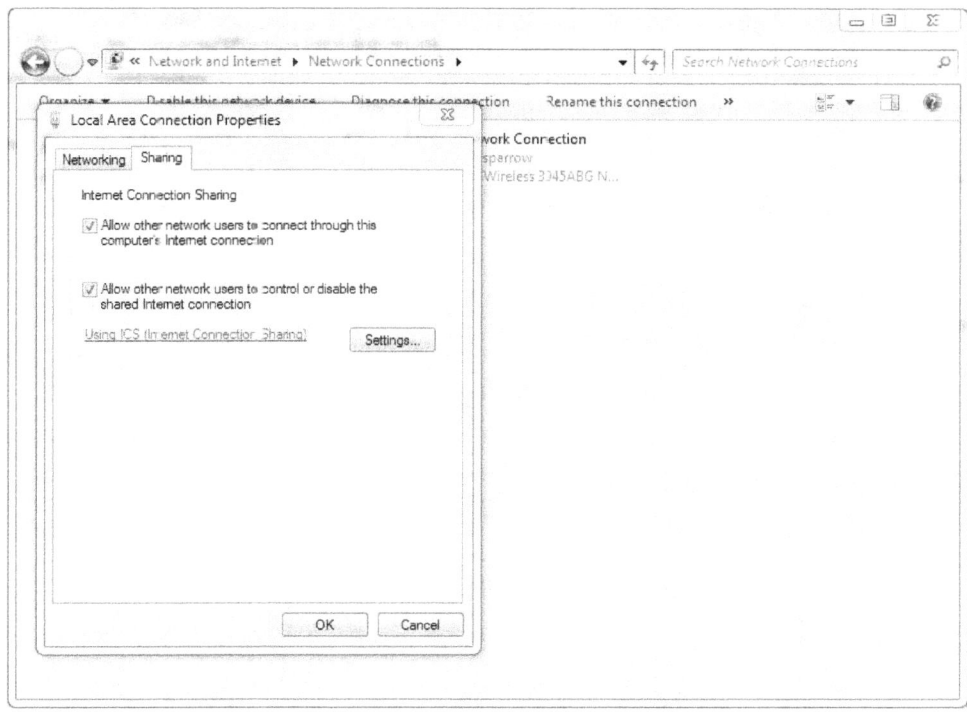

Note: Make sure that other LAN card and all other computers which are connected to Local Area Network are configured to obtain IP address from DHCP server (default configuration).

Manage Password Protected Sharing Feature

password protected sharing is the feature which when enabled requires remote users to authenticate their accounts by providing credentials on the shared computer before they are able to access files or folders on it. When this feature is turned off, Guest account is automatically enabled and whenever remote users try to access files and folders on the shared computer they are assigned with Guest account credentials for a temporary period. By default Windows 7 enables password protected sharing in order to make the computer and its information secured. However in secure environments, for example home networks, this feature can be disabled so that accessing files, folders on the shared computer can easily be done. As an administrator you can disable password protected sharing on a Windows 7 computer by following the steps given below:

1. Log on to the computer with administrator account.
2. Click **Start** button.
3. From the start menu go to **Control Panel** and from the opened window click **Network and Internet** category link.
4. The opened page click **Network and Sharing Centre** category link and on **View your basic network information and set up connections** page in the left bar click **Change advance sharing settings** link.
5. On **Change sharing options for different network profiles** page under **Password pro-tected sharing** section select **Turn off password protected sharing** radio button. (**Note: NOT recommended in production environments. FOR HOME USERS ONLY**).

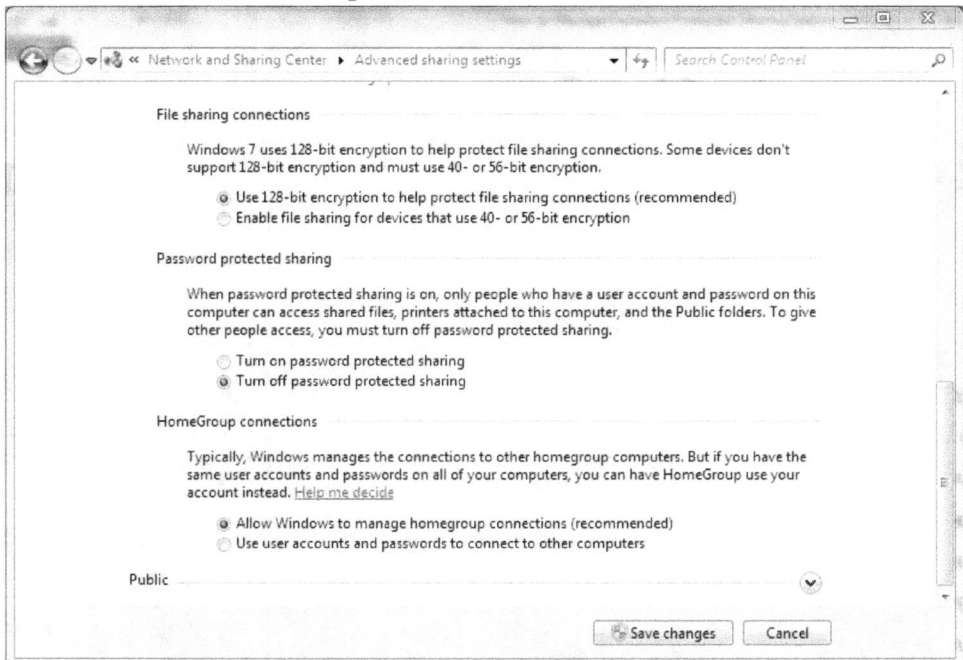

6. Once done, click Ok button to accept and confirm your selection and close the window.

Enable Network Access for Administrative Shares

In older versions of Microsoft operating systems accessing any shared folder was quite simple. However with the simplicity, also came the risks of sensitive information getting stolen. Since Windows 7 and Windows Vista are the operating systems which are considered to be highly secured as compared to the legacy versions, Microsoft has integrated another feature to harden the layers of security in the operating system. By default administrative shares cannot be accessed when Windows 7 or Windows Vista is installed on any computer. In order to make administrative shares available to the users across the network you need to follow the steps given below:

1. Log on to your Windows 7 computer with administrator account and click **Start** button.

2. At the bottom of start menu in search box type **REGEDIT** and press enter key to open **Registry Editor**.

3. On Registry Editor go to: **HKEY_LOCAL_MACHINE\SOFTWARE\Microsoft\Windows\CurrentVersion\Policies\System** location.

4. In the right pane right-click anywhere and point to **New**.

5. From the appeared submenu click **DWORD (32-bit) Value** and type **LocalAccountTokenFilterPolicy** as the name of the new entry.

6. Once done, double click on the newly created entry and from the opened box in **Value data** text box type **1** to enable administrative shares.

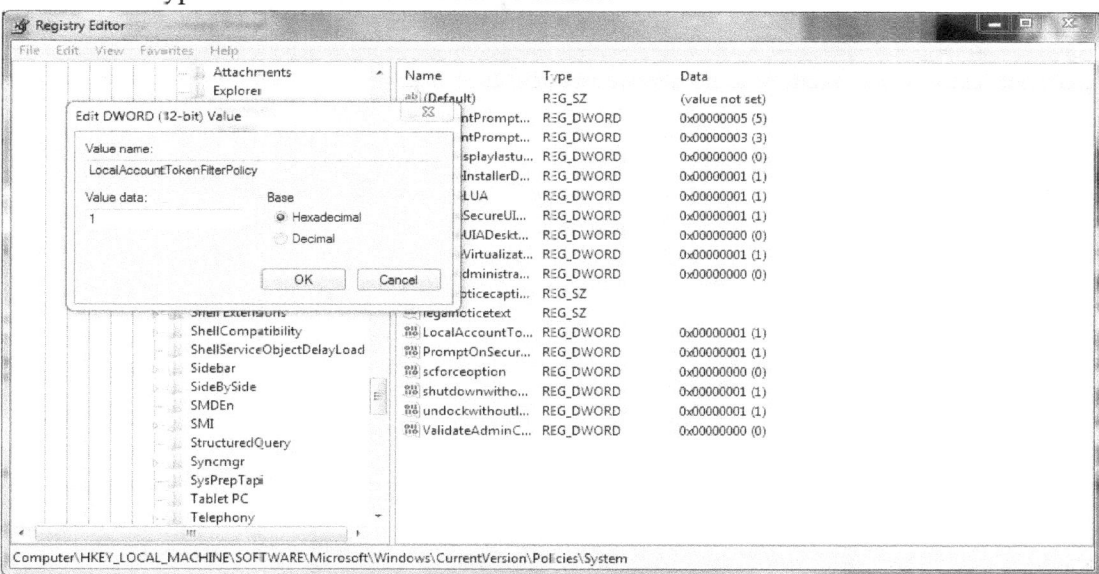

7. Click **Ok** button to confirm your settings and restart your computer to allow the configuration to take effect.

Note: You need to go through the above steps on all the computers on which you want to enable administrative share.

Manage Encryption for File and Printer Sharing

As Windows 7 is quite advanced it supports 128 bit encryption when sharing files or folders. However in some cases, or to be more precise, when communicating with legacy versions of Windows operating systems encryption of this level might not be appropriate as legacy operating systems might not support this type of encryption. When this is the case administrators may want to decrease the encryption bits in order to make Windows 7 computer compatible with lower versions of operating systems. As an administrator if you want to configure this you need to follow the steps given below:

1. Log on to the computer with administrator account.

2. Click **Start** button.

3. From the start menu go to **Control Panel** and from the opened window click **Network and Internet** category link.

4. The opened page click **Network and Sharing Centre** category link and on **View your basic network information and set up connections** page in the left bar click **Change advance sharing settings** link.

5. On **Change sharing options for different network profiles** page under **File sharing connections** category select **Enable file sharing devices use 40- or 50-bit encryption** radio button and click **Ok** button to accept your configuration.

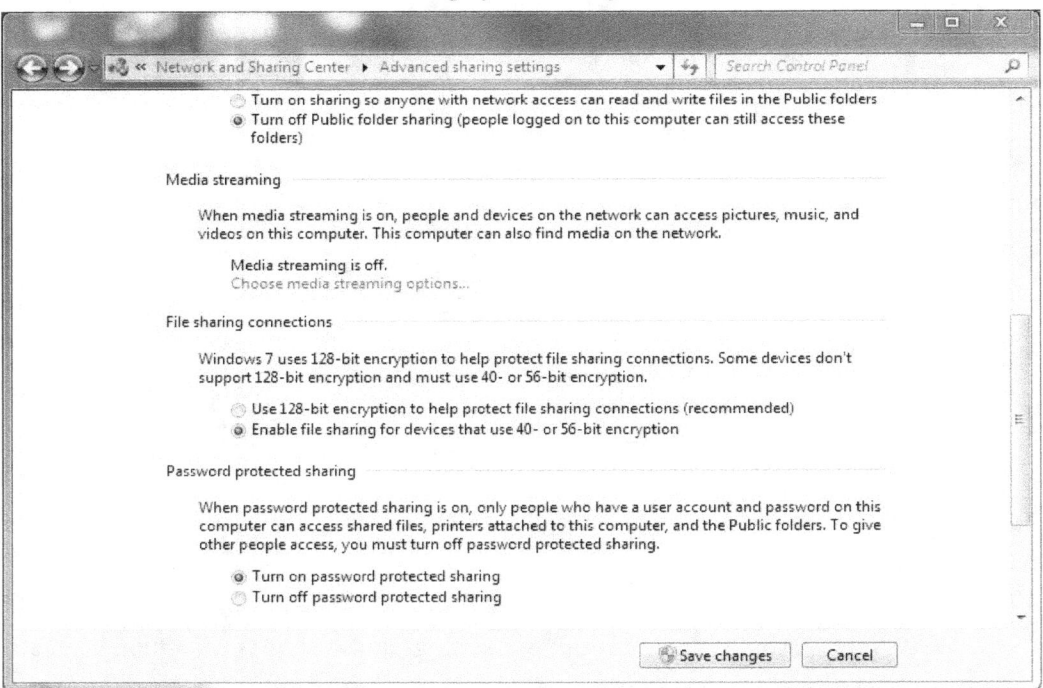

6. Close the opened window.

Share a Folder

Sharing a folder becomes essential when the computer is connected to the network and other users who are sitting on other computers want to access any file or folder which is present on the main computer. In order to access a folder or file located on the main computer, the folder must be shared. This can be done by following the instructions below:

1. Go to the drive where the folder you want to share is located.
2. Right click on the desired folder on which you want to enable sharing and select **Properties**.
3. From the **Properties** page go to **Sharing** tab.
4. On the **Sharing** page click **Advanced Sharing** button.
5. On the **Advanced Sharing** page check the checkbox that says **Share This Folder**.
6. Below the **Share Name** section in the text box you can either leave the default name as it is, alternatively you can type new share name for this folder. This will be the display name of this folder that will be displayed to the people who will access this computer through the network.

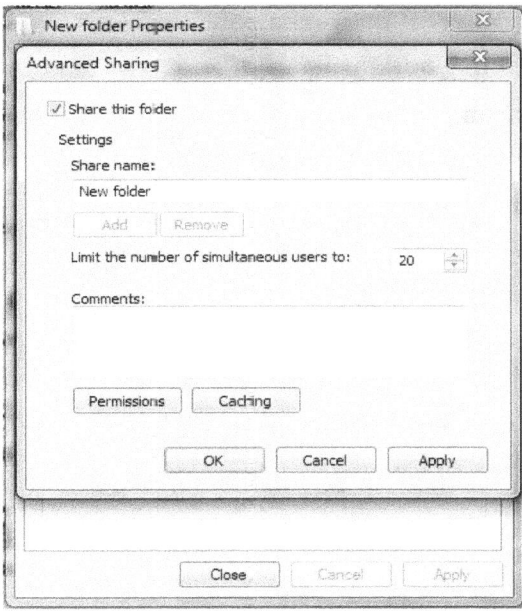

7. If you want other users to only read the contents from this folder from the network you can leave everything else as default and click **Ok** button to accept the selections. However if you want to assign some different permissions, such as enabling other users from the other computers on the network to paste or delete files on this shared folder, you can specify share permissions by clicking **Permissions** button. By default **Everyone** group is assigned with **Read** permissions.
8. Select appropriate permissions from the permissions page.
9. Click Ok button on all windows to accept and confirm your selections.

Share Streaming Media

Home PCs are always expected to contain personal files and other information. These files may include family pictures, home parties' videos, picnic snaps, etc. In home environments where there are two or more PCs these files can be shared as it is considered that home environments are always trustworthy. When this is the case administrators may want to enable streaming media sharing feature in order to make personal video or audio file sharing easier. As an administrator if you want to configure this setting on your computer you need to follow the steps given below:

1. Log on to the computer with administrator account.

2. Click **Start** button.

3. From the start menu go to **Control Panel** and from the opened window click **Network and Internet** category link.

4. The opened page click **Network and Sharing Centre** category link and on **View your basic network information and set up connections** page in the left bar click **Change advance sharing settings** link.

5. On **Change sharing options for different network profiles** page under **Media streaming** section click **Choose media streaming options** link.

6. On the opened page click **Turn on media streaming** button and from **Choose media streaming options for computers and devices** page click **Ok** button.

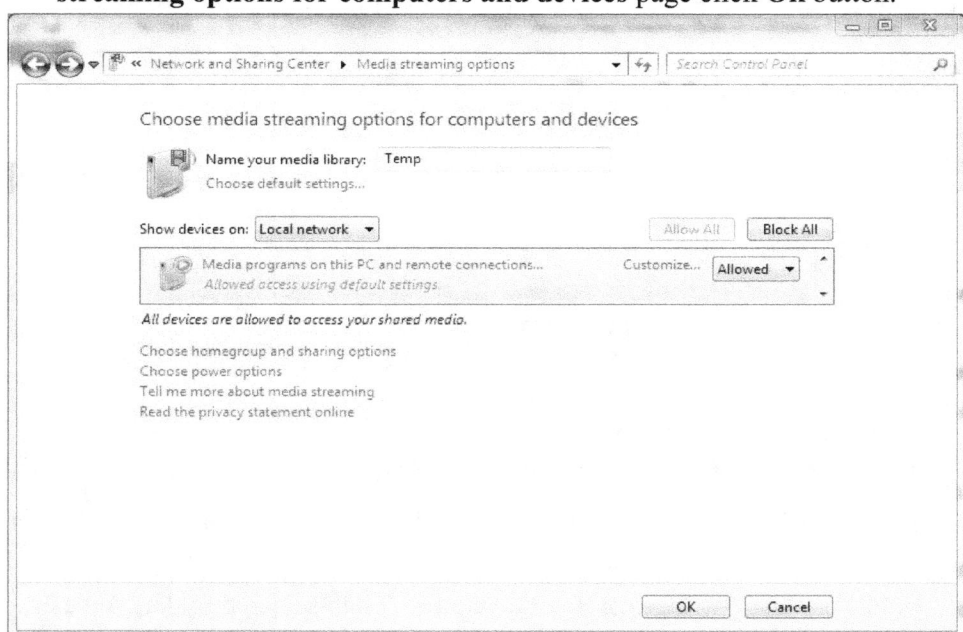

7. Once done, close all opened Windows.

Add a Windows 7 Computer to an Existing Domain

Although Windows 7 is quite user friendly it can also be configured to work as a client computer to any Domain Controller in any client-server network scenario. Except Home series of Windows 7 flavors all other versions of the OS can be added to domain.

There are few prerequisites that a Windows 7 computer must meet before it can be added to a domain. These prerequisites are:

- Computer must not have Windows 7 Starter, Home Basic or Home Premium flavors of operating systems installed as these flavors cannot join a domain.
- Domain Controller must be present in your network.
- DNS server must be present in your network.
- The computer must be connected to the network either via cable or through wireless medium.
- If DHCP server is not present in your infrastructure static IP address should be provided to the computer.
- If DHCP server is not present in your infrastructure static DNS address should be provided to the computer.

Once above prerequisites are met, you can add your Windows 7 computer to the existing domain by following the steps given below:

1. Log on to the computer with the user account that has Administrative privileges.
2. Click **Start** button.
3. In the start menu right-click **Computer** and select **Properties**.
4. In the **View basic information about your computer** page under **Computer name, domain, and workgroup settings** frame click **Change settings** link.
5. In the **System Properties** box ensure that you are **Computer Name** tab and click **Change** button.
6. On the **Computer Name/Domain Changes** box select **Domain** radio button under **Member of** section and type the name of the domain to which you want to add this computer.
7. Click or button.
8. In the opened window provide the credentials of domain administrator and click **Ok** button to accept and confirm your configuration. Alternatively, you can also provide credentials of a domain user account to this computer to the domain.
9. You will be displayed with a message box welcoming you to the domain and Windows will ask you to restart the computer

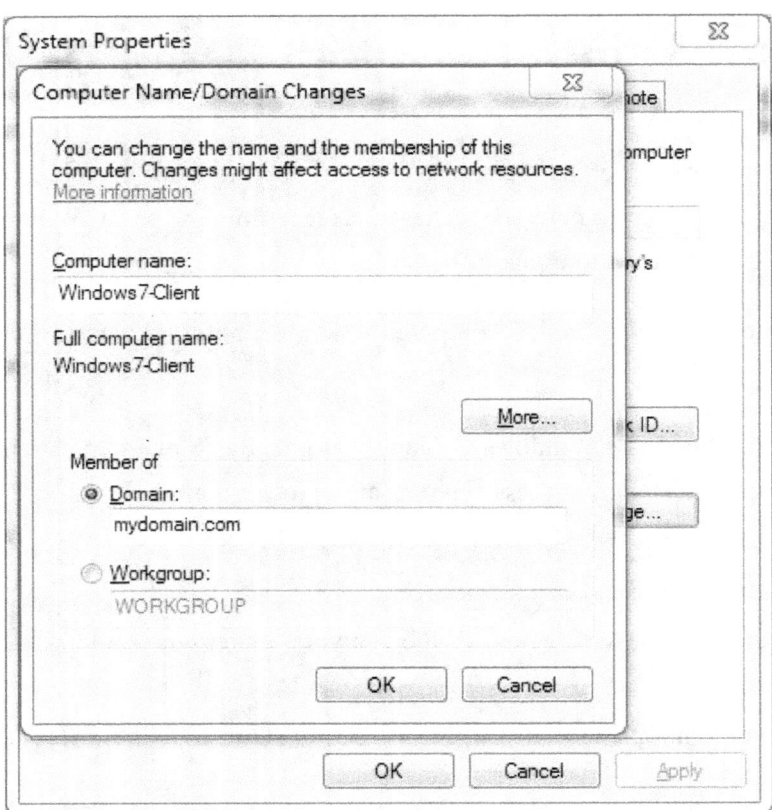

.

Note: Any domain user account credentials can be used to add a computer to a domain. A domain user account can add up to 10 computers (workstations) to a domain using its own credentials.

Use Windows 7 Computer as a Telnet Client

There might be times when you need to connect to another machine or a router through Telnet. If you are Windows XP or Windows server 2003 user you would definitely face problem while using Telnet feature. Unlike Windows XP or Windows server 2003, you need to enable Telnet Client feature before you can use it to connect to another computer or router. Below are the instructions which will tell you how to enable Telnet Client feature in a Windows 7 computer.

1. Click **Start** button.
2. From the menu click **Control Panel**.
3. Click **Programs** link.
4. Under **Programs and Features** category click **Turn Windows features on or off** link.
5. From the **Windows Features** box check **Telnet Client** checkbox and click **Ok** button.
6. Wait until the process is completed.

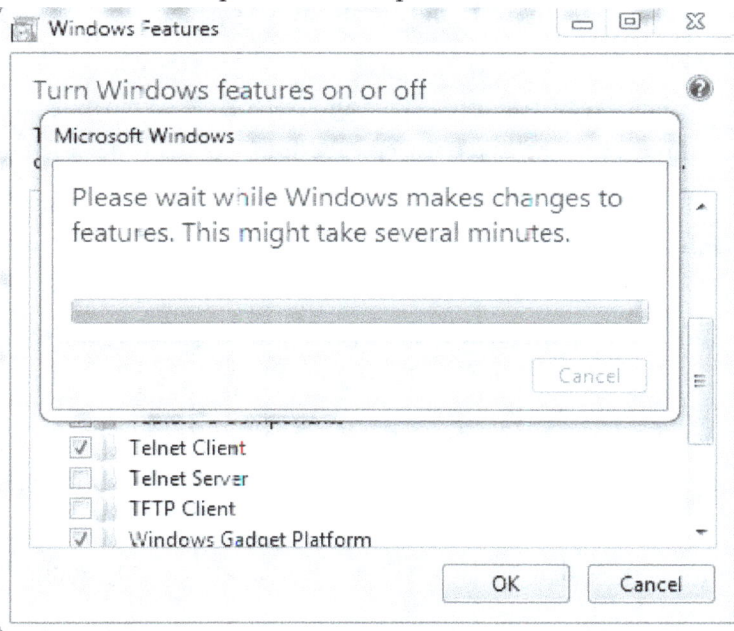

7. Close **Control Panel** window.
8. To check your configuration you can open **Command Prompt** and type "**Telnet**" (without quotes). You will instantaneously be taken to **Microsoft Telnet** prompt. If it happens this means that Telnet client is successfully configured in your machine.

More Info:

Telnet works on port 23 and is an application layer protocol. In Windows XP and Windows server 2003 by default Telnet service was not started and administrators manually needed to start this service from SERVICES.MSC window.

Establish a New Ad-hoc Wireless Connection

Wireless connections have 2 topologies and you can implement any one as per your requirements. The first topology is known as Infrastructure in which there is one Wireless Access Point (WAP) and all wireless clients that communicate with each other use this Wireless Access Point as their central device. This means that every communication that takes place is via WAP. This scenario is best suited in production environments where there are several wireless clients and they need to connect with each other. However in home environments where there two or three laptop PCs which are to be connected with each other, it would not be feasible to purchase Wireless Access Point. On the contrary it is advisable that in these cases people should use Ad-hoc topologies to save money and time. As a home user you can establish an ad-hoc (peer-to-peer) wireless connection by following the steps given below:

1. Log on to the computer with administrator account.
2. Click **Start** button.
3. From the start menu go to **Control Panel** and from the opened window click **Network and Internet** category link.
4. The opened page click **Network and Sharing Centre** category link and on **View your basic network information and set up connections** page in the left bar click **Manage wireless networks** link.
5. On **Manage wireless networks that use (Wireless Network Connection)** page click **Add** button.
6. On **Manually connect to a wireless network** window select **Create an ad hoc network** category.
7. On **Set up a wireless ad hoc network** page click **Next** button.
8. On the next page populate the blank fields as per the desired information and click **Next** button. (Note: If you are trying to join an existing ad hoc network you need to populate these fields with information of that ad hoc wireless setup which may include SSID and pre-shared key).
9. Wait for the process to complete and on the confirmation window click Close button

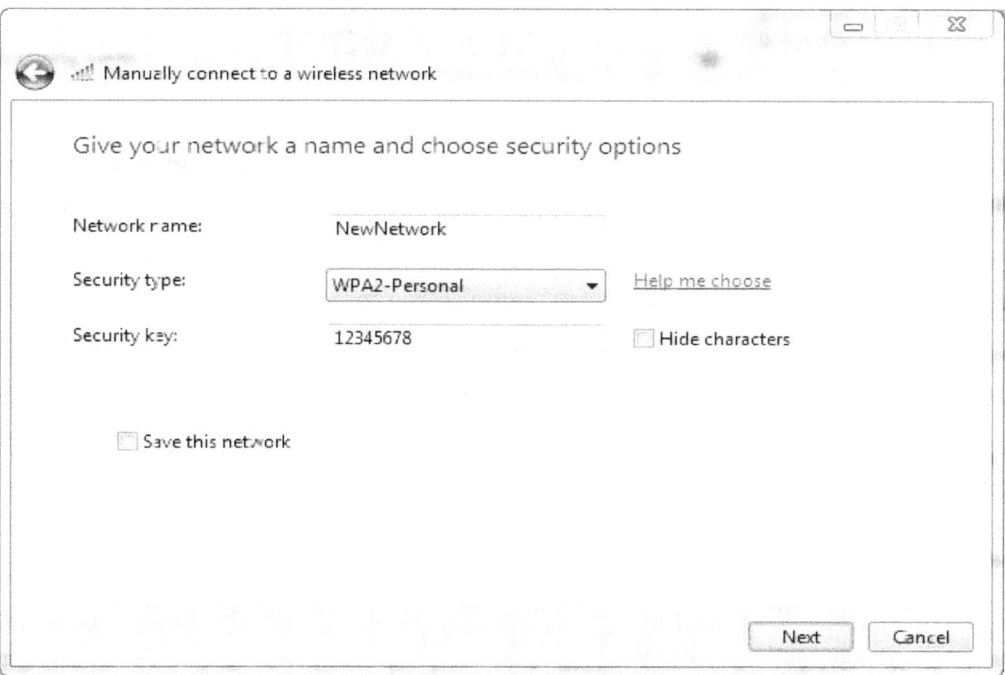

Install Microsoft Loopback Adapter

When you have no network connection available on your computer and still you want your physical machine to communicate with virtual machine, you need to install Microsoft Loopback Adapter on the physical machine and map the LAN card on virtual machine (virtual LAN card) with it. After you have mapped Virtual LAN Card with Microsoft Loopback Adapter of physical machine you need to provide static IP addresses of common range on both the cards to enable communication between them. Below are the instructions using which you can install Microsoft Loopback Adapter on a Windows 7 computer.

1. Click **Start** button.

2. From the start menu right click **Computer** and select **Manage**.

3. On **Computer Management** snap-in in the left pane select **Device Manager**.

4. On the right pane from the device list right-click on the name of the computer and select **Add legacy hardware**.

5. On **Welcome to the Add Hardware Wizard** page click **Next** button.

6. On the next page select **Install the hardware that I manually select from list (Advanced)** radio button and click **Next** button.

7. On the next page select **Network adapters** from the **Common hardware types** list and click **Next** button.

8. On **Select Network Adapter** page under **Manufacturer** section select **Microsoft**.

9. Under **Network Adapter** section select **Microsoft Loopback Adapter** and click **Next** button.

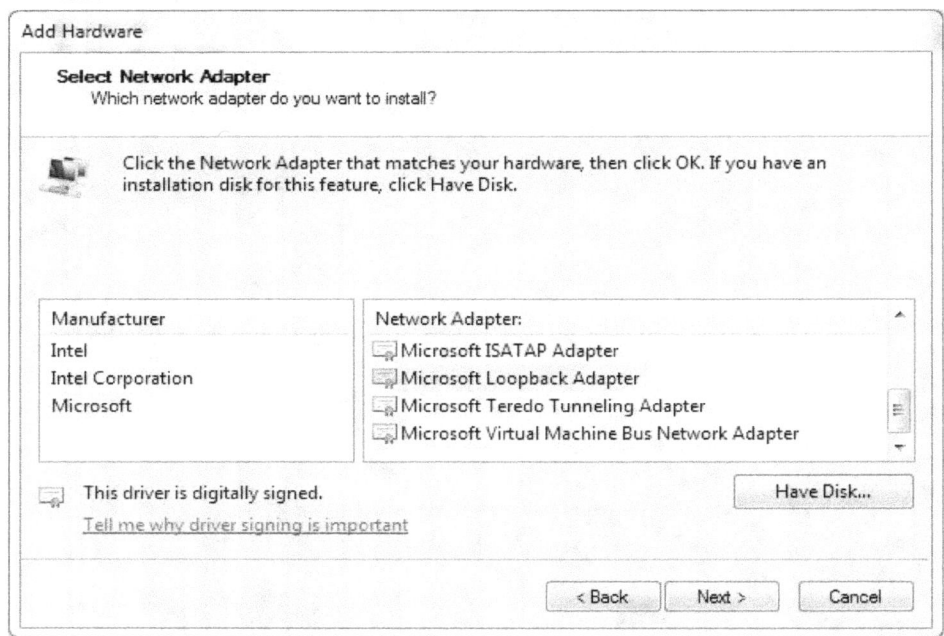

10. On the **Hardware to Install** page click **Next** button to start the installation process.

11. On **Completing the Add Hardware Wizard** page click **Finish** button and finally close **Computer Management** snap-in.

After successful completion of installation of Microsoft Loopback Adapter you can map it with the virtual LAN card of the virtual machine. Once done, you can go to Network Connections page on the physical machine and provide a static IP address to the newly installed Microsoft Loopback Adapter and an IP address of the same range on virtual LAN card to enable communication between Virtual and Physical Machines.

CHAPTER 12
REMOTE DESKTOP CONNECTION

Enable Remote Desktop

Remote Desktop is a feature using which you, as an Administrator of a computer, can access a machine from any other computer which can be located in other room or totally different geographical location. This feature is helpful for those who manage several remote computers from a central location. This feature is also valuable for those who have Small Office Home Office (SOHO) setups and they don't want main computers to be accessed by logging on directly to them.

In order to enable Remote Desktop feature, below instructions are to be followed:

1. Click **Start** button.
2. From the menu right-click **Computer** and select **Properties**.
3. In **System** page in the left pane click **Remote Settings** link.
4. On the **System Properties** box ensure that you are on the **Remote** tab.
5. In the **Remote Desktop** section in **Remote** tab select **Allow connections from computers running any version of Remote Desktop (less secure)** radio button if you want to remotely manage your system from Windows 2000, Windows XP or Windows Vista/7 computers. Alternatively if you want to Remote Desktop your computer from any Windows Vista or Windows 7 computer only you can select **Allow connections only from computers running Remote Desktop with Network Level Authentication (more secure)**.

6. If you want users other than Administrators of your computer to remotely access the machine from other computers you can click **Select Users** button and specify the names of users you want to grant this privilege.

7. Press **Ok** button on all Windows to accept and confirm your configuration and selection.

Technical Info:

Remote Desktop uses TCP 3389 port to connect to other computers and the protocol used is Remote Desktop Protocol (RDP).

Initiate and Use Remote Desktop Connection

When working with large organizations, many people use Remote Desktop connection to perform administrative tasks on remote machines. Remote machines can be either at local premises in some different rooms or campuses or at distant places which might be geographically apart and connected through virtual private networks. Whatsoever the case is, Remote Desktop connection proves to be quite handy feature when it comes to management of multiple computers at different locations. Apart from large organizations, home users can also use Remote Desktop connection feature in order to manage computers which are kept in different rooms. Initiating and using Remote Desktop connection feature is quite easy and the steps do so are given below:

1. Log on to your local computer with any account of your choice. (Since you will be using this computer to connect to remote machine do not require administrative privileges here).

2. Once logged on click **Start** button and at the bottom of start menu in search box type **MSTSC** command and press enter key.

3. On **Remote Desktop Connection** console box in the available text box in front of **Computer**, type the IP address of the remote machine to which you want to connect and click **Connect** button.

4. Once done, you will be asked for the credentials (user name and password) of remote machine. Type in the appropriate information and click **Ok** button.

5. Accept all the confirmation boxes that appear to continue the process.

More Info:

Optionally you can go to **Start > All Programs > Accessories > Remote Desktop Connection** to remote desktop to the remote machine.

Note: To remote desktop any computer you need to have administrator account or any other account who is the member of Remote Desktop Users group on the remote machine. Also, remote computer should be configured to accept Remote Desktop connections which is by default turned off for security reasons.

Customize Remote Desktop Connection (.RDP) File

If you are a frequent Remote Desktop Connection user it might be quite tedious for you to type entire IP address and populate the fields with the credentials every time you want to Remote Desktop to any machine connected to your network. Microsoft understands this problem and therefore it has provided a facility using which you can save Remote Desktop settings and credentials for every computer to which you connect on regular basis. Remote desktop settings which you configure can be saved as an icon on your desktop with .RDP extension. Once you have created the icon you can double-click it and because of the saved credentials you will automatically be connected to the remote computer and the desktop screen of that computer will appear in front of you. In other words you do not have to type IP address, username and password every time you want to connect to the remote computer. You can do so by following the steps given below:

1. Initiate **Remote Desktop Connection** tool after you log on to your Windows 7 computer.

2. On the opened console window click **Options** button to view the hidden features.

3. Once expanded, type in the IP address and the username of the remote computer in their respective fields and check Allow me to save credentials checkbox.

4. Click **Save As** button and on the opened dialog box choose **Desktop** to save the icon after providing the appropriate file name.

5. Click **Save** button to save the dialog box on the desktop.

More Info:

When you will double-click on the saved icon for the very first time Windows will ask for the password for the remote user account. After providing the password you can check the Remember my credentials checkbox to store your username and password permanently.

Increase Remote Desktop Connection Speed

When Remote Desktop Connection is initiated, by default the connection speed to the remote computer is quite slow. The reason behind this is that Microsoft has designed the tool keeping in mind that Remote Desktop Connection tool will mostly be used for the computers which are located at geographically apart locations and will be connected through a slow WAN link. However, not overlooking the possibility that administrators may also want to use this feature in the offices and organizations that have huge campus areas, Microsoft also enables administrators to modify the settings and enhance the performance speed in order to expedite the entire Remote Desktop process. If you want to use Remote Desktop feature with clear graphics and other visual environments you need to follow the steps given below:

1. Log on to the Windows 7 computer with the account of your choice and at the bottom of start menu in search box type **MSTSC** and press enter key to initiate **Remote Desktop Connection** tool.

2. On the appeared console window click **Options** button to configure the additional settings granularly.

3. In the expanded box go to **Experience** tab from the available drop-down list choose **LAN (10 Mbps or Higher)**. Optionally you can check the available boxes as per your choice.

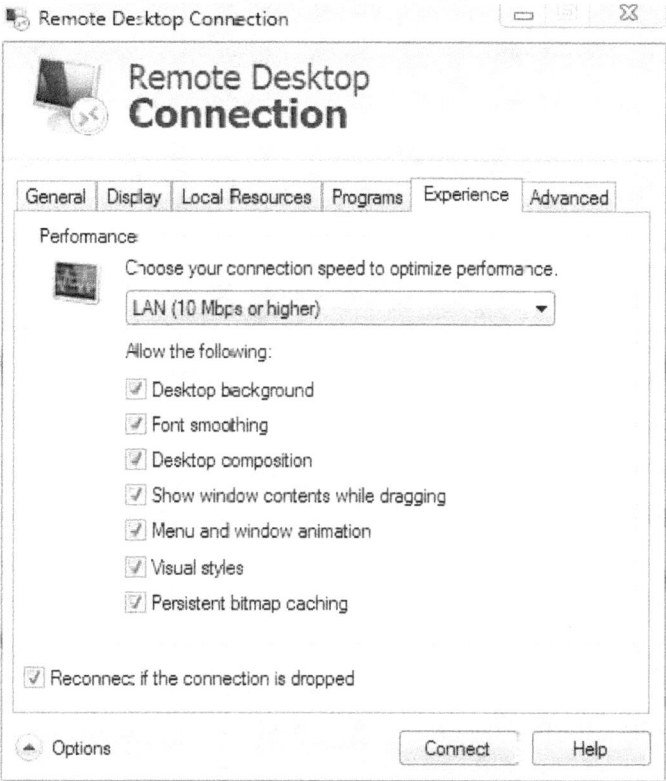

4. Once done, click **Connect** button to connect the remote computer with newly configured settings on your Remote Desktop Connection tool.

Manage Clipboard Mapping

When using Remote Desktop Connection tool in Windows 7, there might be times when you want to copy data from your local computer to the remote machine. In these kinds of situations it becomes quite hectic for the administrators or users to minimize several windows and type Universal Naming Convention path to get the file or folder copied. Many people don't know that when you initiate Remote Desktop Connection in Windows 7, clipboard mapping is initiated as well. This means that if you right click on any file or folder on your local machine and click on Copy option you can directly paste the object to the remote computer. Since this setting is default you need not to alter the configuration. However if you want to change the above settings or you want to confirm that clipboard mapping is enabled on your computer you can follow the steps given below:

1. Log on to your Windows 7 computer with any account and initiate **Remote Desktop Connection** by typing **MSTSC** in the search box at the bottom of start menu.

2. Once opened, click **Options** button to expand the toolbox and view more features.

3. Go to **Local Resources** tab and make sure that **Clipboard** checkbox is checked.

4. Close **Remote Desktop Connection** or click **Connect** button to connect to the remote computer once you are done with your configuration.

Manage Drive Mapping

When using Remote Desktop Connection you can take your local drives to the remote computer virtually. In simple words, you can map your local logical drives so that they can become available on remote computers when Remote Desktop Connection is initialized. Benefit of this is that you do not have to navigate to and fro from your local machine to remote computer every time you need to fetch files and folders that you want to share. Moreover, with the help of this drive mapping feature you can easily copy and paste files or folders to the remote computer as if your local drive is actually the local drive of remote machine. Process for this is quite simple and you can perform the task by following the steps given below:

1. Log on to your Windows 7 computer with the account of your choice and initiate **Remote Desktop Connection** tool by going to **Start > All Programs > Accessories** and clicking **Remote Desktop Connection**.

2. When opened, click **Options** button to view other features offered by the tool.

3. Go to **Local Resources** tab and under **Local devices and resources** section click **More** button.

4. On the opened box expand **Drives** tree and choose the appropriate drive letter which you want to map to the remote computer.

5. Click **Ok** button and finally click **Connect** button to connect to the remote computer with the recently applied configuration **Remote Desktop Connection** tool.

Manage Audio

If your Windows 7 computer is connected to another computer through local area network, using Remote Desktop Connection tool you can play the music on the remote computer and can hear the sound on your local machine. This feature is, although, not very useful for production environments however it can be a great fun for home users. With the help of this setting, users do not have to store music files on every computer available at their homes. On the contrary they can store all music files at a common location and can listen to music on remote computers. You can configure your Remote Desktop Connection tool to hear music from remote computer by following the steps given below:

1. Log on to your Windows 7 computer with the user account on which you want to hear the music and initiate **Remote Desktop Connection** tool by typing **MSTSC** in the search box and pressing enter key.

2. On the appeared box go to **Local Resources** tab and under **Remote audio** section click **Settings** button.

3. On the opened box under **Remote audio playback** section make sure that **Play on this computer** radio button is selected and click **Ok** button to make your settings persistent.

4. Once done, click **Connect** button to initiate the connection to the remote computer and play any audio file that is stored on it.

Note: If remote computer has any Client Operating System, for example, Windows XP, Windows 7 or Windows Vista, installed on it the local user of that computer will automatically be logged off as soon as you will initiate Remote Desktop Connection to that computer.

Use Remote Assistance

Remote Assistance is the feature using which if a person gets stuck with something while working on the computer he can invite someone, who is more knowledgeable than him, to help him out remotely. However, unlike Remote Desktop, Remote Assistance uses the credentials of the user who has invited a person for help. You can invite any one for help using an invitation file that can be created by following the steps below:

1. Click **Start** button.

2. At the bottom of start menu in search box type **Windows Remote Assistance** and press enter.

3. In the opened page click **Invite someone you trust to help you**.

4. In the next page click **Save this invitation as a file** and browse for the location where you want to save the invitation file.

5. Specify the name of the invitation file and click **Save** button.

6. Your invitation file will be saved and you will be prompted with a box displaying a unique password that you need to provide your helper so that he may enter your computer to assist you with your work.

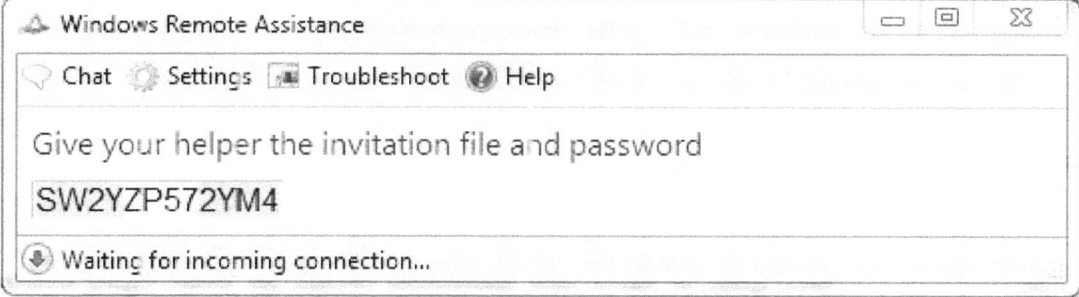

Once the invitation file is created, you can send this invitation file to your helper through mail or through network share. In either case, whenever your helper double clicks the file he is prompted for the password. As he enters the password, a remote assistance session gets initiated and both you and your helper can then see a common desktop and are able to text chat with each other to resolve the issue.

CHAPTER 13
BACKUP AND RESTORE

Backup a Windows 7 Computer

Nowadays backup is an essential part in any IT oriented organization and this custom is now also carried forward to home computers as well. In other words every individual, whether in home or production environment, is now conscious and always tries to create backup for the data that is stored in his/her computer system. With the release of Microsoft Windows 7, backup process is now even simpler and it does not require any technical skills, which indeed is a great advantage for home users. However Windows 7 computer requires a few steps to be taken for the backup process and its scheduling. As a Windows 7 user if you want to set your Windows up for backup you are required to follow the steps provided as below:

1. Log on to Windows 7 computer with administrator account.
2. At the bottom of start menu in search box type **Backup and Restore** and press enter key.
3. On the opened window click **Set up backup** link.

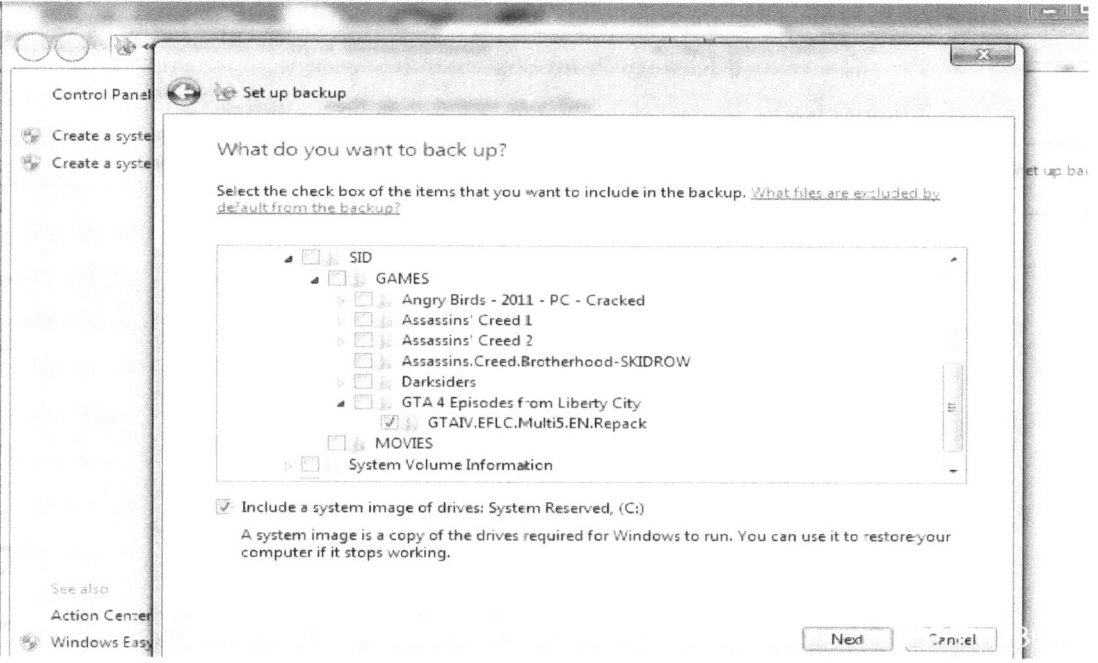

4. On the next page choose the location where you want to store the backup. Alternatively you can click **Save on a network** button to specify a network location for storing backup and click **Next** button.

5. On the next page choose appropriate radio button specifying what data is to be backed up and click **Next** button.

6. On the next page choose the data that is to be backed up by checking the check boxes representing them and click **Next** button.

7. On **Review your backup settings** page click **Save settings and run backup** button to start the process.

Create Restore Points

Windows 7 offers a feature of creating restore points that are quite helpful when your system crashes or behaves abnormally. Main function of these restore points is that it creates and stores the image of the state of your system. When the system starts performing abnormally system state can be restored to the created restore point in order to get exactly the same settings which were present at the time of creation of restore point.

In order to create a restore point below steps should be followed:

1. Click **Start** button.
2. From the menu right-click **Computer** and select **Properties**.
3. From the **System** window in the left pane select **System Protection**.
4. In the **System Properties** box ensure that you are **System Protection** tab.
5. To create a restore point click **Create** button.
6. In the **Create a Restore Point** box enter the description for your restore point. (E.g. Restore Point on Dec 12, 2011)

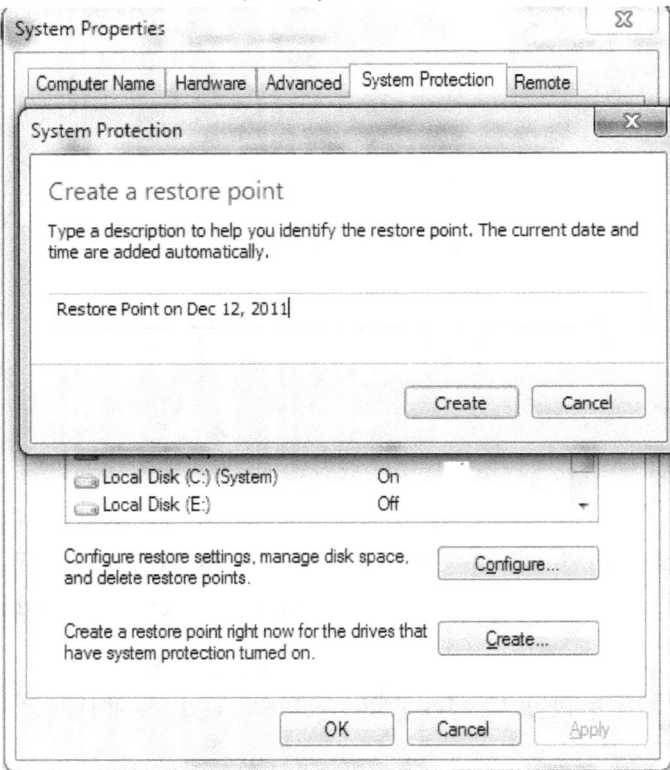

7. Finally click **Create** button to start the process of creation of restore point.

In order to restore your computer to a previously created restore point you need to follow the below steps:

1. To restore your computer to the previously created restore point follow the steps from **1** to **4** as mentioned in the above section.

2. On the **System Properties** box under **System Restore** section click **System Restore** button.

3. On the **Restore system files and settings** page click **Next** button.

4. On **Restore your computer to the state it was in before the selected event** page select the appropriate restore point, which in most cases will be the latest one, and click **Next** button.

5. On **Confirm your restore point** page click **Finish** to start the restoration process.

Create a System Image

In earlier days creating system image was a tedious and hectic task which only administrators were allowed and supposed to do. Because of the complications involved in creating system images home users always used to avoid the process and they normally used to hire a professional service engineer in case their system came across any troubles. With the release of Windows 7 Microsoft has made things easier for home users and now with just a few clicks users can create their own system images which they can use to restore the operating systems if something goes wrong with them. Although steps involved in the process are very simple, administrative privileges on the computer are still required to complete the task successfully. As a Windows 7 administrator if you want to create system image of your computer in both production and home environments you are required to follow the steps given below:

1. Log on to Windows 7 computer with any account that has administrative privileges.
2. Click **Start** button and from the list click **All Programs**.
3. From the new list go to **Accessories** container and from the available applications click **Getting Started**.
4. On the opened window select on **Backup your files** from the options and then click **Backup your files** link that appears.
5. On **Backup or store your files** page click **Create a system image** link from the left bar.
6. On the next page choose the appropriate storage place and click **Next** button.
7. On the pages choose the drives for which you want to create images and click **Next** button.

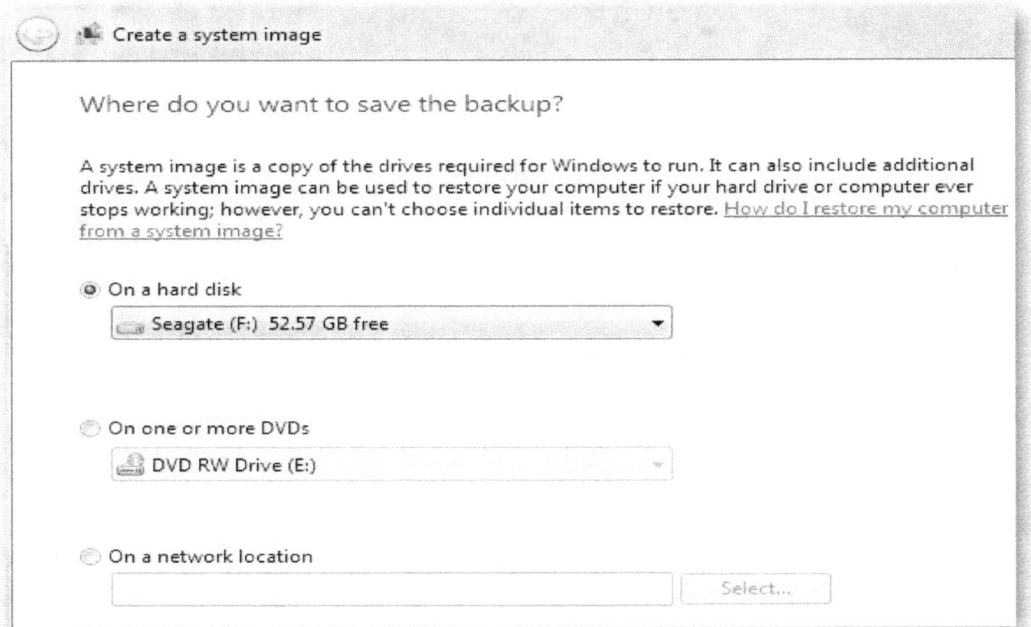

8. On the final page click **Start backup** button to start the process.

Create System Repair Disc

System repair disc is created so that if ever the computer fails to boot or the OS gets corrupted, system repair disc can be used to repair the operating system and bring it back to running state as before. Below are the instructions which can be followed to create a system repair disk.

1. Click **Start** button.
2. From the menu select **Control Panel**.
3. Under **System and Security** category click **Backup Your Computer** link.
4. On the next window in the left pane click **Create a System Repair Disc** link.
5. Make sure that a blank DVD is present in the DVD writer of your computer and on next window click **Create Disc** button to create system repair disk.

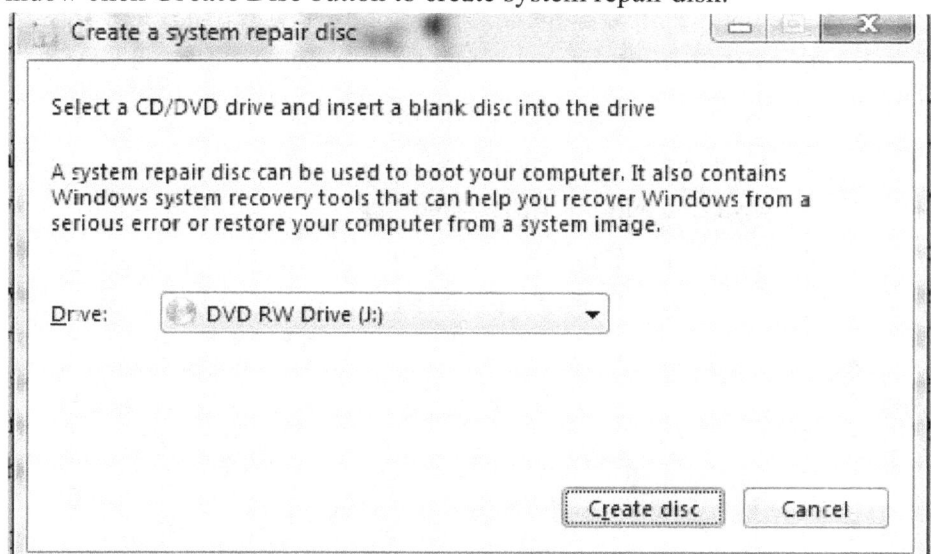

This system repair disc can be used to start Windows 7 computer system allowing it to boot from the disc. Once the system is booted using system repair disc, a previously created system image file can then be located in order to restore the computer to its previous state. Also, this system repair disc contains few recovery tools which can be used to recover your Windows 7 computer in case any critical error occurs in the machine.

Note: In order to use system repair disc you need to create an image of your Windows 7 computer in advance.

Disable Scheduled Backup

When once Windows 7 is configured to create backup, it automatically schedules the backup process that is by default configured to run on a weekly basis. Although backups are essential for all computer systems their creation processes may sometimes be tedious and processor intensive which many home users may want to disable in order to save time. When this is the case users need not to go through any complex configuration process, instead they can follow a few simple steps to disable scheduled backup task at all. The best part is that users can re-enable this process whenever they want to and still the process does not require any complex configuration steps. As a Windows 7 administrator if you want to disable scheduled backup you are required to follow the steps given below:

1. Log on to Windows 7 computer with administrator account.

2. At the bottom of start menu in search box type **Backup and Restore** command and press enter key.

3. From the opened box click **Set up backup** link.

4. Follow on-screen instructions and click **Next** buttons on all the Windows till you reach **Review your backup settings** page.

5. Once there, click **Change schedule** link and on the opened box uncheck **Run backup on the schedule (recommended)** checkbox.

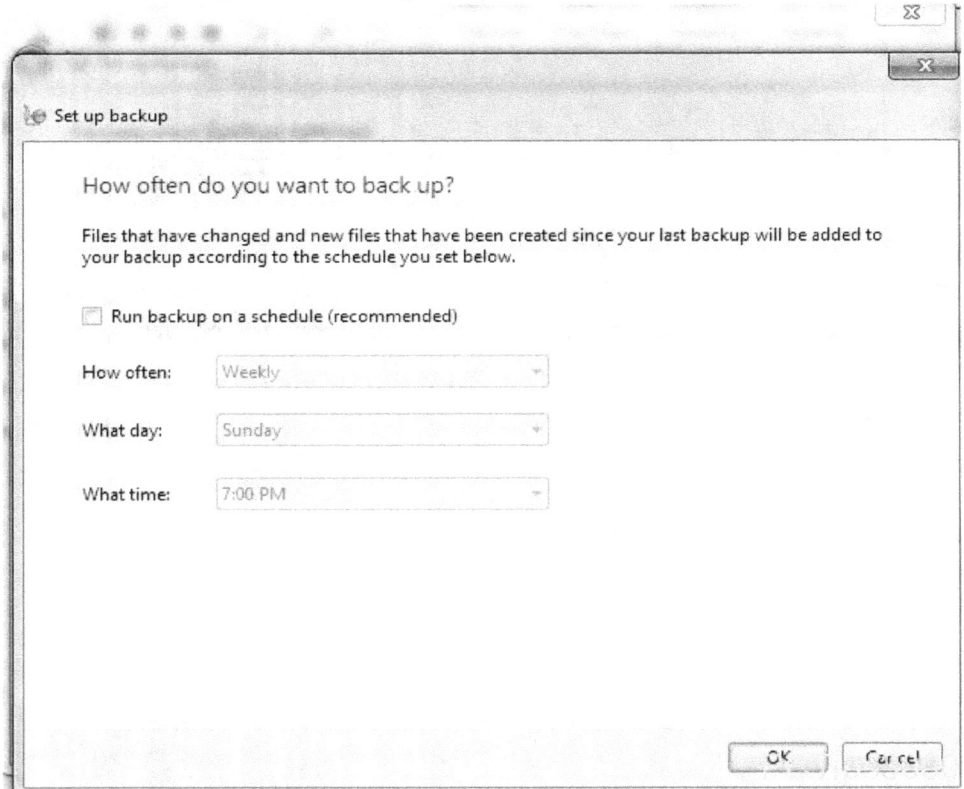

6. Once done, click **Ok** button to save the changes you have made.

Backup Registry

Registry plays an important role in any operating system developed by Microsoft. Registry, in fact, serves as the backbone of Windows which contains complete information about the operating system. Whenever any application is installed its entry is created in the registry file and the entry specifies the nature of the application. For example, if you install an evaluation version of any application its entire information is written in the registry and after the evaluation period is over the registry marks the application as expired. Since, registry is important for any operating system based on Microsoft platform, it becomes essential for a user to back it up in order to protect any stored information in it. You can backup Windows 7 Registry by following the steps given below:

1. Log on to the computer with administrator account. (The process of Registry backup can only be performed by the administrator of the computer).

2. Click **Start** button and from the appeared start menu in the search box type **REGEDIT** and press enter key.

3. In **Registry Editor** window click **File** menu and choose **Export**.

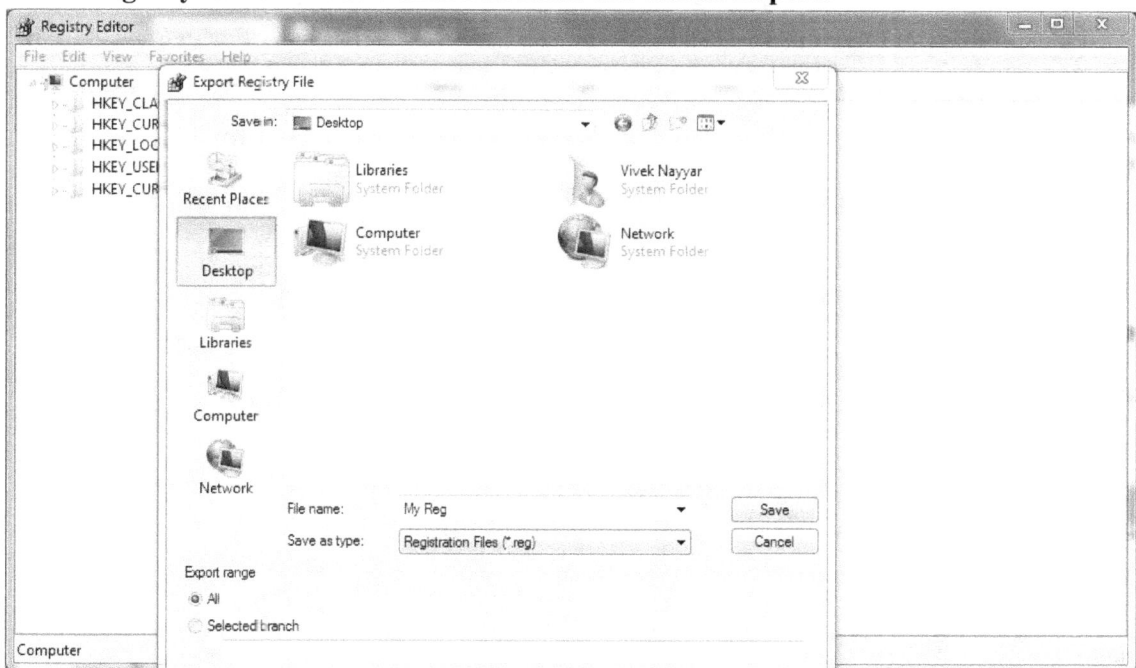

4. In the appeared box choose **All** radio button present at the bottom and specify file name in the corresponding text box.

5. Once done, click **Save** button to back up your registry file and close **Registry Editor** window.

Delete Restore Point

Restore points are the snapshots of any state of the operating system and their creation process is by default scheduled in Windows 7. Restore points help users to revert the operating system back to the state at which it was working flawlessly. Although restore points are automatically created, users can still create their own restore points whenever they want. The process does not require any complicated technical skills and even home users can perform the task. Just like any other object in Windows 7, if users want they can also delete any previously created restore point if they think that it is not required at all. Consequences that users my face in such situations are that they will not be able to restore their computers back to the states at which the deleted restore points were created. As a Windows 7 user if you want to delete previously created restore point you are required to follow the steps given below:

1. Log on to Windows 7 computer with the account that has elevated privileges.
2. From the start menu right click **Computer** and from the available context menu click **Properties**.
3. On the opened page from the left bar click **System protection** link.
4. On **System Properties** box make sure that you are **System Protection** tab.
5. Click **Configure** button and from the opened box click **Delete** button.
6. On the confirmation box click **Continue** button to confirm the deletion process.

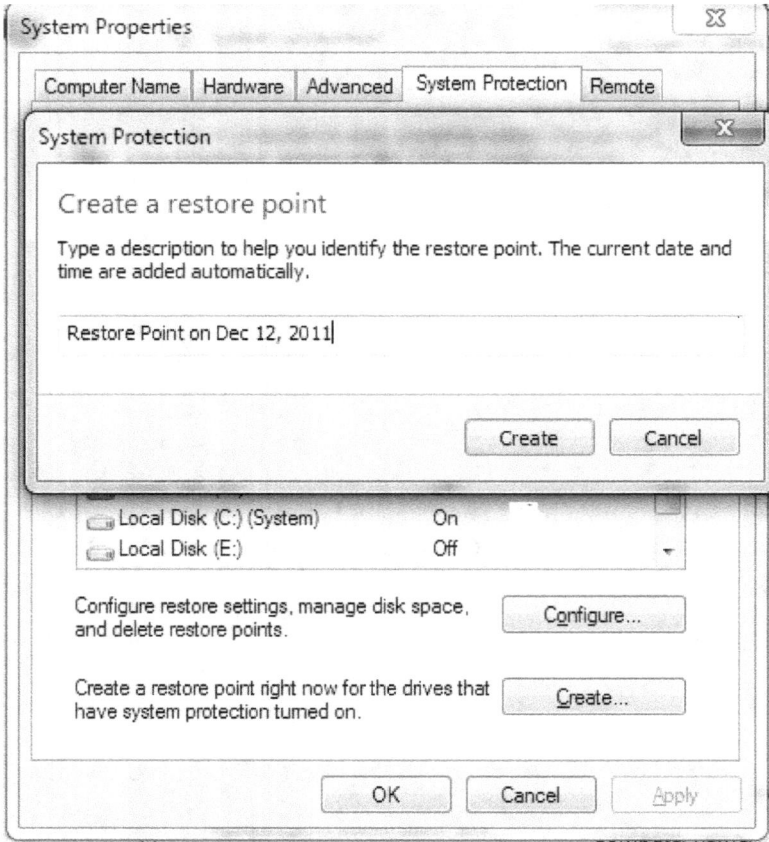

Disable System Restore

Feature of system restore was first introduced in Windows XP which helped users to restore the states of the computers in case any disaster occurred to them. System restore feature captures the image of the running state of the computer. The operating system measures the running state by the successful logon duration and time. This means that whenever a computer successfully starts the operating system captures the image of the state and stores it in its memory. Whenever the disaster occurs, users are able to restore their computers from the previously saved state. This configuration is now carried forward on to Windows 7 with some new advanced features and with the ability of disabling this feature at all. As a Windows 7 user if you want to disable system restore feature you are required to follow the steps given below:

1. Log on to Windows 7 computer with administrator account.
2. Click **Start** button and from the available list click **Computer** option
3. From the available menu click **Properties**.
4. On the opened window from the left bar click **System protection** link.
5. On **System Properties** box make sure that you are **System Protection** tab.
6. Under **Protection settings** list select the desired drive partition on which you want to disable system restore and click **Configure** button.
7. On the opened box select **Turn off system protection** radio button and click **Ok** buttons on all the opened boxes to save the changes.

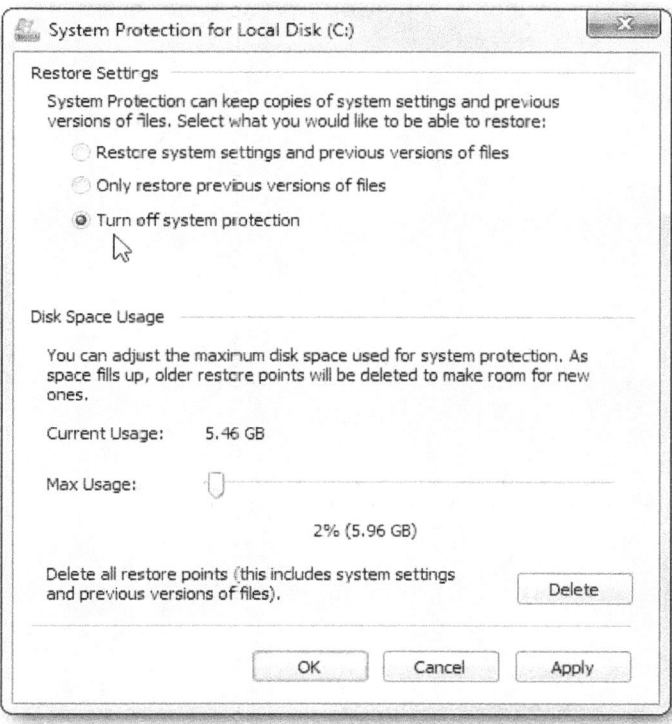

CHAPTER 14
WINDOWS MEDIA PLAYER

Manage WMP Automatic Updates

Just like Microsoft Windows 7, Windows Media Player also checks for updates automatically on a regular basis. It is recommended that automatic updates for Windows Media Player should also be kept on so that users can experience the best quality that is provided by Microsoft. Although it is assumed that people who are using Windows 7 are always connected to the Internet and the Internet connection has unlimited download plan with decent bandwidth. Even though if users still want to use the Internet connection conservatively they can customize the settings for automatic updates for Windows Media Player. As a Windows 7 user if you want to customize automatic update settings for Windows Media Player you need to follow the steps given below:

1. Log on to Windows 7 computer with administrator account.
2. Click **Windows Media Player** icon to initiate the program.
3. From the opened interface click **Organize** menu and from the available list click **Options**.
4. On the opened box go to **Player** tab.
5. Under **Automatic updates** section choose the appropriate radio button as required.

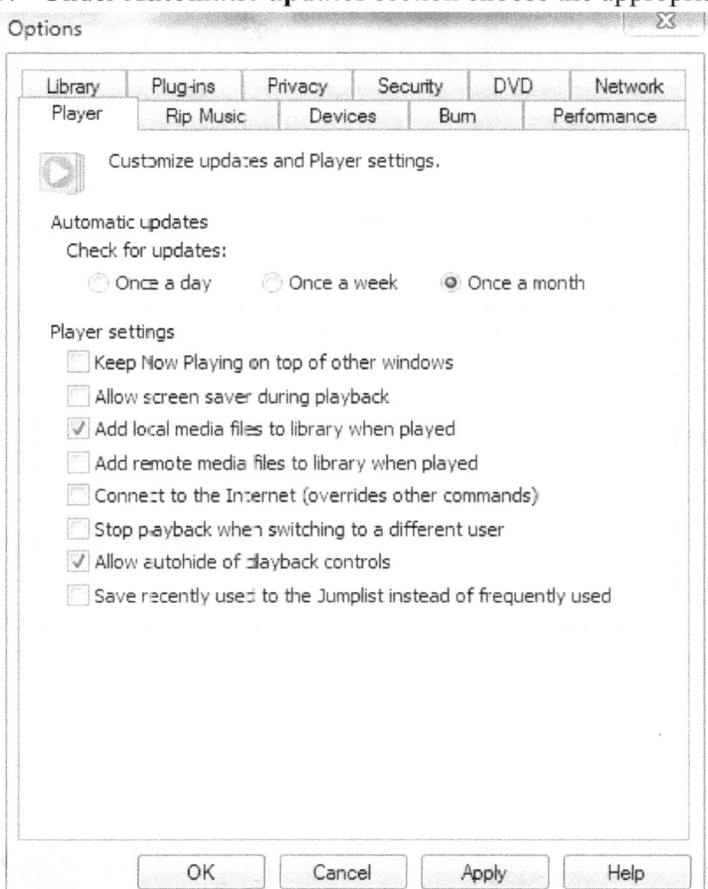

6. Once you are done with the configuration, click **Ok** button to save the changes that you have made.

Manage Screensavers during WMP Playback

Screensavers in Windows 7 only work when the system is in idle position and no user input is detected by the computer. Moreover many people do not know that screensavers stop functioning with any resource intensive application runs in the foreground. An example can be an active Windows Media Player application. In other words if Windows 7 screensaver is set to be initiated if user input is not detected for 10 minutes and Windows Media Player is playing any media file, screensaver would not be initiated at all. Under normal circumstances users do not care about this configuration and by default Windows Media Player is set to stop the initialization of screensaver if it is active. However if users want they can change the settings and as a Windows 7 user if you want to do so you can follow the steps provided below:

1. Log on to Windows 7 computer with the user account for which you want to configure this.
2. Click **Windows Media Player** in the taskbar icon to initialize the application.
3. From the available interface click on Organize menu and from the list click **Options**.
4. On the opened box go to **Player** tab and from the available check boxes under **Player settings** section check **Allow screen saver during playback** checkbox.

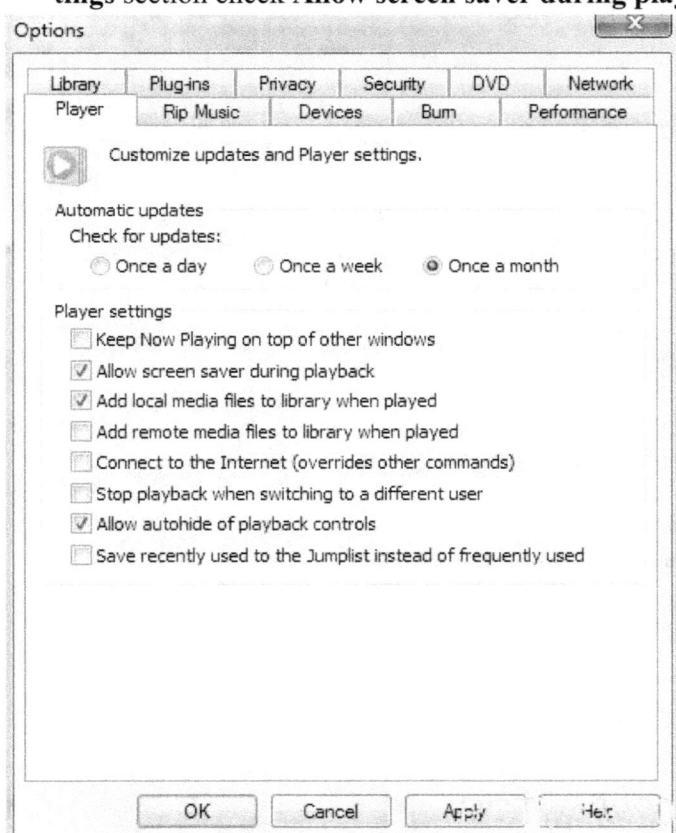

5. Click **Ok** button to save the changes.

Manage Frames in Windows Media Player

By default Windows Media Player is configured to capture every frame that is downloaded from the Internet so that the files can be displayed to the users uninterruptedly. This configuration is considered as the perfect one as users can experience best quality audio and video of media files which are downloaded directly from the Internet. In many cases where Internet connection speed is slow sometimes it takes longer to buffer and therefore users may experience breakage while listening or viewing audio or video files respectively. Windows Media Player allows users to configure the application so that they can experience uninterrupted streaming media even if they have slow internet connection but at the cost of some loss in frames. This configuration is helpful while synchronizing files as well. As Windows Media Player user if you want to configure this you can follow the steps given below:

1. Log on to Windows 7 computer on which **Windows Media Player** application is initialized.
2. On the opened interface click **Organize** menu and from the list click **Options**.
3. On the opened box go to **Performance** tab.
4. Check **Drop frames to keep audio and video synchronized** checkbox.

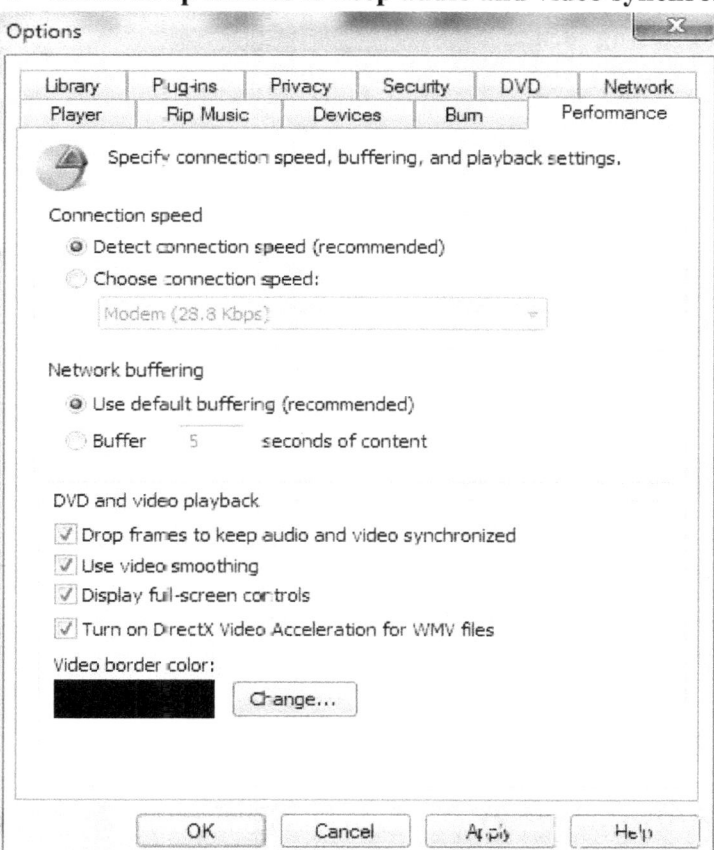

5. Finally click **Ok** button to allow the application to save the changes.

Buffer Time of Windows Media Player Contents

Whenever any content from the Internet is downloaded by Windows Media Player to be played it is automatically buffered and then it is played by the application. Also Windows Media Player is by default configured to use default buffering of the file. Microsoft also recommends this configuration. In some cases however, where Internet connection speed is limited, users can manually specify the duration of the contents which are to be buffered before they are played. The configuration requires just a few simple clicks and even non-technical users can configure their Windows Media Player applications to do so. Moreover, this configuration also allows users to prevent misuse of Internet connection. As a Windows Media Player user in Windows 7 if you want to limit the duration of the contents while buffering you are required to follow the steps given below:

1. Log on to Windows 7 computer.

2. Open **Windows Media Player** application by clicking on the icon available in the taskbar.

3. Once opened, click **Organize** menu and from the appeared list click **Options**.

4. On the opened box make sure that you are **Performance** tab and click **Buffer** radio button under **Network buffering** section.

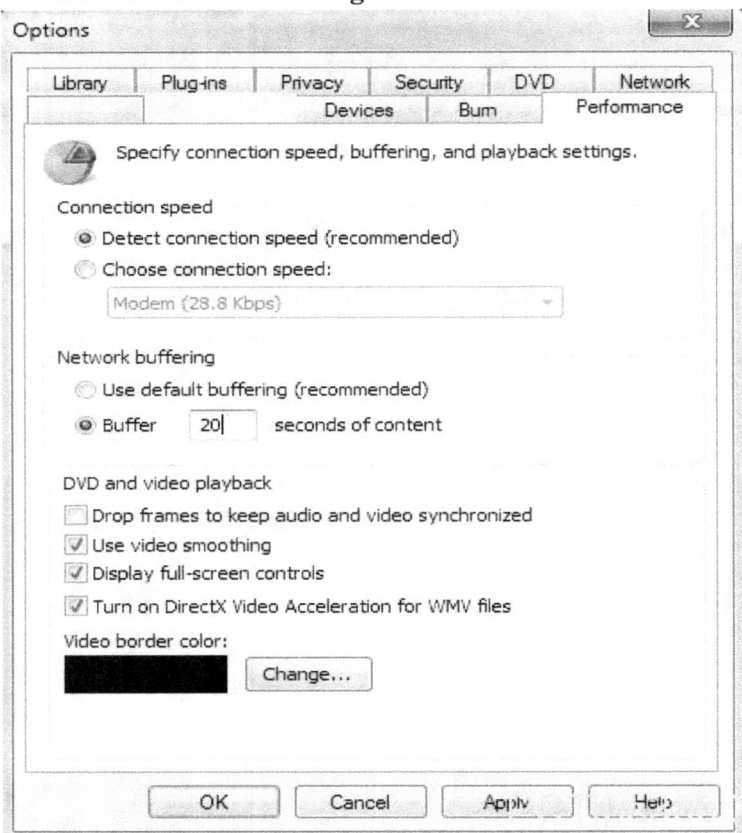

5. On the enabled text box specify the duration for which you want the contents to be buffered and finally click **Ok** button to save the changes.

Keep 'Now Playing' on Top

When Windows Media Player plays any media file, currently playing file is always shown as 'Now Playing'. While playing file if a user initiates another application, 'Now Playing' file is automatically sent to background and the active application is displayed in the foreground. Users can change this configuration so that they can see 'Now Playing' file at every moment. This makes them look at the file and its details so that they can manage it according to their needs. As a Windows 7 user if you want to allow 'Now Available' file to be available on top of all the Windows every time, you are required to follow the steps given below:

1. Log on to Windows 7 computer with the account on which you want this configuration to return.

2. Click **Windows Media Player** icon on the opened interface click **Organize** menu.

3. From the available list click **Options**.

4. On the opened box go to **Player** tab.

5. Under **Player settings** section check **Keep Now Playing on top of other windows** checkbox.

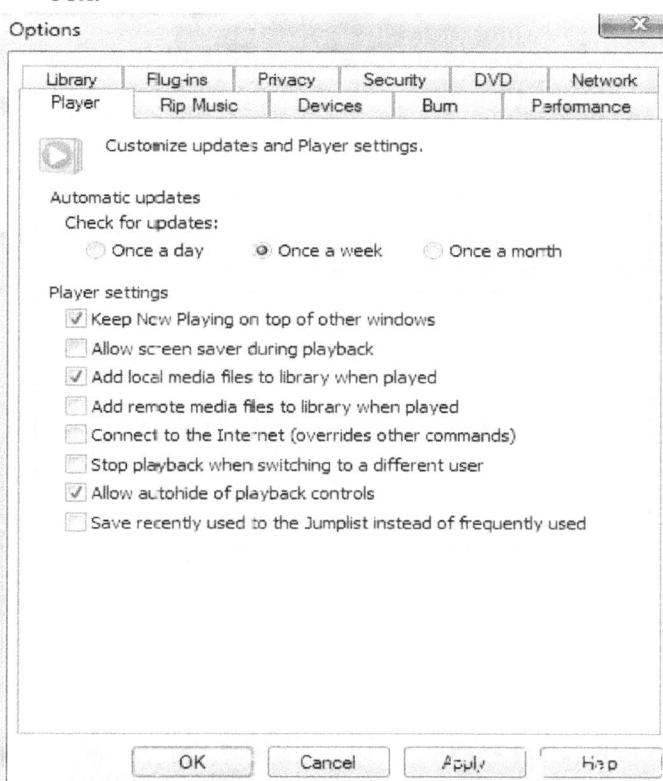

6. Finally click **Ok** button once you are done with the configuration.

Disable Auto Hide Windows Media Player Controls

Windows Media Player that is automatically installed along with the installation of Windows 7 has a unique feature which enables it to auto hide all playback controls whenever user input is not detected by the application for few seconds. This allows users to experience visual effects provided by Windows Media Player uninterruptedly. Moreover, auto hide feature for playback controls also enables users to view video files on a full-screen mode without any unwanted icons displayed on the screen. Automatically hidden playback controls in Windows Media Player automatically become visible whenever the application detects any input from the user's end, that is, whether key press or mouse movement. Although auto hide feature is provided in the application to allow users to experience the best out of Windows Media Player however if users want they can disable this by following the steps provided below:

1. Log on to Windows 7 computer with the user account on which you want to disable auto hide in **Windows Media Player**.

2. Open **Windows Media Player** by clicking on the icon provided in the taskbar.

3. Once opened, click **Organize** menu available at the left corner of the interface of the application.

4. From the available list click **Options**.

5. On the opened box go to **Player** tab.

6. Under **Player settings** section uncheck **Allow auto hide of playback controls** checkbox and finally click **Ok** button to save the changes that you have made.

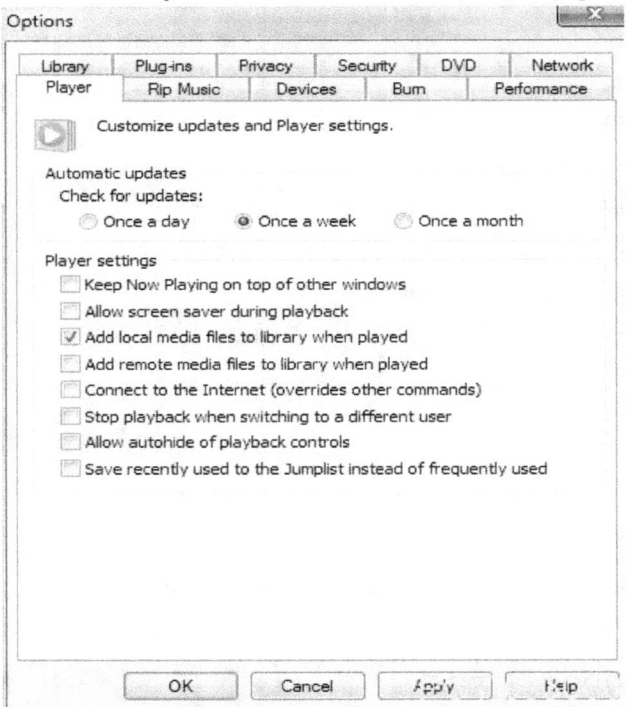

Do Not Store Files in WMP Library

Since Windows Media Player is capable of playing almost every file format, Microsoft has integrated a feature in the application which allows it to store every played file in its library. This configuration ensures that users need not to wander around and hunt for the file every time they want to play it, instead with the help of this feature the files can be centrally located and then can be played at ease. Although this configuration is by default enabled for users' benefit, however users can still disable this if they do not want any local file to be stored in WMP library when it is played. As a Windows 7 user if you want to disable this configuration you are required to follow the steps given below:

1. Log on to Windows 7 computer with any account because this configuration does not require any elevated privileges.

2. Click **Windows Media Player** icon available in the taskbar.

3. On the opened interface click **Organize** menu and from the available list click **Options** to get **Options** box.

4. Go to **Player** tab.

5. Uncheck **Add local media files to library when played** checkbox available under **Player settings** section.

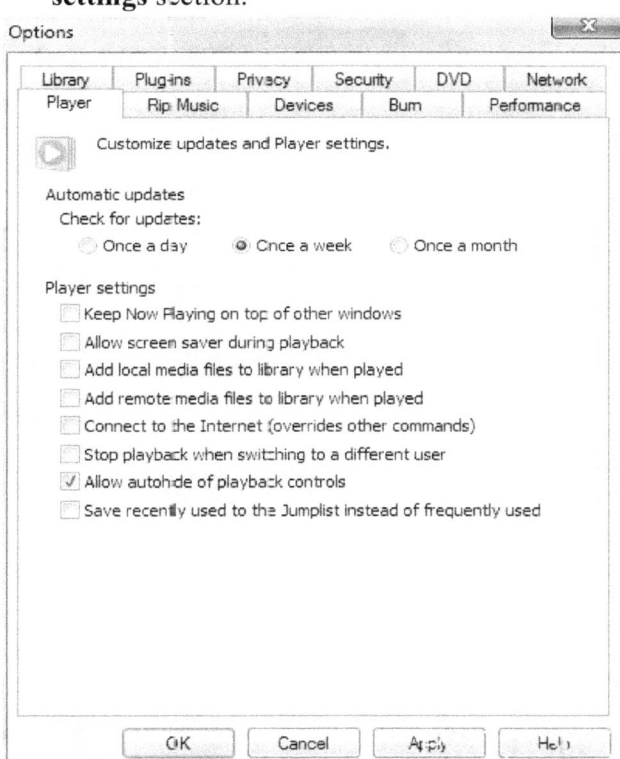

6. Click **Ok** button when you are done with the configuration.

Allow Storing Remote Files to WMP Library

As default configuration of Windows Media Player any local file that is played in it is automatically stored in its library. Just reverse is the case with the files which are located at remote locations. This means that whenever a file that is located at any remote location is played in Windows Media Player it never gets stored in its library. This makes users to go to remote location every time they want to play the file. Windows Media Player has this configuration as default because of security reasons however if users think that storing files from remote locations in Windows Media Player library is safe they can enable this by following few easy steps given below:

1. Log on to Windows 7 computer with any account with or without elevated privileges.

2. Click on the available icon of **Windows Media Player** in taskbar.

3. On the opened interface click **Organize** menu.

4. From the available list click **Options**.

5. On **Options** box which is opened check **Add remote media files to library when played** checkbox.

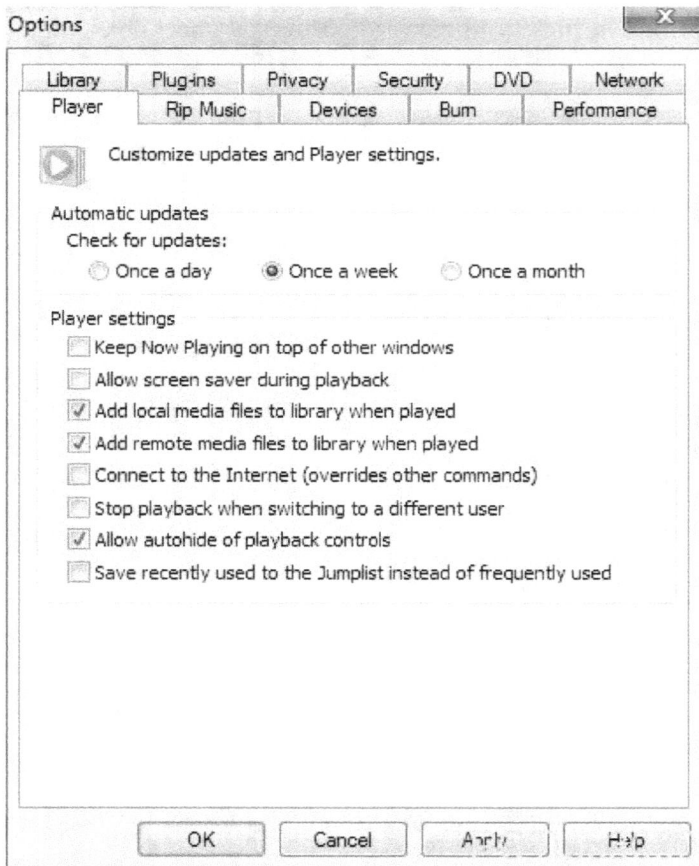

6. Once you are done with the configuration, finally click **Ok** button to save the changes that you have made.

Retrieve All Media Files Information

Whenever a music or video files is played in Windows Media Player by default all its information is automatically gathered by the application. In many cases this information is not at all required by the users as they are not concerned about it. This scenario is most commonly seen in home environments. However in some cases users may require the details of the files and to help these types of users Windows Media Player is configured to automatically go to the Internet and retrieve the missing information of media files almost instantaneously. In order to preserve Internet bandwidth the default configuration of Windows Media Player is that it retrieves only the missing information of the file but if users want they can configure the application to extract every detail of the file, which may also include any updated information that the file may have. As a Windows Media Player user if you want to configure this you need to follow the steps given below:

1. Log on to Windows 7 computer.

2. Open **Windows Media Player** by clicking on its icon on the taskbar.

3. Once opened, click **Organize** menu to get the list.

4. From the available list click **Options**.

5. On the opened box make sure that you are on **Library** tab and select **Overwrite all media information** radio button under **Automatic media information updates for files** section.

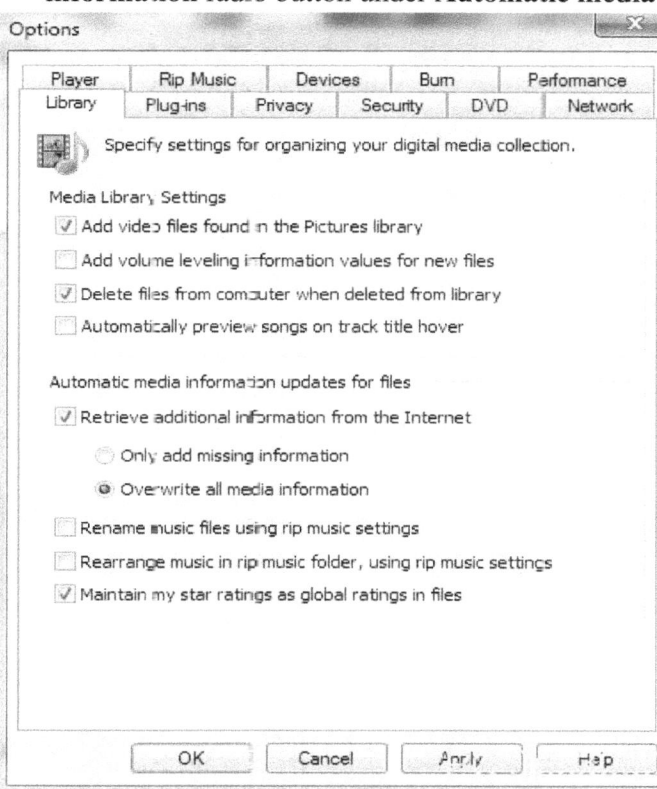

6. Once you are done with the configuration click **Ok** button to save the changes.

Do Not Retrieve File Information from Internet

Whenever a media file is played in Windows Media Player, every detail of the file is available for the users to get view as much information as possible. Many times information of the file, for example, its genre, etc. is missing and users have no way to get its details other than Internet. Mostly users do not care much about these things but sometimes it becomes essential for the users to grab these details from the Internet so that they can categories the locations of the files accordingly. Windows Media Player offers a feature using which missing information of the files can automatically be retrieved from the Internet so that every detail of the file is complete. This consumes a small amount of Internet bandwidth and because of any reason if users do not want this configuration to be left enabled they can follow the steps provided below to disable it:

1. Log on to Windows 7 computer with any account.
2. Click on the icon of **Windows Media Player** available in the taskbar.
3. On the opened interface click **Organize** menu and from the available list click **Options** option.
4. On the opened box make sure that you are on **Library** tab.
5. Uncheck **Retrieve additional information from the Internet** checkbox under **Automatic media information updates for files** section.

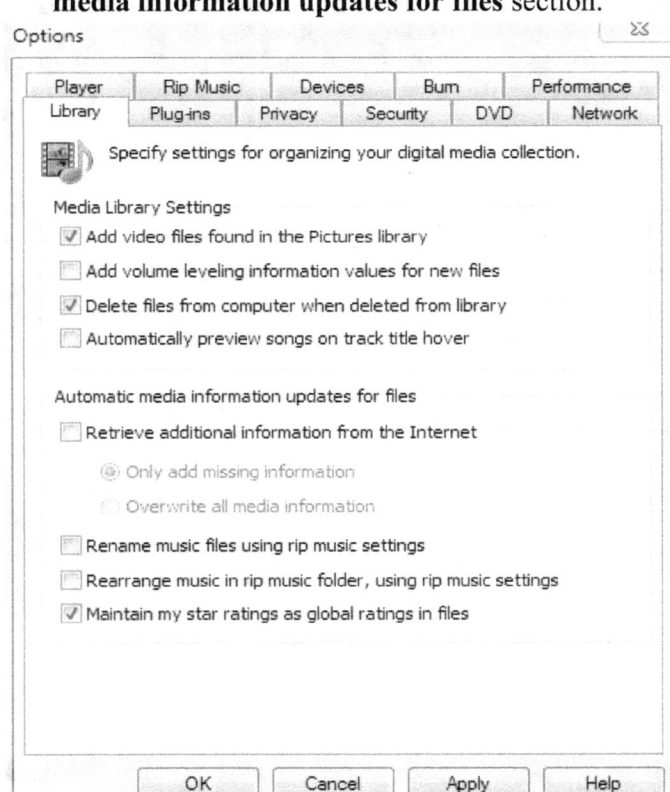

6. Once done, click **Ok** button to save the changes you have made.

Change Save Location of Windows Media Player

Windows Media Player provided by Windows 7 allows users to rip audio CDs and convert the files to MP3 or any other format as selected by the users. Because Windows Media Player is very user friendly and simple to use, users do not require any third-party application for file conversion. Apart from converting audio CDs into MP3 or any other file format, Windows Media Player also allows users to save converted files at the locations of users' choices. Default save location is in the system drive which is not at all recommended if users frequently use the WMP conversion and rip feature. As a Windows 7 user if you want to change the default save location of the converted files in Windows Media Player you are required to follow the steps given below:

1. Log on to Windows 7 computer.
2. Click **Windows Media Player** icon to open it.
3. On the available interface click **Organize** menu and click **Options**.
4. On the opened box go to **Rip Music** tab.
5. Click **Change** button under **Rip music to this location** section.

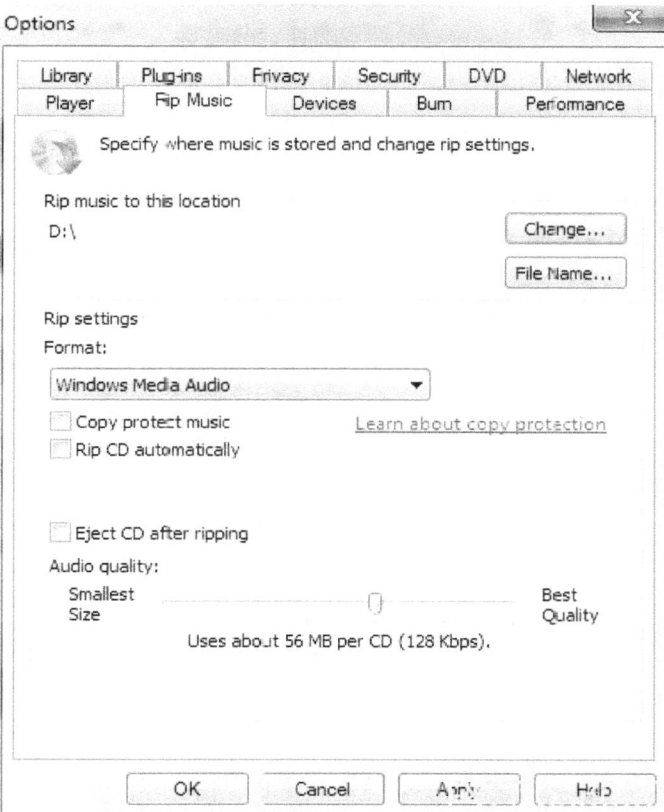

6. Provide the appropriate location as required.
7. Finally click **Ok** button to save the changes you have made.

Convert Files from Audio CD to MP3

Since quite a long time it has been a great complexity for music lovers to convert audio CDs to MP3 file formats. Many users think that an audio CD can easily be copied to a computer and the music files can be played just like that. But when they do this practically they find that no audio files are copied and no music can be heard by playing the files which are copied to the computer. Although there are several third-party applications in the market which allow users to rip music from audio CDs and also allow them to convert music files to any file format they desire Windows 7 provides this feature as a built-in option in Windows Media Player. Windows Media Player allows users to capture and rip music files from audio CDs and convert them to the desired file format quite easily. As a Windows 7 user if you want to capture any audio CD and convert music files to MP3 format you are required to follow the steps given below:

1. Log on to Windows 7 computer.

2. Open **Windows Media Player**.

3. On **Windows Media Player** interface click **Organize** menu and from the available options click **Options**.

4. On **Options** box go to **Rip Music** tab and from the available drop-down list under **Rip settings** section choose **MP3**.

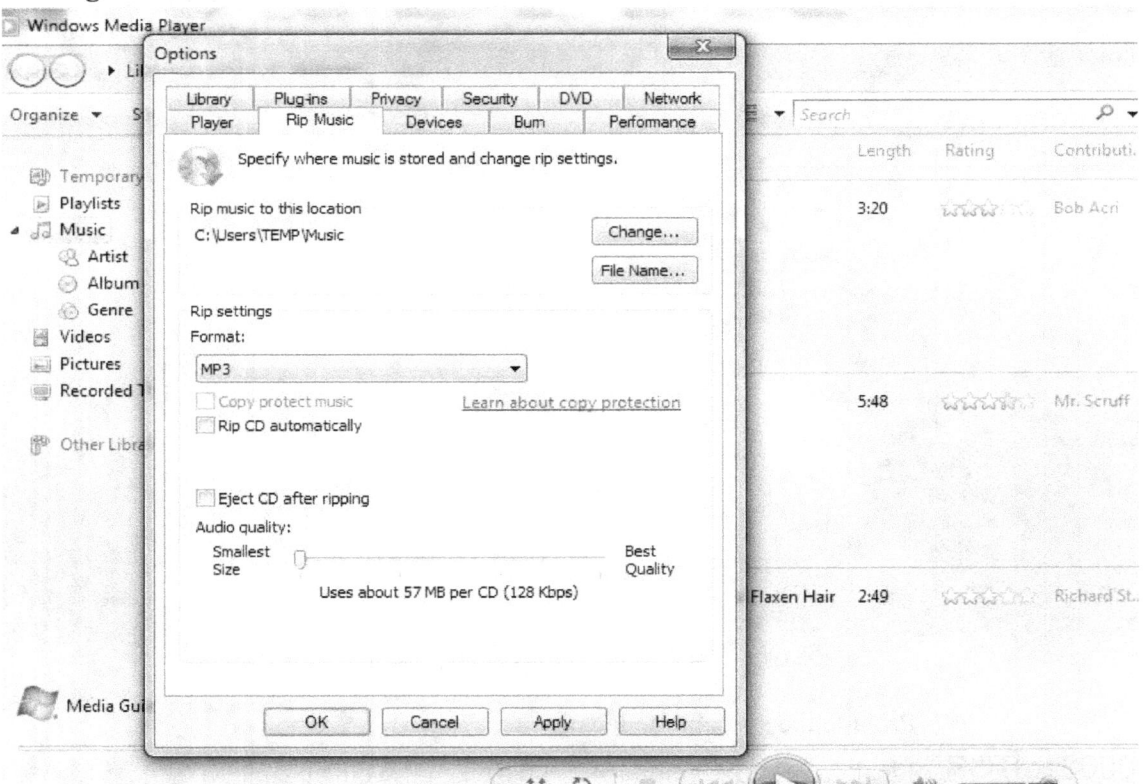

5. Finally click **Ok** button to save the changes you have made.

Manage Burning Speed in Windows Media Player

Windows Media Player is a versatile application which also allows users to burn audio and data discs as desired. Also it is well-known that whenever a disc is burned in the disc burner burning speed must be kept at the minimum to gain best performance. Windows Media Player is by default configured to burn the discs at fastest speed which expedites the burning process remarkably but at the cost of decreased performance (sometimes). If users want they can specify burning speed in Windows Media Player and as a Windows Media Player user if you want to do so you can follow the steps provided as below:

1. Log on to Windows 7 computer with the account that has administrative privileges.
2. Click on the icon of **Windows Media Player** that is available in the taskbar in order to initiate the application.
3. On the opened interface click **Organize** menu and from the appeared list click **Options**.
4. On the appeared box go to **Burn** tab and under **General** section from the available drop-down list select the burning speed as required.

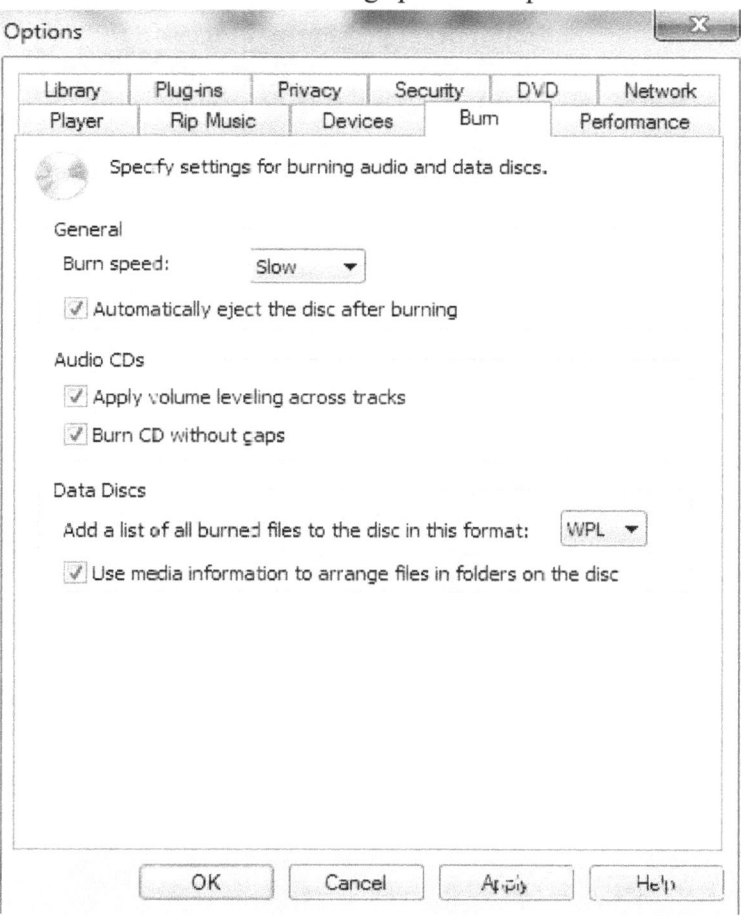

5. Finally click **Ok** button to allow **Windows Media Player** to save the changes.

PCTIPS 3000

Arrange Burned Files in Windows Media Player

When media files are burned on the discs using Windows Media Player application many times users might have noticed that the files are not arranged in the manner they were expected. Even if users try to burn files on the disks by categorizing them in different folders, expected arrangement of the files is still not seen after the burning process is complete. Reason behind this is that Windows Media Player is by default configured to arrange files according to their information stored in them. This makes the arrangement haphazard while burning them to the media. This nature of Windows Media Player can be changed and as a Windows 7 user if you want to do so you can follow the steps given below:

1. Log on to Windows 7 computer with the account that has administrative privileges.
2. Open **Windows Media Player** application by clicking on its icon that is pinned in the task-bar.
3. Click **Organize** menu and from the appeared list click **Options**.
4. On **Options** box go to **Burn** tab.
5. Uncheck **Use media information to arrange files in folders on the disc** checkbox.

6. Click **Ok** button after you are convinced with the new settings of **Windows Media Player**.

Rename Ripped Music Files

Since Windows Media Player offers feature of ripping music files right from audio CDs, it makes WMP even more versatile when it also allows users to convert music files to the formats of their own choices. The biggest challenge in these cases is the name of the files that are being ripped by Windows Media Player as the names sometimes might be quite confusing. To eliminate these problems users can allow Windows Media Player to enforce renaming of ripped music files according to the settings configured. By default Windows Media Player does not allow files to be automatically renamed after they are ripped however if as a Windows 7 user you want to rename the files according to the settings you are required to follow the steps given below:

1. Log on to Windows 7 computer.
2. Click on the icon of **Windows Media Player** that is available in taskbar to open the application.
3. On the opened interface click **Organize** menu and from the appeared list click **Options**.
4. On the opened box make sure that you are on **Library** tab.
5. Check **Rename music files using rip music settings** checkbox.

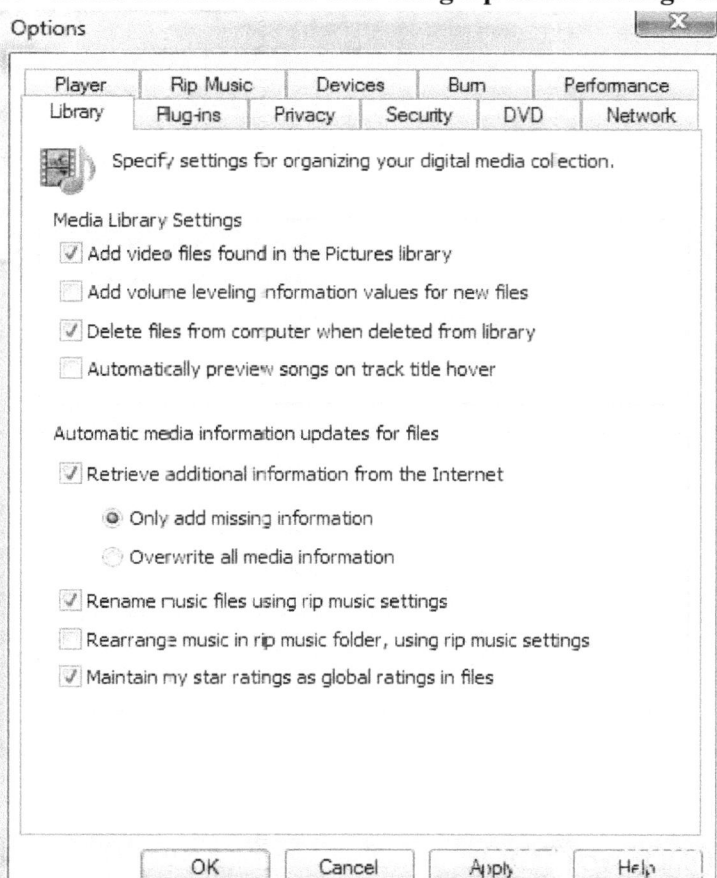

6. Finally click **Ok** button to save the changes.

Do Not Eject Media after Burning

Many third-party disc burning applications that are available in the market or which are downloaded from the Internet have a built-in feature which automatically ejects the optical media when the burning process is complete. This feature works as the notification for the users to inform them that the burning process has been completed successfully and now they can go ahead with the next step. Windows Media Player also has this feature available in it and by default it is enabled. Under normal circumstances this configuration is not supposed to be modified however in some special cases users can change the settings and can prevent Windows Media Player from ejecting the media from the drive after the completion of burning process. As Windows Media Player user if you want to do so you can follow the steps mentioned below:

1. Log on to Windows 7 computer.
2. Open **Windows Media Player** application by clicking on its icon.
3. Click **Organize** menu and from the available list click **Options**.
4. From the box go to **Burn** tab.
5. Under **General** section uncheck **Automatically eject the disc after burning** checkbox.

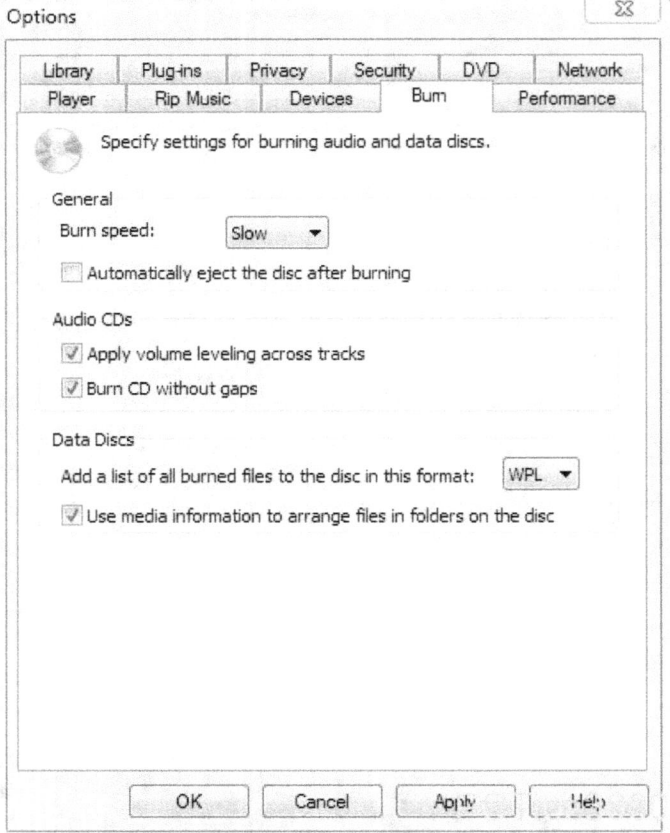

6. Once you are convinced with a configuration, click **Ok** button to save the changes that you have made.

Disable Media Files Deletion from Hard Drive

When a file is stored in Windows Media Player library, automatically or manually, it provides a central point of access for the users. In other words users need not to wander around throughout the system to locate for media files of their choices every time they want to play them. Moreover, there might be times when users may want to delete some media files from the library so that they can make some room for the new ones. When this is the case, default configuration of Windows Media Player automatically deletes the files from the hard drives and the files can never be restored when deleted. Users can change this configuration and they can stop Windows Media Player to delete files physically from the hard drives when they are deleted from the library. As a Windows 7 user if you want to do so you are required to follow the steps given below:

1. Log on to Windows 7 computer.

2. Click on the icon of **Windows Media Player** that is available in the taskbar.

3. Once opened, click **Organize** menu and from the available list click **Options** option.

4. From the opened box make sure that you are **Library** tab and under **Media Library Settings** section uncheck **Delete files from computer when deleted from library** checkbox.

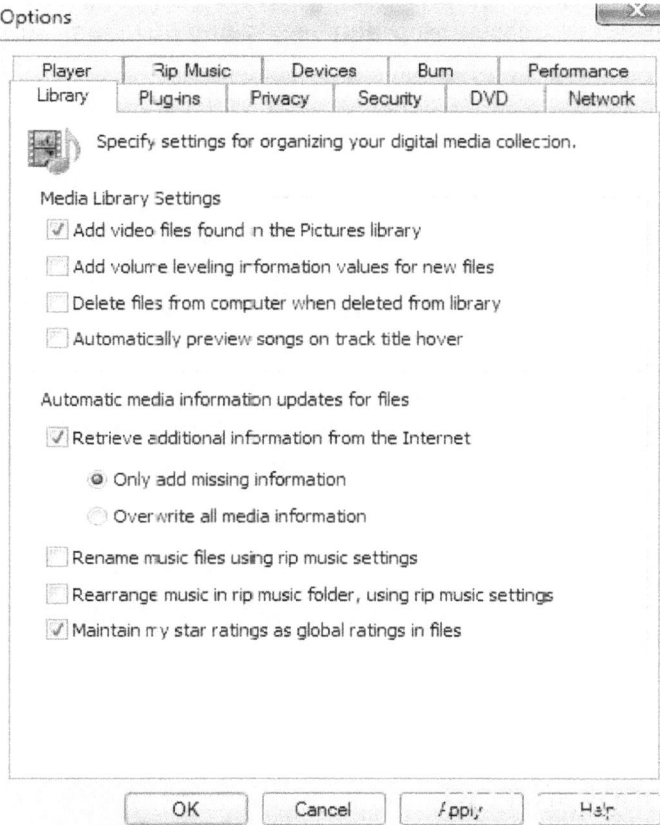

5. Once done, click **Ok** button to make the changes persistent.

Stop Windows Media Player While Switching Users

Switch User is a feature that was introduced with the release of Microsoft Windows XP for the very first time. This feature is now carried forward to almost every operating system that is released by Microsoft. This feature allows users to stay logged on to one user and still allow other users to log on to the same PC. Whenever a user switches from one account to another without logging off, all applications are left intact, i.e. Windows 7 does not close them, so that the user can use them whenever he logs back in. Best example for this can be when a user plays any music file in Windows Media Player and then switches to another user account without logging off from the current one he can notice that media file keeps on running in the background while the user can still work on the other account. In many cases this configuration is quite fine however if users want they can disable playing media file while they switch to another accounts. As a Windows 7 user if you want to do so you are required to follow the steps given below:

1. Log on to Windows 7 computer.
2. Open **Windows Media Player**.
3. From the interface click **Organize** menu.
4. From the available list click **Options** and from the opened box go to **Player** tab.
5. Under **Player settings** section check **Stop playback when switching to a different user** checkbox and finally click **Ok** button to save the changes.

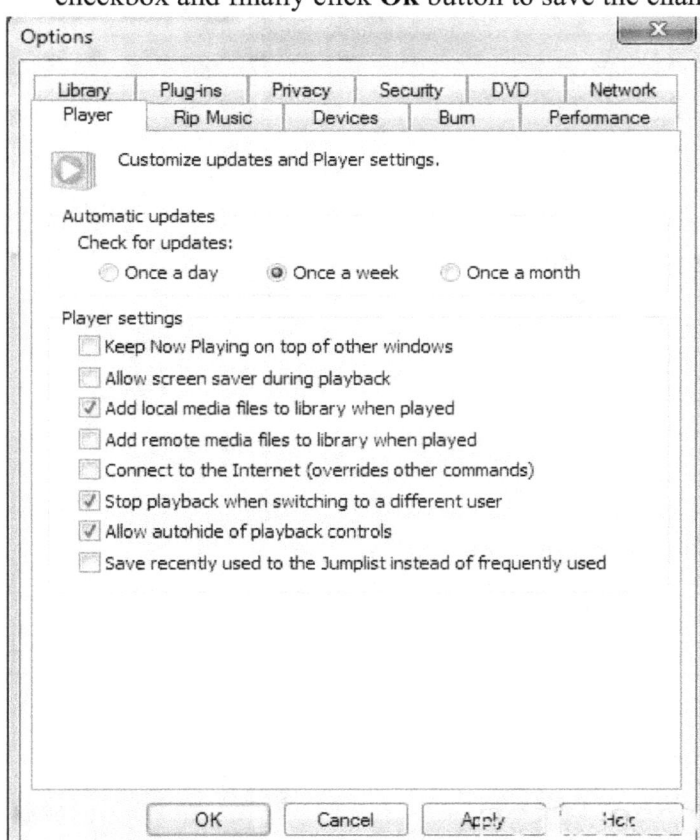

Connect Windows Media Player to Internet

For security reasons by default Windows Media Player is configured not to connect to the Internet automatically. This is because Internet is considered as a place where several hackers are present and are watching out for the loopholes in vulnerable PCs. In case Windows Media Player is connected to the Internet without users' knowledge hackers can get into the systems and can steal or harm sensitive data stored in them. Default configuration of not allowing WMP to connect to Internet automatically is quite suitable for production environments however in homes Windows Media Player can be allowed to connect to the Internet automatically so that users do not have to go through the process every time they need WMP to connect to the Internet. As a Windows 7 user in any home environment if you want to allow Windows Media Player to connect to the Internet automatically you are required to follow the steps given below:

1. Log on to Windows 7 computer.

2. Click on the icon of **Windows Media Player** that is available in the taskbar.

3. From the opened window click **Organize** menu and from the available list of options click **Options**.

4. On the opened box go to **Player** tab.

5. Check **Connect to the Internet (overrides other commands)** checkbox available under **Player settings** section.

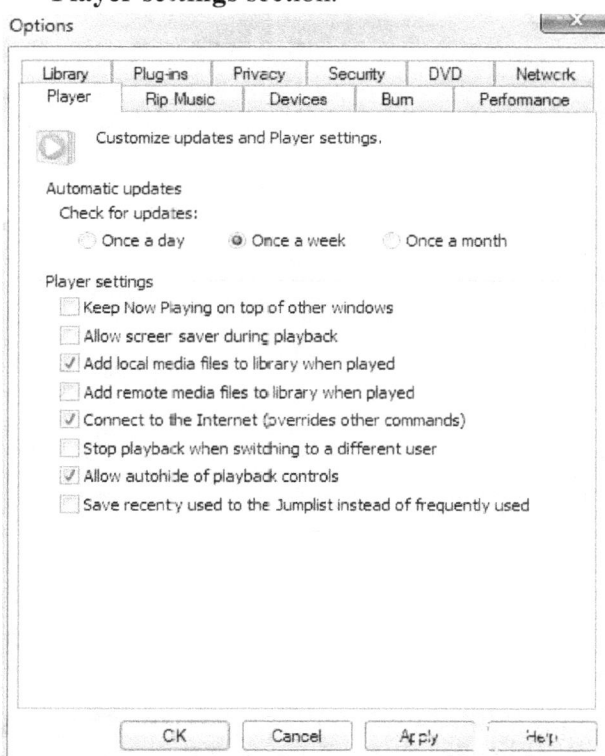

6. Finally click **Ok** button to save the changes.

Specify Internet Speed for Windows Media Player

While using the Windows Media Player in Windows 7 it is assumed that users are always connect to the Internet and any updated information that is available for any media file can be automatically downloaded almost instantaneously. As far as internet connection speed is concerned in many cases this configuration is not supposed to be modified as the default settings are perfect. However in some cases users may need to manually specify the connection speed of the Internet manually so that they can prevent the misuse of the connection. Windows Media Player offers promising controls using which users can limit the speed of Internet connection as desired. As a Windows 7 user if you want to do so you can follow the steps provided below:

1. Log on to Windows 7 computer.
2. Click on the icon of **Windows Media Player** that is available in the taskbar to initiate the application.
3. On the interface click **Organize** menu and from the available list click **Options** option.
4. On the opened box go to **Performance** tab.
5. Under **Connection speed** section select **Choose connection speed** radio button and from the enabled drop-down list choose the appropriate connection speed.

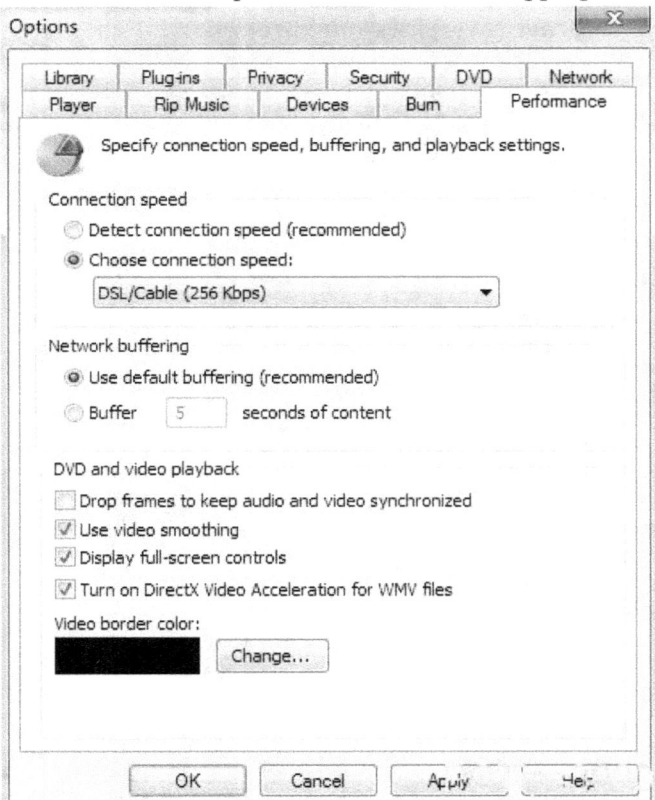

6. Click **Ok** button once you are convinced with the configurations that you have made.

Turn Off/Disable Windows Media Player

Like all other legacy versions of Microsoft operating systems, Windows 7 also has a built in Windows Media Player that allows users to play movies and music while providing promising sound and video quality at the same time. For home users Windows Media Player is a real economical fun as they need not to go for any third-party application to experience good quality while playing any music or movie file. In production environments however administrators may still object if any employee of the company tries to use Windows Media Player during office hours. In these cases the best option, or say, the best solution the administrators may go for is that they can disable Windows Media Player from Windows 7 operating system. As a Windows 7 administrator if you want to disable/turn off Windows Media Player from your computer you are required to follow the steps given as below:

1. Log on to Windows 7 computer with the administrator account.

2. From the start menu go to **Control Panel**.

3. On the opened window click **Programs** category link and from the next window click **Turn Windows features on or off** link under **Programs and Features** category link.

4. On **Windows Features** box expand **Media Features** and from the available list uncheck the check box representing **Windows Media Player**.

5. Click **Yes** button on the appeared confirmation box and finally click **Ok** button to save the changes that you have made.

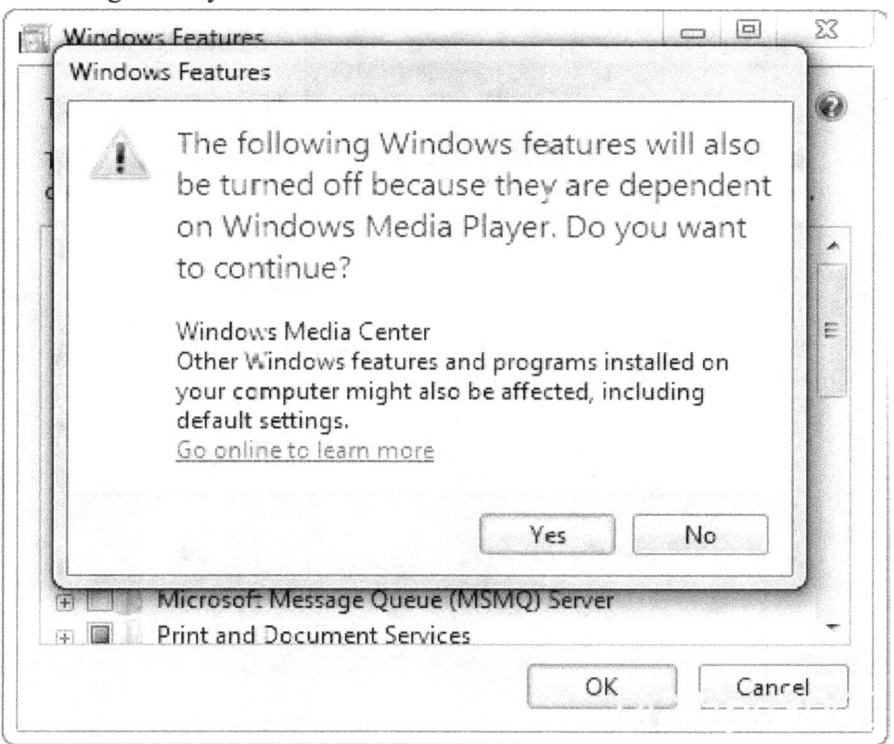

Adding Themes to Windows 7 Media Center

Windows Media Center is a in Microsoft Windows 7 which allows users to experience complete multi-media functions offered by the application in the operating system. Windows Media Center also allows users to watch TV channels in case they have TV tuner card installed in their computers. The default ambiance that Windows Media Center has is very sober and might sometimes become quite boring, especially for fun loving people. To solve this problem, WMC allows users to change themes as per their requirements and individual choices. Changing default theme or color scheme in Windows Media Center application is a simple process and as a Windows 7 administrator or any standard user if you want to do so you need to follow the steps given as below:

1. Log on to Windows 7 computer with any standard user or administrator account.
2. At the bottom of start menu in search box type **Windows Media Center** and press enter key.
3. On opened application interface click **Start** button and from the available list of controls scroll, locate and click **Settings**.
4. On the appeared list click **General**.
5. On the submenu of **General** category click **Visual and Sound Effects**.
6. On the appeared page under **Color scheme** choose the appropriate radio button as required to update color scheme and click **Save** button.

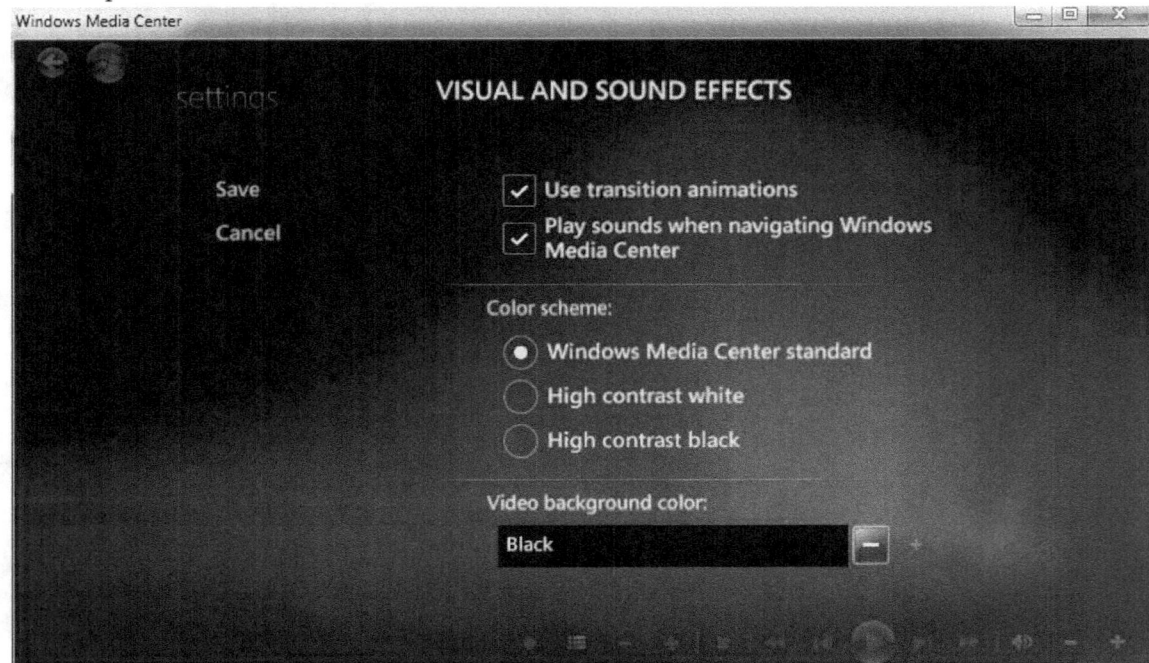

You will find the instantaneous change in the scheme color of Windows Media Center.

Create Music Playlists in Windows 7 Media Center

Almost every computer user loves to hear music and there are several of them who create a separate folder in which they keep audio files of their favorite numbers. This practice is sometimes very useful for new users as they can directly access their music files. This practice is time taking and might consume several megabytes of hard disk space unnecessarily. Better option, which is recommended as well, is to create a playlist which does not require any space at all but is just a collection of links to the favorite music files. Nowadays almost every music player offers the facility of creating playlists in order to provide users instantaneous access to their favorite songs. Same is the case with Windows Media Center in which users can create their own playlists and can listen to music whenever they feel like hence eliminating the requirement of selecting songs every time. As Windows Media Center user if you want to create your own playlists you need to follow the steps as below:

1. Log on to Windows 7 computer with the user account that you frequently use.
2. At the bottom of start menu search box type **Windows Media Center** and press enter key to initiate the application.
3. On the opened interface scroll down to **Music** category and then click **music library** option.
4. On the next screen click **playlists** and click **Create Playlist**.
5. On the appeared box specify the name of the playlist and click **Next** button.
6. On **Select a location to browse for media** window click **Music Library** radio button to select and click **Next** button.
7. Choose the appropriate and required music files and once selected click **Next** button.

8. Finally click **Create** button to create playlist.

Movies in Windows Media Center Media Library

When Windows 7 is first installed on a computer, Windows Media Center is automatically installed which provides almost every multimedia feature that users can think of. Because of its versatile nature the application is capable of playing music, videos, slideshows, etc. Moreover, it allows users to create playlists for music files and video clips. Creating slideshows is also quite easy through this application and before creating any slideshow users can also modify the images if they want. Main focus of this section is on the creation of media library where users can place movie files and can gain instantaneous access to them whenever they need. With the help of easy-to-go wizard offered by Windows Media Center users can place video files at a central location from where they can be played within no time. As a Windows 7 user and Windows Media Center lover if you want to place some movie files in media library you are required to follow the steps given below:

1. Log on to Windows 7 computer.

2. At the bottom of start menu in search box type **Windows Media Center** and press enter key.

3. On the opened application interface scroll down to **Tasks** and click **settings**.

4. On next window click **Media Libraries** option and from the available list on next window click **Movies** radio button to select.

5. Click **Next** button when done.

6. On **Movies** page click **Add folders to the library** radio button to select and click **Next** button.

7. On **Add Folders for Movies** page select **On this computer (includes mapped network drives)** radio button and click **Next** button.

8. On next window choose appropriate folder(s) and click **Next** button.

9. On **Confirm Changes** page choose **Yes, use these locations** radio button under **Are you finished making changes?** section and finally click **Finish** button to start the process.

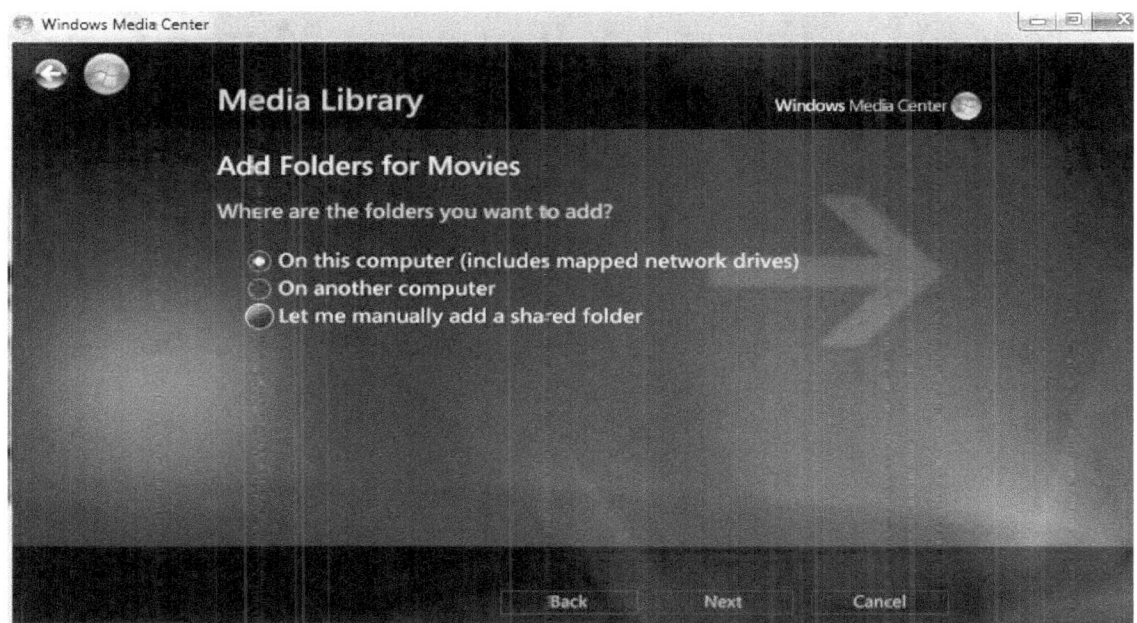

Watch TV without TV Tuner in Media Center

There are several third-party applications in the market that claim that they allow their subscribers to view thousands of TV channels free of cost. These third party applications require legal subscription to the vendors of the applications and sometimes may also require subscriptions to the TV channels they like to view. These steps are, of course, time taking and also require some financial involvement at the same time. Technically speaking, this practice is not considered as practical and many users avoid going for such kinds of solutions. Microsoft understands this and therefore it has included the feature of Internet TV in Windows Media Center in Windows 7. Internet TV feature is required to be installed before it can be used by the users though. The best part is that users are not required to have any TV tuner cards installed on the computers and this feature is mostly beneficial to laptop users. As a Windows 7 user if you want to install Internet TV in Windows Media Center application you are required to follow the steps given as below:

1. Log on to Windows 7 computer.
2. At the bottom of start menu in search box type **Windows Media Centre** and press enter key.
3. From the opened interface scroll down to **TV** category and click **internet TV**.
4. On **Free streaming Internet TV** window check **I have read and understood Terms of Service and Privacy Statement** checkbox and click **Install** button.

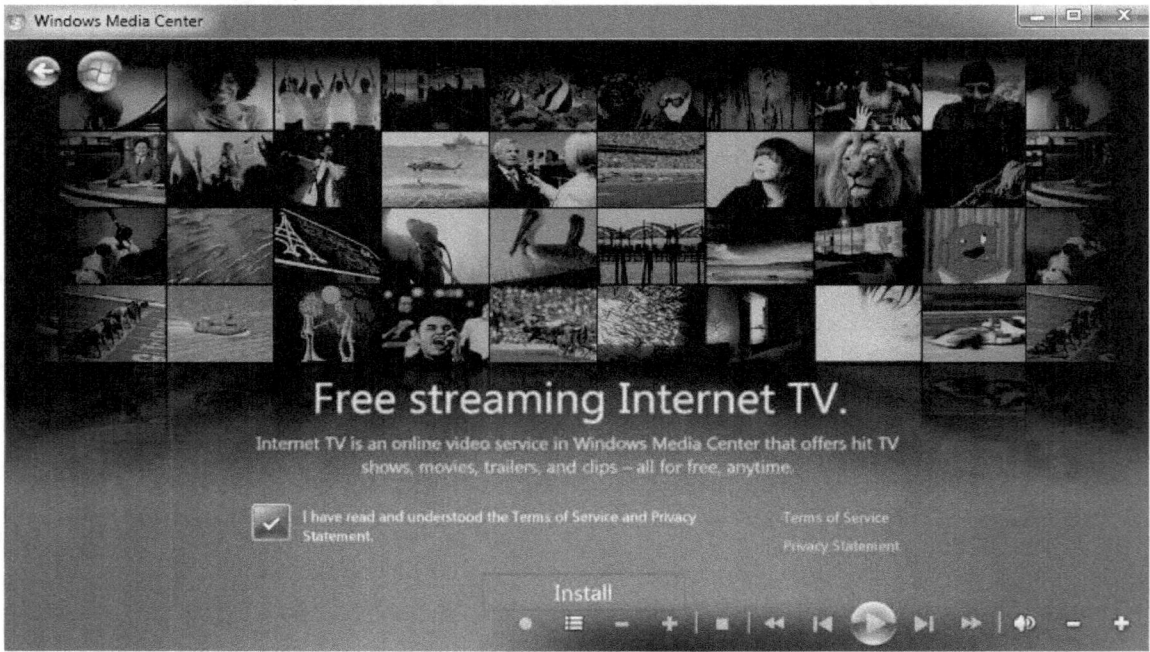

5. Follow the on-screen instructions to complete the installation process.

Edit Photos in Windows 7 Media Center

It would not be wrong if said that Windows Media Center is a complete and versatile application that works as one-stop-shop for multimedia lovers. Reason behind these words is that apart from creating playlists and slideshows, Windows Media Center also allows users to modify image files as per their requirements. Although the application cannot work as a full-fledged image editor developed by third-party vendor users who do not have in-depth technical knowledge about image editing can still use Windows Media Center to modify the pictures according to their will. Moreover, users can also save the images they modify and can also create slideshows out of them. Unlike any full-fledged image editing application, editing images in Windows Media Center is quite easy process and as a Windows Media Center user in Windows 7 if you want to do so you are required to follow the steps guided as below:

1. Log on to Windows 7 computer with the most frequent account that you use.
2. At the bottom of start menu in search box type **Windows Media Center** and press enter key to initiate the application.
3. On the appeared window scroll down and click **picture library** under **Pictures + Videos** category.
4. On the new window click on the appropriate folder that contains images.
5. When opened, right-click on the image that you want to modify and from the available menu click **Picture Details** option.
6. From the available options choose the required ones to modify the image and make appropriate adjustments.
7. Finally click **Save** button to save the changes.

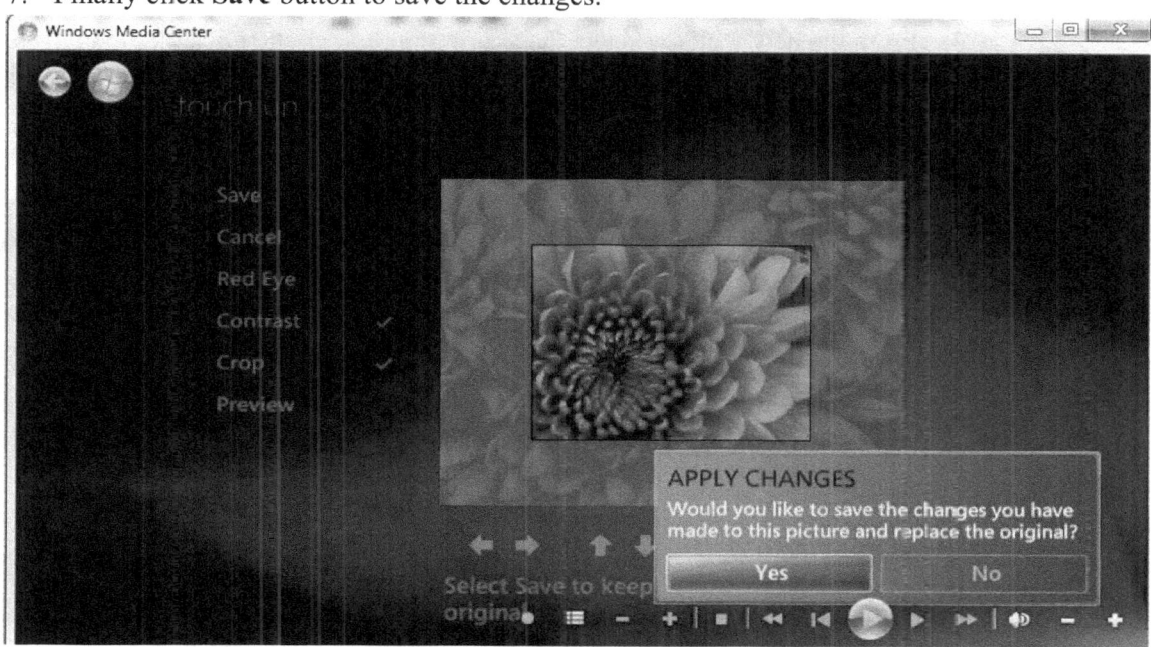

Create a Slide Show in Windows 7 Media Center

In Microsoft Windows 7 Windows Media Center allows users to experience complete multimedia features in a single application. This means that with the help of Windows Media Center users can watch TV, play movies, view slideshows, etc. and they do not require to hunt for any third-party application in order to do such tasks. The matter of fact is that Windows Media Center is not just a viewer but it can also be used to create several things as far as multimedia objects are concerned. Same is the case with slide shows. Windows Media Center allows users to create slideshows of their favorite images and it also allows them to run them at the same time. Although several sideshow makers are available in the market and many of them are absolutely free of cost, however logical thinking can be, why to go for any third-party application (paid or free) if Microsoft has so much to offer. As a Windows 7 user if you want to create slideshow in Windows Media Center you are required to follow the steps given as below:

1. Log on to Windows 7 computer with any account as the process does not require any elevated privileges.

2. At the bottom of start menu in search box type **Windows Media Center** and press enter key.

3. On Windows Media Centre interface scroll down to **Pictures + Videos** category and click **picture library**.

4. On the appeared interface click **<slide shows>** and then click **Create Slide Show**.

5. On the next screen specify the name of the new slideshow and click **Next** button.

6. On **Select a location to browse for media** window click **Picture Library** radio button and click **Next** button.

7. From the new window select the appropriate folder and click on the images to select them.

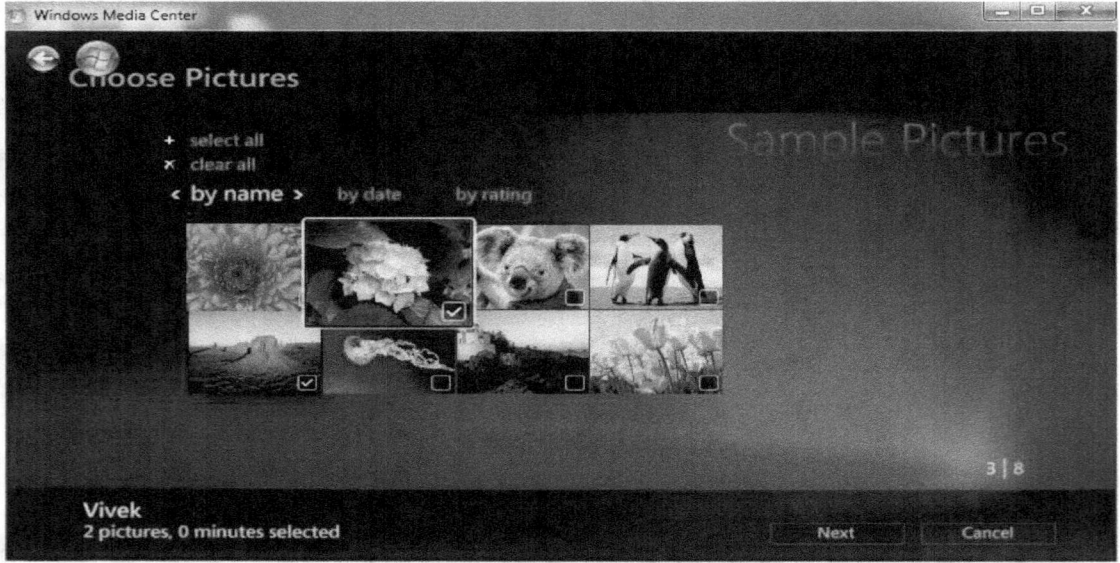

8. Once done, click **Next** button and finally click **Create** button to create the slideshow.

CHAPTER 15
MONITORING, MAINTAINING AND TROUBLESHOOTING

Check if Windows 7 is 64-bit or 32-bit (x64 or x86)

Now-a-days when a laptop is purchased from a vendor it is shipped along with Windows 7 operating system installed on it. In 99% cases it is expected that the Windows 7 operating system which is installed on a laptop PC is of 64 bit. In some cases, however, it can also be of 32-bit which totally depends on the configuration of the laptop. In either case it cannot the expected from any non-technical user that he/she can verify as which flavor of operating system is installed on their laptop PCs. With the help of this section those users will be able to determine whether the operating system is of 64-bit or 32-bit. This verification can be done by just a few mouse clicks and as a Windows 7 user if you want to do so you are required to follow the steps mentioned as below:

1. Log on to Windows 7 computer with any account.

2. From the start menu right click **Computer** and from the available context menu click **Properties**.

3. From the opened window verify the information that is provided in front of **System type** category.

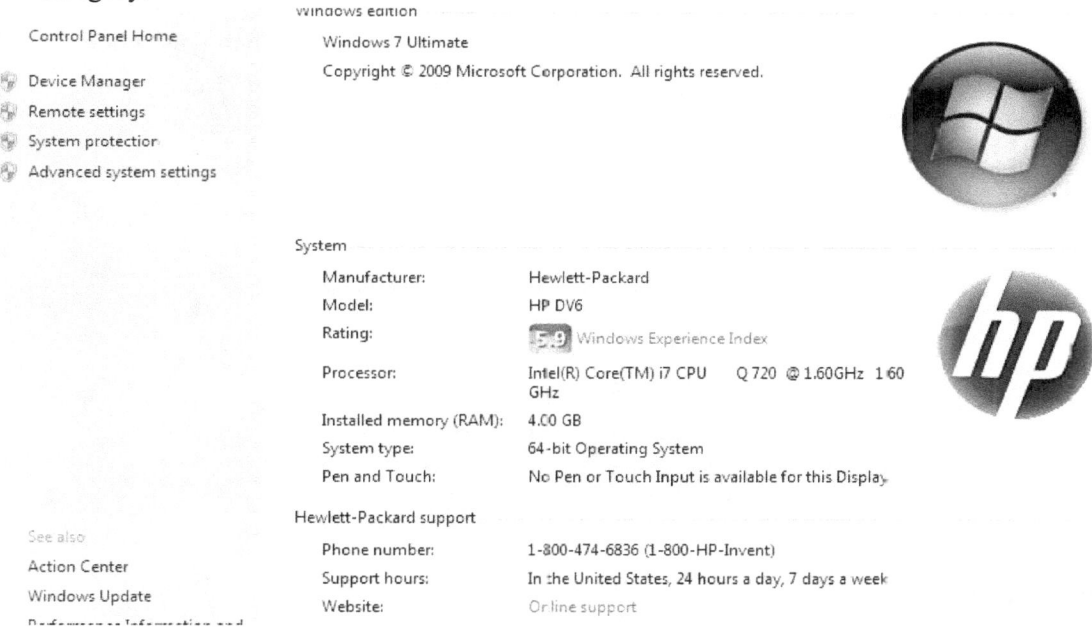

4. Once confirmed, close the opened window.

Note: These steps can also be followed to verify the operating systems on desktop computers and are not limited to laptop PCs only.

Get System Rating

System rating is the feature which was introduced in Windows Vista for the first time and is now carried over to Windows 7. When this feature is initialized, it gathers all the performance related information of your computer according to the hardware devices attached to it. With the help of this information you can determine the exact state of the devices and which of them need to be upgraded to run which applications. System rating can be useful for game lovers and/or for those who are into graphic designing, as with this they can assess if their video graphic card would support any specific game or graphic designing application like 3-D Studio Max or Maya. You can get your system rating information by following the steps given below:

1. Log on to the Windows 7 computer with administrator account.

2. Click **Start** button.

3. From the start menu right-click **Computer** and from the menu click **Properties**.

4. On **View basic information about your computer** page click **System Rating** link available in **System** frame.

5. On **Rate and improve your computer's performance** page click **Rate This Computer** button. Note: Windows Vista users may have to accept User Account Control confirmation.

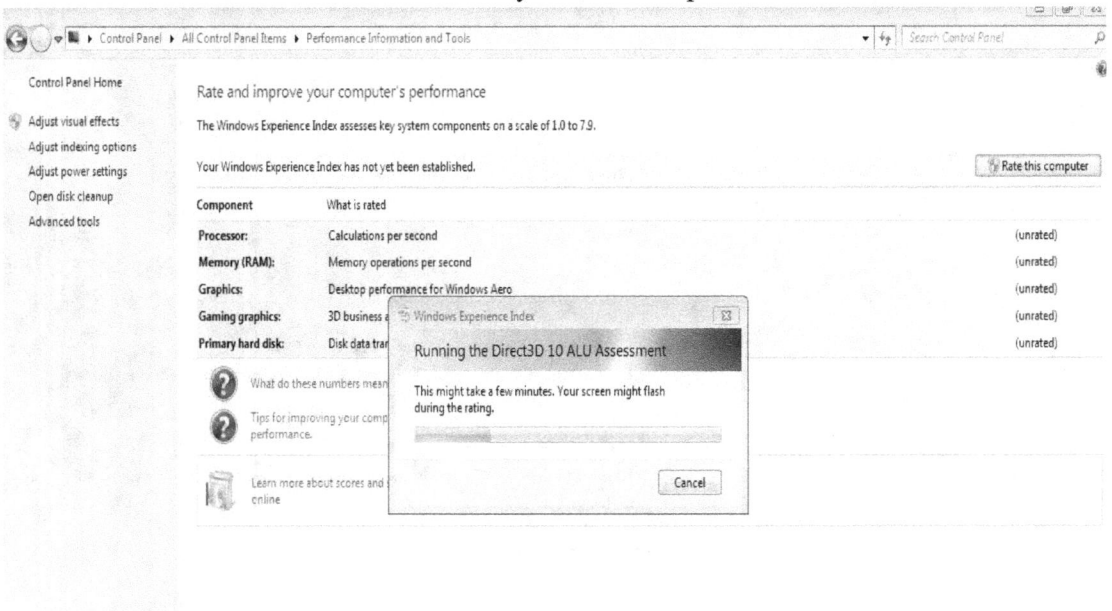

6. You need to wait until the system rating feature gathers the entire information of your computer.

Once the process is complete you can view the overall rating of your system. The overall rating is based on the least performing device attached to your machine. Also, you will get the rating of individual peripherals integrated to your computer as shown in the snapshot below.

Generate System Health Reports

System performance assessment is quite essential for both home users and in offices. Using this feature you can determine the workload on your computer and how the attached devices are performing. It is always a good practice to get a system performance report right after you have installed Windows 7 and use this report as a baseline parameter to compare and assess the performance of your computer which may reduce by the time. You can generate system health report by following the steps given below:

1. Log on to the Windows 7 computer with administrator account.

2. Click **Start** button.

3. From the start menu right-click **Computer** and from the menu click **Properties**.

4. On **View basic information about your computer** page click **No System Rating Available** link present in **System** frame.

5. On **Rate and improve your computer's performance** page in the left bar click **Advanced tools** link.

6. On **Use these tools to get additional performance information** page click **Generate a system health report** link and wait till the report gets generated.

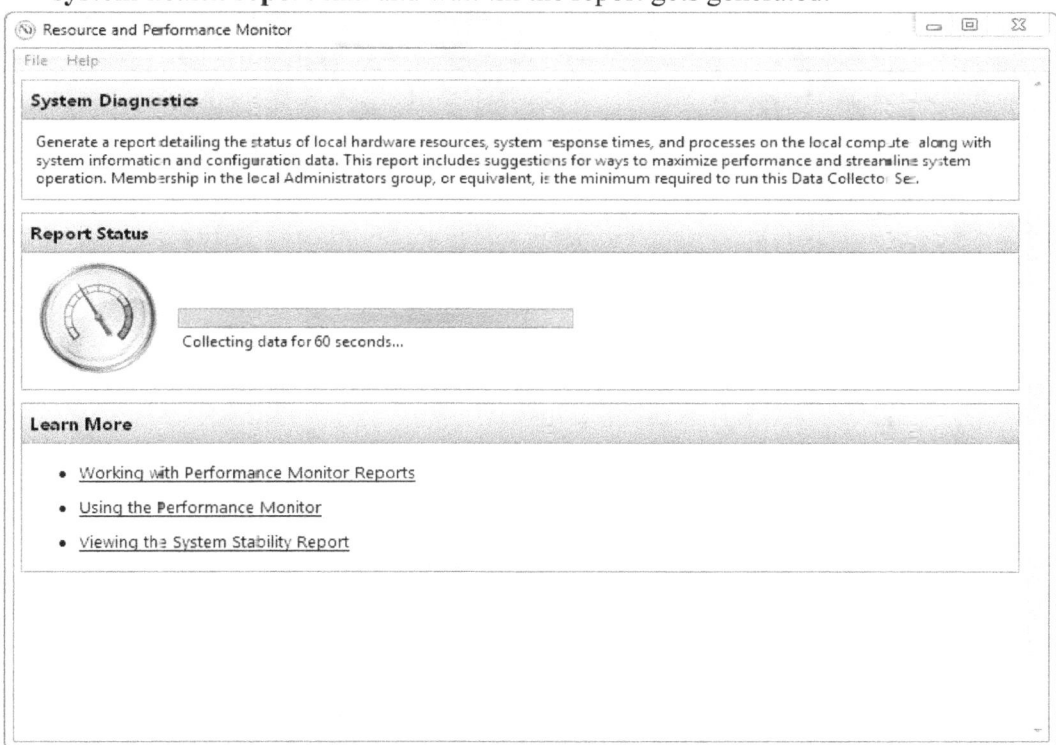

7. Once Windows 7 has gathered all the information regarding the health of your computer you will be displayed with the Resource and Performance Monitor window from where you can get complete information about your system performance. You can then take appropriate action against the issues related to the performance of your Windows 7 computer.

Get Graphical Representation of Hard Disk Usage

Most important part of your computer after microprocessor is your physical hard disk. Without hard disk your computer cannot store even an operating system, hence making it completely unusable for everyone. Directly or indirectly, performance of your computer depends on your hard disk and its working efficiency. In order to maintain consistent and smooth functioning of your hard disk you should monitor its performance on regular basis. Microsoft Windows 7 offers a feature using which you can view the performance of your hard disk graphically. To do this you need to follow the steps given below:

1. Log on to your Windows 7 computer with the administrator account and go to start menu by clicking **Start** button.
2. Right click on **Computer** and from the menu choose **Manage**.
3. On the opened box expand **Performance** and then expand **Monitoring Tools**.
4. From the expanded list choose **Performance Monitor** and from the right pane click on plus (+) sign.
5. On **Add Counters** box under **Available counters** list click on and expand **Physical Disk**.
6. From the available list click **Disk Transfer/sec** and click **Add** button.

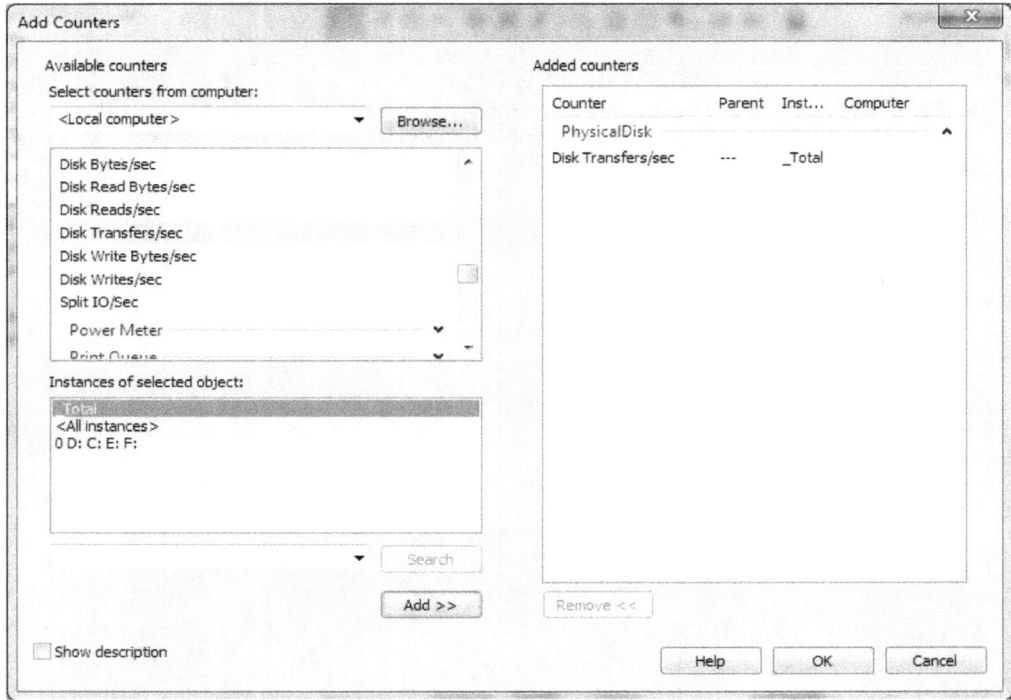

7. Finally click Ok button to add the counter and view the graphical representation of your hard disk usage.

Graphical Representation of Processor's Idle Time

For any computer running any operating system, it is necessary that its processor remains idle most of the times. In other words, the more the processor remains idle the more optimized the computer performance is considered. You cannot protect your computer from virus attacks entirely and neither can you prevent your computer from getting overpopulated, to reduce its performance, by the time. However with some Windows 7 built-in features you can regularly monitor your processor usage and its idle time which can help you assess as when your computer needs hardware upgrades or reinstallation of operating system. You can use Performance Monitor Counters to get the idle time record of the processor. You can add and use this counter by following the steps given below:

1. Log on to the computer with the administrator account and click **Start** button.

2. On the start menu right click **Computer** and from the appeared menu click **Manage**.

3. From **Computer Management** snap-in expand **Performance** and expand **Monitoring Tools.**

4. On the displayed list click **Performance Monitor** and from the right pane click on plus (+) sign to add the counters.

5. On **Add Counters** box under **Available counters** list choose **Processor** category to expand and from the available list click on **% Idle Time.**

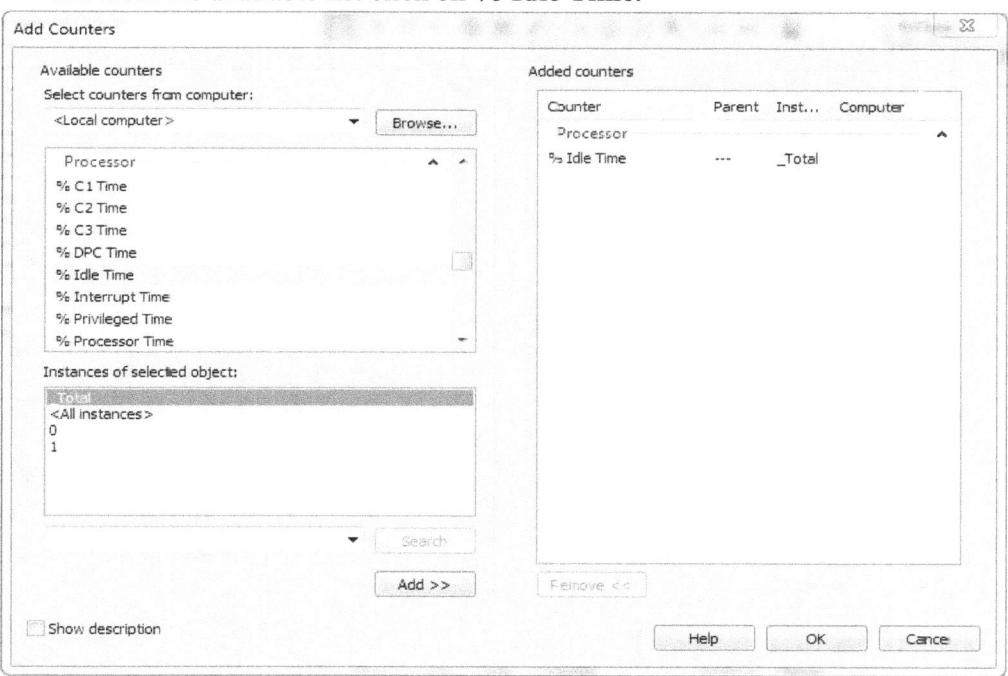

6. Click **Add** button and finally click **Ok** button to accept your configuration.

7. Back on the main window you will find the graphical representation of the idle processor time in %.

DirectX Diagnostic

Well if you really take care of your system and you really give attention towards DirectX you should know from where to get all the information about your installed DirectX. For the first time when you run DirectX Diagnostic tool you will be asked for the WHQL Digital Signature. For that you must click YES. After following these steps, you will be displayed with the DirectX Diagnostic Tool. First tab is the System Tab where you will get all the information about your system and importantly DirectX version. In Windows 7, DirectX 11 (which is the latest version of all DirectX series) is installed at the time of Windows installation. The next tab is Display tab which will show you your display device, manufacture, chip type, monitor, etc. and also the DirectX features like DirectDraw Acceleration, Direct3D Acceleration and AGP Texture Acceleration with the drivers. It also gives you the Sound tab with your Primary and Secondary Sounds Devices. And the last tab is the Input Tab which will show you your input devices such as keyboard, mouse, gamepad, etc. You can run test in all these tabs for optimal settings and results and it will guide you through troubleshooting process as well. To get this follow these steps,

1. Log on to Windows 7 computer with any account.
2. From the Start menu in search box, type **DXDIAG** and press enter.

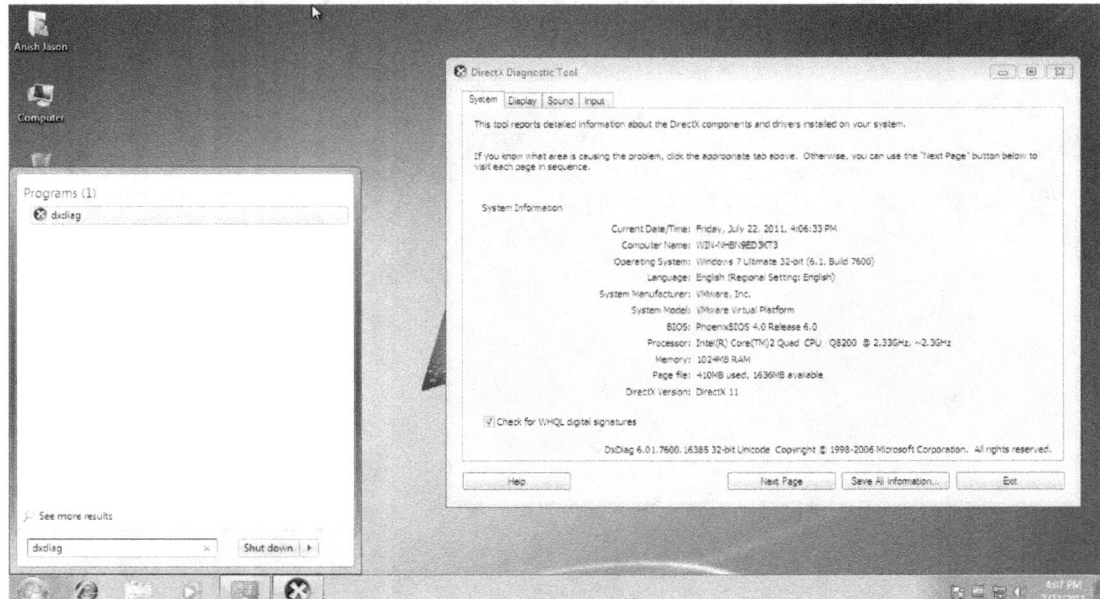

Create Custom Views for Easy Diagnosis

When it comes to troubleshooting or diagnosing Windows errors, most administrators rely on Event Viewer utility provided by the operating system. Although Event Viewer was also available in legacy versions of operating systems, however the updated version offered by Windows 7 has many sophisticated features which allow administrators to locate required logs easily. A great help in this regard is a feature named Custom Views which allows administrators to define the types of logs that they might be interested in. This feature becomes quite handy because administrators need not to go through bulk of logs to find their required information. Instead they can locate filtered logs with the help of Custom Views that contain precise information which are defined to be displayed by the administrators. As an administrator if you want to create Custom Views you are required to follow the steps given below:

1. Log on to Windows 7 computer with the account that has administrative rights.
2. Click **Start** button and from the menu right click **Computer**.
3. From the context menu click **Manage** and from the opened **Computer Management** snap-in expand **Event Viewer**.
4. Right click **Custom Views** and click **Create Custom View**.
5. On the opened box make sure that you are **Filter** tab and configure the fields and check boxes as required.

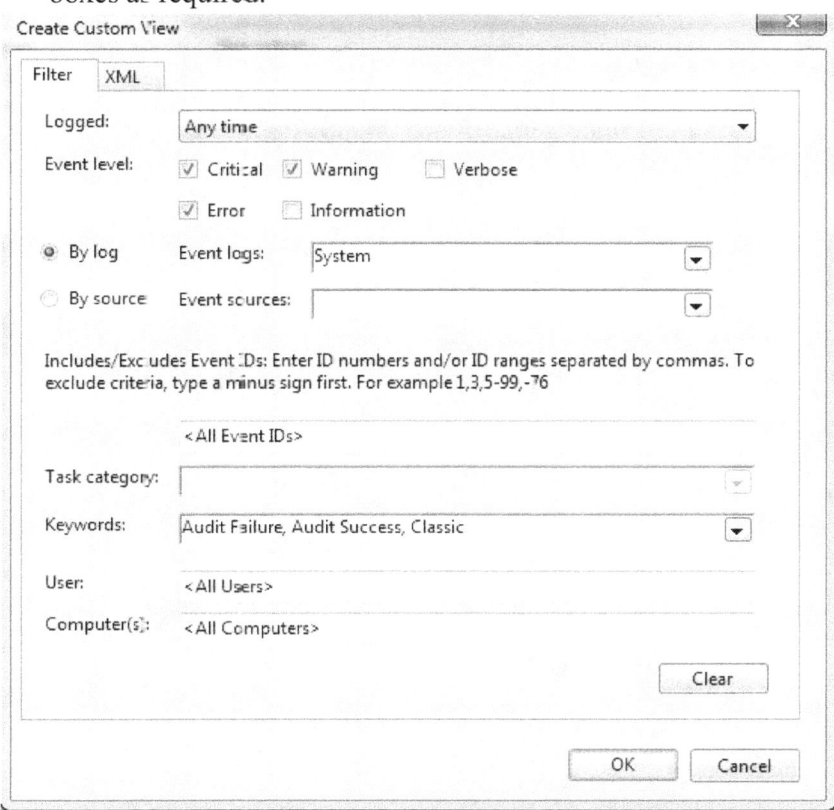

6. Click **Ok** button to save the changes.

7. On **Save Filter to Custom View** box specify the name of the **Custom View** and click **Ok** button to create.

8. You can now locate the logs by expanding Custom Views and clicking on the newly created custom view from the left pane.

Measure CPU Usage from System Tray Icon

Whether Windows 7 is used in home environments or production, every user or administrator is curious to know about the CPU usage of the computer. This is because of the fact that the more the CPU is used the lesser performance it offers. In order to avoid excessive CPU usage users need to reduce the numbers of simultaneously running applications. A user can view CPU usage by going to Task Manager and sometimes, in case of Windows 7 or Windows Vista, he can also place CPU meter gadget on the desktop. However many users do not know that there is another simpler way to place a small icon of CPU usage meter in the system tray by following the steps given below:

1. Log on to Windows 7 computer.
2. Click **Start** button and go to **All Programs**.
3. Locate and right click **Startup** container and from the available menu click **Open**.
4. On the opened window right click anywhere in blank space and go to **New**.
5. From the submenu click **Shortcut** and on the opened box click **Browse** button to locate **TASKMGR.EXE**.

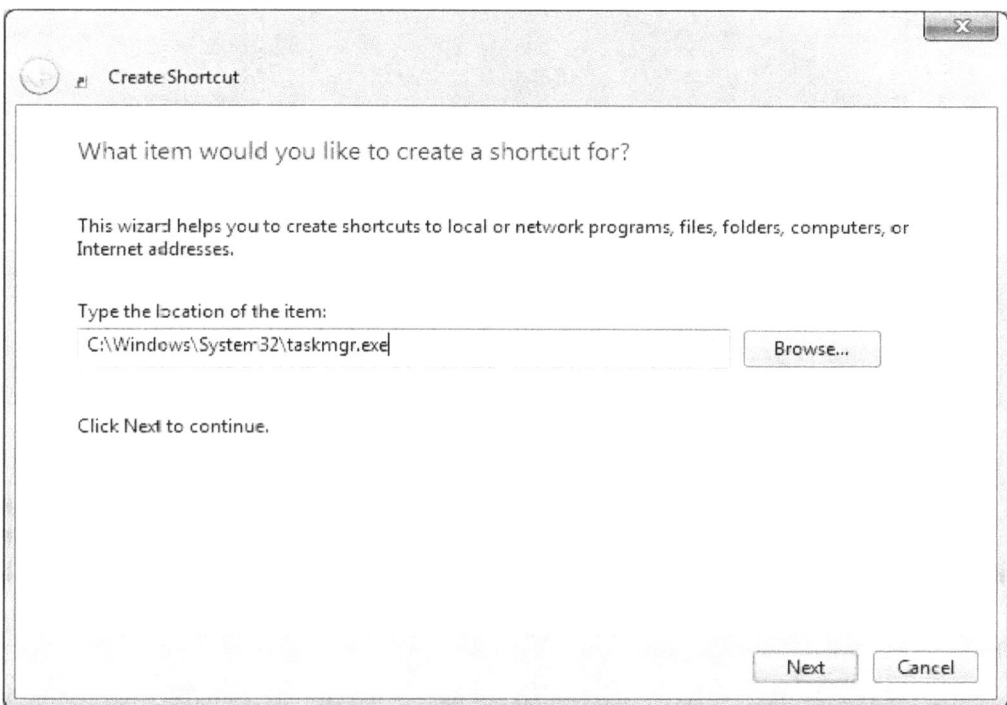

6. Click **Next** button and on the next window specify the name of the shortcut.
7. Click **Finish** button.
8. Right click on the created shortcut and from the menu click **Properties**.
9. On **Properties** box make sure that you are **Shortcut** tab and from the available **Run** dropdown list choose **Minimized**.

10. Click **Ok** button to save the changes.

11. Right click **Taskbar** and click **Start Task Manager**.

12. On **Windows Task Manager** box from the **Options** menu choose **Hide When Minimized** option to select.

13. Close **Windows Task Manager**.

14. Check your configuration by restarting the Windows. You will be displayed with a small CPU meter icon in the system tray.

Using Resource Monitor

When working with Windows 7 or any other operating system it is quite obvious that as the operating system grows older its performance starts decreasing in the same proportion. In earlier versions of Windows, that is, Microsoft Windows 2000 and Windows XP very few diagnostic tools were available and many times in production environments administrators depended on third-party diagnostic tools so that they can assess the health of the systems accurately. With the release of Windows 7 there are several built-in monitoring and diagnostic tools that work in more efficient way as compared to the tools the legacy versions of the operating systems had. Same is the case with Resource Monitor which ships along with Windows 7 and is installed by default. This small application allows administrators of computers to view the usage of resources which they can further use to assess problematic areas of the computer and can take appropriate actions to troubleshoot the problems. As a Windows 7 administrator if you want to use this feature to monitor resource usage you are required to follow the steps given below:

1. Log on to Windows 7 computer with the account that has elevated privileges.

2. At the bottom of start menu in search box type **Performance Info** and press enter key.

3. On the opened page in the left bar click **Advanced Tools** link.

4. On the opened window click **Open resource monitor**.

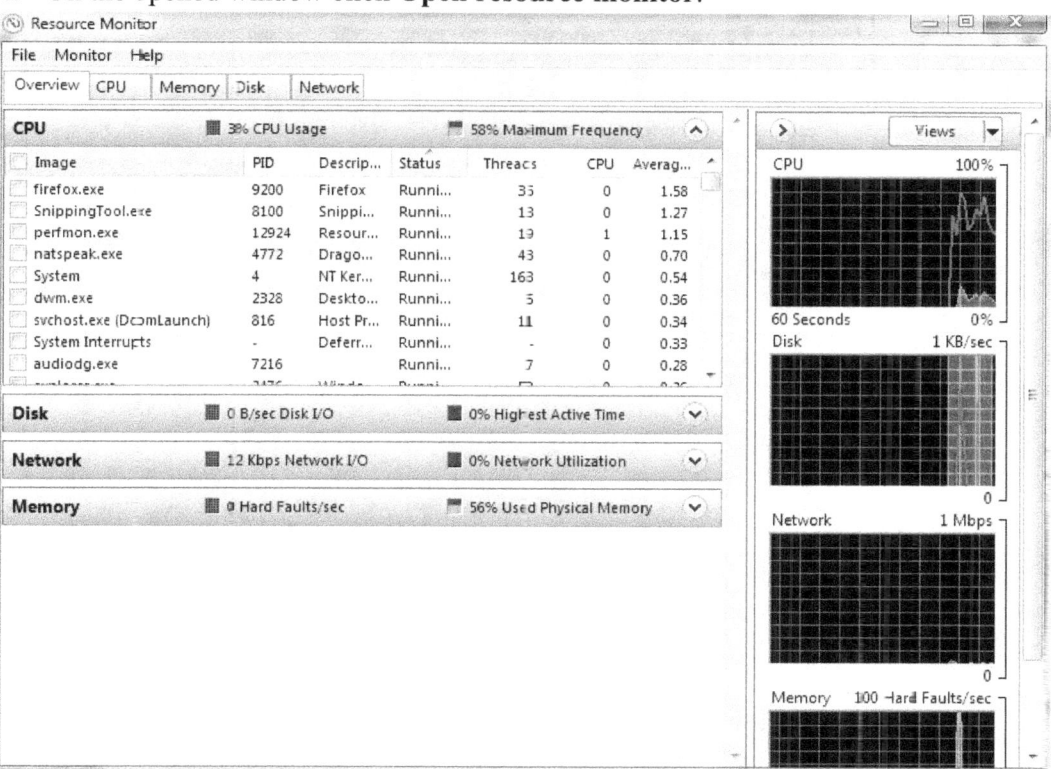

5. You can now view the usage of resources more granularly.

Get Back Windows 7 Desktop If Not Visible

There are times when a user logs on to the computer just to find that there is no desktop screen and other icons visible on the monitor. In most cases users think that their computer system is infected with a virus and they start looking out for a technician who then charges a decent amount from them to rectify the issue. In this section you will learn how to solve this problem without any help from any expensive technician. Whenever you find your desktop screen missing this means that the process associated with it failed to initialize. This may happen either because of unexpected computer shut down or voltage fluctuation. In Windows 7 you can get your desktop screen back by following the steps given below:

1. Log on to the computer with the user account you are facing problem.

2. Right click on the taskbar and click **Start Task Manager**.

3. In **Windows Task Manager** box make sure that you are on **Applications** tab and click **New Task** button.

4. On **Create New Task** box type **EXPLORER.EXE** in the available text box and click **Ok** button to get your desktop screen back on your monitor.

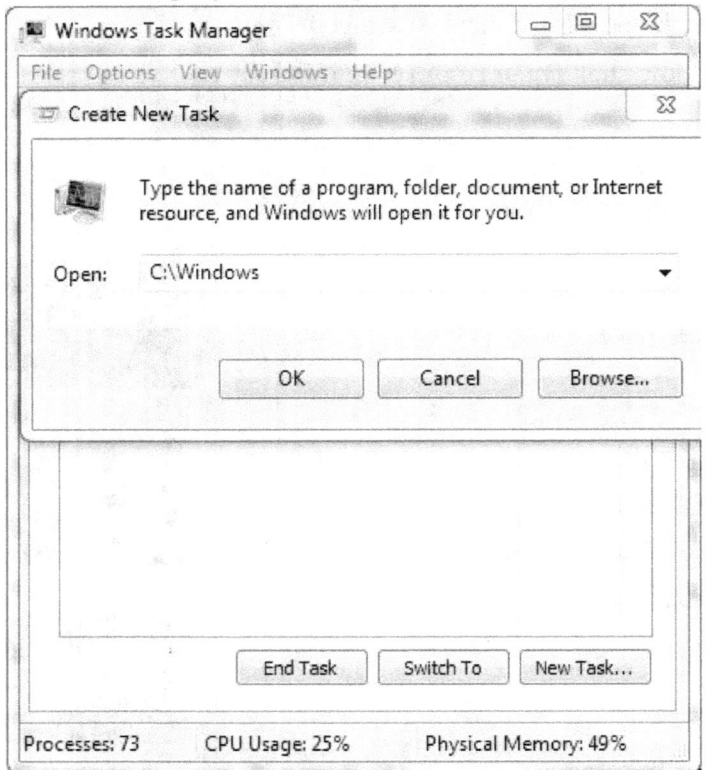

5. Close **Windows Task Manager**.

More Info:

You can run almost any application using the above method. However, for some of them you may require elevated privileges.

End Running Processes

Whenever any application is initialized, Windows starts the process associated with the application in the background. In other words an application only gets turned on because its process runs behind the scenes. However, there are times when users may want to terminate any running application instantaneously. Reasons behind this may include discarding the modifications, eliminating the possibilities of crashing the application, etc. When this is the case users can use Task Manager to end the entire process tree of the application. Users need to be cautious, though, that there are few processes that require System account to run as a service. These processes cannot be terminated by any user even if he is logged on using administrator account. User specific processes can be terminated either by logging on to the computer with the user or administrator account. You can terminate any process instantaneously by following the steps given below:

1. Log on to the computer.

2. Right click on the taskbar and from the menu click **Start Task Manager**.

3. On **Windows Task Manager** box go to **Processes** tab and from the available list right click on the processor you want to terminate.

4. From the available menu click **End Process Tree** and on the confirmation box click **End process tree** button to terminate the process.

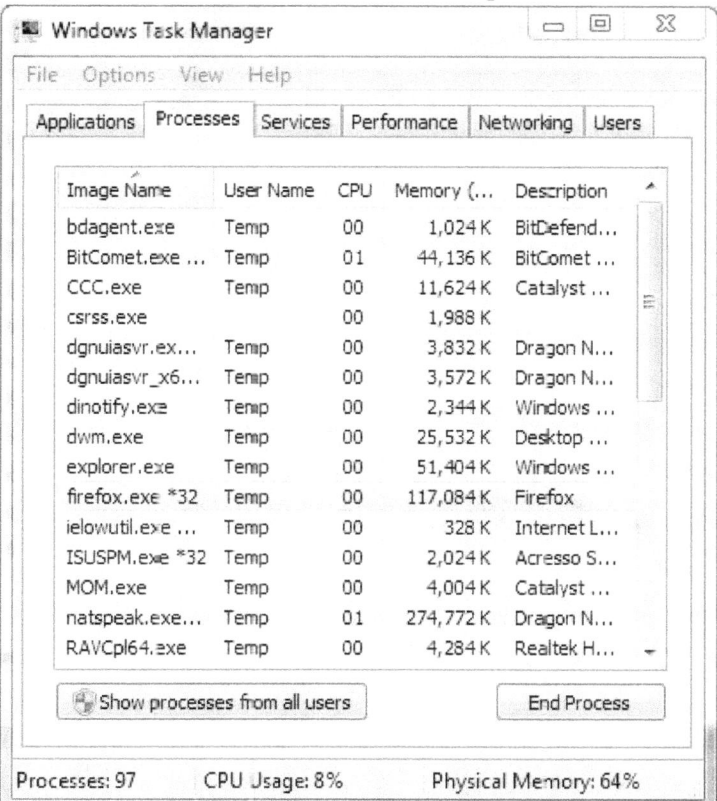

5. Close all opened Windows.

Disable Auto Defragmentation

Defragmentation in a Windows-based computer system is an essential part in order to maintain the efficiency of the operating system. With the release of Windows 7, defragmentation process is by default scheduled to run at one o'clock in the morning every Wednesday. This default configuration is to ensure that the consistency and efficiency of Windows 7 computer is maintained and users need not to go through all the technical configurations. Although this configuration is for users' convenience however it still requires that computer systems should be kept running and should not be in use during that time. Moreover this default process of defragmentation may also take several hours depending on the utilization of the hard disk. Under some circumstances users may want to disable this feature in order to take complete control over the operating system and manually defragment Windows 7 when required and as a Windows 7 user if you want to do so you need to follow the steps given below:

1. Log on to Windows 7 computer with any account that has administrative privileges.

2. At the bottom of start menu in search box type DFRGUI command and press enter key.

3. On **Disk Defragmenter** box click **Configure schedule** button and on the opened box uncheck **Run on the schedule (recommended)** checkbox.

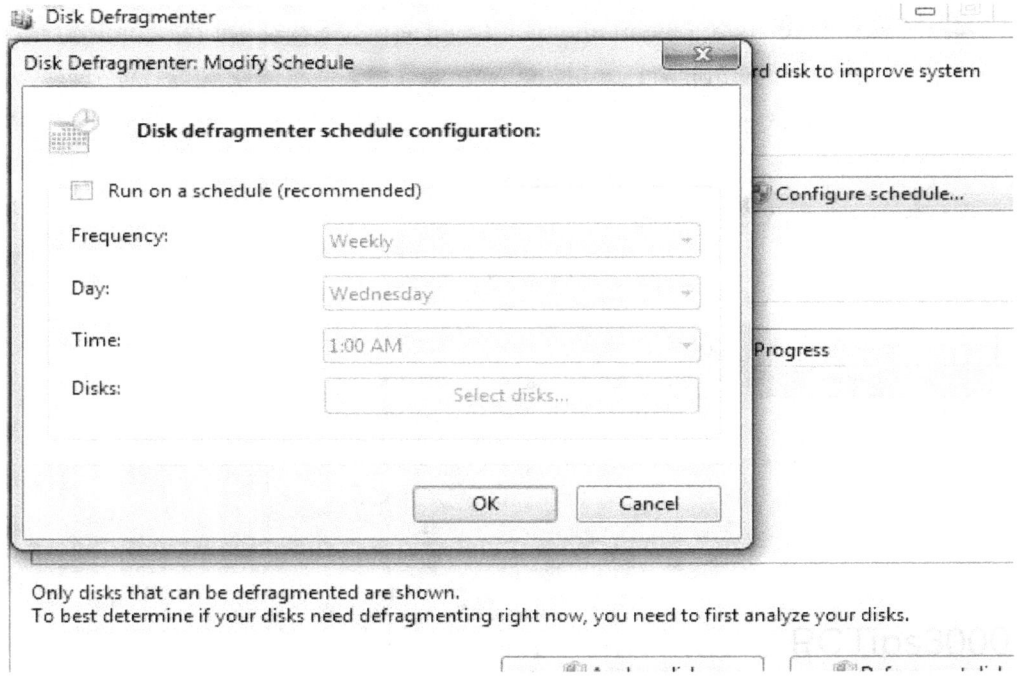

4. Finally click Ok button to save the changes and close all the opened boxes and Windows.

Defragment and Schedule Defragmentation Process

Defragmentation is the process which considerably enhances the speed of your computer. The reason behind this is that when you keep on storing and deleting the files in any particular drive on regular basis the files get fragmented. Because of this the operating system takes more time to collect all the scattered pieces of a file from different locations before opening it. With the help of Defragment, these fragmented files are re-joined together, thus allowing the operating system to eliminate the need of collecting scattered pieces of file from different locations of the hard disk, hence speeding up the system remarkably.

1. To defragment any drive (E.g. C:) you need to follow the steps below:
2. Click **Start** button and from the list and click **Computer**.
3. From the opened window right-click on the drive you want to defragment (Drive C: in this case).
4. From the context menu select **Properties**.
5. From the **Properties** box click **Tools** tab and click **Defragment Now** button.
6. In the **Disk Defragmenter** box you will be displayed with the list of drives in your computer. You can select the drive you want to defragment. (Drive C: in this case) and click **Defragment Disk** button to start the defragment process.
7. Alternatively you can schedule the process of defragmentation so that you don't have to follow this process manually every time you want to defragment any particular drive. To do this follow steps from 1 to 4 as mentioned above and then follow the below steps to schedule the task:
8. Although, defragmentation process for all drives is already scheduled by-default. The default schedule is set on Weekly 1 AM Wednesday as per your time zone. However, if you want to re-schedule the process you need to click **Configure Schedule** button.
9. From the **Disk Defragmenter: Modify Schedule** box ensure that **Run on a schedule (Recommended)** check box is checked and then make appropriate changes from the drop down lists available to modify the schedule.
10. By-default all drives in your computer are selected for defragmentation. However, if you want you can unselect some drives by clicking **Select Disks** button. This step is not recommended though.
11. Finally you can click **Ok** button on every box to accept and confirm your selections.

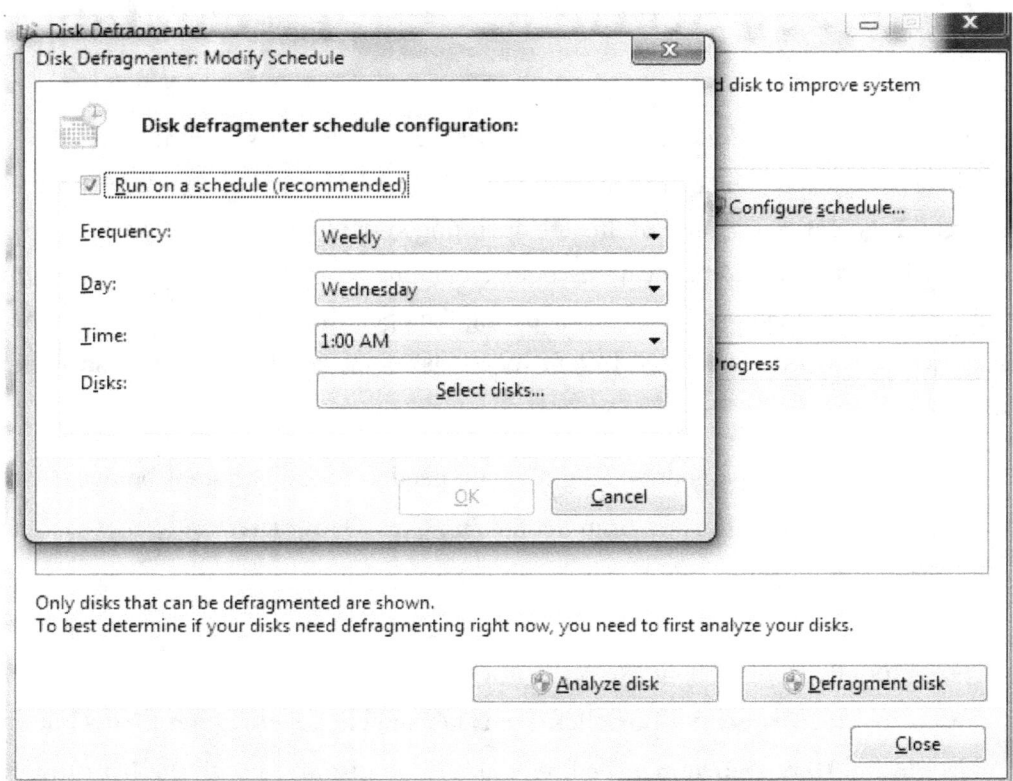

Disk defragmentation is recommended at least once in every 15-20 days. This process helps you automate defragmentation and will eliminate the need of any manual interaction from your side.

Record Problems Easily for Instantaneous Solutions

Every user who works with any operating system installed on the computer is likely to face several problems while working. When this happens, many users call their friends, computer experts, etc. and explain them about the problem they face. In return the experts or friends ask users to detail what they were doing when the problem occurred. Sometimes the user is able to explain but there are times when he cannot describe the things precisely. Microsoft understands this problem and therefore it has introduced Problem Steps Recorder in Windows 7 which can record the occurred problem step-by-step and save it in a single file. This recorded file has several screenshots that explain the problem in detail. You can use this tool by following the steps given below:

1. Log on to your computer and click **Start** button.
2. At the bottom of start menu in search box type **PSR.EXE** and press enter key.
3. **Problem Steps Recorder** tool will be initialized in a floating form on the desktop.
4. To record the steps involved in the problem click **Start Record** button present in the console.
5. Once you are done with the recording, click **Stop Record**.

As soon as you stop recording, the application will ask for the location where you want to save the recorded file. (The file will be saved with .zip extension and the zip file will have another .mht file that can be opened in any web browser)

Fix Device Drivers

As everyone knows, every device that is attached to a computer system is completely depended on the driver that has been developed to make the device work as it does. Some devices are plug and play and drivers for these devices are automatically installed as soon as they are connected on the computer whereas others require manual installation of drivers so that they can be used efficiently. In either case there are times when drivers of the devices may get corrupted and therefore may require some adminis-trative involvement so that they can be fixed. For the devices which are plug and play administrators simply need to uninstall the driver for the devices and restart the computers. During the restart, all plug and play devices reinstall their drivers automatically and administrators do not need to interact with the computers. However for the devices which require manual installation of drivers, as a Windows 7 administrator you can follow the steps given below to rectify the problem:

1. Log on to Windows 7 computer with the account that has administrative privileges.
2. From the start menu right click **Computer** and from the context menu click **Manage**.
3. From **Computer Management** snap-in click **Device Manager** from the left pane.
4. From the right pane right click on the device for which you want to fix the driver and from the available menu click **Update Driver Software** option.

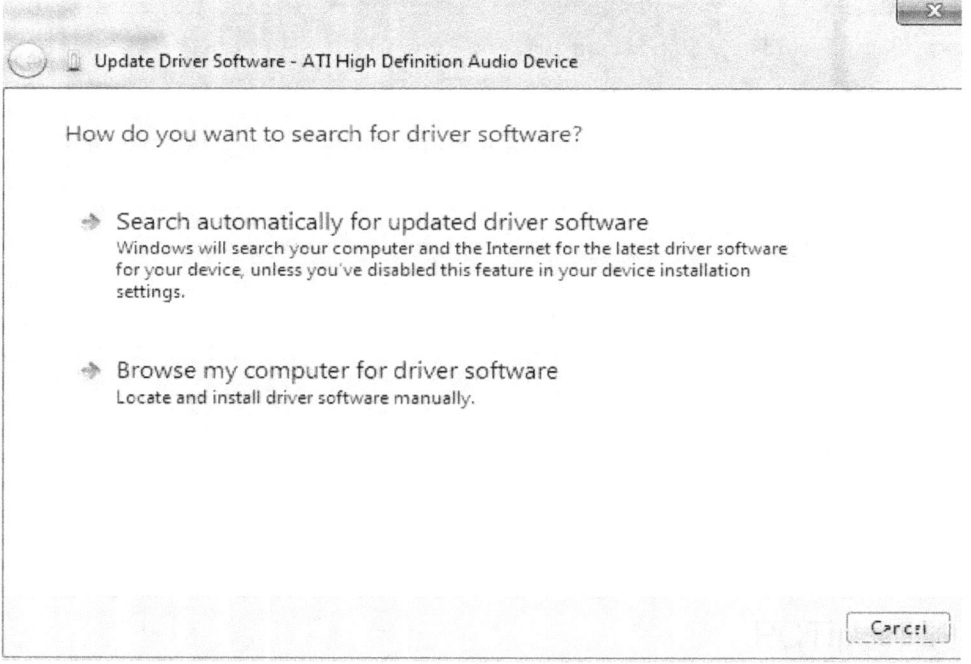

5. Follow the on-screen instructions provided by the wizard to update and fix the device driver.

Monitor LAN Card Usage

When Windows 7 is connected to a local area network or the Internet, it becomes essential to monitor LAN card usage on regular basis to avoid bottlenecks. For home users these monitoring tools are almost useless as it is not expected that there would be a lot of network traffic in the environment. However, when talking about production environment monitoring every hardware peripheral of each computer becomes necessary to get optimum performance from the machine. When using a Windows 7 computer in production environments you need to avoid bottlenecks and for this you need to monitor LAN card usage regularly. You can monitor LAN card usage by following the steps given below:

1. Log on to the computer with administrator account.

2. On the desktop screen right click on the taskbar and from the menu click **Start Task Manager**.

3. On **Windows Task Manager** box go to Networking tab to view the graphical representation of network card usage. (**Note**: When you see that the network interface card is getting heavy traffic, chances are that you will face bottlenecks in the near future. When you see this you need to either manage your network environment to generate less traffic by avoiding the use of unnecessary network services or by adding another network interface card to the machine for load balancing.)

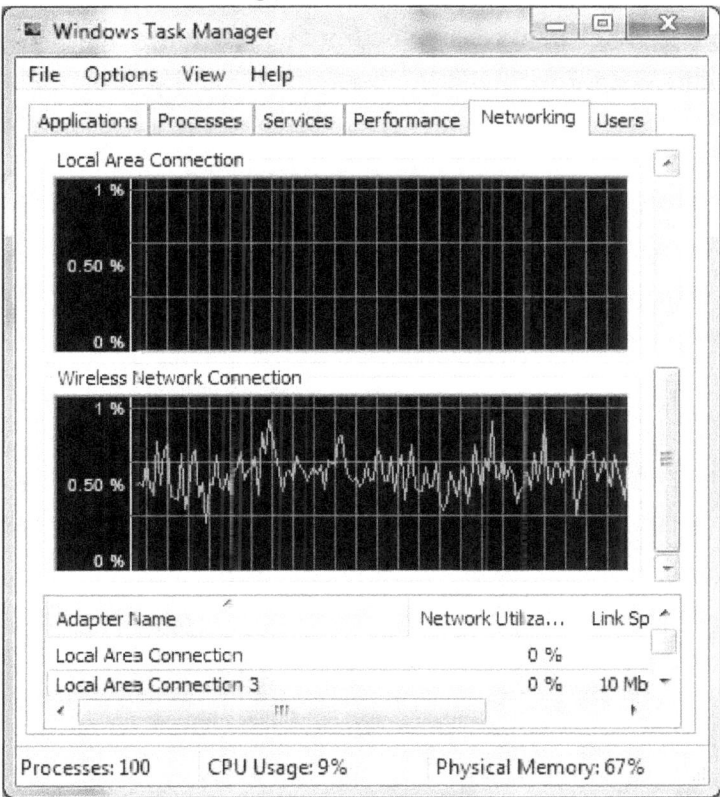

4. Close Windows Task Manager box.

View Amount of Packets Transferred through NIC

Nowadays it is very unlikely that any computer system does not have Internet connection. Even if it doesn't, it might be connected to a local area network for resource sharing purposes. When your Windows 7 computer is in home environment you need not to worry about the bandwidth usage as it is very unlikely that anybody would hack into your LAN and steel any important data, as you might not have any. However when a computer is connected to several other computers in any production environment integrity of data is always at risk. When a company installs an NIC in a computer it expects that the card would transfer some predetermined amount of packets. You need to keep a close eye on incoming and outgoing packets of the NIC card in order to maintain appropriate security. You can do this by following the steps given below:

1. Log on to your Windows 7 computer with administrator account and click **Start** button to get start menu.

2. Right click on **Computer** and from the menu click **Manage**.

3. On **Computer Management** snap-in expand **Performance** and then expand **Monitoring Tools** to get **Performance Monitor** to click on.

4. In the right pane click on the plus (+) sign to add the counter and on the opened box under **Available counters** list click **Network Interface** to expand.

5. From the available list click **Packets/sec** and from the **Instances of select object** list select the NIC you want to monitor.

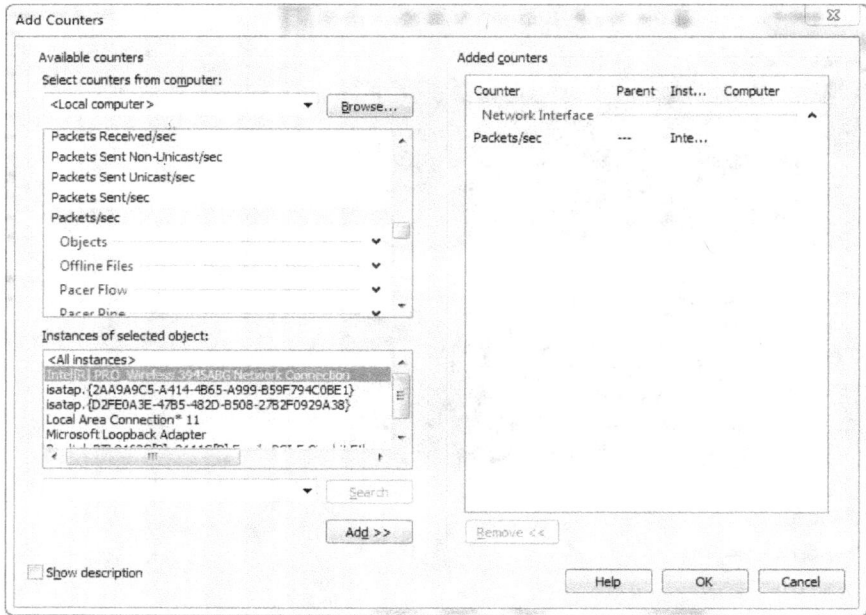

6. Click **Add** button.

7. Once done, click Ok button to add your selected counter and view its graphical usage representation.

Remove Invalid Entry from Bootloader File

During the installation of Windows 7 on a computer there might be times when administrators may misconfigure something and to rectify the problem they may reinstall the operating system right from scratch. Because of this, many times two entries of Windows 7 operating system are written in the bootloader file and whenever user starts the computer he/she gets the screen displaying two operating systems and is asked to select

to restart the computer. Best solution in this situation is to remove invalid entry of Windows 7 operating system from the list. This requires elevated privileges and therefore administrator account should be used to log on to complete the process. As a Windows 7 administrator if you want to do so you are required to follow the steps given below:

1. Log on to Windows 7 computer with the account that has administrative privileges.
2. At the bottom of start menu in search box type **MSCONFIG** command and press enter key.
3. On **System Configuration** box go to **Boot** tab.

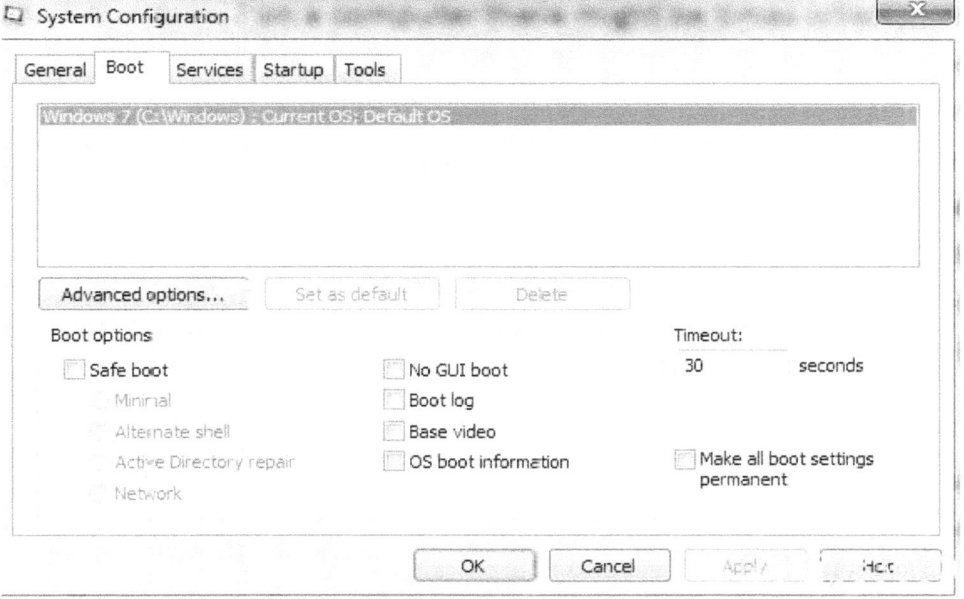

4. From the available list of entries select the invalid one and click **Delete** button.
5. Finally click Ok button to save the changes and when asked click Restart Now to restart the computer.

Create System Repair Disc

In the early days of Windows 98 administrators used to create a bootable disk so that they can repair Windows 98 computers in case anything goes bad with them. Creating these types of repair discs ensured that administrators do not get stuck anywhere when computers failed. Same concept is now carried forward in Windows 7 and the operating system also allows administrators to create repair discs so that they can be used in case Windows 7 computers fail to boot. Repair disks created by Windows 7 not only ensure that the systems boot successfully but also allow administrators to restore the operating systems from any backup image file. As a Windows 7 administrator if you want to do so you are required to follow the steps given below:

1. Log on to Windows 7 computer with administrator account.
2. At the bottom of start menu in search box type **System Repair Disc** and press enter key.
3. Make sure that a blank CD or a DVD is in CD/DVD burner and the device is connected to the computer (in case the burner is external).
4. From the available drop-down **Drive** list choose the current burner.

Create a system repair disc

Select a CD/DVD drive and insert a blank disc into the drive

A system repair disc can be used to boot your computer. It also contains Windows system recovery tools that can help you recover Windows from a serious error or restore your computer from a system image.

Drive: DVD RW Drive (G:)

Create disc   Cancel

5. Once done, click Create disc button to start the creation process.

Fix MBR

Master Boot Record in Windows 7 is a record that contains all bootable files which are required to be loaded into memory in order to boot the operating system successfully. Although this MBR is by default protected by the operating system however because of some reasons sometimes it gets corrupt. When this is the case most administrators simply reinstall the operating systems on the computers and the process is typically knows as clean installation. This practice is mostly used by non-technical users. This section focuses on repairing MBR which will guide users through the process to rectify MBR related issues on their own hence eliminating the need of getting depended on the service engineers, at least in home environments. The process requires Windows 7 bootable media and if as a Windows 7 user or administrator you have the media you can follow the steps given below to repair MBR on your own:

1. Start the computer and insert Windows 7 bootable media into DVD-ROM drive.

2. Boot computer with DVD ROM and on the first screen specify the appropriate information as required and click **Next** button.

3. Click on **Repair Your Computer** button and from the next window click **Command Prompt**.

4. On the opened command window type **bootsect /nt60 C:** and press enter key.

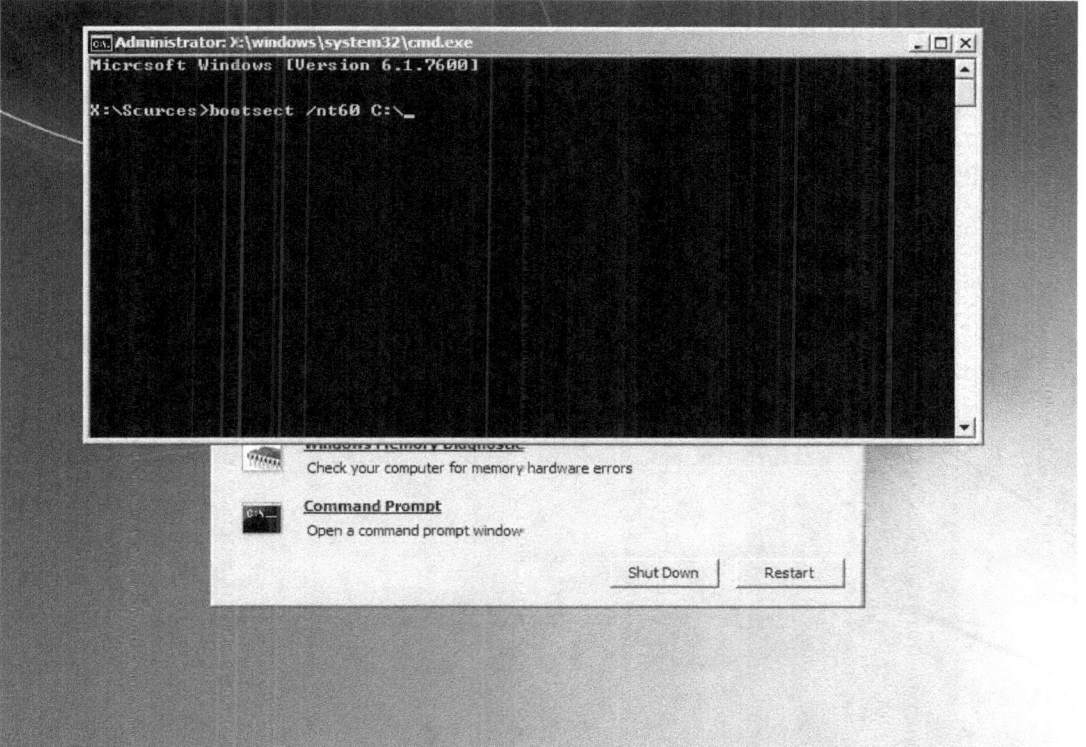

5. Once done, restart the computer and remove the bootable media from the drive to start it in normal mode and find the problem fixed.

Fix Bootloader File

Many times a Windows 7 computer fails to boot. There might be several reasons behind it but one of the major reasons which are mostly encountered by the experienced professionals is corrupt bootloader file. In fact bootloader is the only file that allows Windows 7 operating system to boot whenever the computer is started. Many inexperienced administrators prefer reinstallation of entire operating system when the operating system fails to boot but this section will guide you through the process using which as an administrator or a home user you can fix the corrupt bootloader file easily. The process requires Windows 7 bootable media and a CD/DVD-ROM drive directly connected to the computer. The computer should also be configured to boot from CD/DVD-ROM. As a Windows 7 administrator, in order to repair the bootloader file you need to follow the steps given as below:

1. Insert Windows 7 bootable media into the CD/DVD-ROM drive.
2. Start the computer with DVD support.
3. On the appeared screen click **Repair your computer**.
4. After scanning is complete click **Windows 7 Installation** and click **Next** button.
5. On **System Recovery Options** box click **Command Prompt**.
6. On the opened command window type **bootrec.exe /FixBoot** and press enter key to repair the file.

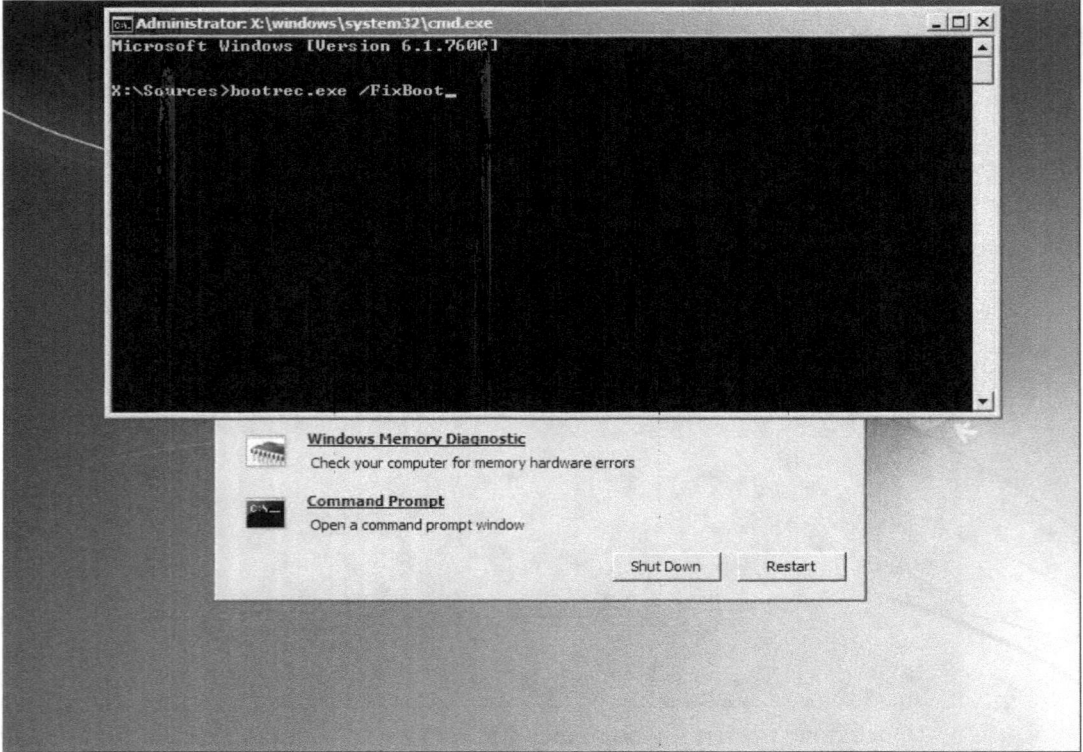

7. Take out the bootable media from CD/DVD-ROM drive and restart the computer normally.

Start Windows 7 in Safe Mode

Safe Mode in Windows 7 is a mode in which the operating system starts where only essential services and drivers are loaded into the memory. When the operating system is booted in normal mode, almost all services and drivers are automatically initialized and if the computer is infected with some viruses they are also initiated at the same time. When this happens, users are not able to delete those virus applications and even if they run any antivirus program to remove them, they fail to do so as well. The reason behind this is that when a file is being the used by the Windows, Windows does not allow the file to be modified or deleted whatsoever. In order to delete these files or remove any unwanted drivers users need to boot Windows 7 in safe mode and as a Windows 7 user if you want to do so you are required to follow the steps given as below:

1. Make sure that your computer is connected to the power supply.
2. Power on the computer and start pressing **F8** key repeatedly till the time a list of boot options is displayed.
3. On the list of boot options, the very first option that is displayed will be Safe Mode and it will be selected as default.

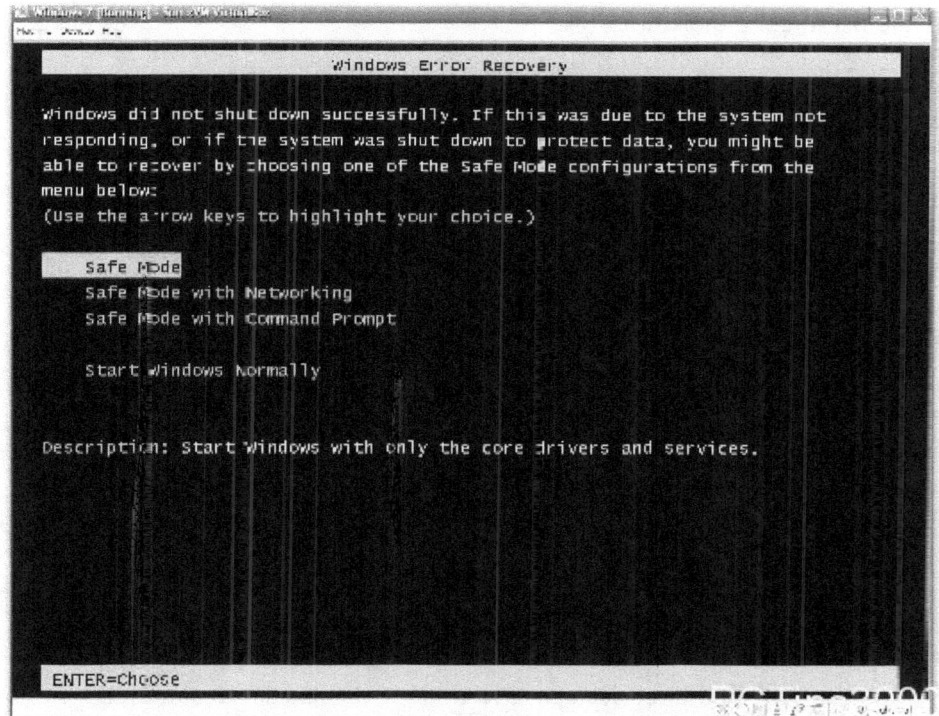

4. Hit enter key to boot Windows 7 in Safe Mode.

Delete Windows Services

Since quite a long time Microsoft operating systems are completely based upon the services that run in the background. In fact, there are several services which are automatically installed along with operating system and are automatically initialized whenever the computer starts. These services play an important role to provide several useful options to the users in order to make their tasks easy. However there are still many services which are not automatically initialized and some of them are even those which are not at all required in home environments or sometimes in production environments as well. In later cases if administrators want they can delete such services with a small command which can be written in an elevated DOS prompt. In order to delete any service administrators are required to know the exact name of that service which they can know by typing SERVICES.MSC in the search box in start menu and double-clicking the desired service in the opened window. As Windows 7 administrator, if you want to completely delete any service using command prompt you are required to follow the steps given below:

1. Log on to Windows 7 computer with the account that has administrative privileges.
2. Click **Start** button and click **All Programs**.
3. From the available list click **Accessories** container and right-click **Command Prompt** from the list to get the menu.
4. From the available options click **Run as administrator**.
5. In the opened window type in **sc delete** command followed by the name of the service and press enter key. For example, **sc delete TapiSrv**.

6. You can refresh the services page to find the deleted service missing.

Rectify MSI Installer Problem to Install Software

When Windows 7 is installed on a computer and has grown mature, it starts decreasing its performance by the time. In other words, when users keep on using the operating system on a regular basis, after sometime registry files and other executable files start getting corrupt and sometimes they may fail to run at all. Another very common problem that old Windows 7 operating system generates is that it does not allow users to install any software application. Most common error that users experience in these cases is the problem with MSI installer. Many users do not know how to rectify this problem and therefore, in home environments, they call for service engineers which many times charge a decent amount and they simply do a clean install of the operating system. This problem can easily be rectified by running a small command in the command window and this can be done even by home users. As a Windows 7 user if you want to do so you need to follow the steps mentioned as below:

1. Log on to Windows 7 computer with the account that has elevated privileges.

2. Click **Start** button and click on All Programs.

3. From the available menu click **Accessories** container and right click **Command Prompt**.

4. From the menu click **Run as administrator** and click on Yes button on **User Account Control** confirmation box.

5. In the command window type **reg delete HKLM\SOFTWARE\Microsoft\SQMClient\Windows\DisabledSessions /va /f** command and press enter key to execute it.

6. If required restart the computer to allow the changes to take effect.

Cannot Open a Webpage (DNS Cache)

There might be times when you are connected to the Internet and you see that everything is working just fine, however you are still not able to open any web page. When this is the case, the problem might be with the DNS cache of your computer. DNS cache is a temporary storage area in your computer where all the IP addresses of the webpages which you have visited are stored for a specific period of time. With the help of DNS caching, computers do not have to look out for IP addresses of already visited webpages with the DNS servers. In some cases though, DNS cache of a computer might get poisoned with fake entries. When this happens it becomes essential for a user to clear the DNS cache in order to make computer contact DNS servers to repopulate the cache with genuine entries. You can clear DNS cache of your Windows 7 computer by following the steps given below:

1. Log on to the Windows 7 computer using administrator account.
2. Click **Start** button.
3. From the start menu click **All Programs** and from the list click **Accessories** folder to expand it.
4. From the contents right-click **Command Prompt** and from the context menu click **Run as Administrator**.
5. On **User Account Control** confirmation box click **Yes** button to allow computer to open command prompt using elevated privileges.
6. In the opened command window type **IPCONFIG /FLUSHDNS** and press enter key.

7. Close command window.

More Info:

You can view the entries in DNS cache by typing IPCONFIG /DISPLAYDNS in the command window.

www.ingramcontent.com/pod-product-compliance
Lightning Source LLC
Chambersburg PA
CBHW081430170526
45166CB00008B/2155